"This book will become the 'go to textbook' for an up-to-date history of the International Mission Board for many years to come. It uniquely looks at the IMB through the lives of key individuals prior to the formation of the Foreign Mission Board (chapter one) and the administrations of the mission organization's leadership right up to the present. I found this approach both fascinating and informative. I am glad to commend this work to all who desire to obey the final marching orders of King Jesus."

—Daniel L. Akin, President,
Southeastern Baptist Theological Seminary

"Where you find Southern Baptists, you find a denomination committed to taking the gospel to the ends of the earth. This has been our heritage for 175 years—and this essential volume reminds Southern Baptists today of this crucial stewardship. There are serious historical, moral, and theological questions that arise in any honest reckoning with the past. The contributors in this book have done Southern Baptists a great service by tracing both the unwavering commitment to the Great Commission that has been the hallmark of Southern Baptists and the issues that history presents us. The reader will grow in appreciation for Baptists and their missionary convictions—and for the SBC and its global missions force, now serving Christ for 175 years."

—R. Albert Mohler, Jr., President,
The Southern Baptist Theological Seminary

"Southern Baptists are at our best when we are focused on taking the gospel message to as many people as possible in as many places as possible. This book tells that story! It is a compelling saga of a mission-focused people, motivated by the love of God for the nations. It is also a story of perseverance through all kinds of hardship and opposition—sometimes created by our mistakes and shortcomings. Through it all, we have remained on mission, telling the good news about Jesus to many people who have never even heard his name. May God inspire you to join this movement!"

—Jeff Iorg, President,
Gateway Seminary

"*Make Disciples of All Nations* recounts the remarkable history of SBC global missions. The accomplished contributors relate important stories about the origins, presidents, settings, turning points, identity, theology, finances, challenges, and more. Along the way, readers will gain insight into Baptists, missions, and the global context."

—Christopher W. Morgan, Dean and Professor of Theology, School of Christian Ministries, California Baptist University;
author of *Christian Theology: The Biblical Story and Our Faith*

"If you love Baptist history, and more specifically the history of Baptist missions, then this is exactly the book you will want. Carefully broken into the most important moments and eras, each section provides a detailed look into the most important moments of our missiological history. I'm grateful to see this volume and trust that Southern Baptists will find it to be an enormously helpful resource for the next generation of missiological work."

—Jamie Dew, President,
New Orleans Baptist Theological Seminary

"*Make Disciples of All Nations: A History of Southern Baptist International Missions* is an expansive look at the work of the International Mission Board across 175 years of history. It provides insights into the leaders who led the organization and the strategies they employed. Today, under the leadership of Dr. Paul Chitwood, the IMB continues to serve Southern Baptists in this 'one sacred effort'—leading the next generation of mission advance in obedience to the Great Commission, with the vision of Revelation 7:9 ever before us."

—Todd Lafferty, Executive VP and COO,
International Missions Board, SBC

"*Make Disciples of All Nations* is an encouraging—though not sanitized—historical account of Southern Baptist cooperation focused on faithfulness to the Great Commission. The authors of this volume do not write as disimpassioned historians, but all in various ways are both the beneficiaries and contributors to the history about which they are writing. While any time is a good time to be encouraged by churches aiming to cooperate to advance the kingdom of God, perhaps today—more than any other time—we need to be reminded of how God's mission to make his name known unites us. I am glad to commend this excellent volume to you to that end."

—Matthew Bennett,
Assistant Professor of Missions and Theology,
Cedarville University

"What an incredible gift this book is to all those who wish to know and learn about the remarkable missions heritage that has been passed along through the years by Southern Baptists through the Foreign/International Mission Board. We are forever indebted to the leaders and staff who navigated the crises, changes, and challenges that took place over the many years. But most of all, we are reminded of the missionary heroes who have served—often nameless and faceless—so courageously and faithfully. God has used them mightily and he is still working through them today. May Southern Baptists always hold this mission to take the gospel to the ends of the earth with the highest priority and regard."

—Kevin Ezell, President,
North American Mission Board

"From our beginnings in 1845, Southern Baptists have always been a people deeply committed to global missions. Even today, many would argue it remains the most important 'glue' that holds our convention of churches together. A new history of Southern Baptist global mission efforts has been long overdue, so I couldn't be more excited about *Make Disciples of All Nations*. This volume is denominational history at its best. The authors focus upon key individuals, themes, controversies, and initiatives. They are sympathetic to the subject, because they each love the Great Commission, but they avoid hagiography. When it is regrettably necessary to be critical, the authors never venture into cynicism. I trust this book will introduce a generation of Baptists to our missionary heritage. More importantly, I pray the Lord will use this book to call thousands of men and women to embrace God's call to make disciples here, there, and everywhere."

—Nathan A. Finn, Provost and Dean of the University Faculty,
North Greenville University

"International missions may be a core part of Southern Baptist identity, but few in our denomination know the story of how we got there. *Make Disciples of All Nations* is a clearly told account of God's provision and providence in Southern Baptist missionary efforts, highlighting our personalities, our strategies and successes, and even our failures and warts. This book is a God-send for pastors, students of history, and anyone passionate about fulfilling the Great Commission."

—Rhyne Putman
Associate Vice President for Academic Affairs
Director of Worldview Formation, Professor of Christian Ministries
Williams Baptist University

"The story of Southern Baptist missions through the International Mission Board is a testimony to the power of the Holy Spirit mobilizing God's people to fulfill the Great Commission. Our cooperative missions efforts have planted seeds of the gospel around the world, and countless lives have been transformed by the power of Jesus Christ. What a blessing it is to be a part of a body of churches that is unified in its purpose to preach the gospel among all the nations."

—Ben Mandrell, President and CEO
Lifeway Christian Resources

"*Make Disciples of All Nations* provides a fresh perspective to the development of Baptist missions in general and Southern Baptist missions in particular. It presents the historical context preceding the formation of the Southern Baptist Convention, the founding of the Foreign Mission Board, and its development into the International Mission Board in a readable, engaging style. The historically curious and the serious historian will both find this work a valuable addition to their libraries."

—Lloyd A. Harsch, Professor of Church History and Baptist Studies
Associate Dean of Theological and Historical Studies
Director, Institute for Faith and the Public Square
Occupying the Cooperative Program Chair of SBC Studies
New Orleans Baptist Theological Seminary

"What a joy it is to read this recounting of the challenges, controversies, and successes of Southern Baptist missionary workers and leaders. This book is a must-read to understand our cooperative missionary endeavor. It also serves to recall us to our charter for obedience and cooperation—to the orders that Christ has given his church."

—Gregory A. Wills
Director, B. H. Carroll Center for Baptist Heritage and Mission
Research Professor of Church History and Baptist Heritage
Southwestern Baptist Theological Seminary

MAKE
DISCIPLES
OF ALL
NATIONS

A History of Southern Baptist
International Missions

JOHN D. MASSEY, MIKE MORRIS,
and W. MADISON GRACE II

EDITORS

KREGEL
ACADEMIC

Make Disciples of All Nations: A History of Southern Baptist International Missions

© 2021 by John D. Massey, Mike Morris, and W. Madison Grace II

Published by Kregel Academic, an imprint of Kregel Publications, 2450 Oak Industrial Dr. NE, Grand Rapids, MI 49505-6020.

ISBN 978-0-8254-4558-3

Printed in the United States of America

21 22 23 24 25 / 5 4 3 2 1

*To Southern Baptist missionaries
and those who sacrificially support them*

CONTENTS

ABBREVIATIONS

BMS   Baptist Missionary Society

BP   Baptist Press

FMB   Foreign Mission Board

FMBM   Foreign Mission Board Minutes

FMJ   *Foreign Mission Journal*

HFJ   *Home and Foreign Journal*

IMB   International Mission Board

IMBA   International Mission Board Archives

LML   Lottie Moon Letters

NAMB   North American Mission Board

SBC   Southern Baptist Convention

SBCA   Southern Baptist Convention Annual
(Proceedings of the SBC)

TC   *The Commission*

WMU   Woman's Missionary Union

Note: Many of the resources could be accessed at the time of writing at these two websites: https://www.imb.org/research-archives and http://www.sbhla.org/digital_resources.asp.

FOREWORD

I'VE HAD THE PRIVILEGE of viewing Southern Baptist missions from a host of roles and relationships. Growing up in a Southern Baptist church, I learned of the love and admiration that people in the pew have for their missionaries, heard their prayers voiced for the lost around the world, and witnessed their sacrificial giving to support the work. As a ministry student in a Baptist college and Southern Baptist seminary, I learned about our denomination's mission history and sat under the teaching of former missionaries. As a local church pastor and seminary professor, I taught about that history and led our church and my students to partner with our missionaries. As trustee of the International Mission Board, SBC, I learned about the inner workings of Southern Baptists' most revered missions entity and began to see its vast reach among the nations.

None of these roles or relationships compares, however, to the view that I now have as IMB president. How I wish every Southern Baptist could see what I see! The cumulative impact of 175 years of churches working together to fulfill the Great Commission is staggering not only in terms of the fruit that remains from that work but also in terms of the new pathways that are being forged. Every year, hundreds of thousands of lost people overseas hear the gospel, tens of thousands of new believers are baptized, and thousands of new churches are planted as Southern Baptists undertake their cooperative mission work among the nations.

The vision of heaven that John describes in Revelation 7:9–10 includes a vast multitude from every nation, all tribes, peoples, and

languages. For 175 years, Southern Baptists have faithfully steward-
ed our part of the vision. As we learn about those who have gone
before us, may we be inspired to go ourselves, even to the nations.

—Paul Chitwood, PhD
President, International Mission Board

INTRODUCTION

IN THE YEAR 2020 the International Mission Board of the Southern Baptist Convention celebrated its 175th anniversary of making disciples of all nations as a denomination of SBC churches. Since its formation by the newly formed Southern Baptist Convention in 1845, the Foreign Mission Board (which would later become the IMB) has represented the enduring commitment of Southern Baptists to engage cooperatively the task of the Great Commission around a common confession of faith through times of many internal and external challenges. The history of SBC missions is a great adventure, one of survival and expansion, conflict and resolution, trials and triumph, sacrifice, and the planting of gospel churches to the ends of the earth. From its beginning the FMB has endured, adapted, and grown significantly in the midst of all the changes and upheavals that the United States and the world have experienced. The FMB survived the Civil War, Reconstruction, two world wars, economic boom and bust, and widespread civil unrest during the decades of the 1950s, 1960s, and 1970s. The SBC and its missions agency persevered in orthodoxy during the theological downgrade of many mainline denominations during the so-called modernist-fundamentalist controversy, the rise of the ecumenical movement, and the theological challenges faced in various quarters of SBC seminary and denominational life that surfaced in the 1960s and 1970s. The IMB has faced the tragic events of 9/11 and the subsequent "war on terror" that has lasted until this day, the hyperpolarization of politics, postdenominationalism, denominational tribalism, the challenges and opportunities of globalization, and now the COVID-19 pandemic. In all of these periods of American and world history, the FMB/ IMB has by God's grace survived, adapted, and thrived through its commitment to cooperative missions founded on a common confession of faith. This book tells the story of SBC missions efforts and progress to make disciples of all nations.

The following book was born out of the need to update and retell the history of Southern Baptist missions from a contemporary perspective for a new generation in light of the dramatic changes in the world and in the SBC over the last twenty-five years. William R. Estep wrote the last comprehensive history in 1994 in his *Whole Gospel Whole World: The Foreign Mission Board of the Southern Baptist Convention 1845–1995*. Much has transpired over the last twenty-five years in SBC denominational life and missions. The name has changed from the Foreign Mission Board to the International Mission Board. The IMB has implemented major strategic and organizational changes. The IMB board of trustees has elected three new presidents. The manner in which the IMB relates to churches and funding missions has evolved. The SBC landscape has become more diverse in approaches to ministry, theological subgroups, and demographic composition. Globalization has led to the nations migrating to the large urban areas of the world, including North America. Missions is no longer only "over there" but also in the cities of the United States, where immigration has brought about significant demographic shifts in local populations. As a result, the IMB now works closely with the North American Mission Board to develop strategies and equip churches to reach diaspora peoples in North America. Churches of the SBC and other evangelical churches are in need of thinking missiologically like never before in order to reach their own internationally diverse neighborhoods with the gospel of Jesus Christ. A retelling of the story of SBC missions will be one way to help shape missions strategy today.

One of the most significant changes to the context of SBC missions is the rise of global Christianity and the multiplication of Baptist and evangelical missions partners worldwide. Since the mid-twentieth century the epicenter of global Christianity has shifted to the Global South. Baptist churches and conventions are present on every continent because of the tireless efforts of FMB/IMB missionaries and their national partners. More than two centuries of the evangelical Protestant missionary movement has borne fruit. From its beginning, the FMB has been a part of the larger evangelical missions movement that has sown the seeds of the gospel, leading to a shift in the epicenter of the evangelical world from its traditional strength in the West to Asia, Africa, and Latin America. Rethinking the role of the IMB in the age of global evangelical Christianity is a pressing need that can be partly met by an updated review of SBC missions history.

The time has arrived for a fresh examination and reflection on where we have been in order for us to understand where we now stand in our cooperative missions efforts and where we should go into the twenty-first century in the Great Commission ministries of the people called Southern Baptists. We have chosen to utilize the basic approach of Estep in his *Whole Gospel Whole World* by telling the story of Southern Baptist missions through each administration of the FMB/IMB. The content of this work differs, however, in emphases, perspective, and content. *Making Disciples of All Nations*, as an edited work, includes contributions from across SBC life. We decided at the beginning to utilize the perspective of historians, theologians, and missiologists to retell the story. This work presents chapters that are unique but when taken together provide a rich mosaic of SBC missions in all its diversity. We asked each contributor to write from his academic strength. Missiologist contributors address issues of missions strategy more than others. Historians do a deeper dive into historical details that shed light on the events and personalities involved in the advancement of SBC missions. Theologians offer more color on internal and external theological challenges and issues that gave shape to SBC missions. A guiding assumption for this work is that SBC missions activity does not exist in a vacuum; the contexts of world events, denominational life, American cultural developments, and the broader evangelical Christian world have shaped it deeply. The viewpoints of the historian, theologian, and missiologist offer a more complete picture of how and why the FMB has evolved over time and the driving forces that have molded it.

The present work is meant to be celebratory of 175 years of cooperative missions while also being critically reflective. This book is a family portrait painted by members of the SBC family, each committed to cooperative missions founded on a common confession of faith. Southern Baptists, along with all believers, are works in progress both individually and corporately. Authors have sympathetically yet often directly addressed both the strengths and weaknesses present in SBC missions history. Such history is replete with inspirational sacrifices of those whom God has called to serve cross-culturally and of the faithful "rope-holders" who have made SBC missions possible through sending, praying, and sacrificial giving. A renewed narrative of SBC missions will hopefully inform current missions practice and strengthen the ties of cooperation among SBC churches.

In chapter 1 Jason Duesing begins our narrative with an examination of SBC pre-beginnings—the missionary roots that ultimately led to the formation of the SBC and, consequently, the FMB. He suggests a change in methodology in the way historians look at the origins and progress of Baptist missions. He acknowledges three prevailing positions on the genesis of Baptist history and missions: the single-source view, the multi-source view, and the genetic view of Baptist history and missions. Rather than only considering who came first in Baptist missions, Duesing argues that an assessment of the Baptist missions movement cannot be reduced to an oversimplified chronological approach and is not fully captured with the multi-source or genetic views. He argues, however, for a "symphonious" view of Baptist missions that is composed of many contributions and movements. While Duesing acknowledges multiple contributions to Baptist missions, he narrows his biographical sketches to three key figures who represent significant movements in this symphony of Baptist missions: (1) the African

American George Liele, (2) the Englishman William Carey, and (3) the American Adoniram Judson. While Duesing covers all three of these men in chronological order, he notes that their contributions to Baptist missions go far beyond their era. In chapter 2 W. Madison Grace II chronicles the beginning of the SBC, the FMB, and the contribution of its first corresponding secretary, James B. Taylor (1846–1971). Grace rightly points out that SBC missions are a part of a larger evangelical missions narrative but has its own unique beginning and subsequent associational-denominational approach to missions funding and administration. He identifies Adoniram and Ann Judson's embrace of New Testament baptism, and their resulting break with the Congregationalist missions sending agency that appointed them, as the spark that led Baptists in America to form a denomination for the support of missions at home and abroad. Fellow Congregationalist missionary Luther Rice also converted to Baptist views on baptism and took up the task of raising support for the Judsons and other Baptist missionaries who would follow. Rice's efforts led to the formation of the General Missionary Convention of the Baptist Denomination in the United States for Foreign Missions, on May 18, 1814, also known as the Triennial Convention because it met every three years. The Triennial Convention united Baptists in the North and the South for the cause of missions through its Baptist Board of Foreign Missions but ultimately split in 1845 over the controversial practice in the South of appointing slaveholding missionaries, a practice supported in the South but rejected in the North. Grace identifies the pro-slavery stance of Baptists in the South and their unwillingness to reject the practice as the underlying issue that led to the split in 1845. This birth in sin, as Grace points out, marked the beginning of the SBC and consequently of SBC missions.

J. B. Taylor served a lengthy and distinguished tenure as the first corresponding secretary of the FMB. As Grace notes, he was a foundation stone for the FMB that set the direction for its growth and expansion into new fields. Taylor was a pastor with a heart for reaching the nations for Christ. He led the FMB to exert its initial efforts in China, a mission that would become the single greatest investment in dollars and personnel until the communist insurgency expelled the last remaining missionaries after the establishment of the People's Republic of China in 1949. Grace recounts that Africa soon became a new field of service for the FMB as Taylor addressed two of the greatest challenges of the new missions agency: recruiting new missionaries and raising funds to support the work. The FMB made attempts to open a Japan mission but to no avail. It did manage, however, to open new work in Italy at the close of Taylor's tenure as corresponding secretary. Taylor and the FMB would face and overcome many obstacles; the largest and most obvious challenge was the devastation and interruption of support for SBC missions due to the Civil War. The money quickly dried up, but many missionaries found a means of sustaining their work and presence on the field until funding resumed after the war. Taylor also skillfully led the FMB through the opposition of the Landmarkers, led by J. R. Graves, and the anti-missions movement that opposed boards managing missionaries, a duty they believed belonged solely to the local churches. Taylor and other SBC leaders gave a hearing to Graves's concerns and formulated a solution that drew Graves's praise and support while also preserving the denominational approach to missions. Taylor ended his leadership at the FMB after having laid a foundation that enabled the SBC to strengthen and expand its missionary efforts.

In chapter 3 Anthony Chute picks up the story of SBC missions after Taylor under the leadership of his successor, Henry A. Tupper (1872–1893). Tupper grew the missions force from nineteen to ninety-two and initiated new work in three new countries: Japan, Mexico, and Brazil. He is also known as the FMB leader who supported and encouraged the appointment of single female missionaries; Lottie Moon is the best-known single female missionary who was appointed under his tenure. During Tupper's leadership, the Woman's Missionary Union, inspired by Lottie Moon, established an annual Christmas offering for its overseas operations—an offering that would later be named the Lottie Moon Christmas Offering. He also emphasized the importance of the missionary wife in reaching women with the gospel of Christ and thereby reaching the entire family. Chute notes that Tupper believed reaching one woman for Christ would be greater in its influence on the family and society than reaching two men.

The FMB work in Brazil would become the second-largest SBC missions investment, second only to China, during Tupper's tenure and beyond. The appointment of William and Ann Bagby in 1881 proved to be consequential for the expansion of SBC missions work in Brazil and led to a multigenerational impact by the Bagby family on missions efforts in this country.

Chute notes that Tupper demonstrated his doctrinal and diplomatically driven leadership by skillfully handling the appointment recension of John Stout and T. P. Bell, both former students of Crawford Toy at The Southern Baptist Theological Seminary. Both men embraced Toy's higher-critical view of the Bible, which viewed Scripture as containing errors. Tupper also led the FMB through the termination of T. P. Crawford and his Gospel Mission Movement, which many believed was rooted in Landmarkism. The administration of Tupper strengthened the foundation of FMB missions that was laid by Taylor and set the stage for the future.

In Chapter 4, Mike Morris examines developments within the FMB during the leadership tenure of R. J. Willingham (1893–1914), successor to Tupper. Morris recounts that Willingham was the pastor of First Baptist Church in Memphis when he received the call to serve as corresponding secretary of the FMB. By the time of Willingham's appointment, the FMB was already involved in China, Japan, Africa, Italy, Brazil, and Mexico. Willingham's administration would continue a focus on China that contained the largest share of missionaries in any field of service. He inherited the controversy initiated by T. P. Crawford's Gospel Mission Movement and the controversy over methodology that ensued. Morris helpfully points out that John Nevius and the self-supporting principle for new churches influenced Crawford and many in the China mission, including Lottie Moon. The FMB, however, did not fully embrace the principles of Nevius, choosing instead to continue to offer financial support to local leadership with gradual reductions over time but remaining committed to evangelism, education, publishing, and medical ministries that characterized FMB work from the beginning. Willingham was in leadership when Lottie Moon died on Christmas Eve 1912, aboard a ship bound for home in the harbor of Kobe, Japan. Morris points out that by the time of his death in office in 1914, Willingham managed to grow the number of missionaries from ninety-four to three hundred during his tenure and expand into Argentina and Uruguay.

In chapter 5 David S. Dockery explores the monumental changes within the SBC with the formation and implementation of the Cooperative Program during the tenures of J. Franklin Love (1915–1928), successor to Willingham, and T. Bronson Ray (1928–1933); and the issuing of the 1925 Baptist Faith and Message. Dockery also offers a look at how the broader national and international context of the FMB during these two administrations shaped SBC missions. J. F. Love began his administration at the beginning of World War I. Concurrently, American Christianity was engaged in a war of its own over the "faith once for all delivered to the saints" and biblical authority. The so-called modernist-fundamentalist controversy was underway among Northern Baptists and Presbyterians. This controversy prompted the publication of *The Fundamentals* in 1915; Southern Baptists were among its contributors and signatories. Southern Baptists responded to the debate by issuing in 1925 the Baptist Faith and Message, an update of the 1833 New Hampshire Confession. This publication demonstrated the long-standing practice of the SBC to cooperate together for missions around a common confession of faith. As Dockery observes, in the same year as the adoption of a new confession of faith, the Cooperative Program was also adopted by the SBC; this occurrence brought about a significant advance in the way Southern Baptist churches carried out cooperative ministries. Churches would give to the Cooperative Program, and then money would be distributed to the various boards and entities from this central fund. This practice eliminated the need for agents of boards to inundate local churches with solicitations of support. These significant doctrinal and administrative changes took place during the tenure of J. Franklin Love and eventually led to the great eras of growth for SBC missions in the post–World War II economic boom. Following J. Franklin Love, T. B. Ray served a short stint as corresponding secretary.

In chapter 6 John Massey covers the administration of Charles Maddry (1933–1944), who immediately followed T. B. Ray. Maddry served during a time of great global crises: the Great Depression, the Sino-Japanese wars, the rise of Hitler and Nazi Germany, and the rise of a militarized and expansionist Japan. Maddry was an eyewitness to the bombing of Pearl Harbor and the entrance of the United States into World War II. He worked tirelessly to eliminate crippling FMB debt, restructured the FMB to distribute leadership through regional secretaries, and moved the FMB home office to its current location. In many ways Maddry was a pivotal figure. He led during a time when business practices were being more widely adopted in ministry and more modes of international travel had become readily available. He was known as the traveling secretary, who made many overseas trips to check on the progress of the work and minister to FMB missionaries. The FMB work in China and Brazil continued to hold prominence of place during Maddry's administration; but the FMB also intensified its work in many other fields, including but not limited to Africa.

In chapter 7 Keith E. Eitel highlights the important legacy of leadership established by the administration of M. Theron Rankin (1945–1953). Rankin served at key moments in world history as an FMB missionary and later as FMB executive secretary. As Eitel notes, Rankin was the first field missionary to serve as executive secretary; this pattern was followed by the FMB for the next four administrations. He served with distinction as a missionary in China during its days of conflict and turmoil. FMB executive secretary Charles Maddry met Rankin for the first time during one of his trips to China and was greatly impressed with Rankin. Eventually,

Maddry elevated Rankin to the position of secretary of the Orient. As Maddry's service to the FMB came to an end, the board set its sights on Rankin to follow Maddry, and he did so in January 1945. Rankin is credited with laying the foundation for the great period of missions advance that would come to full flowering in the administration of his successor, Baker James Cauthen.

In chapter 8 Thomas Nettles covers the expansive and consequential FMB period under the leadership of Baker James Cauthen (1954–1979). He also, like Rankin before him, served as a missionary to China and as the secretary of the Orient before becoming executive secretary. He presided over the FMB when its missionaries had been expelled from communist China in 1951; these missionaries mostly scattered to serve among the Chinese diaspora all across Asia. By the end of Cauthen's tenure, China had begun to show a new openness to the West and to move away from the extremes of Mao's policies and system of governance. Cauthen oversaw the largest period of growth in SBC missions until that time, building on the Advance program begun by Rankin and being a part of implementing the SBC-wide initiative, Bold Mission Thrust. As Nettles notes, by 1978 the FMB had missionaries in ninety-four countries. Under Cauthen many new categories of service were initiated that had not existed in previous administrations. One example was the well-known Journeyman program. Cauthen led the FMB during widespread domestic unrest—the push for racial equality, the aftermath of the Korean War, the Vietnam War, and many other major crises, both domestic and international. He was a steady hand during the theological crises that arose in the 1960s and that continued until the end of his tenure. In his twenty-six years of service as executive secretary of the FMB, Cauthen proved to be a true statesman in SBC life and the embodiment of the convention's global missions commitments.

In chapter 9 John Mark Terry and Micah Fries introduce the administration of Keith Parks (1980–1992). They note that Parks, before his appointment as FMB president, served as an FMB missionary assigned to the Indonesian Baptist Seminary and later in various leadership positions within the organization. Parks led the FMB to embrace a focus on unreached people groups, a new concept at the time, and to establish a global strategy group that sought the best methods for advancing the Great Commission with focused attention on the unreached. Parks helped with the implementation of Bold Mission Thrust prior to his election as president and continued the program implemented across the SBC while serving as president. Terry and Fries highlight the creation of the nonresidential missionary model and the formation of Cooperative Services International (CSI) as two important contributions made by Parks to FMB strategy. Parks formed CSI and the nonresidential model to serve the unreached with creative and new strategies for communicating the gospel; this model would carry forward under the administration of Jerry Rankin, Parks's successor. Terry and Fries note that Parks also brought in Anglican David Barrett to help with identifying unreached people groups and developing strategies for reaching them. Barrett's impact on Parks and the work of the FMB was seismic and enduring. The focus on unreached people groups became ensconced in FMB strategy and continues as a primary emphasis of the IMB today. Parks established himself as an innovative missiologist, but his tenure ended in controversy. His criticisms of the Conservative Resurgence in the SBC would eventually lead to his resignation in the midst of controversy and conflict with the board of trustees.

In chapter 10 Robin Dale Hadaway offers a review of Jerry Rankin's lengthy and transformational tenure as FMB president (1993–2010). Hadaway highlights the many significant changes that Rankin made to the structure, strategy, and overall operations of the FMB, one of which was changing the name from FMB to IMB. Rankin dissolved CSI and mainstreamed its strategy and ethos into the overall operations of the IMB. The focus on the unreached that began under Parks was refined and furthered during the Rankin years. This focus led to the deployment of personnel to fields of service with less than 2 percent of an indigenous, evangelical Christian witness. The IMB gradually shifted personnel and efforts from traditional fields of service to those they deemed underserved by the gospel. The FMB-localized mission structure was abolished in favor of a regional leadership model under Rankin. Rankin oversaw the introduction of new strategies such as Church Planting Movements, as outlined in a booklet authored by David Garrison; the Camel Method, a strategy designed by Kevin Greeson for Muslim contexts; and Training for Trainers, created by Steve Smith and Ying Kai. As Hadaway notes, each of the major changes that Rankin made to the IMB was met with debate and controversy. Perhaps more than any other president before him, Jerry Rankin made the most significant and lasting changes to the IMB.

In chapter 11 Hadaway discusses the brief but important presidency of Tom Elliff (2011–2014), who followed Rankin at the IMB. As Hadaway notes, Elliff was a third-generation pastor who served for two years with his wife, Jeannie, in Zimbabwe. They returned to the United States after their daughter's automobile accident in order to provide further medical care for her. Prior to his election as president, Elliff served as senior vice president for spiritual nurture and church relations under Jerry Rankin. Elliff's presidency of the IMB was marked by pastoral guidance of IMB personnel, an emphasis on the doctrinal preparation of missionaries for service, and a challenge to all SBC churches to adopt and work toward reaching an unreached people group.

In chapter 12 Paul Akin covers the relatively brief but significant presidency of Elliff's successor, David Platt (2014–2018). As noted by Akin, Platt at thirty-six years of age was the youngest IMB president ever to serve in the role. Since the time of M. Theron Rankin, Platt represented the first IMB president who did not serve as a field missionary but brought gifts and skills needed for the moment to guide and direct the work of the IMB. Platt represented a generational shift in leadership within the SBC and the IMB. Akin notes that he inherited an organization that was greatly affected by the economic recession that occurred between 2007 and 2009. Platt skillfully helped to align the organization's financial realities with the number of staff and field personnel employed by the organization.

He brought the number of field personnel down from approximately 4,700 to 3,700, mostly through incentives for voluntary separations. Platt was also deeply concerned about grounding IMB missions strategy in clear biblical teaching and principles. He commissioned the *Foundations* document, which outlined how IMB strategy would operate within doctrinal parameters. As Akin notes, Platt was also concerned to mobilize SBC churches for the task. He often used the example of the Moravians to set out his vision for mobilizing a "limitless" number of Southern Baptists to join IMB efforts around the world for the cause of the Great Commission. Platt continued the emphasis on reaching the unreached peoples of the world by launching a new emphasis on reaching large urban centers of the Global South. The pull of the pastorate eventually led to Platt's transition from the IMB to serve as the teaching elder of McLean Bible Church in Virginia.

Akin in chapter 12 also introduces David Platt's successor, Paul Chitwood, who was elected as IMB president in 2018. As Akin mentioned, like Platt, Chitwood never served as a missionary but was uniquely prepared for the role as IMB president through the pastorate, as an IMB trustee, and as the executive director of the Kentucky Baptist Convention. In an era of flatline Cooperative Program giving, having a seasoned champion for the Cooperative Program will prove to be an advantage for the IMB. Chitwood has established a leadership team to carry out his vision for the IMB as it moves deeper into the twenty-first century, building on a 173-year legacy of missions leadership and missions service before him.

Now we turn to the pre-beginnings of SBC missions.

PRE-BEGINNINGS

Jason G. Duesing

WHO'S ON FIRST?

WHEN HISTORIANS CLASSIFY historical figures in terms of who was first to do something, even when the figures did not think of themselves by such classifications, sometimes the historical accounts can read like the famous Abbott and Costello skit, "Who's on First?"[1] This is very much the case with the ongoing scholarship surrounding who was the first modern missionary or who should be termed "the father of modern missions." Sometimes, when I read these, a skit like this comes to my mind:

---

1 "'Who's on First?' by Abbott and Costello," *The Baseball Almanac*, https://www.baseball-almanac.com/humor4.shtml (accessed May 11, 2020).

Who was on the mission field first?

That's what I am asking, who?

Exactly.

Exactly what?

What's on second?

I thought Judson was second.

No, what's on second. I don't know is on third.

Who's on first?

Exactly.

Who *is* on first, Liele or Carey?[2]

Who's on first. I don't know Liele or Carey.

So you don't know Liele, Carey, or who's on third?

Who's on first!

Ah!

To give some context to what I mean, here are just a sampling of quotations:

> 1991—"Books written in English have frequently spoken
> of William Carey (1761–1834) as 'the father of modern

---

2   The name Liele can also be spelled as Leile or Lisle.

missions,' and of the work that he brought into being as the first Protestant missionary of modern times. Our earlier chapters have shown that this is a misunderstanding." [3]

1998—"Thus by the time William Carey—often mistakenly perceived to be the first Baptist missionary—sailed for India in 1793, Liele had worked as a missionary for a decade."[4]

2002—"William Carey . . . is most deserving of the title, 'Father of the Modern Mission Movement.' . . . However, he should not be considered the first Baptist foreign missionary! That distinction should be reserved for certain African-American Baptists who left their homes, journeyed to new lands, and started churches a decade before Carey went to India."[5]

2010—"The man often regarded as the first Baptist missionary, George Liele . . . a slave and ordained preacher."[6]

2012—"William Carey may have been the greatest missionary since the time of the apostles. He rightly deserves the honor of being known as 'the father of the modern missions movement.' . . . The man I believe is the pioneer of Baptists missions was a black man and a former slave by the name of George Leile. . . . Here is a modern missions grandfather."[7]

3   Stephen Neill, *A History of Christian Missions*, 2nd ed. (London: Penguin, 1991), 222.

4   Alan Neely, "Liele, George," in *Biographical Dictionary of Christian Missions*, ed. Gerald H. Anderson (New York: Macmillan Reference USA, 1998), 400–401.

5   Christopher Ballew, "The Impact of African-American Antecedents on the Baptist Foreign Missionary Movement: 1782–1825" (PhD diss., Southwestern Baptist Theological Seminary, 2002), 218.

6   David W. Bebbington, *Baptists through the Centuries: A History of a Global People* (Waco, TX: Baylor University Press, 2010), 242–43.

7   Daniel L. Akin, *10 Who Changed the World* (Nashville: B&H, 2012), 1, 86.

2015—"[Liele] should, therefore, probably be considered the first Baptist missionary, though some historians of mission would demur, since a 'missionary,' by definition, is sent out by a church."[8]

2018—"Even though William Carey may be called the father of the modern missionary movement, George Liele left America and planted the gospel in Jamaica a full ten years before Carey left England."[9]

2019—"George Liele (c. 1750–1820) was America's first cross-cultural missionary."[10]

These observations aside, what is taking place among historians is important, for it reveals that the entire story has not been told of who all helped propel Protestants to contribute to the growing task of global evangelism in the late eighteenth century. The purpose of this chapter is to answer the questions, Who's on first? and, Does it matter when assessing the history of missionary involvement by Baptists? That is, this chapter will acknowledge that George Liele was the first modern Baptist missionary and that it is right to consider William Carey the father of modern missions and Adoniram Judson as the pioneer American Baptist missionary. But I hope to do more than that.[11] Yes, who did what on which day is vital for understanding the historical task, but George Liele's contribution is far greater than just being first. In our efforts to reclaim him, we've also limited him. And then there is the matter of how he, Carey,

---

8 Anthony L. Chute, Nathan A. Finn, and Michael A. G. Haykin, *The Baptist Story* (Nashville: B&H Academic, 2015), 98.

9 Lesley Hildreth, "Missionaries You Should Know: George Liele," *IMB*, June 26, 2018.

10 Edward L. Smither, *Christian Mission: A Concise Global History* (Bellingham, WA: Lexham, 2019), xiii.

11 For the purposes of this chapter, I define *missionary* as "one who crosses cultures to share the gospel." See Jason G. Duesing, "The Pastor as Missionary," in *Portraits of a Pastor*, ed. Jason K. Allen (Chicago: Moody, 2017).

or Judson considered themselves. What would they make of all these titles? This chapter will answer this question by providing a brief background of the history of the beginnings of the modern missions movement in order to suggest a new methodology for missions historians and theologians to consider, and then it will give a biographical treatment of each figure and their missions strategies to illustrate the methodology.

THE MODERN MISSIONS MOVEMENT

From 1937 to 1945, church historian Kenneth Scott Latourette published his seven-volume *A History of the Expansion of Christianity*.[12] What is remarkable about this massive undertaking is that three of the volumes are dedicated just to the nineteenth century. Following Latourette's emphasis and organization, Ralph Winter classified the history of Christian missions into epochs; the last, which covered 1800–2000, he titled "Modern Missions."[13] What then is premodern missions, or, what happened to missions after the Reformation?

Following the Reformation, Protestants were slow to assemble any kind of organized missionary approach that would rival the Roman Catholic orders. To be sure, the Reformers themselves did engage in some global evangelism, but the movement could not yet sustain the transportation of churches or missionaries.[14] In the seventeenth century, the German Pietist movement influenced Dutch Protestantism and shaped those sent as chaplains throughout their trading colonies. In the early eighteenth century, the Pietists

---

12   Kenneth Scott Latourette, *A History of the Expansion of Christianity*, 7 vols. (New York: Harper, 1937–1945).

13   Ralph D. Winter, "The Kingdom Strikes Back: Ten Epochs of Redemptive History," in *Perspectives on the World Christian Movement: A Reader*, eds. Ralph D. Winter and Steven C. Hawthorne, 3rd ed. (Pasadena, CA: William Carey Library, 1999), 195–213.

14   See Glenn S. Sunshine, "Protestant Missions in the Sixteenth Century," in *The Great Commission: Evangelicals and the History of World Missions*, eds. Martin I. Klauber and Scott M. Manetsch (Nashville: B&H Academic, 2008), 12–22; Michael A. G. Haykin and C. Jeffrey Robinson Sr., *To the Ends of the Earth: Calvin's Missional Vision and Legacy* (Wheaton, IL: Crossway, 2014).

shaped Count Nicolaus Ludwig von Zinzendorf, who gave refuge to persecuted Moravian Christians. This colony would awaken to the missionary task and take the gospel to the West Indies, Greenland, the Americas, South Africa, Egypt, and Tibet. The Moravian effort coincided with the Great Awakening in England and America through John Wesley, who had some connection to the Pietists. In New England among the Puritans, there had been some cross-cultural work done among Native Americans by John Eliot and then David Brainerd. The accounts of this expansion of the gospel as well as further development of the need for participation in global evangelism were fueled by the writing and ministry of Jonathan Edwards and George Whitefield. As Protestants entered the nineteenth century, they organized their efforts in several mission societies and agencies to enable their churches to fund and send their missionaries. Thus, as George Liele and William Carey were taking the gospel to other cultures in their respective parts of the world, they were doing so on the eve of what we know now as the modern missions movement.

The term *father of modern missions* originated following William Carey's death in an admiring biography by George Smith:

> Yet we, ninety-three years after he went forth with the Gospel to Hindostan, may venture to place him where the Church History of the future is likely to keep him—amid the uncrowned kings of men who have made Christian England what it is, under God, to its own people and to half the human race. These are Chaucer, the Father of English Verse; Wiclif, the Father of the Evangelical Reformation in all lands; Hooker, the Father of English Prose; Shakspere, the Father of English Literature; Milton, the Father of the English Epic; Bunyan, the Father of English allegory; Newton, the Father of English Science; Carey, the Father of the Second Reformation through Foreign Missions.[15]

---

15   George Smith, *The Life of William Carey, D.D., Shoemaker and Missionary* (London: John Murray, 1885), 439.

Had Carey been alive, he likely would have discouraged this assessment. When writing his *Enquiry* in 1792, he chronicled the spread of the gospel from the apostle Paul to the Reformation. He then depicted the modern era by recognizing the work among Native Americans by Eliot, Brainerd, and Carey's contemporaries, Mr. Kirkland and Mr. Sergeant. Carey included mention of the mission work of the Dutch and then lauded the work of the Moravian Brethren.[16] Nathan Finn mentions that Carey "was keenly aware that he was in continuity with a movement that had already commenced."[17]

This is not to say that no one was aware of Liele's contribution. Many in England were aware due to the publication of Liele's letters in John Rippon's *The Baptist Annual Register*. While there is no evidence that Carey read *The Register*, there is a high likelihood that he did because of the notices about his own works that appeared at the same time. *The Register* chronicled the first notice of the publication of Carey's *Enquiry* in 1792, a notice concerning Carey's ordination, and the minutes of the Northamptonshire Association that documented the formation of what would become the Baptist Missionary Society (BMS). These reports are interspersed in and around the ongoing correspondence of George Liele to John Rippon, a local pastor and editor.[18] As the historian Brian Stanley notes, "Thus, even before the formation of the BMS, Jamaican Baptists were brought to the attention of Particular Baptists in England."[19]

---

16   William Carey, *An Enquiry into the Obligation of Christians to Use Means for the Conversion of the Heathens* (Leicester, 1792).

17   Nathan A. Finn, ed., *Help to Zion's Travellers* (Mountain Home, AR: BorderStone, 2011), xvn9.

18   John Rippon, *The Baptist Annual Register for 1790, 1791, 1792, and Part of 1793* (London, 1793), iv. "Having had a wish therefore to gratify the Brethren at home and abroad; and hoping, under a Divine blessing to be the instrument of bringing many of the churches so far acquainted, That that they may have an opportunity of *relieving* one anothers wants, of *praying* for each other when the ways of Sion mourn, and of *praising* God in the enjoyment of prosperous circumstances—I determined in the year 1790, God willing, to print a periodical work, which should be intitled, The Baptist Annual Register."

19   Brian Stanley, *The History of the Baptist Missionary Society, 1792–1992* (Edinburgh: T&T Clark, 1992), 69–70.

A SUGGESTED METHODOLOGY

Among Baptist historians, there has been an ongoing methodological discussion about how one can best interpret the Baptist
tradition. Some have argued for a single source, or "monogenesis,"
of great authority that anchors the Baptist tradition, which I argue
in another essay is largely an unhelpful contribution, especially
as it finds expression in ultra-successionist forms.[20] Most have,
instead, acknowledged that there is a multi-source, or "polygenesis," influence that comprises the Baptist tradition.[21] Baptists are a
product of the Reformation, yes, but their organizational formation
comes in England later, for example. In addition, another historian,
William Brackney, has argued that a better way is to think of the
various epochs of the Baptist movement as a "genetic approach
that attempts to make a historical connection between the various
streams of Baptist thought, while allowing for diversity in evolved
thinking."[22] This idea of searching for shared DNA, if you will, has
merit, but I am afraid it sometimes loses theological precision.
Timothy George also used a genetics metaphor when describing his
methodology: "Historical theology is the genetic study of Christian
faith and doctrine ... [that] investigates the nuances and modalities,
the developments and deviations, of the efforts of all Christians."[23] I
like the specificity here best as it attempts to find common doctrinal
commitments and seeks to leave no person behind.

What does this have to do with an assessment of the beginnings of the modern missions movement? What I am suggesting

---

20   Jason G. Duesing, "Baptist Contributions to the Christian Tradition," in *Baptists and the Christian Tradition*, eds. Matthew Y. Emerson, Christopher W. Morgan, and R. Lucas Stamps (Nashville: B&H Academic, 2020).

21   See James M. Stayer, Werner Packull, and Klaus Deppermann, "From Monogenesis to Polygenesis: The Historical Discussion of Anabaptist Origins," *Mennonite Quarterly Review* 49, no. 2 (Apr 1975): 83–121; and Malcolm B. Yarnell, *The Formation of Christian Doctrine* (Nashville: B&H Academic, 2007), 7.

22   William H. Brackney, *A Genetic History of Baptist Thought* (Macon, GA: Mercer University Press, 2004), 2–3.

23   Timothy George, "Dogma beyond Anathema: Historical Theology in the Service of the Church," in *Review and Expositor* 84, no. 4 (Fall 1987): 691.

is that historians are thinking in an unhelpful way about modern missions leaders when thinking merely in terms of the chronology of progeny. However, this is not to say it is unhelpful to identify who might be the first to do something or from whom a tradition developed. I affirm those clarifying efforts. Rather, I am saying that when assessing the modern missions movement, we need to do more than that if we are going to capture with faithfulness the movement itself.

Thus, instead of monogenesis, polygenesis, or a genetic approach, I present what I call a symphonious approach for assessing the modern missions movement. This era in history is, after all, a movement, and much like the musical use of that term, we see similar themes—there are many diverse and complementary components that make up a symphony. For the symphony to achieve its desired sound, all must play their part. Symphonies usually are composed of four movements, each of which tells part of the story at different speeds and intensity.

For example, when considering the Protestant Reformation, historians and theologians do not often speak in terms of who was the first Reformer or who is the father of the Reformation. Rather, those events and people in church history made up a symphonic movement. Like its musical counterpart, it had a prelude in Wyclif and Hus, struck its opening notes with Luther, and saw further development and deployment in Zwingli, Calvin, and Cranmer. Complementing these major sections were a host of other Reformers, with their own social and cultural events, advancements in technology, translation, and specific convictions that added to the color and depth of the symphony that was the Reformation.

So it is with the modern missions movement. The Reformers themselves played some parts of the initial piece, but the Moravians and others opened the overture in its beginning. George Liele, then, represents the first movement with a unique and influential contribution that many have overlooked, yet he mobilized and influenced many. Carey, shaped by all who went before, gave a full, well-organized presentation; the DNA of such serves as a refrain for later movements that include Americans Adoniram and Ann Judson and many other missions societies, organizations, and work. What is more, there are other figures who contribute to this symphony who have yet to be acknowledged. Timothy George notes the underappreciated John Sutcliff.[24] Many women advanced the cause of global missions from 1800 to 2000 who have not yet received full study. In addition, there is a need to research the churches involved, those sent by the churches to check on the missionaries and send reports, and the printers and distributors of letters and pamphlets from the field—and much more.

Thus, as far as titles and assessing the right chronology of the movement, I am arguing that it is more helpful to think of the modern missions movement like other movements in church history and to minimize the emphasis on titles in favor of assessing all the component parts and their unique contributions that serve to make up the movement as a whole.

GEORGE LIELE (CA. 1750–1828)

George Liele made a significant mark on American Christian history long before he left America for Jamaica as a missionary. Born as a slave in Virginia, Liele's father is thought to have been the earliest believing slave in America. They were owned by Henry Sharpe, who relocated the family to Georgia in 1770. In 1773, at the age of twenty-three, Liele was converted at Buckhead Creek Baptist Church, where Sharpe was a deacon. Liele would later share with the English Baptist pastor John Rippon that after hearing the gospel,

the more I saw that I was condemned as a sinner before God, till at length I was brought to perceive that my life was held by a single thread. . . . I saw my condemnation

---

24 Timothy George, "Let It Go: Lessons from the Life of William Carey," in *Expect Great Things, Attempt Great Things*, eds. Allen Yeh and Chris Chun (Eugene, OR: Wipf & Stock, 2013), 8.

in my own heart, and I found no way wherein I could escape the damnation of hell, only through the merits of my dying Lord and Saviour Jesus Christ. . . . I felt such love and joy as my tongue was not able to express. After this I declared before the congregation of believers the work which God had done for my soul, and the same minister . . . baptized me.[25]

According to Albert Raboteau, Liele experienced "an inward, experiential realization of the doctrines of human depravity, divine sovereignty, and unconditional election made vividly apparent to the imagination and the emotions."[26] By May 1775, Liele was set apart by the church for the ministry after preaching before the congregation, and as a result, he was given his freedom by Henry Sharpe.[27]

Traveling near Savannah, Liele started meeting with a group of believers in Silver Bluff and soon established a church, the first African American Baptist church in America. One of his earliest converts was David George, who would eventually move to Sierra Leone to serve as the first Baptist pastor in Africa.[28] With the onset of the Revolutionary War, Liele was helped to move to Jamaica in

---

25   Rippon, *Register*, 332–33.

26   Albert J. Raboteau, *Slave Religion: The "Invisible Institution" in the Antebellum South* (New York: Oxford University Press, 2004), 268.

27   Edward A. Holmes, "George Liele: Negro Slavery's Prophet of Deliverance," *Baptist History & Heritage* 1 (August 1965), 28.

28   William Haun, "Missionaries You Should Know: David George," *IMB*, October 2, 2018. Lamin Sanneh, "George, David," in Anderson, *Biographical Dictionary of Christian Missions*, 238–39. Ballew, in "The Impact of African-American Antecedents," considers both Liele and David George as the first Baptist missionaries and joint precursors to the modern missions movement, citing David George's relocation to Nova Scotia with the British at the time or just before Liele was deployed to Jamaica. However, while certainly a contemporary preacher who crossed cultures to preach the gospel, David George's Nova Scotia ministry was distinct from George Liele's in terms of its transient circumstances, whereas Liele's Jamaican work was indigenous from the start. That said, a case can be made for David George's role, and he should not be overlooked as a part of a symphonious approach. Regardless of how one assesses Nova Scotia, his missionary legacy as the first Baptist pastor in Africa due to his landing in Sierra Leone in 1792 is a vital component to the history of the early modern missions movement.

1783, where, once he fulfilled his financial obligations, he began a
new church and ministered to the slaves while working as a farmer. Liele's cross-cultural missionary service came to him due to
circumstance, but it led to years of fruitful engagement and gospel
advance among the people living in Jamaica. His establishment of
the church in Kingston helped shape the development of the Baptist
movement in that country and beyond, for Liele's church covenant
and vision for reaching people would encourage the BMS to focus
on sending missionaries to Jamaica in 1814.[29] The covenant was
designed to work with both slave and owner, emphasizing the need
to settle disputes among believers, the need for slaves to have a
recommendation from their owners before joining, and the mutual
pursuit of charitableness between the two.[30]

As Alan Neely explains, "While [Liele] never openly challenged
the system of slavery, he prepared the way for those who did."[31]
Slavery would come to an end in Jamaica in 1838, and by that
time there were over twenty thousand believers on the island as a
result of Liele's ministry.[32] As a testimony to Liele's labors, Thomas
Nicholas Swigle wrote the following to John Rippon in England:

> We have great reason in this island to praise and glorify
> the Lord, for his goodness and loving kindness in send-
> ing his blessed Gospel amongst us, by our well-beloved
> minister, Brother Liele. We were living in slavery to sin
> and Satan, and the Lord hath redeemed our souls to a

---

29 Horace O. Russell, "Prologue," in George Liele's Life and Legacy, ed. David T. Shan-
    non (Macon, GA: Mercer University Press, 2012), 10.

30 "1796 Covenant of George Liele," in Charles W. Deweese, Baptist Church Covenants
    (Nashville: Broadman, 1990), 190. For analysis of the covenant, see Russell, "Pro-
    logue," 10–11.

31 Neely, "Liele, George," 400–401.

32 Sylvia R. Frey and Betty Wood note, "The direction and approach of the devel-
    oping African independence movement, to the extent that they can be attributed
    to a single individual, were determined by the power and personality of George
    Liele." Sylvia R. Frey and Betty Wood, Come Shouting to Zion: African American
    Protestantism in the American South and British Caribbean to 1830 (Chapel Hill:
    University of North Carolina Press, 1998), 115.

state of happiness to praise his glorious and ever blessed name. . . . The blessed Gospel is spreading wonderfully in this island; believers are daily coming to church, and we hope, in a little time, to see Jamaica become a Christian country.[33]

In my assessment, it is right and good to refer to George Liele as the first Baptist missionary and the first American missionary, but by taking a symphonious approach, there is far more to Liele's contribution to the modern missions movement than his place in line.

WILLIAM CAREY (1761–1834)

Born in a small village to a devout Anglican family, Carey regularly attended church but experienced no major life transformation.[34] By his teens he apprenticed as a shoemaker in a neighboring town, and through the persistent witness of his coworker John Warr, Carey saw his need for a Savior. Soon after his conversion, he left the Church of England and attended a Congregationalist church while intently reading and studying the Scriptures. When faced with the quandary of defending from the Bible his own infant baptism, Carey sought aid from John Ryland Sr., the pastor of College Lane Baptist Church in Northampton. In October 1783, Carey received believer's baptism from the pastor's son, John Ryland Jr. Shortly thereafter, another pastor encouraged Carey to preach for a small congregation while maintaining his shoemaking trade. As he contemplated pastoral ministry, he wrote this to his father, "I see more and more of my own insufficiency for the great work I am called to. The truths of God are amazingly profound, the souls of men infinitely precious, my own ignorance very great."[35]

---

33 Rippon, *Register*, 542.
34 Portions of this section are presented with permission in a revised form from Jason G. Duesing, *Seven Summits in Church History* (Spring Hill, TN: Rainer, 2016).
35 Timothy George, *Faithful Witness: The Life & Mission of William Carey* (Birmingham, AL: New Hope, 1991), 25.

By 1785, Carey had accepted a vocational pastorate in Moulton. There he established a friendship with Baptist pastor Andrew Fuller of neighboring Kettering. During this time, Carey's regular reading of the voyages of Captain James Cook opened his eyes to the world. In addition, Robert Hall Sr.'s *Help to Zion's Travellers*, a doctrinal primer molded from the evangelical theology of Jonathan Edwards and distinct from the hyper-Calvinist climate in England among Baptists, helped shape Carey's theological thinking more than any other book outside the Bible. With a theology that held the sovereignty of God in balance with the responsibility of man and a growing zeal to see the saving message of the Lord Jesus taken to the ends of the earth, Carey set out to organize his thoughts for accomplishing this task. After wrestling with the Great Commission in Matthew 28, Carey raised the notion of global evangelism at a minister's meeting in 1785 but was told he "was a most miserable enthusiast for asking such a question." Despite the discouraging response, Carey continued his planning, and as Timothy George notes, his "concern for the unevangelized heathen in distant lands did not slacken his zeal to share the good news of Jesus Christ with sinners at home."[36]

In 1789, Carey went to pastor the Harvey Lane Church in Leicester. By May 1792, he published *An Enquiry into the Obligations of Christians to Use Means for the Conversion of the Heathens*, an argument that the Great Commission remained as a mandate for all churches. This argument was novel in Carey's day, for the accepted understanding was that the Great Commission was fulfilled by the apostles and no longer applicable to believers. Carey, instead, read the text plainly and, as Nathan Finn argues, merely applied what he first learned from Robert Hall's doctrinal primer to foreign missions. In the *Enquiry*, Carey answered common objections to the idea of cross-cultural evangelism as well as documenting, in great detail, the vast numbers of people outside of Christ. As

---

36   George, *Faithful Witness*, 28.

George explains, "Carey's statistics were more than mere numbers on a chart. They represented persons, persons made in the image of God and infinitely precious to Him."[37] At the next meeting of the Baptist Association, Carey preached a sermon from Isaiah 54 calling for the transmission of the gospel overseas, encouraging his hearers to "expect great things. Attempt great things."[38] Lest one think the staid work of church association meetings, convention sermons, and denominational resolutions are a hindrance for gospel advance, consider that the launch of a missions society that would contribute to the most wide-reaching missions movement began in a small free-church association meeting following a sermon with the formal passing of a resolution that read, "Resolved, that a plan be prepared against the next Ministers' meeting at Kettering, for forming a Baptist Society for propagating the Gospel among the Heathen."[39]

In October 1792, the Baptist Missionary Society was formed, and Carey stepped forward to join the first deployment to India. Of that day Fuller recounted:

> Our undertaking to India really appeared to me, on its commencement, to be somewhat like a few men, who were deliberating about the importance of penetrating a deep mine, which had never before been explored. We had no one to guide us; and, while we were thus deliberating, Carey, as it were, said, "Well, I will go down if you will hold the rope." But before he went down, he, as it seemed to me, took an oath from each of us at the mouth of the pit to this effect, that while we lived we should never let go the rope.[40]

37   Timothy George, quoted in *Seven Summits*, 97.
38   William Carey, quoted in *Seven Summits*, 100.
39   William Carey, quoted in *Seven Summits*, 100.
40   Andrew Fuller, in *The Complete Works of Rev. Andrew Fuller*, ed. Joseph Belcher (Philadelphia: American Baptist Publication Society, 1845), 1:68.

Carey made preparations to depart, and when writing to his father, he resolved, "I have many sacrifices to make. . . . But I have set my hand to the plough" (Luke 9:62).[41]

Carey and family arrived in Bengal in November 1793 and endured immediate hardship. In October 1794, the Careys lost their five-year-old son, Peter, to illness; this tragedy, along with other trials, wreaked havoc on both Careys, especially his wife. Paul Pease explains, "Over the past sixteen months Dorothy had suffered many hardships, hurts, losses, and fears: the sad and frantic farewells in England, the long voyage with a young baby, the culture shock of India, the uncertainty of the numerous moves, the humiliation and pain of dysentery, her sister left in Debhata, and now the death of her five year old son. It all became too much for her, and she seemed to retreat from all reality."[42]

Further, the first seven years saw very little spiritual fruit. Writing to his sister in November 1798, Carey said, "No one expects me to write about experience, or any of the common topics of Religion; nor to say anything about the Doctrines of the Gospel, but News, and continual accounts of marvelous things are expected from me. I have however no news to send, and as everything here is the same, no Marvels. . . . At best we scarcely expect to be anything more than Pioneers to prepare the Way for those who coming after us may be more useful than we have been."[43]

In 1799, however, Carey moved his family to Serampore and joined with two other missionaries, Joshua Marshman and William Ward. Known now as the Serampore trio, the three established the Serampore Mission and, in 1800, saw their first convert.

In October 1805, Carey and his fellow missionaries, like Liele, also adopted a covenant to guide their work. "The Serampore Form

---

41 Eustace Carey, *Memoir of William Carey, D.D.* (London: Jackson and Walford, 1836), 64.

42 Paul Pease, *Travel with William Carey* (Leominster, UK: Day One, 2005), 84–85.

43 "William Carey to Ann Hobson," November 27, 1798, in *Baptist Autographs in the John Rylands University Library of Manchester, 1741–1845*, ed. Timothy D. Whelan (Macon, GA: Mercer University Press, 2009), 91–92.

Agreement" gave guidance to the Serampore Mission but would also guide future missionaries.[44] Organized around ten principles, the Agreement discussed preferred methods for sharing the gospel, learning the culture, and the primacy of planting indigenous churches. The Agreement starts, "In order to be prepared for our great and solemn work, it is absolutely necessary that we set an infinite value upon immortal souls; that we often endeavor to affect our minds with the dreadful loss sustained by an unconverted soul launched into eternity."[45] Their plan was to read the agreement publicly three times a year "to keep these ideas alive in our minds."[46]

While Carey's legacy grew chiefly through Bible translation and as the trailblazer for scores of future missionaries, he, like Liele, also influenced the culture and country where he lived. In one instance, Carey wrote first about observing the practice of suttee (*sati*), wherein the wife would cast herself on the funeral pyre of her dead husband. In April 1799, Carey wrote:

> As I was returning from Calcutta I saw ... a Woman burning herself with the corpse of her husband, for the first time in my life.... I asked [the people assembled] what they were met for. They told me to burn the body of a dead man. I inquired if his Wife would die with him, they answered yes, and pointed to the Woman.... I asked them if this was the woman's choice, or if she were brought to it by an improper influence? They answered that it was perfectly voluntary. I talked till reasoning was no use, and then began to explain with all my might against what they were doing, telling them it was a shocking Murder.... But she in the most calm manner mounted the Pile, and danced on it with her hands extended as if in the utmost tranquility of spirit.[47]

---

44   Zane Pratt, *Introduction to Global Missions* (Nashville: B&H Academic, 2014), 120.
45   "The Serampore Form Agreement," *Baptist Quarterly* 12, no. 5 (January 1947): 130.
46   "The Serampore Form Agreement," 138.
47   William Carey to Ryland, Mudnabati, April 1, 1799, in *The Journal and Selected Letters of William Carey*, ed. Terry G. Carter (Macon, GA: Smyth & Helwys, 2000), 79–80.

Carey did not give up his advocacy. In December 1829 he wrote, "On the 4th of this month a regulation was passed by The Governor General in Council to forbid the burning or burying alive of Hindu Widows with their husbands. This is a matter of utmost importance and calls for our loudest thanks."[48]

William Carey died in 1834, leaving instructions that his tombstone read, "A wretched, poor, and helpless worm, On thy kind arms I fall." In my assessment, it is also right and good to refer to Carey as the father of modern missions when appropriate, but a symphonious approach shows there is much more to Carey's contribution to modern missions than just his paternal organizational and inspirational role in history.

ADONIRAM JUDSON (1788–1850)

In the summer of 1806, several dedicated young men attending Williams College in Williamstown, Massachusetts, began to gather regularly to pray and read reports of the burgeoning work of Andrew Fuller, William Carey, and the new Baptist Missionary Society in England. On one occasion, while meeting in a field adjacent to the college campus, the students, trapped by a thunderstorm, took shelter in a haystack. Haystacks in 1806 were not the tightly bound bales we see today. Rather, they were piled as high as possible with only a pitchfork and a sundown deadline. Thus, as with a quickly assembled snow fort, the young men of Williams dove into and carved out a hay-lined shelter to continue their meeting. What they found, though, was far more rewarding than had they discovered a missing needle.

The "Haystack Prayer Meeting," as it came to be called, resulted in the dedication of these young men to personal participation in the global missions task, and the ensuing years led to the entry of formal American participation with the sending of Adoniram and Ann Judson along with several others to the East. Herein we can see a

---

48   William Carey to Sisters, December 17, 1829, Serampore, in Carter, *Journal and Selected Letters of William Carey*, 84.

dotted line from 1806 to the present, for the Haystack Prayer Meeting is, in many ways, the Wittenberg door of American evangelicalism's awakening to the need and universal call for all believers to support, organize, and send many for global gospel proclamation. To be sure, Liele and Carey were formative examples and inspirations, but the organizing force that came after the Haystack Prayer Meeting is what sustained American involvement in global evangelism.

Recognizing the significance of that 1806 prayer meeting, later missions supporters dedicated in 1867 a monument on the grounds of Williams College, where it still resides in the college's Mission Park.[49] In recent years, Protestants have rightly remembered the five-hundredth anniversary of the actual Reformation events the door in Wittenberg helped to launch, events that would encourage the later formation of Williams College and many Protestant churches in New England. Therefore, in the spirit of the Reformation's gospel recovery, it is good and right also to consider the contribution of a group of praying students, heirs of Wittenberg themselves, in a symphonious approach to understanding the modern missions movement.

After meeting the Haystack leaders while studying at Andover Seminary, Adoniram Judson helped form the first missions sending agency in American history despite initial opposition by the culture around him.[50] While only a few were contemplating

---

49   The monument reads, "The Field is the World. The Birthplace of American Foreign Missions." The selection of the phrase "The Field is the World" is an intriguing one, but not unique given the time and missionary context. Taken from Matthew 13:38 and the Lord Jesus's explanation of the parable of the weeds, the correlation of the harvest field to the world appears first as merely background information, a description of the stage on which the parable would take place. However, as many would rightly note, the acknowledgment that the boundaries for the proclamation of the gospel are global is good and significant news for all dwellers in time and space distant from the land of Israel in the era of the New Testament. An example of how a missionary-minded preacher interpreted and applied Matthew 13 in the mid-nineteenth century is Gardiner Spring (1785–1873), and his sermon "The Extent of the Missionary Enterprise" (1840).

50   The next two paragraphs are adapted from Jason G. Duesing, "Standing Like a Steersman in a Storm: Courage to Act Like Men in a Culture that Says Otherwise," in *Nelson's Annual Preacher's Sourcebook*, ed. O. S. Hawkins (Nashville: Thomas Nelson, 2014), 4:300–303.

the idea of personal participation in the global missions task, and only a small group of churches in England had formally sent any missionaries by this time, Judson and his friends blazed a path that many Americans would follow. Therefore, it is appropriate to consider Judson as the pioneer American missionary.[51] As a student, he read a sermon by an English preacher that moved him to "break the strong attachment I felt to home and country, and to endure the thought of abandoning all my wonted pursuits and animating prospects."[52] This resulted in the following personal resolution: "The command of Christ, 'Go into all the world, and preach the gospel to every creature,' was presented to my mind with such clearness and power, that I came to a full decision, and though great difficulties appeared in my way, resolved to obey the command at all events."[53] Yet, there was no one to send him. Even though only a young man with young, supportive friends, Judson managed, by sheer courage and harnessed ambition, to persuade the older church leaders of the need to create a missions sending agency. Though he faced delays and criticism, eventually he saw the formation of the American Board of Commissioners for Foreign Missions (ABCFM) arise out of a network of New England Congregationalist churches.

While traveling to Asia, Ann and Adoniram Judson became convinced that the practice of infant baptism by their own Congregationalist churches did not fit with what they came to see as clear teaching from the Bible on the matter. Thus, when the Judsons arrived in India, they sent word that they could no longer serve in good conscience with the very mission board Judson helped found and on whose financial support they depended. Judson explained, "In a word, I could not find a single intimation in the New Testament, that the children and domestics of believers were members of the

---

51   See Jason G. Duesing, ed., *Adoniram Judson: A Bicentennial Appreciation of the Pioneer American Missionary* (Nashville: B&H Academic, 2012).

52   Adoniram Judson to Stephen Chapin, December 18, 1837, quoted in Francis Wayland, *A Memoir of the Life and Labors of the Rev. Adoniram Judson, D.D.* (Boston: Phillips, Sampson, and Company, 1853), 1:51–52.

53   Judson to Chapin, in Wayland, *Memoir*, 1:51–52.

church, or entitled to any church ordinance, in consequence of the profession of the head of their family. Everything discountenanced this idea. When baptism was spoken of, it was always in connection with believing. None but believers were commanded to be baptized; and it did not appear to my mind that any others were baptized."[54] When the Judsons joined the Baptists, they did so without any clear path of financial security or even a plan to carry out their missionary task. Judson cut off the only lifeline he had and trusted the Lord to provide. His wife, Ann, wrote home defending their decision and concluded, "Thus, my dear parents and sisters, we are both confirmed Baptists, not because we wish to be, but because truth compelled us to be."[55] Judson could have asked for a short-term provision from the ABCFM until they landed on their feet or arrived at their destination. He also could have downplayed the issue as a mere ecclesiological variance, not a major departure of doctrine. But here the Judson's biblical courage appeared as they moved forward by faith in their newfound convictions even though, like Abraham, "[they] went out, not knowing where [they were] going" (Heb. 11:8 ESV).

Luther Rice received an appointment from the ABCFM alongside Judson in 1812 and traveled to India in the second wave of new missionaries. Upon his arrival, he learned of the Judsons' change of mind regarding baptism, and though arguing with Judson at first, Rice, after listening to Judson preach on the doctrine in September 1812, soon thereafter accepted believer's baptism in November. In the ensuing months, Judson and Rice wrote to Baptist churches in America to enlist support to enable them to stay on the field, but Rice's deteriorating health led them to conclude that Rice should return to the United States and seek to organize Baptist churches in a formal missions board. En

---

54 "A Letter to the Third Church in Plymouth, Mass," August 20, 1817, in Adoniram Judson, *Christian Baptism: A Sermon on Christian Baptism, with Many Quotations from Pedobaptist Authors*, 5th American ed. (Boston: Gould, Kendall & Lincoln, 1846), 100.
55 James Knowles, *The Memoir of Mrs. Ann H. Judson* (Boston: Lincoln & Edmands, 1829), 75.

route, Rice started his tireless work, writing to a Baptist pastor in Massachusetts that they were "under a sincere conviction that the missionary cause would be more advanced by the formation of a Baptist Society in America . . . [for] our brethren in the United States have equal love for the Lord Jesus; and certainly not less zeal for diffusing the savour of his precious name among those who must, otherwise, *perish for lack of vision.*"[56]

When Rice arrived home, he traveled north and south on horseback going from Baptist church to Baptist church, proving his giftedness for the task of mobilizing support and calling for a national society to unite all the churches.[57] Though not accepted or encouraged by all Baptist churches, Rice's efforts bore fruit in a short amount of time.[58] The Philadelphia Baptist Association and Baptists in Massachusetts and South Carolina were compelled to organize to "provide funds for foreign missions" and to gather to establish a unified national organization.[59] In May 1814, three dozen church leaders from eleven states gathered in Philadelphia to form the General Missionary Convention of the Baptist Denomination in the United States of America. This "Triennial Convention" met every three years and would serve as the forerunner to the Southern Baptist Convention that would originate, sadly, in 1845 over a disagreement among Baptists in the North and South over the tragic and evil practice of slavery. At its start, however, the Triennial Convention remained focused on its task and started to send other missionaries, including John Peck, to the frontier land of Missouri and Lott Cary, a former slave and leader of the African Baptist Missionary Society, to Liberia.

---

56 Massachusetts Baptist Missionary Society, *The Massachusetts Baptist Missionary Magazine*, September, 1813, 332.

57 Robert G. Torbet, *Venture of Faith: The Story of the American Baptist Foreign Mission Society and the Woman's American Baptist Foreign Mission Society, 1814–1954* (King of Prussia, PA: Judson, 1955), 26–30.

58 One of his leading critics was John Taylor and his anti-missions society following. See John Taylor, *Thoughts on Missions* (Franklin County, KY: n.p., 1820).

59 Massachusetts Baptist Missionary Society, *The Massachusetts Baptist Missionary Magazine*, December, 1813, 354.

So, why did Baptists first form a national denomination? Here is the actual wording from the Triennial Convention's first constitution: "We the delegates from Missionary Societies, and other religious Bodies of the Baptist denomination, in various parts of the United States, met in Convention, in the City of Philadelphia, for the purpose of carrying into effect the benevolent Intentions of our Constituents, by organizing a plan for eliciting, combining, and directing the Energies of the whole Denomination in one sacred effort, for sending the glad tidings of Salvation to the Heathen, and to nations destitute of pure Gospel-light."[60] Simply put, this shared idea of marshaling the energies of churches "in one sacred effort" to take the gospel of Christ to "nations destitute of pure Gospel-light" served as the primary motive for early American Baptists to organize and gather on a national level. This is no small point for our denominationally averse age to miss: the reason why Baptist churches sought to cooperate at a national level, with all of its necessary machinery, politics, stresses, and strains, was for the purpose of uniting to send the gospel to those who have never heard (Rom. 15:21).

In my assessment, it is also right and good to refer to Adoniram Judson as the pioneer American Baptist missionary, given his role in helping to organize the Baptist Foreign Mission Board, but the employment of a symphonious approach reveals there is much more to Judson's contribution to modern missions, and from those who served before, with, and after him, than just Judson's pioneering organizational vision alone.

CONCLUSION

This brief overview of the lives and ministries of George Liele, William Carey, and Adoniram Judson reveals that these men had a lasting impact on those they reached for Christ, the immediate culture and

---

60 American Baptist Foreign Mission Society, *Proceedings of the Baptist Convention for Missionary Purposes Held in Philadelphia, in May, 1814* (Philadelphia, 1814), 3.

context, and the future of the modern missions movement. As I have argued, when historians and theologians analyze the modern missions movement in the ways they quantify other movements in the history of Christianity, seeing these leaders playing their unique parts in one grand symphony allows their voices and legacies to be appreciated for their ongoing influence. This perspective distinguishes itself from attempts to summarize one missionary or the other as "the first" or "the father" while minimizing their much larger contribution. David Bebbington says, "The most important development in which Baptists participated during their four centuries of existence was the foreign missionary movement."[61] My argument has been that a symphonious approach to assessing that movement allows current researchers to see the full value and beauty of what the movement's leaders were able to do in their lifetimes, not to mention all the supporting figures and trends that helped to strengthen the movement and that have yet to be studied and shared. As Stratford Caldecott reminds us, "Every great change, every rebirth or *renaissance* in human culture, has been triggered by the retrieval of something valuable out of the past, making new, creative developments possible."[62] I hope this assessment serves to help foster new and creative assessments of the modern missions movement for the sake of those who do not yet have a missions history.

Candidly, here at the end, many historians might respond to my clarifications and say, "Enough already. I don't care who is on first or how is the best way to put it all together, just as long as the missions movement and its overlooked figures are studied and shared." With that bottom-line sentiment I would agree—but then would also point out that "I don't care" . . . well, he is the shortstop.

---

61   Bebbington, *Baptists through the Centuries*, 215.
62   Stratford Caldecott, *Beauty for Truth's Sake* (Grand Rapids: Brazos, 2009), 12.

BEGINNINGS

Southern Baptists, the Foreign Mission Board, and James Barnett Taylor

W. Madison Grace II

EVERY STORY HAS A BEGINNING, yet rarely is that beginning the start of a new story; rather, it is a new chapter in a larger narrative. In looking at the IMB we find that its story is merely a chapter in the larger narrative of Baptist missionary efforts and the greater missionary enterprise. The roots of the beginnings of Southern Baptist missionary work are in this larger history of Christianity. Southern Baptist missionary endeavors are not unique and set apart from others who also are, and have been, taking the gospel to the uttermost. However, we rightly should narrow the focus to the particular stream of missionary work that has been part of Baptist work. The IMB is a Baptist organization and is connected to those of that confessional stripe. So we must recognize that Southern Baptist mission work is connected to broader Baptist work. Our previous chapter oriented us to those particular connections in George Liele, William Carey, and Adoniram Judson. Others could be added there as well, such as J. G. Oncken, who rightly understood that every Baptist is a missionary. Southern Baptist mission work stands on the shoulders of the broader missionary work of our forefathers and theological cousins throughout history. We must not forget that as we engage the history of Southern Baptist missions.

Our particular purpose, however, is to tell the story of Southern Baptist missions. This chapter aims at engaging our particular beginnings. The question of how the FMB/IMB began, however, is attached to the larger question of how the Southern Baptists came into being. The reason many Baptists, who hold to the autonomy of the local church, cooperate beyond their locality is due to missions. David Bebbington rightly claims that the "most important development in which Baptists participated during their four centuries of existence was the foreign missionary movement."[1] So the beginnings of SBC denominational structure are closely connected to the beginnings of SBC missionary work. However, this is a tale that begins long before a gathering of 327 delegates in Augusta, Georgia, on May 8, 1845.[2] We will begin where our previous chapter left off, looking at the formation of the Baptist Board of Foreign Missions and the

---

1   David W. Bebbington, *Baptists through the Centuries: A History of a Global People* (Waco, TX: Baylor University Press, 2010), 215.

2   The exact number of persons involved can be confusing, as McBeth states: "These 327 delegates included only 293 persons since some represented more than one church or society, a fact which has created no end of confusion in reporting. This was hardly a representative assembly; of the 293 present, 273 came from the three states of Georgia, South Carolina, and Virginia. Significantly, the American Baptist Publication Society had representatives in Augusta, which means that one of the Northern Baptist agencies helped form the Southern Baptist Convention." Leon McBeth, *The Baptist Heritage: Four Centuries of Baptist Witness* (Nashville: Broadman, 1987), 388.

General Convention of Baptists in the early nineteenth century. Here we will see that there was a zeal for missions from all Baptists that was entangled with competing ideas of what cooperative work should look like, especially in light of the horrendous institution of slavery in the United States. Ultimately those differences caused a division that led to the formation of a new convention and a newly formed mission board. Finally, we will look to the first long-lasting leadership of this board in the person of James Barnett Taylor, who was the first corresponding secretary of the FMB.

DENOMINATIONAL BEGINNINGS

In the previous chapter Jason Duesing examined the initial missions work of George Liele, William Carey, and Adoniram Judson. The missions work these men and their families engaged in was made widely known and spurred a variety of mission societies in England and the United States. Just as Congregationalists were being prompted for foreign missions, as was seen with the Haystack Prayer Meeting and the Judsons, so too were Baptists interested in engaging in this "new" enterprise. Help was soon to come that would excite and organize this newly found missions fervor, which would lead to the founding of the General Convention of Baptists in America. This help would come through one of Judson's fellow missionaries who also had recently become a Baptist—Luther Rice.

General Convention

Luther Rice was born in 1783 in Northborough, Massachusetts, where he would eventually join the Congregationalist church. He attended Williams College, where he participated in the discussions there surrounding missions. The longing for engagement for foreign missions was on his fellow students' minds, and their efforts for missions aided the establishment of the Congregationalist board that sent both Judson and Rice. Though Rice did not travel with Judson to India, he was on a ship not far behind him, and he would also soon follow him in his desire to become a Baptist. In 1812, a few months after his arrival in Calcutta, Rice was baptized by William Ward and soon came home to seek funds for the missionary work of the Judsons.

When Rice returned to the United States, his goal was to help promote missions and provide support for the Judsons and others on the field. We should not think, however, that he was coming to create the first missions organization among Baptists. In his home region of Boston there already was a Baptist missions society that was more than happy to take on Rice and send him out across the country to excite the public for missions. Rice's work paid off with not only increased interest in missions but also interest in organizing a national system that would become the General Missionary Convention of the Baptist Denomination in the United States for Foreign Missions (General Convention), established on May 18, 1814. The convention was presided over by the South Carolinian pastor Richard Furman. It was decided that this convention would meet every three years and, as such, is often referred to as the Triennial Convention. This convention formed a board to manage the interest of foreign missions called the Baptist Board of Foreign Missions, with Thomas Baldwin of Boston presiding. Rice was appointed as a missionary for the new board and asked to continue his efforts at home. The board also appointed the Judsons as missionaries.

Tensions
From the beginning of the General Convention unity was weak among the various churches represented across the land. The United States was still focused on the individual states rather than a federal vision for the nation. This was true for the Baptists as well. Though many wanted to see greater unity in their denomination, there were still many differences between Baptists of different regions. The clearest regional differences were found between the North and the South, which we will address later on. Whether north/south or east/west, the way of life was so different in these regions that fundamental disagreements existed about what the new denomination should look like.

An early tension was the purpose for which the convention itself existed. William Estep points out, "Whether they realized it or not, Baptists in America had not only organized for missions, they had become a denomination, for the Triennial Convention was something other than a missions society."[3] Many pushed against the denominational idea due to the concern of centralized power. Would a denominational structure usurp the authority of the local churches? This was the question on the minds of many who mostly lived in the North. The big difference was between understanding the convention in the older associational model or the newer societal model. Robert Baker helpfully defines these two methods of connectionalism: "The associational method was . . . a denominational program based upon the participation of *churches* in a formal connection."[4] In this method issues of doctrine, discipline, and education were all considered. The joining of these varying works solidified an authority that was unattractive to many. The society approach removed these concerns. "Instead of having missions as a secondary interest, the missionary society was organized *solely* for missionary purposes; and instead of a constituency composed of churches in formal connection, the missionary society was based upon *individuals* whose participation was completely voluntary."[5] Both of these approaches were represented in the newly formed convention, but the associational method was initially implemented. Not only would there be a Foreign Mission Board but also a Home Mission Board and the establishment of Columbian College in Washington, DC. However, there were movements to redefine the purpose of the convention and thus highlight the larger issue. This is clearly seen from Francis Wayland, president of Brown University:

---

3   William R. Estep, *Whole Gospel Whole World: The Foreign Mission Board of the Southern Baptist Convention, 1845–1995* (1994; repr., Eugene, OR: Wipf and Stock, 2001), 37.

4   Robert A. Baker, *Relations between Northern and Southern Baptists*, 2nd ed. (n.p.: 1948), 12.

5   Baker, *Relations between Northern and Southern Baptists*, 12.

An attempt was made, pretty early in the history of this organization, to give it the control over all our benevolent efforts. It was proposed to merge in it our Education Societies, Tract Societies, Home Mission Societies, and our Foreign Mission Societies, so that one central Board should have the management of all our churches, so far as their efforts to extend the kingdom of Christ were concerned. After a protracted debate, this measure was negatived by so decided a majority that the attempt was never repeated, and this danger was averted. We look back, at the present day, with astonishment that such an idea was ever entertained.[6]

The various works of the convention were slowly separated from the work of the General Convention until the sole purpose of the convention was foreign missions, and thus the convention moved to a societal method from an associational one.

Clearly persons like Wayland had strong opinions about the nature of the work of the convention—many who thought like him were from the North. Southerners like Richard Furman and W. B. Johnson were involved in the establishment of the General Convention and argued from the start for the associational model. This tension in approach became a tug-of-war in authority between Baptists and did not help create unity. Baker points out that these issues along with other concerns highlight the sectionalism that existed in America at the time.[7] The competing interest for power from one section over another is clearly seen in this issue. However, as we will see below, though tension did exist over the structure and purposes of the convention, there were many who desired to work as a unified body—that is, until the sectional issue of slavery came to a head.

---

6   Francis Wayland, *Notes on the Principles and Practices of Baptist Churches* (New York: Sheldon, Blackman, 1857), 185.

7   Baker, *Relations between Northern and Southern Baptists*, 16–17.

Slavery

Leon McBeth, following Baker, claims that "sharp differences had arisen between Northern and Southern Baptists before the slavery issue became crucial among them."[8] We have seen that these differences did exist, but we question how divisive they really were. Furthermore, as one looks into the various histories[9] of the Southern Baptist Convention, there is agreement that slavery played a role in the divide between Northern and Southern Baptists. However, some presentations do not always present the enormity of the role the South's "peculiar institution" played in the division from the North. Though tensions other than slavery have rightly been presented as reasons for the split from the General Convention, from beginning to end those reasons are all linked to the issue of slavery.

Initially, many Baptists were not too conversant about slavery because most of them could not afford the practice. As time marched on, however, more and more Baptists would become accustomed to the institution of slavery, with some of them becoming slaveholders themselves. There were always those who were against slavery, but there came a larger acceptance of the institution, especially in the South, whose economy was largely dependent on a slave workforce.

In 1833, slavery was abolished in the United Kingdom, and at this time British Baptists began imploring their American cousins to abolish the horrendous practice in the States. This encouragement was coupled with a broader humanitarian movement that became abolitionist in nature. The argument for abolitionism was not uniform, and different parties argued for their own plan to eradicate the practice. Thus, a spectrum of thought was created between those who wanted immediate abolition and those who wanted a long-term loosing of the practice. Many Baptists, especially in the North,

---

8 McBeth, *The Baptist Heritage*, 347.

9 Barnes states, "The formation of the Southern Baptist Convention grew out of the division in the Home Missions Society and the General Convention (foreign missions) over the question of slavery. But the tendency to division in American Baptist life was in evidence before slavery became an issue." W. W. Barnes, *The Southern Baptist Convention, 1845–1953* (Nashville: Broadman, 1954), 12.

would join these different groups as well as make abolitionism a requirement in some of their societies. One group in particular that heightened the abolitionist effort was the American Baptist Anti-slavery Convention, formed in 1840. The broader humanitarian movement was gaining steam in the convention and had many followers who served on the boards.

McBeth contrasts the sectional difference of the nation at this time: "While the South moved toward militant defense of the slave system, the older Northern states one by one outlawed slavery, and the newer Northern states refused to allow the system to be introduced into their areas."[10] At the 1841 meeting of the Triennial Convention, the issue of slavery was explicitly addressed. A compromise was drawn up, though, that made the boards of the convention neutral on the issue of slavery. Some members of the convention found the approach of some of the abolitionists to be too strong and forceful. These same abolitionists had come to the opinion that it was not just unethical but unchristian for one to hold slaves. No longer was there a mounting divide between parties, but there was now a strong discord between abolitionists and those unwilling to argue against the practice of slavery. One should note, of course, at these meetings only white men were invited to participate even though a good number of their own constituents were women and nonwhite. Though compromise was reached, there was little trust that such a concord would be upheld, and the agreement did indeed come to be tested.

This testing came in two forms from those in the South who distrusted the boards managed mostly by Northerners. The first test came from Georgia with a missionary applicant named James E. Reeve. Reeve was applying to be a missionary with the Home Mission Society, and he held slaves. His application was neither accepted nor denied, in part due to the neutrality statement and in part due to the knowledge that it was a test since it was openly acknowledged that his application was put forward to "stop the

---

10   McBeth, *The Baptist Heritage*, 384.

mouths of gainsayers."[11] The second test came from the Alabama convention who inquired of the Foreign Mission Board whether someone owning slaves could be accepted as a missionary. McBeth rightly points out that what they were seeking to know was how much authority the board was willing to wield over the process of accepting missionaries.[12] The answer was a strong no: "One thing is certain; we can never be a party to any arrangement which would imply approbation of slavery."[13]

In response to these two events, the Virginia Baptists issued a call for a meeting of Baptists in the South to address the issues of the divide between the North and the South on the issue of slavery. This call was the beginning of the official break from the North. In the *Religious Herald* on March 13, 1845, the Virginia Baptists addressed their concerns regarding the actions following the Alabama Resolution. In summary, they claimed that the board's decision not to allow slaveholders to be missionaries was "unconstitutional," a violation of the compromise of the 1844 convention meeting, "inconsistent," "unjust" to Southerners, and "unwise." Given these arguments the following resolutions were presented:

1. Resolved, That this Board have seen with sincere pain the decision of the Board of the Baptist Triennial Convention, contained in a recent letter addressed to Rev. Jesse Hartwell, of Ala. and that we deem the decision unconstitutional, and in violation of the rights of the Southern members of the Convention; and that all farther connexion with the Board, on the part of such members is inexpedient and improper.

2. Resolved, That the Treasurer of this Board be required to deposit in one of the Savings banks of the city, any funds which may be in hands or which may come into them, to be disposed of as the Society, at its annual meeting, may direct.

---

11   McBeth, *The Baptist Heritage*, 386.
12   McBeth, *The Baptist Heritage*, 387.
13   McBeth, *The Baptist Heritage*, 387.

3. Resolved, That this Board are of opinion, that in the present exigency, it is important that those brethren who are aggrieved by the recent decision of the Board in Boston, should hold a Convention to confer on the best means of promoting the Foreign Mission cause, and other interests of the Baptist denomination in the South.
4. Resolved, That in the judgment of this Board, Augusta, Geo., is a suitable place for holding such a Convention; and that Thursday before the 2nd Lord's day in May next is a suitable time.
5. Resolved, That while we are willing to meet our Southern brethren in Augusta, or any other place which may be selected, we should heartily welcome them in the city of Richmond—and should it be deemed proper to hold it in this city, the Thursday before the 4th Lord's day in June next will be a suitable time.[14]

The tone of this article, signed by the president of the Virginia Board, J. B. Taylor, clearly shows that the sentiments of those in the South were such that a division was necessary. The upcoming meeting, at least from the perspective of those in Virginia,[15] was less about determining a path forward in the Triennial Convention and more of presenting a plan for a new convention—a convention that would not argue for the abolition of the institution of slavery.

The real divide between the North and the South was over continuing with the peculiar institution or abolishing it. This is, as McBeth calls it, "a blunt historical fact."[16] When the break officially happened, it was acknowledged that there was no difference in creed with those in the North, there was no difference in organization of

---

14   H. Leon McBeth, *A Sourcebook for Baptist Heritage* (Nashville: Broadman & Holman, 1990), 263–64.
15   Not everyone in the South was ready to head into a division from the North. For instance, J. L. Waller offered a dissenting opinion in *Baptist Banner and Pioneer*, which he edited. See McBeth, *Sourcebook*, 265–67.
16   McBeth, *The Baptist Heritage*, 382.

the missions boards, and there was no real break with the ongoing ministry. The break had to do with those who were unwilling to engage in the cause of abolitionism. Some claimed to be anti-slavery but not abolitionist, but these claims were of the cowardly middle that was more concerned with keeping the status quo or obtaining their own minuscule piece of power. As we will see, Southern Baptist beginnings are solely, and horrendously, based on the deplorable anthropology of Baptists in the South.

THE FORMATION OF THE FOREIGN MISSION BOARD

The FMB has always been a board of the Southern Baptist Convention. Though other boards have come and gone within the convention, the FMB has always, by necessity, been part of the SBC. So its beginning is connected to the beginning of the SBC. The board's initial leadership was present at the formation and, as we will later see, was intricately involved in establishing the convention in the South. The beginnings for both the SBC and the FMB occurred in Augusta, Georgia, May 8–12, 1845.

Augusta

As we have seen, slavery was the reason for the creation of the Southern Baptist Convention. The belief that the rights of Southerners had been violated was expressed not only in the South but also from those in the North like Francis Wayland. This is evidenced in a famous letter Wayland wrote to J. B. Jeter: "You will separate of course. I could not ask otherwise. Your rights have been infringed. I will take the liberty of offering one or two suggestions. We have shown how Christians *ought not* to act, it remains for you to show us how they *ought to* act. Put away all violence, act with dignity and firmness and the world will approve your course."[17] This sentiment was shared by Jeter as he presented the letter to the convention in

---

17 *Daily Chronicle and Sentinel*, May 10, 1845.

1845. Jeter at this time offered three courses of action—cooperate with the decision of the board, wait until the next Triennial Convention to address the issue, or separate immediately.[18] By the second day the Augusta convention resolved the following: "That for peace and harmony, and in order to accomplish the greatest amount of good, and the maintainance [*sic*] of those scriptural principles on which the General Missionary Convention of the Baptist denomination of the United States, was originally formed, it is proper that this Convention at once proceed to organize a Society for the propagation of the Gospel."[19]

Within a few days a constitution was written that established the Southern Baptist Convention "for the purpose of carrying into effect the benevolent intentions of our constituents, by organizing a place for eliciting, combining and directing the energies of the whole denomination in one sacred effort, for the propagation of the Gospel."[20] The debate concerning whether the new convention was going to be a society was discussed at the meeting. They concluded that it would follow the associational method. During the meeting they established two boards, "a Board of Managers for Foreign Missions, and also one for Domestic Missions, and that a committee be appointed to nominate members of such Boards." It was further decided that the FMB would reside in Richmond, Virginia, while the Domestic Mission Board would reside in Marion, Alabama. A collection was taken up for both boards to begin the work of Southern Baptist missions. In addition, it was requested that state conventions and other bodies present who had monies for missions send that money to these boards. The convention also requested that the FMB communicate with the Triennial Convention about any claims they may have with them and to report back at the next meeting in 1846.

At the end of the convention, W. B. Johnson, the new president of the convention and its architect, as well as a slave owner himself,

---

18   *Daily Chronicle and Sentinel,* May 10, 1845.
19   SBCA, 1845, 13.
20   SBCA, 1845, 3.

wrote of the newly formed convention and the reasons for its existence. Previously Johnson had served in a variety of capacities, including president of the General Convention, where he worked for unity with the North and the South, but after the report of the Alabama Resolution, he was ready to support a different work. In Johnson's address we clearly see again that the issue for Baptists in the South was slavery. He began by referencing the "painful division" that had occurred in Baptist missions, and he wanted to present the "peculiar circumstances" that led to this division.[21] Johnson clearly established that there was no real difference between Baptists in the North and the South and that they were still brethren, though others have tried to exclude the South "from Christian fellowship."[22] Any sense of disunion was due to the actions of those in the North, for the General Convention's constitution "knows no difference between slaveholders and non-slaveholders."[23] He, like so many before him, cited again the resolution of the convention of neutrality on slavery. And he further claimed that there had been "an usurpation of ecclesiastical power quite foreign to our polity."[24] Bringing the issue of slavery back into the foreground, Johnson posited, "These brethren, thus acted upon a sentiment they have failed to prove— That slavery is, in all circumstances, sinful."[25] Johnson put the onus completely on the North and claimed that those in the South had not "receded" one step from the original purpose of missions that the General Convention set out to do. He claimed, "It is they who wrong us that have receded."[26] He concluded, "Our brethren have pressed upon every inch of our privileges and our sacred rights— but this shall only urge our gushing souls to yield proportionately of their renewed efforts to the Lord, to the church universal, and to the dying world."[27]

---

21   SBCA, 1845, 17.
22   SBCA, 1845, 17.
23   SBCA, 1845, 17.
24   SBCA, 1845, 18.
25   SBCA, 1845, 18.
26   SBCA, 1845. 19.
27   SBCA, 1845, 20.

Johnson and others at the convention were very clear about the purpose of the division with the North. Rights had been violated, but those rights were, ironically, built on the right to deny rights to others—namely slaves, but also women. The circumstances of the beginning of the SBC are difficult to comprehend. How could people who clearly seem to want to take the gospel to the uttermost, who argue and have fought for religious liberty, still make claims for the enslaving of others created in God's image? Further, why did it take 150 years for those in the SBC to apologize publicly and rightly for these sins?[28] These are questions that will not be satisfactorily answered. The history that follows about the incredible work of the SBC and especially its missions work cannot and should not divert us from the fact that the convention was birthed in sin, and we, who are no better than they, can easily commit similar sins. It is by the grace of God that the SBC has done what it has done, in spite of ourselves.

The Foreign Mission Board

However misguided the reason for the split between Baptists, we should also acknowledge that they were seriously interested in mission work, a work Estep describes as "the new convention's breath of life."[29] The FMB immediately began meeting and working toward building the foreign mission work from the South. At the Augusta meeting the officers for the two boards were established, and J. B. Jeter, lifelong friend of J. B. Taylor, was selected as the president of

---

28   See Resolution No. 1 "On Racial Reconciliation on the 150th Anniversary of the Southern Baptist Convention," SBCA, 1995, 80–81. Notice in particular: "Be it further RESOLVED, that we lament and repudiate historic acts of evil such as slavery from which we continue to reap a bitter harvest, and we recognize that the racism which yet plagues our culture today is inextricably tied to the past; and Be it further RESOLVED, that we apologize to all African-Americans for condoning and/ or perpetuating individual and systematic racism in our lifetime; and we genuinely repent of racism of which we have been guilty, whether consciously (Psalm 19:13) or unconsciously (Leviticus 4:27); and Be it further RESOLVED, that we ask forgiveness from our African-American brothers and sisters, acknowledging that our own healing is at stake; and Be it further RESOLVED, that we hereby commit ourselves to eradicate racism in all its forms from Southern Baptist life and ministry."

29   Estep, *Whole Gospel Whole World*, 58.

the board, which may be in part why the location of Richmond, Virginia, was chosen since it was his home city. At the Augusta meeting, the FMB met and established its direction.[30] At the May 20 meeting, the board convened in Richmond and officially began work, which addressed a variety of issues, including the request from the convention to communicate with the General Convention in Boston about "the pecuniary relations of the Triennial Convention and the equitable division of missionary labor."[31] This task fell to the president and to Taylor, whose relations with the northern board were close. Throughout the next few meetings, decisions about the direction and future of the FMB were made by the various members of the board; an important decision was to mark China as the major emphasis of their missions effort.[32] The board then went about the simple work that would be its focus for the foreseeable future: finding missionaries and continuing to raise funds.

The first missionaries of the new board were to meet qualifications that were identical to those of the General Convention. Article 10 of the new constitution stated, "Missionaries appointed by any of the Boards of this Convention must, previous to their appointment, furnish evidence of genuine but fervent zeal in their Master's cause, and talents which fit them for the service for which they offer themselves."[33] Taylor and Jeter did correspond, as directed, with the General Convention about the South's interests in the missions efforts of the General Convention but were denied a transference of any funds. The missionaries themselves, however, were given the choice of which convention they wanted to serve. Most stayed the course with the General Convention, but a few joined ranks with the FMB. In July the board began conversations with I. J. Roberts, who was serving with the General Convention in Canton, China. Shortly thereafter S. C. Clopton contacted the board and expressed his interest in joining with them. By September the

30 FMBM, May 8, 1845.
31 FMBM, May 20, 1845.
32 FMBM, June 30, 1845.
33 SBCA, 1845, 4.

board had interviewed Clopton and appointed him as their first missionary, and soon, while working with the "China missionary board of Kentucky," the board secured Roberts as a missionary.[34] Soon more missionaries would join, including George Pearcey, Lewis Shuck, and Matthew T. Yates. The board was able to find missionaries for the work, but the difficult task was finding funds to support the work.

The task of raising funds for any cause is always a difficult endeavor. It was particularly difficult for the new board at the beginning, and a great deal of effort was spent traveling to elicit funds. At the close of the Augusta meeting, the FMB requested Johnson "to make a tour among the churches in behalf of the Foreign Mission Enterprise."[35] This task he took up, but more agents (regional fundraisers) would be needed to join in the effort to raise monies for the missionary enterprise. Over the next few months, the board would appoint a variety of agents across the South. There was not a larger plan in place to elicit funds more effectively, and this was especially the case because of not having a corresponding secretary.

In Augusta C. D. Mallory was initially chosen as the corresponding secretary of the FMB and was offered an annual salary of $1,200. However, Mallory declined the offer to serve. It would be the beginning of a difficult search for the corresponding secretary. There is no doubt that the job was a difficult one not only in finding missionaries but also, and more importantly, in raising the necessary funds to send the missionaries. A few competent pastors were offered the position, men like W. B. Johnson and R. B. C. Howell, but they all rejected the offer. Finally, Jeter led the board to offer his friend James B. Taylor from Grace Street Baptist Church in Richmond the position of corresponding secretary of the FMB. Taylor had been serving with the board since the Augusta meeting. He was selected for his experience in convention and mission society work, as will be seen below. Like the previous candidates,

---

34   FMBM, August 4, 1845, and September 1, 1845.
35   FMBM, May 8, 1845.

he too declined the invitation to serve. However, he did provide a word of hope: "If no competent individual can be found who will be likely to give satisfaction to the whole self and who may be certainly expected to accept this office I am willing until the first of June, to devote two entire days in each week, to the duties of the Secretary and if it be necessary I am willing to take a journey to the South."[36] Taylor of course did accept this role, but his part would not remain as limited as he first desired. He would continue as the corresponding secretary of the FMB until his death in 1871. To his part in this story we now turn.

JAMES BARNETT TAYLOR

The life of the first corresponding secretary (and then president) of the FMB began in England on March 19, 1804. He was born to George and Chrisanna Taylor, who were not believers at the time of his birth, though his mother had him baptized into the Church of England. His fraternal grandparents, however, were Baptists, and it was in those Dissenters' home that his father was reared, and against which he possibly rebelled due to the social status that was afforded Baptists in England in the late eighteenth century. When James was still an infant, his parents decided to immigrate to the United States to try for a better life. If it was better horizons they sought, the timing was not ideal, for as they landed in New York they arrived at the height of the yellow fever outbreak. George's trade at the time was to make coffins, and he was never out of business. He caught the fever one day, and his coworkers thought he would never return. But he was determined to beat it, and he did. Though the family had employment, it did not produce much, and the childhood that James had in New York was one of poverty.

However low the funds were for the family, it was during this time that his father turned his life away from seeking certain "infidelities" and soon sought God. George and his wife were baptized

---

36 FMBM, December 29, 1845.

in 1807 at the First Baptist Church by William Parkinson. With the family regularly attending the Baptist church, James, though of little wealth, did not suffer from a spiritually impoverished youth. In fact, at thirteen, he and some friends sought the counsel of their pastor about "religious impressions," which culminated in James being baptized into First Baptist Church.[37]

The next year the family moved from New York to Virginia, where James would spend his remaining life, especially near Richmond, where his father had some work and where he himself would labor for years and be buried. It was here in Virginia, at the age of sixteen, that he desired to fulfill the call to preach. By 1824 he was licensed to preach and became connected with another young man with a similar desire, J. B. Jeter. The two quickly became friends and soon were traveling together preaching across Virginia and beyond. Jeter writes of his initial impression of Taylor, "He was strikingly frank in his disposition, gentle in his manners, confiding in his spirit, and plain and neat in his personal experience. In less than twenty hours after our first meeting we had entered fully into each other's views, sympathies, and plans."[38]

This itinerant preaching was part of the ministry of the Virginia General Association, which called on young James to be a missionary "to occupy the lower section of Meherrin District for six months, making a tour once a month and to render a particular account of his labors."[39] This task and its tours would be the first of many missionary endeavors in Taylor's life. During this time the question was also put to him about being ordained, since many of the churches he was visiting desired that he administer the ordinances. He was ordained on May, 2, 1826, at Sandy Creek in Charlotte County.[40] Soon after this ordination, James was called to

---

37   George B. Taylor, *Life and Times of James B. Taylor* (Philadelphia: The Bible and Publication Society, 1872), 20.

38   Taylor, *Life and Times of James B. Taylor*, 39.

39   Taylor, *Life and Times of James B. Taylor*, 34. Taylor was paid $25 for this work, but completed only three months of the service, resigning in December of 1825.

40   Taylor, *Life and Times of James B. Taylor*, 43.

his first pastorate at Second Baptist Church in Richmond, where he would serve for the next thirteen years. Elder J. A. Chambliss reported on that call,

> The eyes of the church were turned to him as the most suitable man for the pastorate which they were now called upon to fill; but their efforts to secure his services, though marked by all the well-known determination and persistence of Deacon William Crane, who conducted the correspondence with the church, were promptly and steadily discouraged. Mr. Taylor could not be persuaded that it would be wise for him, a mere boy, without training or experience, to undertake the task of building up a church which was then small, weak, without a congregation, badly located in the city, and mightily opposed by the old and influential mother-church.[41]

Though Taylor rejected this offer, the church was persistent that he was the man for the job and convinced him to become their pastor.

The description above of the state of the church was quite accurate, and Taylor's work as a pastor was difficult. In fact, this congregation, seven years in existence, had never had a pastor. Quickly Taylor went about the work of orienting the church toward the preaching of the gospel, organizing Sunday schools for education, and beginning a deeper involvement in missions. Though he had a gift in the pulpit, his major work was that of a pastor. His biographer—George B. Taylor, his son—states that he "seems even then to have believed, with Dr. Chalmers, that 'a house-going preacher makes a church-going people,' and to have acted upon the maxim."[42] This care for his people was a central characteristic of Taylor that would continue throughout his life. Whether members of his church or missionaries, Taylor felt the responsibility of caring for these souls.

---

41   Taylor, *Life and Times of James B. Taylor*, 45.
42   Taylor, *Life and Times of James B. Taylor*, 52.

This young minister was greatly involved in the care of his church, but he was also courting a young lady at the time. On October 30, 1828, Taylor was wed to Mary Williams of Beverly, Massachusetts. Much of his correspondence throughout his life is to his wife, where he recollects the journeys and workings of the ministry for associations, education, and ultimately the FMB. Throughout all of these, we see a consistent desire to love and care for his family. This desire can especially be seen in his diary only a few weeks after his wedding: "I will endeavor to administer to all the wants and alleviate all the sorrows of my dear Mary. I will seek to control my temper under all circumstances, subduing fretfulness, anger, and impatience, that she may thereby be rendered happy in committing her earthly destinies to my hands. I will strive to please and cheer her, and above all to promote her spiritual welfare. O Lord, direct and support me in doing thy will in all the relations of life, for the Redeemer's sake! Amen."[43]

The work that Taylor labored in during his first church was indicative of the type of ministerial engagements he took on throughout his life. Not only was he concerned for his home and for providing pastoral care for his church, but he was also engaged in many societies, boards, and associations as well as keeping an itinerant preaching ministry throughout the region and beyond. These extra-ecclesial endeavors illustrate the type of ecclesiology that Taylor and others had at the time. Though Baptist ecclesiology contains a strong independency, there also is a necessary desire to cooperate with other churches and believers for the great cause of God's kingdom. This was the approach of Taylor throughout his life and one reason why he was the ideal person for leading the FMB. The contacts and networks created during these times were of great value later on, but of more value than that was his persistence to work diligently for the sake of the gospel wherever he went.[44]

---

43 Diary entry November 27, 1828, cited in Taylor, *Life and Times of James B. Taylor*, 62.
44 See Taylor, *Life and Times of James B. Taylor*, 78–81. Taylor highlights this aspect of Taylor's ministry well: "It is one thing to reach your destination at ten A.M. and have the day to rest for the night's service, and quite a different thing to ride forty miles, get off your horse at dusk, and 'preach at early candlelight,' and then perhaps

The broader cooperative work of Taylor also allowed him to engage in the educational effort of Baptists during this time. In the first half of the nineteenth century, a variety of Baptist schools were established.[45] Taylor helped create the Virginia Baptist Educational Society and through it the Virginia Baptist Seminary, which would become Richmond College. His particular involvement was in raising funds for the school, but it was a cause he found to be greatly worthy of his time and efforts. He claimed, "My mind has been so deeply interested in this subject that I am sometimes ready to give up every other employment and labor specifically in this department of usefulness. Something must and will be done for elevating the standard and improvement among the ministry of our denomination."[46]

This desire to improve the denomination was connected with his desire to see the gospel advance. He personally made sure that was happening at home, but he also pondered the work on the foreign field. On January 19, 1833, he illustrated this desire in his journal:

> How pressing the need of more laborers to scatter the seed of the kingdom, to teach the wretched Burmese the way of life! Oh that I could go!—that my qualifications were sufficient to allow me a place among the little band who are wearing out their lives there! I should account it a rich privilege to be permitted to assist them in any way. But this I can do here. If I may not myself tell the love of a Saviour

---

rise at day to make twenty or twenty-five miles in order to fill an appointment at eleven in the morning. Whole pages of a memorandum-book kept by Mr. Taylor tell of such riding and preaching."

45 "In about ten years from that time, however, no less than five institutions of learning, which have grown into colleges and theological seminaries, were founded, at Hamilton, N.Y., in 1819; Waterville, Me., in 1820; Washington. D.C., in 1822; Georgetown, Ky., in 1824; and at Newton, Mass., in 1825; while, during the next ten years, five other centres caught the same impulse, resulting in the founding of the Richmond College, Va.; Wake Forest, N.C.; Furman University. S.C.; Mercer University, Ga.; and New Hampton Institute, N.H." William Cathcart, ed., *The Baptist Encyclopædia* (Philadelphia: Louis H. Everts, 1881), 252.

46 Taylor, *Life and Times of James B. Taylor*, 100.

to the benighted heathen, I can see to it that something be done for the support of those who do go. This I will do. May God prosper the Burman mission and all other missions, and fill the whole earth with his glory!"[47]

The desire for missions pushed Taylor to be involved in the General Convention's missions efforts. He made raising support for missions a perennial effort on the part of his church and with those with whom he came in contact. He helped the Boston board gain many supporters throughout the years, was called on for help by the board, and even was offered a position, which he declined.[48]

Beyond the itinerant preaching ministry, Taylor also grew his church in such a way that allowed it to help in establishing other churches. One in particular that Second Baptist planted was Third Baptist, which would later become Grace Street Baptist under Taylor's ministry there. His preaching travels also included his helping to start churches. In 1835 in Baltimore he helped in the forming of Calvert Street Church. Clearly Taylor's vision was for a ministry that was bigger than the church to which he was called. He closely managed his time so that he could ensure every effort for the gospel would be achieved.

In addition to all of these works, Taylor also spent time writing. He wrote for the *Religious Herald* and even edited that publication for a time. He wrote many pages on the lives of Virginia ministers as well as a memoir of Luther Rice that was well received at the time. This later work was accomplished after Taylor left the pastorate at Second Baptist and took on the role of chaplain at the University of Virginia for a year ending in July 1840. After this time Taylor accepted a call to the pastorate at Third Baptist in Richmond. It was while he was pastor of this church that he further led in broader denominational issues and ultimately the split from the North in 1845.

---

47   Taylor, *Life and Times of James B. Taylor*, 106.
48   Taylor, *Life and Times of James B. Taylor*, 109.

Taylor's biographer stresses that there was not any real animosity from Taylor toward the Baptists in the North. He claims "he wrote no word which breathed in a spirit of bitterness and wrath."[49] In fact, his journals of the time are more concerned with raising funds for the new building at Grace Street Baptist Church than the larger denominational issues.[50] That was true until March 3, 1845, when he wrote, "To-day received the intelligence that the Foreign Mission Board have decided slaveholder to be ineligible to appointment. The Lord, I trust, will guide his servants at the South, and overrule all to his glory. A Southern organization will now be necessary."[51] On March 8 he also wrote about this news: "Yesterday the Board of the Virginia Foreign Mission Society determined to recommend the call of a convention to consider the expediency of a Southern organization, distinct and separate from the North, in carrying on the cause of missions. Secured one hundred dollars in subscription for meeting house."[52] The coming break with the North was difficult for Taylor, who had spent a good bit of time and energy working for the board and with those ministers in Boston and beyond. He claimed that he could not sleep at all after hearing this news and called the separation "painful," as W. B. Johnson would do a few months later.[53] He prepared remarks on this looming split that are helpful in understanding his thoughts about the whole ordeal:

> In these remarks I speak not as a slaveholder: I have never held a slave, and I do not expect to sustain this relation.

---

49 Taylor, *Life and Times of James B. Taylor*, 149.
50 The entries do show that he wrote about broader concerns. Consider the entry for February 28, 1845: "Prayer-meeting at night. The firing of guns announced the fact that by a majority of two in the Senate, Texas is to be annexed to the United States. It is not possible to determine the results growing out of this measure. May it not lead to a dissolution of the Union—to a way with Mexico or Great Britain? The Lord overrule all for his glory!" Taylor, *Life and Times of James B. Taylor*, 150.
51 Taylor, *Life and Times of James B. Taylor*, 150–51.
52 Taylor, *Life and Times of James B. Taylor*, 151. The last line shows again of his concern and record for raising funds for his church's building.
53 Taylor, *Life and Times of James B. Taylor*, 151. See President Johnson's address, SBCA, 1845.

But I must close my eyes against the strongest and clearest demonstrations of love to Jesus and the souls of men
on the part of my Southern brethren ere I can say they
should be excluded from any position within the gift of
the acting Board. . . . And now my heart is sick in view of
the future. A separation is to take place. We are not more
to mingle together as we have done in sweet fraternal
intercourse, while, encircling the cross, we contemplated
the woes of our race and labored for their removal. I fear
that the sectional heart-burnings and jealousies which
a few restless, reckless spirits have been aiming to excite
will be fearfully increased. May the Lord prevent it! May
overrule all for good!

I could not be satisfied without giving this frank expression of my views and feelings. I believe the Board
have erred. I felt bound to remonstrate. Though writing
in plainness, I am not sensible of a particle of unkind
feeling. I close by praying that, whatever may become
of us, the heathen nations may all speedily see the salvation of our God.[54]

Though one may see the inner turmoil of Taylor in this address,
he was adamantly in favor of the split. On March 4, 1845, just after
hearing the news of the board's decision not to allow slaveholders
to be missionaries, he wrote to W. B. Johnson,

We cannot consent to remain idle while so much is to
be effected in the spread of Messiah's kingdom throughout the earth. I trust we shall have grace to preserve us
from unholy animosity, and even unkindness, toward
our Northern brethren, while with becoming energy we
betake ourselves to the work of abiding to evangelize
the world.

---

54   Taylor, *Life and Times of James B. Taylor*, 151–52.

> I rely much, my dear brother, on your experience and
> discretion in the trying emergency. With but a short re-
> move from the blessed world above, you may be expected
> with less of carnality and prejudice to contemplate the
> bearings of this whole subject. May the Lord direct us![55]

Taylor, along with Jeter, traveled a few weeks later to Providence, Rhode Island, to meet with the mission board. There they were treated cordially by their host Francis Wayland and others like Dr. Gillette, but Taylor reported that the meetings themselves were "far from being pleasant."[56] He traveled back home after this meeting only to travel soon to Augusta, Georgia, for the upcoming meeting. Given the enormity of the situation that was upon him as well as the short amount of time home, he did endeavor to raise more funds for the building of Grace Street Church. In understanding this history let us not forget that Taylor (and many others) were pastors who primarily cared for the flock entrusted to them as well as the broader kingdom concerns.

Taylor's analysis of the meeting in Augusta is typical of many of his journal entries. He did not provide much information about the outcomes but did provide his own take on the meetings, which he found to be unified and pleasant. His final analysis was that this meeting was "on the whole one of the most pleasant meetings of the kind I have ever attended."[57] He was committed to the new work of Baptists in the South, but he was not aware of the extent of the work his role would entail for him.

First Corresponding Secretary

Locating the FMB in Richmond allowed Taylor to attend the meetings of the board in the first year and to be initially involved in the conversations on strategy and focus of the board as well as serving

---

55 Taylor, *Life and Times of James B. Taylor*, 153.
56 Taylor, *Life and Times of James B. Taylor*, 154.
57 Taylor, *Life and Times of James B. Taylor*, 155.

on committees. This was work that Taylor would do in conjunction with his pastoral care. The diary entries of this time consistently show the mixture of church affairs with other concerns. On July 7, 1845, he attended the board's meeting whose minutes state that he had been assigned "to correspond with the Mission Board in Kentucky in reference to taking under their care and patronage Brother Roberts now a missionary in China."[58] However, George Taylor states in his biography that this move was a part of the overall strategy of the board, as "it was determined to commence, as soon as possible, an independent mission in China."[59]

These meetings would continue throughout the rest of the year, and Taylor would be privy to the consistent declines of persons to take the role of corresponding secretary. No doubt his love for missions and his present involvement with the board impressed upon him the need to fill this important role for the new board. On December 1 of that year, the board came to him and asked him to consider the job. He wrote in his diary, "Attended a meeting of Foreign Mission Board, at which the appointment of Corresponding Secretary was conferred on me. I find myself placed in circumstances which render it difficult to determine my duty. The call is an urgent one, and yet my relations to the church are so peculiarly endearing that I know not how to dissolve them. O Lord, guide!"[60] The conferring of the appointment of the secretaryship came by letter from Jeter, who implored him to take the position, offered a variety of reasons why he was the best person for the job, and concluded with more than a bit of cajoling:

> We cannot succeed without a Secretary, and no man is fit for this office who cannot find readily other and important employment. But if a sacrifice is to be made, who is to make it? No man is more fairly committed, by the

---

58   FMBM, July 7, 1845.
59   Taylor, *Life and Times of James B. Taylor*, 156.
60   Taylor, *Life and Times of James B. Taylor*, 158.

course which he has already taken, than yourself to place the offering on the missionary altar. Shall we confess that we have been deceived—that the South cannot conduct a foreign mission enterprise? This will never do. Should you decline the appointment, we must press forward, but certainly we shall be embarrassed.[61]

Taylor was torn. His love for the ministry at the church and his love for the mission work that he also had been so involved with before were somewhat at odds with one another. When he discussed the matter with his church, they implored him to stay. His journal shows that he was quite perplexed during this time and filled with prayers to God to help him see the way. Finally, he determined that he could not take the position, but he did offer to do the work part-time until a proper secretary could be found. For six months he provided two days a week and one tour of the South to help raise funds for the board. At the end of this time, two things occurred: First, the new building at Grace Street was dedicated, thus ending the need over the last few years to raise funds for the building, which had been a large part of his ministry. Second, he finally came to the realization, as others already had, that he was indeed the man for the secretaryship. He resigned from his church on June 21, 1846, and that summer began work as the full-time corresponding secretary of the FMB. A. M. Poindexter aptly reflected on Taylor's decision to leave the pastorate and enter into the work of the board:

When elected to and urged to accept the office, he encountered one of the greatest trials in his life. He loved and rejoiced in the pastoral relation. He had been remarkably successful as a pastor. In no other sphere could he, with so much personal satisfaction, serve his Lord. . . .

On the other hand, though regretting deeply—none more deeply—the causes which led to the organization

---

61   Taylor, *Life and Times of James B. Taylor*, 158.

of the Southern Baptist Convention, he thought that measure right and desirable. It had his fullest sympathy and support. He knew that, to succeed, the Boards of the Convention must adequately be represented. If his brethren thought him the most suitable representative of the Foreign Mission Board, should he not yield to their judgment? . . . His interest in the foreign mission cause was not the product of official relation. Often there is a suspicion that the zeal of agents results not from appreciation of their objects, but their desire of success. However this may be of others, it was not true of him. His sympathy had long been enlisted for the perishing heathen, and his sound practical judgment taught him that the work of foreign missions was not only the most direct, but the most efficient, means of carrying out the commission of our Lord. . . .

A sense of duty led him to accept the office of Secretary, and its duties were thenceforth the work of his life.[62]

Taylor's Initial Work with the FMB

When Taylor finally decided to step into the role of corresponding secretary, he was the first in the position but was not new to the board. The tasks that correspond to many of the changes in later leadership in the FMB/IMB were not the primary concerns of the new board. As mentioned earlier, the two major issues that needed to be addressed were finding missionaries and raising funds. China had already been chosen as the primary place of mission work, but soon other locations such as Africa and Italy would be added. More missionaries would be added to the board, and Baptists in the South would slowly begin to support Taylor and the FMB.

In 1846, the first regular Southern Baptist Convention meeting occurred in Richmond, Virginia. The board Jeter had been leading, and the work that Taylor had been advancing for the last

---

62   Taylor, *Life and Times of James B. Taylor*, 176–77.

few months, were now to become official. The recommendation of Taylor as the corresponding secretary passed by unanimous vote, and committees were formed to focus on important aspects of the mission work: agencies for fundraising, publication, finances, the China mission, the African mission, and theological education in China. Taylor was also able to present to the convention the work the board had been doing. He acknowledged to the convention that the board's anticipation in the first year was merely to begin the process of mission work; however, they were able to accomplish more than they had hoped. He reported that they had contacted the General Convention, as requested, about transference of claims and received the word back that no transference would occur of property or debts. Missionaries also would not be transferred from the General Convention to the SBC; however, they would allow, "in the spirit of fraternal regard," any missionary to resign and join the SBC.[63] Taylor also clearly defined the role of corresponding secretary of the FMB at this meeting (he had not officially been elected when giving the report), claiming that this role was the essential link between churches in the South for the cause of foreign missions. He saw it as a monumental task that "will require no ordinary measure of intelligence, discretion and energy, aright to fill this duty."[64] This claim was no mere speculation since he had lived it the last few months; he felt the weight of the job into which he was stepping. Raising funds would be the primary role. He reported that in the first year the board collected $11,735.22 and spent $2,231.09, but any balance remaining would be used to cover the new missionaries appointed by the board to China and Africa.

Also at the meeting, a copy of the *Southern Baptist Missionary Journal* was presented as a publication to aid in telling mission stories and to include material "to quicken and encourage our churches

---

63   SBCA, 1846, 21.
64   SBCA, 1846, 22.

in the sublime work."[65] The *Southern Baptist Missionary Journal* was intended for pastors, but Taylor also wanted a publication for a general audience. Eventually, *The Commission* came into existence to fill this role and had a circulation upwards of eight thousand. From this early meeting we can see a more direct involvement of the SBC in the affairs of the FMB than would later be the case. As Jesse Fletcher notes, "In fact, it was not the Foreign Mission Board but rather the Convention which did the directing in the early years through its special committees on China, Africa, expansion (Committee on New Fields of Labor), and agencies."[66]

Taylor also announced the appointments and upcoming departure of Clopton and Pearcy within the month, as well as the appointments of J. L. Shuck and I. J. Roberts, who had been serving with the General Convention as missionaries in China. In October of 1845, the board reached out to both of them and requested that they consider joining the FMB. At the time, unbeknownst to the board, Roberts had sent a communication requesting to join it, and the board accepted him.[67] Shuck was in the States at the time traveling with Yong Seen Sang. Shuck not only accepted the offer to join the FMB but also agreed to help raise funds for the cause while he traveled across the United States, thus delaying their trip back to China.[68] This commitment to aid the cause of the FMB at home was due in part to the reception and presentation of Shuck and Sang at the 1846 convention meeting in Virginia, where both addressed the convention about their work.

China

The board did not want to overextend themselves at the beginning of their work, which is why they restricted their focus to the China and Africa mission fields. As we have seen, there were several

---

65   SBCA, 1846, 23.
66   Jesse C. Fletcher, "Foreign Mission Board Strategy," *Baptist History & Heritage* (October 1974): 213.
67   SBCA, 1846, 25.
68   Estep, *Whole Gospel Whole World*, 73.

missionaries to China already prepared to travel, but an additional need was for help in two other areas: theological education and health care.[69]

The early focus of the China mission was on the city of Canton. Roberts was joined by the Cloptons and Pearcys to continue the work in the region, while Shuck eventually moved on to Shanghai. The request for a theological educator resulted in the appointment of Francis Johnson, and the physician J. Sexton James was also sent. The Whildens would also soon join the work going on in China. As good as the outlook was for this mission, soon tragedy would occur. Within the first year Clopton died of fever, the Jameses drowned in the Hong Kong harbor, Pearcy moved from Canton to Shanghai because of failing health, Mrs. Whilden died, and their children were sent back to the States. The board also had to remove Roberts as one of its missionaries due to his inability to work well with the FMB's personnel in China.[70] The work continued on despite these setbacks, and others—the Gailards, R. H. Graves, and the Schillings—would soon join the work. It was Graves himself who would be the anchor of the Canton mission; he served there for fifty-six years. The Shucks soon partnered with M. T. Yates, who arrived, along with his wife Eliza, in Shanghai in 1847 and would serve for the next forty-two years, eleven of which were with T. P. Crawford, who worked in Shantung.

---

69 In 1846 it was reported "that the Board be instructed to secure at the earliest practicable period, a suitable individual to devote himself chiefly to the theological training of such native converts in China, as may be employed in the christian [sic] ministry." SBCA, 1846, 15. The board also requested, "That it is expedient to send to the China field, as soon as possible, a christian [sic] physician, who shall also be engaged in imparting the knowledge of divine truth." SBC Annual, 1846, 15.

70 See J. Winston Crawley, "East Asia," in Baker J. Cauthen, et al., *Advance: A History of Southern Baptist Foreign Missions* (Nashville: Broadman, 1970), 80–81. Estep provides more detail on the decision to part ways with Roberts. Apparently, Shuck had warned the board of Roberts, and it was soon discovered why. "Shortly after his appointment, the Foreign Mission Board became aware that Roberts was attempting to raise money through the Kentucky-based China Mission Society and learned that he was, at the same time, receiving support from a Canton Missionary Society." Estep, *Whole Gospel Whole World*, 90.

Africa

At the 1846 meeting, it was reported that work in Africa should begin soon. Taylor reported, "Many of her sons are among us, and from them we may hope, in process of time, to select those who will become eminently qualified to preach to their countrymen 'the unsearchable riches of Christ.'"[71] The work in Africa by the FMB was modeled after the General Convention's work there by missionaries like Lott Carey. When given the opportunity to move to the board in the South, John Day requested to transfer and became one of the first FMB missionaries in Liberia, thus becoming the first FMB missionary to Africa. This work soon grew, though only partially supported, and additional missionaries would join. In 1849 the board reported that there were thirteen missionaries, of whom six were teachers or interpreters serving in Liberia.[72] One of those missionaries was B. J. Drayton from the First African Baptist Church of Richmond, Virginia. In 1849 his report from Monrovia was given to the convention:

> During the last three months, I have traveled one hundred and twenty miles; preached thirty-seven sermons; lectured seven times; attended fifteen prayer meetings; visited one hundred and seventy-eight families; distributed two hundred and fifteen tracts, and attended four concerts of prayer for the spread of the gospel. My Bible class contains thirty-four males and twenty-seven females. This department of my labor is doing well; much interest seeming to be manifested. The Sabbath school is yet in a healthy condition; the children, both Americans and natives, are rapidly improving. This is an interesting location, and if sustained properly, much good can be done. Pray for me.[73]

---

71   SBCA, 1846, 24.
72   SBCA, 1849, 54.
73   SBCA, 1849, 55.

The work in Liberia was growing, and soon Sierra Leone would be added to the African mission. By the time of the American Civil War, there were eighteen pastors with 1,258 members in twenty-four stations in Liberia and Sierra Leone.[74] However, the effects of the Civil War on the FMB had direct effects on the board's work in Africa, which was left without support for many years.

The board was also sending missionaries into central Africa, including Thomas J. Bowen, who was appointed in 1849. He was joined by Harvey Goodale and Robert F. Hill. The three traveled the next few months surveying the land. Goodale unfortunately fell ill and died. Hill remained in Liberia while Bowen moved further south, eventually near modern-day Nigeria, where he was invited to Ijaiye, where he settled. Many others would join him in the work. Most would not remain. During the Civil War, the mission would not be supported by the board, but the missionaries continued with their tasks.

Japan and Italy

China was not the only field in East Asia the board wished to engage in missions. Early on Japan was also chosen as a field. In 1859 the board appointed J. Q. A. and Sarah Rohrer, Crawford H. Toy, and J. L. Johnson to Japan. The Rohrers sailed for Japan but were lost at sea, and Toy and Johnson never departed due to the American Civil War.

Though China and Africa were the main locations of work during Taylor's tenure at the board, in 1870, at the end of his leadership, the board began a new work in Italy. At its meeting on June 18, 1870, the board began to focus on Europe, as directed by the convention. It was acknowledged that the "Board has been anxious for years, as opportunities might offer, to carry out the sense of the Convention. Hitherto the way was not open."[75] At this meeting, the board appointed Dr. William M. Cote as a

---

74   SBCA, 1861, 53.
75   FMBM, June 18, 1870.

missionary to Europe to a place that he would think would be most suitable.[76] His choice was Rome due to Italy's new openness. Cote noted the shift in the country: "One fact is certain, Rome is now open to the Gospel. The power of the Anti-Christ has come to an end, and his spiritual power is fast decreasing.[77] In January of 1871, a Baptist church was established in Rome, and no less than John Broadus was in attendance. He writes of this occasion, "I had no idea beforehand how interesting and promising a field Rome would now be, and had not thought much about this mission. I am now thoroughly satisfied that the Board has acted wisely in establishing this mission, and I should exclaim vehemently against any idea of abandoning it."[78]

Struggles

Taylor and the FMB were making strides in sending and supporting their work internationally, but back in the States, there were a few problems that they would have to overcome. One of these problems was the pushback on their work by others in the convention. Criticism of associational mission work was nothing new for Baptists. The anti-missions movement had left its mark, but now Taylor and company would have a new challenge with the work of J. R. Graves and the rise of Landmarkism.

Landmarkism began in the early 1850s and soon had a number of followers, growing especially through Graves's paper, *The Tennessee Baptist*. On September 4, 1858, he wrote in the paper concerning the missionary boards,

> No man has lower views of the authority of a Missionary Board to dictate to missionaries or churches than we have. . . . The scriptural plan is clearly exemplified in the New Testament, and it is simple and effectual, and the

---

76   FMBM, June 18, 1870.
77   SBCA, 1871, 48.
78   SBCA, 1871, 49.

sooner we return to it as a denomination, the better for us and for the world. . . .

We do not believe that the Foreign Board has any right to call upon the missionaries that the churches send to China or Africa, to take a journey to Richmond to be examined touching their experience, call to the ministry, and soundness of faith. It is a high handed act, and degrades both the judgment and authority of the Church and presbytery that ordained him, thus practically declaring itself above both.[79]

At the 1859 annual meeting, Graves presented his case for another plan for foreign missions, one that would be less structured, less dependent on a board, and more reliant on the churches. A committee was formed to address the issues that Graves presented. Taylor and Poindexter listened to Graves and discussed his plan for the FMB throughout the evening until the sun rose the next day. The following day the committee reported to the convention the outcomes of the meeting. It presented two resolutions: First, it would be "inexpedient" to make any changes to the FMB. Second, if a church or association desired to send their own missionaries and raised their own funds for the missionaries, then the FMB would become a "disbursing agent" for the missionary.[80] This report was adopted, and Graves approved of the outcome. In an editorial he said, "There is no reason why our denomination may not co-operate harmoniously in missionary matters. . . . Here are two plans of operation submitted to the brethren. Let them make their election. Let them remember that they have no good excuse for doing nothing."[81]

---

79 J. R. Graves, *The Tennessee Baptist*, September 4, 1858, as cited in Robert A. Baker, *The Southern Baptist Convention and Its People, 1607–1972* (Nashville: Broadman, 1974), 216–17.

80 SBCA, 1859, 95–96.

81 J. R. Graves, *The Tennessee Baptist*, May 21 and May 28, as cited in Baker, *Southern Baptist Convention and Its People*, 218–19.

Landmarkism was a small problem for Taylor and the board compared to the issues that would arise from the Civil War. Before the war the board was functioning quite well. Missions work was expanding, and funds were coming in from the churches. All would come to a halt in a short period of time. Taylor's diaries in 1861 attest to the difficulties that would only increase over the next few years for the board. It was becoming more and more difficult to secure contributions for the board, and over time he had to limit his own travels and rely on correspondence for his work. What pushed him to continue the work was the missionaries on the field—they were in his charge, and he had a responsibility to help support them.

The financial problems continued as the war marched on. There was not enough money coming in to cover the thirty-eight missionaries the board had at this time. This trying time led the board to seek loans to cover the expenses of the missionaries. The board also attempted to send cotton to London to fund the missions work, a plan that failed. Poindexter even resigned his position so that the work would not be hindered. Ultimately the board could not afford to pay the salaries of its missionaries, and many of them had to find other trades on the field in order to make ends meet and continue the mission's work. Yates, for example, became a translator for the US Embassy. Joseph Harden, in Africa, turned to making bricks. All were cut off from the board and left alone throughout the duration of the war. Additionally, the FMB invested deeply in Confederate bonds that quickly lost all value. At the meeting of the board on March 12, 1866, the treasurer said that in December the board had a balance of $1.78.[82]

The war wreaked havoc on the South and the FMB. Before the war there had been great hope and zeal for missions; that hope and zeal were not snuffed out, but after the war there was greater work needed to regain what had been lost. The FMB was in debt for $10,000, but the board was quick to rebuild. By 1871 all debts

---

82   FMBM, March 12, 1866.

were paid off and the board raised $25,700 and was able to add to its treasury. Estep states this well: "In spite of wars in America, China, and Africa, and in spite of the loss of so many missionaries, the work had survived."[83] These difficulties were part of the work that went into the beginnings of the FMB. Taylor managed them all as best he could as well as having to deal with the tragedies of losing missionaries on the field. In his biography, his son aptly wrote about his fastidiousness in his charge as secretary:

> At times he suffered much solicitude with reference to the pecuniary support of the missionaries, and cherished so close a personal sympathy with them in their sufferings and provisions as in some good sense to share them; and he did this all the more intensely because he could not help seeing that so few bore the missions and the heathen on their hearts. Borrowing Carey's well-known figure, it may be said that he held *hard* to the rope which held those whom he helped to let down into the well, so that he often felt the strain upon mind and heart.[84]

Pastoral Care

As we have seen above, Taylor's work as a minister was central to his vocation. His work for the FMB operated as a continuation of his pastoral role, not as an alternative to it. He was no longer the pastor of a congregation, but he saw to it that he was pastoring a much broader flock: the SBC and especially the missionaries of the FMB.

This care that he offered to the missionaries is evidenced in how he related to them. He saw it as his duty to ensure that those the SBC was sending out understood the role that they were entering. Consider his words as he charged the newly appointed missionaries: "You go out, not as ambassadors from an earthly government, but as ministers of the kingdom of Christ—not to treat with secular

---

83   Estep, *Whole Gospel Whole World*, 101.
84   Taylor, *Life and Times of James B. Taylor*, 203.

powers on great national questions, but to *bear communications of divine love*, beseeching the heathen to be reconciled to God."[85] Taylor also made sure to take care of their needs. He personally traveled with many of the missionaries as they made their way to the vessels that would carry them to their mission locations. George Taylor notes that this was the normal case: "The Corresponding Secretary personally contracted for the passage, purchased the necessary articles, and superintended the embarkation. This involved heavy responsibility and required business ability, while it often subjected him to peculiar cares and labors. But it is not too much to say that he was eminently successful in the discharge of these duties, while he endeared himself to the hearts of his missionary brethren and sisters by his kind attentions to their comfort and solicitude for their welfare."[86]

Taylor also kept regular communication with all the missionaries not only to check in on the mission but also to make sure that they themselves were doing well. In a letter to George Taylor, C. F. Sturgis (a pastor from Alabama) relates how other missionaries thought of J. B. Taylor's letters: "The letters of Brother Taylor especially seemed more like the loving epistles of a father to his children than the mere perfunctory communications of the Secretary of the Board."[87] In another instance, a former missionary mentioned the correspondence of Taylor: "Yes, I feel that I do know him, though I have never seen him. I was a missionary in China, and often read the letters he wrote to the missionaries of his Board, and loved him from them. Indeed, all of the missionaries at that station used to look for his letters with interest, and we all read them with delight and profit."[88]

Taylor's care for the missionaries was as great as his care for the FMB itself. This was his work unto the Lord. He traveled countless miles and raised thousands of dollars to send out workers for the

---

85   Taylor, *Life and Times of James B. Taylor*, 178.
86   Taylor, *Life and Times of James B. Taylor*, 182.
87   Taylor, *Life and Times of James B. Taylor*, 198.
88   Taylor, *Life and Times of James B. Taylor*, 198.

harvest. At the end of Taylor's ministry at the FMB he had accomplished much. By the numbers he helped raise $628,180.93 and sent out eighty-one missionaries into China, Liberia, Sierra Leone, Nigeria, and Italy.[89] His last year of service found him feeling weaker and wanting to resign from the work, but he pressed on until December 11, 1871, when he resigned from the board. In response, the board made this report:

> During the whole period of its existence, extending through twenty-six years, he has performed the duties of this office with a diligence, fidelity, and disinterestedness never excelled, and with a judgment, prudence, and efficiency rarely equaled. He has been, in truth, the life and motive-power of the Board. In all this time his relations with all its members have been most fraternal and pleasant. Nothing has ever occurred, in their business transactions, in their complicated interests, or in their earnest discussions, to disturb, for a moment, the reciprocal confidence and affection between the Board and their Secretary.[90]

Eleven days later, with his family present, James B. Taylor died.

CONCLUSION

The beginnings of the Foreign Mission Board of the Southern Baptist Convention are intricately tied together with the environment in which they were birthed. The world of the Southern United States in the nineteenth century was one that tolerated and warred over an unjust practice and unbiblical anthropology that so shaped Baptists in the South that the Southern Baptist Convention still

---

89 Data from Eugene L. Hill, "Administering Southern Baptist Foreign Missions," in Cauthen, et al., *Advance*, 29.
90 Taylor, *Life and Times of James B. Taylor*, 297.

feels its contours to the present day. This history cannot be denied but only learned from in the hopes of knowing and doing better in the future.

Despite this blight, the beginnings also birthed a mission board that zealously went about the task of exciting the churches to be involved in taking the gospel to the uttermost. Though many churches, missionaries, and pastors were involved in this process, it is to J. B. Taylor that Southern Baptists owe much in leading and shaping the FMB throughout many challenges from its inauguration to a quarter century later. Never did he waver from the desire to accomplish the task of engaging the world with the gospel. No better words could conclude this work on him and the FMB than those spoken at his funeral by J. L. M. Curry: "Whatever of history belongs to the foreign missions work of the Southern Baptist Convention is closely, inseparably interwoven with Brother Taylor. . . . The history of foreign missions under his patronage is his monument."[91]

---

91   C. E. Maddry, "World Outreach of Southern Baptists," quoted in Hill, "Administering Southern Baptist Foreign Missions," 28.

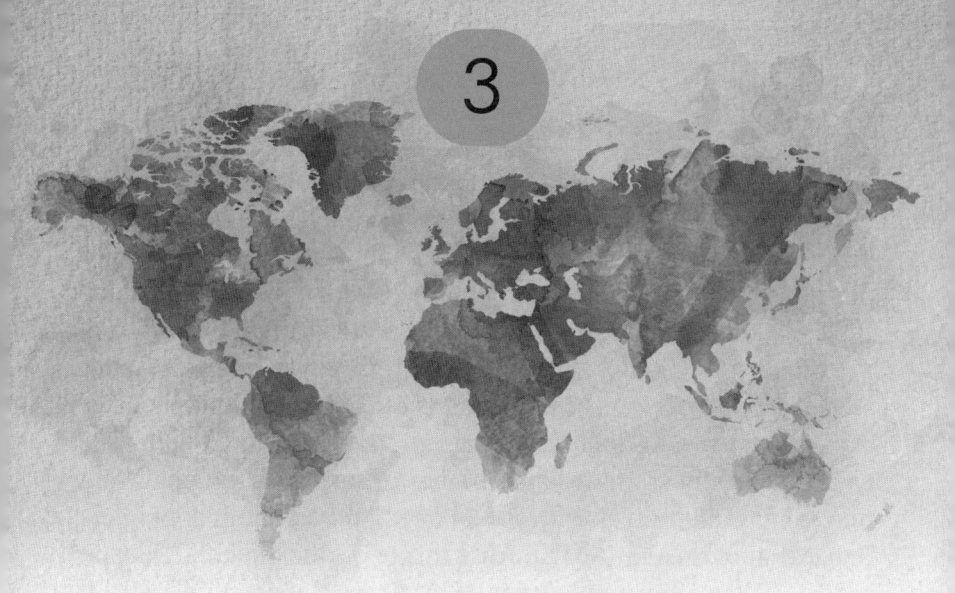

GROWTH AND CONTROVERSY
The Administration of
Henry Allen Tupper, 1872–1893

Anthony L. Chute

HENRY ALLEN TUPPER was born in 1828 on a date that occurs only once every four years—February 29. Whether he considered February 28 or March 1 his birthday during non-leap years is unknown, but perhaps it is an appropriate date nonetheless in that he was both behind and ahead of the times in which he lived. He served as a chaplain for the Confederate Army, yet he paved the way for women to become missionaries without requiring them to be married. He had ties to Baptist royalty, including Richard Fuller and James P. Boyce, yet he expressed high hopes for John Stout and T. P. Bell, two men who had been relieved of missionary service after denying the plenary inspiration of the Bible. He once belonged to the oldest Baptist church in the South, First Baptist of Charleston, South Carolina, yet he distanced himself from the older, less historic claims of Landmark Baptists.

Tupper served as corresponding secretary of the FMB from 1872 to 1893. During his term, the number of missionaries grew from nineteen to ninety-two, with a total of 147 missionaries appointed. Expansion of mission work during this period included Mexico in 1880, Brazil in 1881, and Japan in 1888. At the close of his final fiscal year in 1893, the Foreign Missions Board raised over $150,000, up from $25,000 the year before Tupper assumed office. In addition to these numerical examples, his significance as a pastor and administrator was such that each time he felt led to submit a resignation letter, both church and governing bodies refused to accept it. Despite his impressive efforts in raising awareness and funds for reaching the world for Christ, most Southern Baptists remain unaware of his work. Instead, they remember a missionary appointed under his tenure—Lottie Moon.

The purpose of this chapter is to examine the work of the Foreign Mission Board under the leadership of Henry Tupper. Though not a biographical portrait, this chapter will highlight the personal perspective and strategies that Tupper implemented as he served in this role. As such, it will be helpful to introduce the material with an overview of Tupper's early life, including the events that shaped his thinking regarding missions. Both advancements and controversies will be addressed with respect to Tupper's involvement and the larger purposes of the Foreign Mission Board. Finally, this chapter will examine the Tupper era's historical impact and practical implications for missiology today.[1]

---

1   Special thanks to Jonathan McCormick, Regional Librarian at Gateway Seminary, for assistance in locating materials relevant to this chapter.

TUPPER'S BACKGROUND FOR MISSIONS

Henry Tupper was born in Charleston, South Carolina, to Tristam and Eliza Tupper. At his professional peak Tristam was president of the South Carolina Railroad, thus providing a substantial income for the family and introducing his son to the world of business and bookkeeping. An excerpt from Tupper's diary states, "In the midst of my college course [my father] took me into his office, much to the distress of mother and my own dissatisfaction, and kept me there for two years of my education. . . . For thirty years I have kept a cash book and can tell at any time my income and expenditure at any period during that time."[2] Henry's innate sense of fiscal responsibility would serve him well as pastor of churches and corresponding secretary of the FMB.

The Tuppers were active members at the First Baptist Church, Charleston, a congregation that Henry affectionately called his spiritual alma mater. Henry's earliest memories of the church included a deep devotion to its pastor, Basil Manly Sr. He later recalled, "I thank God that I was born under the ministry of one whom I always regarded the holiest man I ever knew. At my mother's knee I was taught to believe that Dr. [Richard] Furman was a saint, and that his mantle had fallen fairly on the shoulders of Dr. Manly."[3] Henry's reference to his mother's impressing him with a love for the church and its pastors indicates a formative period in his life that would come to further fruition as he recognized the influence mothers had in the family, thus leading to a greater need for female missionaries.

Tupper was also shaped by the transition of pastors at First Baptist Charleston, as William Brantly Sr. succeeded Manly. The next seven years, from 1837 to 1844, became known as the "Innovation Pastorate" whereupon the congregation shared Brantly's pastoral duties with his administrative responsibilities as president

---

2   George Braxton Taylor, *Virginia Baptist Ministers: Fifth Series, 1902-1914 with Supplement* (Baltimore: H. M. Wharton, 1916), 17.

3   H. A. Tupper, ed., *Two Centuries of the First Baptist Church of South Carolina, 1663-1883, with Supplement* (Baltimore: R. H. Woodward, 1889), 157-58.

of Charleston College. Tupper later noted how this arrangement put Brantly "in a position for a wider range of influence, and gave him the honor of re-organizing a cherished institution of learning, of sending out, as graduates, several of the most brilliant and useful men of the State."[4] Being in a position to reorganize an institution and send others forth was precisely the role in which Tupper himself served as he penned those words.

Moreover, during the Innovation Pastorate, several other changes took place that influenced Tupper's view of progressing beyond the past to accommodate the future. He recalled that the "gown and bands were laid aside; the sounding board over the pulpit, regarded as a sacred thing, was taken down; the south gallery was fitted for white attendants; and the cross aisles leading to side doors were built up with pews, while the Sunday-school was removed from the church to the newly-built lecture room."[5] Although such changes seem minor on paper, in reality the congregation was introduced to and embraced the innovations introduced by Pastor Brantly. Tupper took note, displaying a keen eye for lessons learned: "In reference to these last innovations, let me remark . . . that the changes in the externals of the church only prepared for greater material modifications, which suggests the truth that neither this mountain nor Jerusalem is essential to the worship of the Father."[6] Tupper learned early in life that change was necessary for progress.

Other changes were needed, however, that were not as readily apparent to Tupper or his family. As white citizens of Charleston, the Tupper family embraced slavery as a normal way of life. During his childhood, Henry did not seem to recognize the evils of slavery but noted instead how African Americans were included in every facet of gospel ministry, even under leadership from his family: "The colored Sunday-school, superintended from its origin to its conclusion by members of the writer's [i.e., Tupper's] family, was a prominent feature

---

4   Tupper, *Two Centuries*, 184.
5   Tupper, *Two Centuries*, 166.
6   Tupper, *Two Centuries*, 167.

of the church and the germ of more extensive work among the colored people themselves."[7] The proximity with which Tupper engaged fellow church members in the African American community left a lasting impression on him: "With several of these practical deacons or elders of the church, the writer had, in his childhood, personal acquaintance, and subsequently he had occasion to hold them in high esteem."[8] Such reminiscences may ring hollow today in light of a more concentrated focus on America's past sins, but Tupper was sincere in his love for African Americans, such that when he presented himself for membership in the church, he announced his intention to become a missionary to Africa. His plans were immediately tabled by Richard Fuller, who, upon baptizing him, announced that Henry's labors would prove more useful in America. As an adult, Tupper's relations with the African American religious community were such that he frequently preached and taught among them: "Before the War I preached every Sunday and Thursday night to the colored people and had appointments on the plantations in the vicinity. This was service in which my heart rejoiced."[9]

Tupper's pastoral labors among African Americans brought forth different realities with the outbreak of the Civil War. He was present at the opening salvo, having been in the boat that carried orders to open fire on Fort Sumter. His positioning was no accident, as he later stated: "In the principles on which the War was fought, I was a South Carolinian thoroughly imbued."[10] He was appointed by Jefferson Davis as chaplain of the North Georgia Regiment, which he served without compensation. Like many white Baptists in the South during this time, Tupper viewed the war as an interruption in otherwise good relations between black and white congregants:

> And known is it to not a few, from personal knowledge,
> that this work of the Old First Church was as good seed

---

7   Tupper, *Two Centuries*, 316.
8   Tupper, *Two Centuries*, 315.
9   Taylor, *Virginia Baptist Ministers*, 25.
10 Taylor, *Virginia Baptist Ministers*, 26.

which, when the relation of the races was changed by the war, was springing up in self-denying projects for the spiritual profit of the negroes, which perhaps may be more perfectly realized by the Providence which has made them free to serve God "under their own vine and fig-tree." But never will the time come when negroes shall have truer friends and more devoted laborers for their religious welfare than was the Old First Church, with regard to which it shall be said of many a rejoicing African in the other world, "This and that man was born in her."[11]

The fact that Tupper was a sinner in the midst of a sinful world should surprise no one.[12] The same gospel that he proffered to African Americans for their salvation was the same gospel that he himself came to embrace. Having been raised in a Christian home afforded him the advantage of attending church regularly, and thus frequently being exposed to the gospel, but he encountered and resisted the conviction of sin for nearly a decade before giving his life to Jesus Christ. Such encounters led him to sit in the gallery during church services for fear that he would be exposed as an unbeliever. In 1846, Richard Fuller led a protracted meeting and took a special interest in Tupper. He provided a copy of John Angel James's *The Anxious Inquirer after Salvation Directed and Encouraged* for Tupper's benefit, which he read one evening. The following morning Tupper shared with Fuller his fear of having a false hope, to which

---

11 Tupper, *Two Centuries*, 318.
12 The struggle to understand such a context where people advanced the gospel while enslaving other people, while failing to see the disconnect between the two, is perhaps best explained by John B. Boles as he attempted to place the work of Thomas Jefferson in a similar context: "We should not expect him [Jefferson] to have embraced the values of a cosmopolitan, progressive person of the twenty-first century. How could he possibly have done so? Instead, we should try to understand the constraints—legal, financial, personal, intellectual—under which he lived. To understand certainly does not mean to approve or even forgive; rather, it means to comprehend why Jefferson made the kinds of decisions he made and saw the world as he did." See John B. Boles, *Jefferson: Architect of American Liberty* (New York: Basic Books, 2017), 3.

Fuller replied with an encouraging but theologically lackluster promise: "If you go to hell I will go with you and we shall preach Jesus there until they turn us out, and then where will we go?"[13] Tupper was converted several weeks later after meeting with Francis Johnson, the son of William B. Johnson, who encouraged him to read and claim the promise of Romans 10:9. According to Tupper, "the whole world was changed. It was a delight to live."[14] He was baptized on February 17, 1846, along with a friend whom he had led to the Lord immediately after his conversion. Tupper's evangelistic instincts were also on display two months later when his childhood friend, James P. Boyce, returned to Charleston from his studies at Brown University during spring vacation. After Tupper related his own experience, Boyce "felt himself a ruined sinner, and like the rest, had to look to the merits of Christ alone for salvation."[15] Boyce was baptized by Fuller on April 22, 1846, later becoming one of the founders of The Southern Baptist Theological Seminary.

Tupper and Boyce had become brothers in the Lord, but they also became brothers-in-law when Tupper married Boyce's sister, Nancy (Nannie). Henry and Nannie were also childhood friends, as their parents owned pews almost opposite to each other. He admired her early on, noting that she frequently dressed in white, which "was a fit and beautiful emblem of her simple and pure character."[16] Their marriage on November 1, 1849, enhanced Henry's life, ministry, and income significantly. Nannie was active in her faith from a young age, as Henry noted: "She was really the 'pious, consistent little member of the church.' She visited the poor, sought children for the Sabbath school, and was ready for every good word and work."[17] She served in many roles during Henry's tenure

---

13   Taylor, *Virginia Baptist Ministers*, 22. Again in this episode, Tupper references the wise counsel and encouragement he received from his mother.
14   Taylor, *Virginia Baptist Ministers*, 22.
15   John A. Broadus, *Memoir of James Petigru Boyce* (New York: A. C. Armstrong and Son, 1893), 45. Cited in Thomas J. Nettles, *James Petigru Boyce: A Southern Baptist Statesman* (Phillipsburg, NJ: P&R, 2009), 54.
16   Taylor, *Virginia Baptist Ministers*, 24.
17   Taylor, *Virginia Baptist Ministers*, 24.

as corresponding secretary, including president of the Female Missionary Society at the First Baptist Church of Richmond, and vice president of the Women's Missionary Society of Richmond. Her father, Ker Boyce, was one of the wealthiest men in South Carolina, having made a fortune through business practices and wise investments. When Henry wed Nannie, he was in a position to receive nearly half a million dollars from her father's estate.[18] Together they had twelve children.

Prior to becoming corresponding secretary, Tupper served as pastor of two churches. His first pastorate, from 1850 to 1853, was First Baptist Church in Graniteville, South Carolina, and he described his work there as "partly missionary and entirely gratuitous and this greatly delighted me."[19] An issue with his health led him to spend the winter of 1852 in Florida, and even though he was told that he would never preach again, he accepted the pastorate of First Baptist Church, Washington, Georgia, in April 1853. The church was noted for its founder, Jesse Mercer, and its location in Wilkes County, which attracted a number of wealthy and educated inhabitants. Mercer's pastorate, lasting from 1827 to 1841, established and encouraged support for missions, as First Baptist, Washington, led the Georgia Association for decades in its giving to mission work. Tupper continued the tradition, both in word and in deed: "The church was thoroughly indoctrinated on the subject of missions, as their large contributions indicated. But frankness requires me to say that in the report of those donations were included my support of a missionary among the Indians and another in Africa, or amounts equivalent to such support."[20] In point of fact, Tupper viewed the promotion of evangelism and missions as an ongoing priority for every pastor: "The minister must realize that he was called to publish the glad tidings of salvation—which are to all people—before he was called to the pastorate of any church; and consequently, when

---

18   Robert Alton James, "A Study of the Life and Contributions of Henry Allen Tupper" (PhD diss., New Orleans Baptist Theological Seminary, 1989), 25.
19   Taylor, *Virginia Baptist Ministers*, 24.
20   Taylor, *Virginia Baptist Ministers*, 25.

he becomes the pastor of a church in our land, he should make all his labors and all his prayers and all his successes bear upon the fulfillment of his original vocation before God."[21]

It was also during this period that Tupper became involved in Baptist denominational life, serving on numerous committees at both the local and state level, thus sharpening his administrative skills.[22] He preached the missionary sermon for the Georgia Association in 1854, and he delivered the opening sermon for the annual meeting in 1869. He served as a trustee of Mercer University, and he was elected on nine occasions to represent Georgia Baptists at the annual meeting of the Southern Baptist Convention. His work on behalf of the convention mainly dealt with home missions. On several occasions he was appointed as a representative of the American Baptist Home Missionary Society.

Tupper received numerous offers to leave his pastorate in Washington, including two separate occasions when Boyce invited him to teach theology at The Southern Baptist Theological Seminary. Tupper declined both offers, citing his love for the pastorate and the people of Washington. His refusal to "exchange in a measure the office of preaching for that of teaching," or to sever the "sacred and happy relation" he had with his congregants could not be overridden by his brother-in-law's pleas. However, the opportunity to expand his influence in missions had the opposite effect.[23] As much as Tupper loved the pastorate and the people of his church, he seems to have never relinquished his desire to be more engaged in missions. In his own words, "The subject of missions haunted me."[24] Because of his desire to do something more, he once proposed a plan to James B. Taylor (his predecessor as corresponding secretary) to form a self-sustaining mission work in Japan. He estimated the cost to be a quarter of a million dollars and may have offered part

---

21   H. A. Tupper, *A Decade of Foreign Missions, 1880–1890* (Richmond, VA: Foreign Missions Board of the Southern Baptist Convention, 1891), 773.

22   See James, "A Study of the Life," 41–46.

23   Broadus, *Memoir of James Petigru Boyce*, 102.

24   Taylor, *Virginia Baptist Ministers*, 26.

of his personal fortune to bring the proposal to reality. The onset of the Civil War prevented him from pursuing this interest further, which, as he noted, was not new to him: "The cherished plan, like my others for mission work, was unrealized."[25]

Tupper's plan to become a missionary to Africa may have simply been the idealistic dream of a young man hoping to make a difference in the world, but his desire to go to Japan as a missionary was born from his developed understanding of the need for more missionaries to enter the harvest. He also knew that sacrifices were necessary for unreached people to hear the gospel, hence his willingness to exchange the comforts of his own life for the people of Japan. Even though he was unable to go himself, Tupper personally felt the cost paid by others who did answer the call to missions. Such was the case with Mary E. Canfield, who made a profession of faith at First Baptist, Washington, and subsequently sensed a call to become a missionary to Africa. Her mother was opposed to Mary leaving for Africa and blamed Tupper for her daughter's apparent confusion. Tupper spoke to Mary's mother, informing her that a greater separation between mother and daughter would occur unless she too confessed Christ as her Savior. Not only did Mary's mother become a believer, but she also consented to her daughter's departure to Africa. One year later, Tupper visited Mary's mother to inform her that her daughter had died on the mission field. She received the terrible news while packing a box to send overseas to the African mission.[26]

In December 1871, James B. Taylor announced his resignation as corresponding secretary of the Foreign Mission Board. The committee searching for his replacement announced its intention to find a person who was "pious, an earnest friend of foreign missions, of popular, at least respectable, speaking talents, discreet,

---

25   Taylor, *Virginia Baptist Ministers*, 26.

26   Unbeknownst to Mary's mother, Tupper had personally pledged to support Mary and her husband, T. A. Reid. The standard annual salary was $600, but Tupper added $150 for Mary to send back to her mother. Even after Mary's death, Tupper continued his support to her husband and her mother.

industrious, of business habits, of financiering skill, acquainted with the world . . . free from objections in all sections and among all parties . . . fitted to be a wise counselor of the Board, and to make a favorable impression everywhere in behalf of foreign missions."[27]

Tupper described receiving the news of his election to succeed Taylor as "a flash in a cloudless sky" that provided him with "perhaps the realizing of all my missionary hopes and preparations."[28] Given that Tupper had been taught business methods with integrity by his father, had a loving relationship and lifelong respect for his mother, was eager to share the gospel personally and encourage churches to do the same pastorally, and had experience in denominational circles as a friend of missions and understood the great sacrifices made by those on the mission field, it is not too much to say that he had been preparing for the task long before the opportunity arose.

TUPPER'S PLAN FOR PROMOTING FOREIGN MISSIONS

Tupper felt the tremendous weight of following Taylor's twenty-six years in leadership as corresponding secretary. In his first report to the board, Tupper stated, "This report might well be draped in mourning. The prospect of the future and the retrospect of the past are gloomed by the remembrance that the moving spirit of our Foreign Mission cause . . . is passed away, and the ponderous work, which he so meekly and successfully carried forward, is transmitted to other and untried shoulders."[29]

Tupper's untried shoulders were now responsible for work already underway in Africa, China, and Europe. Tupper was gratified that the $6,000 needed to send a team to China was raised early in his administration and a sum of $20,000 was received to fund

---

27 "Secretary of the Foreign Mission Board," *Religious Herald*, January 25, 1872, 2. Cited in James, "A Study of the Life," 56.
28 Taylor, *Virginia Baptist Ministers*, 29.
29 H. A. Tupper, *The Foreign Missions of the Southern Baptist Convention* (Philadelphia: American Baptist Publication Society, 1880), ix.

a Baptist chapel in Rome. Such was not the case with the African mission, which reported the following year that it was "in distress, and calls for prompt support by prayer, by men, and by money."[30]

Though he was untried in this role, Tupper soon had definite ideas about the direction of the Foreign Mission Board. He quickly backed the growing call to support single women on the mission field, stating, in light of Lula Whildon and Edmonia Moon's departure for China, that "the necessity of Christian women to carry the word of God, as men cannot do it, to the women of heathen lands, is increasingly felt. Women societies are organizing to support Bible-women at our Missionary stations. God helping them, our sisters on the way, will do good work. The sisterhood of our Southern Zion should be aroused to the grand mission of redeeming their sister-woman from the degrading and destroying thraldom of Paganism."[31]

He also set out to improve the *Home and Foreign Journal* (later, *Foreign Mission Journal*) since "knowledge of the world's necessity goes before the quickening of Christian conscience to give the gospel to all mankind." The paper, as he envisioned, would be "mechanically improved, ably edited, faithfully managed, and generally circulated."[32] Though there were disagreements regarding the need for such a journal and further problems related to its financing, Tupper believed it was an essential medium for communicating mission stories which would, in turn, spur readers to pray and give: "The cause of missions will progress only as pastors and other active friends bestir themselves to promote the circulation of missionary literature."[33]

The following year, 1873, Tupper provided a more thorough plan for missionary work under his administration. In an article titled "Plan for Promoting Foreign Missions," Tupper suggested the formation of executive committees at the state level that would coordinate and cooperate with the Foreign Mission Board to advance the following:

---

30   SBCA, 1873, 34.
31   SBCA, 1872, 42.
32   SBCA, 1872, 43.
33   SBCA, 1883, v.

1. Circulating the Home and Foreign Journal.
2. Establishing and fostering the monthly concert of prayer for missions.
3. Arranging for stated and occasional meetings and addresses in the interest of Foreign Missions.
4. Aiming to have communication with every church in their respective States, and to secure some regular contribution from every member of the church, and of the Sabbath school.
5. Encouraging "Woman's Mission to Woman," and distributing "Mite Boxes," with the plan of using them, throughout the churches, and Sabbath-schools, collecting funds, and advancing the interest of the work by such other agencies and instrumentalities as may be deemed expedient, in consultation with the Richmond Board.

Tupper requested that each committee follow up with quarterly reports to the board, and to "let comprehensive views of the duty of God's people to the perishing nations be taken, and trusting to their liberality and the promised presence of the Saviour of the world, let our work of evangelization be vigorously pressed in the four great corners of the earth."[34]

In fulfilling the first item of his five-point plan, Tupper invested himself and his finances in the journal. He served as sole editor from 1878 to 1882 and supplied the journal without charge to pastors who were unable to afford a subscription. The journal contained letters from missionaries, news from abroad, pleas for assistance, and missionary sketches that, according to Tupper, "would quicken the interest of the churches."[35]

The focus on prayer was a constant in Tupper's administration as he often challenged Baptists to pray to the Lord of the harvest and called for concerts of prayer to that end. Tupper regularly held

---

34 H. A. Tupper, "Plan for Promoting Foreign Missions," *HFJ* 6, no. 1 (July 1873): 2. See James, "A Study of the Life," 116–39, for a robust examination of the outcomes of each of these proposals and from which the following section is indebted.
35 Taylor, *Virginia Baptist Ministers*, 31.

a monthly concert of prayer when he was a pastor in Washington, Georgia, and he continued to encourage Southern Baptists to do the same. He stressed the importance of prayer even when concerts of prayer were considered less practical. In response to the Foreign Mission Report at the 1883 Southern Baptist Convention, which called for monthly missionary meetings similar to concerts of prayer, the Committee on Conclusion of the Boards submitted the following:

> The outpouring of the Holy Spirit is the one great and constant necessity of all our missionary work. The laborers of the field need the anointing of the Spirit, and the churches need His moving power, that they may give liberally, regularly and devoutly to missions in foreign fields. The Holy Spirit is promised in answer to *prayer*. Let us then hold more special services of prayer for missions. . . . At such meetings the promises of God can be read, information from the fields occupied by the Board in distant places given; and above all, united, earnest and special prayer for the Holy Spirit. Thus shall we receive the grace of giving, and means to support more missionaries.[36]

In addition to circulating the journal and calling for collective gatherings for prayer, Tupper also made it a priority to arrange meetings for missionary discussions. He traveled extensively to this end, describing such times as "delightful in some respects but great crosses in others."[37] While he enjoyed the time with pastors and missionaries, he knew the cost his family bore in his absence. Toward the end of his tenure, and in light of the centennial celebration of the foreign missions movement, Tupper proposed a goal "to send out one hundred new missionaries and to build one hundred simple chapels in foreign fields—one missionary and a chapel for

---

36   SBCA, 1883, 26–27.
37   Taylor, *Virginia Baptist Ministers*, 31.

each year of the centenary."[38] Such an ambitious goal required extensive travel and communication with churches.[39]

Raising funds for missions proved more difficult apart from such periodic celebrations. Upon taking the role of corresponding secretary, Tupper was approached by J. L. Burrows, then president of the board, who asked, "How can every member of every Baptist Church of the South be induced to give something regularly to the cause of foreign missions?" Tupper later wrote, "This I have kept constantly in mind."[40] Tupper often alternated between optimism and unmet expectations in his pleas for financial support. In a brief article titled "Sixty-Eight Thousand Dollars," the number corresponding to the financial needs of the board for 1873–1874, Tupper casually noted, "A little labor on the part of pastors and the more active members, and a little self-denial and liberality on the part of the churches, will cause the money to be raised. It is not too much for us to do so."[41] However, that same year, in a report to the Southern Baptist Convention, Tupper decried the continuous requests for money as being beneath the dignity of Christ's work: "That the grand object for which our Saviour died should be sustained by incessant begging instead of by the voluntary and stated offerings of His people, discords with the spirit of self-consecration and the experienced power of Divine Grace."[42] If each Baptist in the South would give one penny per week, he observed, it would "stop our appeals for money, save a percentage to agents of one-third of their collections, and enable the Board to quadruple their missionary efforts."[43]

That full participation was an unlikely possibility did not deter Tupper; instead, he proposed a more reliable system of

---

38   SBCA, 1890, xliii.
39   The goal was not reached, but it resulted in substantial increases. Forty missionaries were appointed between August 4, 1890, and March 20, 1893, and a record of nearly $155,000 was raised. See James, "A Study of the Life," 127.
40   Taylor, *Virginia Baptist Ministers*, 31.
41   H. A. Tupper, "Sixty-Eight Thousand Dollars," *HFJ* 6, no. 1 (July 1873): 2.
42   SBCA, 1873, 40.
43   SBCA, 1873, 40.

financial support, which led to the formation of a committee to study the matter further. The committee determined that instead of simply depending on commissioned agents to raise money, executive committees in each state could make the needs of the board known in advance according to its expected expenditures. The committee also proposed that missionaries be paid quarterly in advance and that the board be allowed to borrow money on their behalf if the funds were unavailable. This proposal marked a major change as the convention attempted to move from dependence on commissioned agents to local churches providing regular offerings. As it turned out, the plan was not sufficient for the times, and agents were still utilized. Tupper described the struggle to balance income and expenditures accordingly: "Thus the outflow, month by month and quarter by quarter, is as nearly uniform as that of a broad, deep river. The supply, on the contrary, is variable and unsteady as the rains of heaven that feed the sources of the river, flowing and ebbing like the ocean tides from which the clouds are born."[44]

Still, there were successes. An additional element in raising funds, as suggested in Tupper's "Plan for Promoting Foreign Missions," included the use of "mite boxes." The mite box received its name from the account in Luke 21:1–4 of the widow who cast her "two mites" (KJV) into the offering and received commendation from Jesus as having given "more than they all." Mite boxes became a staple in Baptist life after being adopted by the Woman's Mission to Woman society. The success of mite boxes was such that distribution totals were printed in convention minutes under "Woman's Work." In 1884, for example, records indicate that in a ten-year period, 28,520 mite boxes had been distributed "for the use of societies organized for co-operation with our missionary enterprise," resulting in nearly $75,000.[45]

---

44 H. A. Tupper, "An Ebb Tide," *Alabama Baptist*, February 1, 1883, 3. Cited in James, "A Study of the Life," 130.
45 SBCA, 1884, 11.

Two more observations can be made regarding Tupper's involvement in the financial matters of the board. First, he was extraordinarily conscientious of the need for integrity in financial matters. Owing perhaps to his father's training both in business and church life, Tupper stated, "I believe the money accounts of the Mission Rooms are kept with absolute precision. My rule and direction is that, should death overtake me any day, there would be nothing in my affairs as Corresponding Secretary which would require the least explanation."[46] Second, Tupper's integrity was matched by his generosity. James notes that Rebecca Lokey, a granddaughter of Tupper, recalled, "The Foreign Mission Board's financial concerns received special attention during family worship as Tupper prayed that the Lord would lead someone to give generously. Tupper was often compelled to be the giver. She remembered seeing Tupper, on one occasion, contribute a special check for foreign missions through the First Baptist Church of Richmond. Later, one of Tupper's sons, Tristam, informed her that it was for the amount of $8,000. The Board again finished the year out of debt."[47]

In sum, Tupper's plan to promote foreign missions was simple but effective. The circulation of the *Home and Foreign Journal* informed thousands of Baptists of the advances and needs of missionaries on the field. The continued calls for prayer reminded Baptists that their work was not their own, but rather a privileged participation in the global work of missions. His travel to churches to promote missions was physically taxing, but it enabled him to state the case for missions more personally. Along these lines, he wrote, "I try to make the missionaries feel that I am one of them. They certainly seem like my family—my family in the Lord. Their sorrows are my sorrows. Their joys are my joys."[48] Finally, his expectation that every Baptist should give to missions, even if only a penny, demonstrated a singular purpose of building obedience and generosity from the ground up.

---

46   Taylor, *Virginia Baptist Ministers*, 30.
47   James, "A Study of the Life," 129.
48   Taylor, *Virginia Baptist Ministers*, 31.

TUPPER'S ACCOMPLISHMENTS
ON THE FOREIGN MISSION BOARD

Tupper's tenure as corresponding secretary led to advances in missions in at least two areas: the opening of new mission work in Mexico, Brazil, and Japan; and increased visibility and participation of women in missions. Despite constant pleas for personnel and funds for the ongoing work in Africa, China, and Europe, the board determined to advance the gospel by opening three additional mission stations during Tupper's tenure, thus doubling its extension in the foreign mission field. The work in Mexico came about in 1880 with the appointment of John Westrup. Baptists already had a foothold in the territory as early as 1864, but support was lost from the American Baptist Home Missionary Society in 1873. Despite the assassination of Westrup the same year of his appointment, the work continued through his brother, Thomas. The death of a missionary, while solemnly observed, did not dampen the hopes of Baptists: "Our people have responded to the Mexican mission with a unanimity before unknown, and with the close relations soon to exist between the two countries, I [O. C. Pope] regard Mexico as a most promising field for work."[49] Tupper was instrumental in raising funds for the mission and securing land for what would become the Madero Institute of Saltillo, an orphanage and school for girls.

The work in Brazil was also a continuation of an earlier commitment that had yet to come to fruition. Thomas Jefferson Bowen was sent by the FMB in 1859, but the work ceased two years later due to his failing health, which necessitated a return to America. A Baptist church was later organized in 1871 by a group of "exiled" Southerners living in Sao Paulo. Strangely, it was said that Southerners were especially desired in Brazil, given their experience with slavery: "Here let it be said, that some missionary efforts in Brazil have failed because

---

49   SBCA, 1881, 39. William D. Powell was initially sent to investigate the death of John Westrup, but he became so moved by reading Westrup's account of his work there that he offered himself for appointment in Westrup's stead in 1881.

labor was done with the negro slaves of that country, unmindful of the delicate relation between master and slave. We are not slaveholders now; but we know about that relation, and Southern ministers, other things being equal, are the best missionaries that can be sent to Brazil."[50] William and Ann Bagby were appointed by the FMB to serve in 1881, which they continued to do for well over a half century. Tupper published letters and reports from the Bagbys illustrating the challenge and promise of missions in Brazil:

> So, steeped in atheistic materialism, and deified *humanism*, thousands go down to an eternal midnight. Thus, the man who comes to this land to preach the gospel, finds himself encountered not only by priestcraft and ritualism, but by skepticism, atheism, and rationalism, under innumerable forms. Yet, notwithstanding all these human creeds and human fictions, the people in many places are not only willing, but *anxious* to hear the gospel, and pay respectful and earnest attention to the missionaries. In some places, it is true, preachers have been *stoned*, but the better class frown down these things, and give full liberty to proclaim the gospel.[51]

The anticipated entrance into Japan as a mission field began prior to Tupper's administration, but a series of unexpected events prohibited Southern Baptist missionaries from reaching their destination. In 1859, John and Sarah Rohrer were appointed to the work, but their ship was lost at sea. Two other missionaries, Mr. and Mrs. J. L. Johnson, were scheduled to travel on the same ship, but they missed their journey due to illness.[52]

Southern Baptists approved of mission work in Japan in 1888, due in part to the continued pleas from Matthew T. Yates, a missionary

---

50   "Our Missionaries to Brazil," in Tupper, *A Decade*, 161.
51   "Brother Bagby on Brazil and Its People," in Tupper, *A Decade*, 207.
52   Leon McBeth, *The Baptist Heritage: Four Centuries of Baptist Witness* (Nashville: Broadman, 1987), 422.

in China. As with the previous expansions, the needs for ongoing mission work could have easily taken precedence over new work. In 1888, the situation in Africa was depicted as having languished "until we scarcely have left to us 'a local habitation and a name,'" while in China, "the necessity for enlargement is still more urgent and alarming."[53] And yet, apparently without hesitation, the convention added Japan as another field of service: "The Committee especially commend to the Convention the establishment of a mission in the long-neglected but progressive empire of Japan. . . . To carry out the views of the Board the least amount that can be asked for is $100,000 as against the $86,000 contributed the past years. We should not rest satisfied with even double that amount."[54] The husband-and-wife team of John and Drucilla McCullum along with John and Sophia Brunson were appointed in 1889.

The doubling of foreign mission fields during Tupper's administration was not the result of his initiative, coming as it did on the heels of previous efforts. However, the leadership required to manage existing fields of service while adding new opportunities for missions certainly required a corresponding secretary of unusual talent. Tupper's extraordinary efforts in this regard did not go unnoticed: "We have—the writer of this paragraph will say in the absence of the Secretary, and will print before he can see it— one of the most accomplished, untiring, wise and self-sacrificing Secretaries with whom a Board was ever blessed. The Board are unanimous in feeling that he has done and is doing his work grandly, although he has on his shoulders burdens under which two such men might well falter."[55]

The advancement of missions during Tupper's tenure was driven significantly by the progressive acceptance of single women on the mission field, the rise of women's missionary societies, and the formation of the WMU. As noted earlier, Tupper's mother played

---

53   SBCA, 1888, 21.
54   SBCA, 1888, 22.
55   "Pray for the Secretary and the Board," *FMJ* 17, no. 12 (July 1886): 1.

a key role in shaping his love for the church and providing wise counsel. Upon becoming corresponding secretary, he encouraged women to increase their involvement in mission work, believing they were competent for the task. He was also aware that foreign missions essentially required women to do more than accompany their husbands to the mission field as they would have unique opportunities to share the gospel. Women were particularly needed as missionaries in China:

> Men have no access to the families of China, to convey to them the gospel of Christ. As in all countries, the children are under the influence of the mother. The women unreached, Paganism is necessarily perpetuated by the maternal instruction of the children; and the women can only be reached by women. This woman's work is imperative, not only to elevate their degraded sex, and by that elevation to give new tone to the moral character of society; but as the rational means, under God, of undermining the fabric of heathen superstition and blasphemy. The conversion of one woman in China is worth, in its influence, as much as that of two men.[56]

In light of such possibilities, Tupper queried, "And why may not woman's missionary societies spring up all over our land, fired with the desire to give the gospel to the women of heathen lands? Let these societies be formed; and let them band together for the simple and grand purpose of sending the ennobling and saving gospel to women."[57] Tupper's views were not just maternally motivated or practically stated, but theologically informed as well: "Daughters of Zion, mothers in Israel, if you have love for the Saviour of your race, who has honored your sex above all humanity, in becoming the son of a woman, now is the time to show that love by making

---

56 "Necessity of Women's Work," in Tupper, *Foreign Missions*, 152.
57 "Necessity of Women's Work," in Tupper, *Foreign Missions*, 152.

your free-will offerings to him, which, though less costly, may be
no less acceptable than that which won for Mary the imperishable
phrase: 'She hath done what she could.'"[58]

The advance of foreign missions was especially helped by the
appointments of Edmonia Moon and her sister, Charlotte Diggs
"Lottie" Moon, as missionaries to China in 1872 and 1873, respectively. Edmonia first contacted Tupper to inquire whether single
women could be appointed as missionaries. Tupper personally
visited Edmonia to become better apprised of her plans, and he
then solicited financial assistance on her behalf through Mary Jeter,
wife of Jeremiah B. Jeter and organizer of a women's missionary
society in Richmond. Edmonia's pastor, J. C. Long, wrote, "When
we heard that she proposed to go as a missionary to China, we
were not surprised. We knew that she had been thinking of and
pitying the Chinese, and that her heart burned to teach them the
way of life. It was not like her to be appalled by the difficulties in the
way."[59] She was joined by her sister Lottie the year following, and
the two immediately made a positive impression on Baptist men
and women alike: "Miss Lottie enters on her new life with firm and
sober delight. The two sisters are of one purpose and one heart, and
if God grants them health and strength, we may reasonably expect
them to make a deep impression on the hearts of these heathen
women. I do trust the sisterhood will prayerfully, conscientiously
and constantly take a lively interest in their missions."[60]

Edmonia's missionary career was cut short in 1876 due to
health reasons, with Lottie accompanying her on the return trip
to America. Lottie returned to Tengchow on December 24, 1877,
where she became the most visible of all female Southern Baptist
missionaries. Moon was a gifted linguist whose intention to become
a schoolteacher was set aside after she responded to a missionary
sermon, telling her pastor that she had long known that God wanted

---

58   "Necessity of Women's Work," in Tupper, *Foreign Missions*, 152.
59   "Edmonia Harris Moon—Conversion and Missionary Spirit," in Tupper, *Foreign
     Missions*, 217.
60   SBCA, 1874, 34.

her in China. Lottie's dedication to serving the Lord in a strange land was demonstrated by her willingness to adopt Chinese customs and by her refusal to accept well-deserved furloughs until her post could be filled in her absence. Regarding the latter, Tupper was in the unfortunate position of having to remind Lottie to do what she needed but did not prefer:

> The main thing on my mind is to ask you, my Sister, when are you coming home? You know that I have warned you, most respectfully, more than once, against staying too long at your post. It is quite refreshing to see one so brave, so heroic—if I do not offend by the word—but I cannot forget Miss Whilden, who prompted by the same motive that prompts you, did stay too long and has not recovered in six years. And yet, how I wish that some of your spirit could be infused into others, who seem to be fretting away life by petty cares, which wear down health and spirit, and are the sure precursors of "breaking down" and coming home too soon. I commend the middle course, in the way of wisdom—bravery, self-denial, and yet care of life and health.[61]

Tupper's concern for Lottie's refusal to take a furlough had lasting ramifications. In 1887 Moon wrote to a group of Baptist women in Virginia, suggesting a week of prayer followed by a mission offering during the Christmas season: "Is not the festive season, when families and friends exchange gifts in memory of The Gift laid on the altar of the world for the redemption of the human race, the most appropriate time to consecrate a portion from abounding riches and scant poverty to send forth the good tidings of great joy into all the earth?"[62] Lottie's suggestion was heartily embraced by

---

61   H. A. Tupper, Letter to Lottie Moon, July 12, 1890.
62   Catherine B. Allen, *The New Lottie Moon Story* (Nashville: Broadman, 1980), 170. Cited in McBeth, *Baptist Heritage*, 418.

the newly formed WMU (1888). Tupper also proposed a special offering to fund a missionary who could replace Lottie for one year. His discussions with Annie Armstrong, corresponding secretary of the WMU, led to her recommendation that the Christmas offering be named in Lottie Moon's honor.[63] The influence of women was most strongly felt at home. A spate of women's missionary societies had sprung up prior to Tupper's administration, including the Women's Union Missionary Society in New York (1861), the Baltimore Auxiliary of the Women's Missionary Society (1870), and the Woman's Mission to Woman (1871), also organized in Baltimore. The appointment of Edmonia Moon essentially led to the formation of the Richmond Woman's Missionary Society (1874), whereas support for Lottie Moon arose among ladies in Georgia, including Cartersville (where Lottie had been teaching) and Washington (where Tupper had served as pastor).

Such efforts were welcome but scattered. Tupper's interest in connecting various female mission societies with the larger purposes of the Foreign Mission Board resulted in his proposing central committees in each state. The societies would thus benefit through better organization, enabling them to communicate ideas and needs with one another and to the convention more efficiently. At the 1876 meeting of the Southern Baptist Convention, Tupper's views on promoting women in missions became policy for the board: "Pious women are fitted in a peculiar sense to be evangelists and the educators of the household. The policy of the Board will be to multiply this class of laborers at our various missionary stations."[64]

Such change had not come easily for all Southern Baptists: "We have been slow to learn. Offering the gospel almost exclusively to *adults*, we were for a long time blind to the interests of *children*. Awake to the necessity for a large number of laborers in

63   Jesse Fletcher, *The Southern Baptist Convention: A Sesquicentennial History* (Nashville: Broadman & Holman, 1994), 96.
64   SBCA, 1876, 16.

heathen lands, and for the collection of funds for their support; we were similarly blind to the fitness and efficiency of Christian women for these noble undertakings."[65] Indeed, a significant obstacle to female participation in the convention meetings occurred in 1885, when the terminology for membership was changed from "delegates" to "brethren."[66] Though not allowing women to attend as delegates was consistent in principle with Southern Baptist practice at the time, the intentional change in language may have been the final indicator that women would have to organize apart from the convention in order to continue their missionary momentum.

Women's work on behalf of missions became self-sustaining through the formation of the WMU in 1888. The WMU's roots went back two decades prior, when Ann Graves of Baltimore arranged for a meeting of women at her home during the annual meeting of the Southern Baptist Convention. She read letters aloud from her son, Roswell, who described his efforts in sharing the gospel among the Chinese at the Canton mission. In subsequent years the women continued to meet during, but outside of, the convention to foster support for missions. Tupper's idea of a central committee in each state contributed to the formation of the WMU when, in 1887, Annie Armstrong called for delegates from each state committee to attend the 1888 annual meeting. The ladies in attendance voted to organize under the auspices of an auxiliary, thus preserving the right to determine their own direction while at the same time declining to compete with the established Home and Foreign Mission Boards. Tupper celebrated this work, noting in his 1888 report, "From all indications our Christian women were never more enlisted, heart and hand, in giving the Gospel to the perishing. . . . There are *almost as many women as men in the foreign missions of the world.*"[67]

---

65   SBCA, 1877, 27–28.
66   SBCA, 1885, 30.
67   SBCA, 1888, xiv–xv.

TUPPER'S CHALLENGES ON THE
FOREIGN MISSION BOARD

To be sure, there were ongoing and unique challenges faced by Southern Baptists during Tupper's tenure. The various mission stations required entirely different sets of needs according to their context such that success and distress were ongoing realities for the board and its missionaries. A comparison between the Italian mission and the central African mission during the midpoint of Tupper's tenure illustrates the polarity well. Under the leadership of G. B. Taylor, superintendent of Italian missions, the work was described as moving steadily forward, with "solid foundations having been laid and evangelical principles in reception of members, and in the discipline of the churches becoming more firmly settled and more clearly understood."[68] A chapel costing nearly $30,000 was completed and occupied by 1878. In terms of setbacks, the Italian mission was affected by the death of Taylor's wife in 1884, described as "a distressing calamity viewed from the human side, to the mission and to the cause of Christ in Italy."[69]

By contrast, the central African mission's situation was particularly distressful, as noted in the 1885 report: "There are but few results that promise permanence. Indeed, there is little that is permanent in Central Africa, except its mountains and forests, its rivers and deserts. Again and again our missions have been broken up by raids from hostile tribes, property destroyed or left to natural rapid decay, and so-called cities, with 50,000 or 100,000 inhabitants, swept from their homes leaving their sites degenerated into jungles."[70] The report closed with a particularly revealing comment summarizing the perspective of the nineteenth-century Baptist worldview: "Still nothing but Christianity can raise this barbarism into civilization, and therefore our Lord has commanded us to carry His gospel into the darkest and

---

68   SBCA, 1885, 48.
69   SBCA, 1885, 48.
70   SBCA, 1885, 48.

most unpromising regions of earth. The brightest hopes for Africa seem now based upon European and American colonization."[71]

In addition to addressing the ongoing needs of the mission field, Tupper was responsible for recruiting missionaries who would support or succeed their fellow workers, or perhaps engage in new fields of service. This process proved to be a delicate balance between the willingness of workers to participate and the willingness of churches to provide financial support. Tupper worked both ends of the system, encouraging young people to become missionaries and challenging churches to increase their giving. However, the disparity was such that it was hard to recruit new missionaries when those on the field still lacked full financial support: "A serious question embarrasses the Board. By the report from our missionaries, it is seen how inadequate are the means in men and places of worship for the work pressing upon missions. Should the Board affirm that it has scarcely a mission half equipped for its necessary work, the affirmation would be within bounds of sober variety."[72]

Navigating support for existing mission work, recruiting new missionaries, and financing missionary endeavors were not the only problems Tupper faced during his years as corresponding secretary. As an employee of the FMB, coming under the auspices of the SBC, Tupper was responsible for ensuring that missionaries appointed to the field were in agreement with Southern Baptist principles. There were no problems in this regard with the vast majority of appointments during his tenure; however, such problems, when they did occur, were of a higher profile coming as they did when a person's name was already made public. Baptists united around the appointment of missionaries, but the recension of an appointment or the removal of a missionary threatened to divide them.

In 1881, John Stout and T. P. Bell were appointed as missionaries to China. Tupper had great respect for the men as both were leaving their pastorates for the mission field and both were

---

71   SBCA, 1885, 48.
72   SBCA, 1888, xlvi.

educated, having graduated from The Southern Baptist Theological Seminary. He was not alone in rejoicing over their future work, as "their praise [was] in all the churches."[73] Stout and Bell addressed the 1881 convention, "making fine impressions."[74] James Boyce, however, had a different impression of the men due to their relationship, as students, to Crawford Toy, a professor at Southern Seminary who had resigned two years prior because his view of biblical inspiration "was at variance with those held generally held by the denomination."[75] When he was hired to teach Old Testament interpretation and Oriental languages in 1869, he professed to be in full agreement with the seminary's Abstract of Principles, even delivering an inaugural address in which he claimed the Bible was absolutely and infallibly true. However, his growing interest in German philosophical theology led him to differentiate between the truth of spiritual matters and the fallibility of historical assertions. In the classroom, students became acquainted with his preference of Darwinian evolution over the creation account in Genesis, his rejection of Mosaic authorship of the Pentateuch in favor of the documentary hypothesis, and his reinterpretation of messianic predictions from a more rationalistic perspective.

Boyce wrote to Tupper expressing his concern over Stout's and Bell's appointments. To his dismay, Boyce was informed that the board had not questioned the men about their views of inspiration. Evidently, their reputations as pious young men, their willingness to serve, and the great need for support on the field led Tupper and the board to assume their compatibility. When Boyce pressed the matter, Tupper requested that Stout express his views on inspiration in writing. In his response, Stout admitted to being sympathetic with Toy's views, conceded that there were errors in the Bible, and stated that he would teach accordingly if allowed to serve on the mission field. His response forced the board's hand:

---

73 SBCA, 1881, 54.
74 SBCA, 1881, 157.
75 J. B. Jeter, "The Southern Baptist Convention," *Religious Herald*, May 22, 1879, 2. Cited in Nettles, *James Petigru Boyce*, 349.

> Whereas Rev. John Stout has candidly and courteously presented to the Board of Foreign Missions his views on Inspiration, and whereas his views do not seem to the Board to be in accord with the views commonly held by the constituency of the Southern Baptist Convention. . . . Resolved, That, while the Board distinctly and emphatically disclaim the least right over the conscience or Christian liberty of any man, they have not the right to consent to any missionary teaching or printing anything regarded by them as contrary to the commonly received doctrinal views of the constituency of the Southern Baptist Convention.[76]

Bell sided with Stout, and in the month following their celebrated appearance at the convention, the board deemed it necessary to rescind the appointments. Tupper remained in a difficult position, as Lottie Moon threatened to resign over the decision. According to Thomas Nettles, "Men were needed and these two men had great promise. Tupper had to use all his skills as a diplomat and administrator to assuage the feelings of his star missionary, even assuring her of his personal affection for Toy."[77] Stout and Bell never went to China as missionaries, but they remained, according to the board, "beloved and honored for their piety, zeal and ability, [and they] are esteemed among the most earnest and efficient friends of our missionary enterprise."[78]

The dilemma with Stout and Bell was complicated by the fact that the board had not previously stipulated a particular view of inspiration as a requirement or disqualifier for missionary appointments. Yet Tupper and the board understood that their missionaries belonged to the convention, which belonged to the churches, which ultimately belonged to Christ. Thus, the incompatibility of their views overrode any concern over the previous policy.

---

76   FMBM, June 17, 1881.
77   Nettles, *James Petigru Boyce*, 381. For a summary of Tupper's views on inspiration, see James, "A Study of the Life," 99–102.
78   SBCA, 1882, 53.

Another high-profile incident occurred with the removal of
Tarleton Perry ("T. P.") Crawford from the mission field over the
question of whether convention boards should support missionaries.
Crawford and his wife, Martha, had long been associated with the
FMB upon their appointment as missionaries to China in 1851. He
began the "Gospel Mission Movement," a title which overtly suggested
that the FMB, and other such organizations, were not based on New
Testament principles.[79] The ecclesiological underpinnings of the
Gospel Mission Movement were similar to those of Landmarkism,
which promoted the idea of the local church as the only authorized
body to send and support missionaries. J. R. Graves, one of the main
proponents of Landmarkism, had publicly challenged the biblical
foundations of the FMB in 1859, but he was unsuccessful.

Crawford was particularly concerned that missionary funds
should not be used to support native preachers. In his 1875 report
to the board, Crawford stated, "We have never paid native preachers
with mission funds. We believe the system will retard the growth of
vital Christianity in China and all other heathen lands. We desire to
see the church grow from the healthy root of faith in Christ and love
for His cause."[80] Crawford believed that funding from an outside
source (i.e., the FMB) incentivized native preachers to accept and
promote the gospel for financial gain. He championed the idea of
self-supporting churches not only as biblical but also as a deterrent,
thus excluding insincere workers and preserving the integrity of the
mission. Crawford wrote to Tupper, advocating that this position
become the norm not only in China but in all mission fields:

> We wish the denomination to thoroughly abandon the
> idea of working through mission money in the hands of
> native Christians in all their foreign fields. . . . We wish
> the denomination to feel that the work can only be done

79   James notes that Crawford attributed the title to Tupper himself, who referred to it
     as such in his final report at the 1893 Southern Baptist Convention. See James, "A
     Study in the Life," 194.
80   SBCA, 1875, 60.

by the chosen ones going forth from her own warm bosom, imbued with her spirit, under the power of her convictions, permeated with her doctrines and inspired by her aims; that through these alone can she erect her moral power, bring the heathen to her standard, and accomplish her mission in the world.[81]

Crawford's position did not reflect that of the majority of missionaries who were employed by the board, but he doubled down on his strategy after receiving a copy of Chaplin H. Carpenter's *Self-Support, Illustrated in the History of the Bassein Karen Mission from 1840–1880.*[82] Robert Alton James notes that the board mailed copies of the book to its missionaries but did not intend it as an endorsement of future policy.[83] Crawford was therefore misguided into thinking that his arguments had taken root, and thus he reengaged the discussion. He met with the board on October 12, 1885, in which he presented the case for self-support becoming the policy of the board. The board concluded that self-support was ideal but not practical; therefore, it would be encouraged but not mandated.[84] Crawford resumed his work in China, alternately conflicting with the board and reporting on the positive work of the mission.

The break between Crawford and the board came in 1892, when copies of his book *Churches to the Front!* arrived in the United States. In it, Crawford remonstrated the convention and board, referring to their work as unscriptural, underperforming, and outdated:

The general impression that Churches, as such, are incapable of conducting missions . . . casts reproach not only upon them but also upon Christ and the Apostles,

---

81   T. P. Crawford, Tengchow, China, to H. A. Tupper, Richmond, December 21, 1877. Cited in James, "A Study of the Life," 199.
82   C. H. Carpenter, *Self-Support, Illustrated in the History of the Bassein Karen Mission from 1840 to 1880* (Boston: Rand, Avery, 1883).
83   James, "A Study of the Life," 200–201.
84   See FMBM, November 6, 1885.

their original founders. The truth of the matter is this: the work of foreign missions, when freed from the care of "subsidy money," its accompanying host of "native employees," "schools" and other "worrying adjuncts" and confined to Gospel or spiritual things as it should be, is comparatively simple. But, like the work of home pastors, it is of such a nature that it cannot be clearly understood or intelligently superintended by any outside party whatever. Yet, painful to say, these erroneous conceptions gave origin to our two great Conventions. Their very existence and course of action throw discredit upon the Churches by taking the work out of their hands and by claiming superior managing ability for the Boards of their appointment. However, the unwritten history of their operations fails to sustain the claim, or to free them from the charge of serious blunders in the selection of men, the adoption of measures and the expenditures of funds. Not only so, our foreign missions, relative to the growth of the denomination, are weaker to-day than they were thirty years ago. These results—without any reflections upon individual men—show clearly that the system is not adapted to our people. Whatever may be said of the past, it is now wholly out of correspondence with its environments.[85]

Despite his attempt to separate concerns about the board from people on the board, the people on the board severed their ties with Crawford, informing the delegates at the 1892 convention that "Dr. T. P. Crawford's name, also, will no longer appear on our list of missionaries."[86] Interestingly, the same report stated that "Miss Lottie Moon, who has endured the heat and toil of many continuous years in her field, has yielded at last to the invitations of the Board,

---

85   Tarelton Perry Crawford, *Churches to the Front!* (n.p., 1892), 8–9.
86   SBCA, 1892, xxxvii.

and is taking needed rest in this country."[87] The Gospel Missions Movement, known by this time as "Crawfordism" by its detractors, was all but forgotten by the end of the century, whereas the work of Lottie Moon is still remembered annually with love offerings taken up in her name.

TUPPER'S LEGACY FOR TODAY

Tupper retired from the board on June 30, 1893, but lived on until March 27, 1902. During this time, he was elected as a trustee of a women's college and became Bible chair at Richmond College. He also devoted about eight to ten hours a day studying modern languages and preparing a Hebrew primer, with the prime object being "a more perfect knowledge of the Scriptures."[88] The board accepted his retirement, referring to him as "an officer courteous in bearing, wise in counsel, diligent and self-sacrificing in effort and from whom we part with sincere regret."[89] A summation of his work appeared in *Southern Baptist Foreign Missions* with the following commendation:

Between these dates—February 20, 1872 and June 30, 1893—the voluminous records of the Board and of the Southern Baptist Convention contained on almost every page some proofs of the zealous, assiduous, faithful, incessant labors of this very modest, quiet, Christian gentleman. In every state of our vast domain and in every continent of the globe, his autograph letters have carried wise advice couched in terms of kind sentiment and courtly politeness, while his unwritten record stamped upon the minds and hearts of members of the Board and missionaries under our appointment is beyond the

---

87   SBCA, 1892, xxxvii.
88   Taylor, *Virginia Baptist Ministers*, 35–36.
89   FMBM, May 23, 1893.

power of human language to represent. Eternity alone will suffice to estimate the power of his faith, his calmness, his prudence, his consecration.[90]

Without waiting for eternity to appreciate fully Tupper's impact on foreign missions during this period, we can now appropriate some lessons from his life and tenure. First, Tupper had been preparing for the role of corresponding secretary long before he anticipated it as a career move. His father had trained him to have an eye for detail, particularly in business, which became an invaluable asset as he raised and accounted for mission dollars. Second, Tupper's love for the church was instilled at a young age, specifically by his mother, whose influence also led him to value the work of women on the mission field. Without sidestepping scriptural admonitions regarding complementarian roles of men and women, Tupper found ways to incorporate both on the mission field. Third, Tupper operated with the understanding that the work of the Spirit in missions did not negate the responsibility of believers to recruit, send, and solicit support for missionaries. Tupper called churches to prayer, not as a matter of rote, but in light of the difficult tasks missionaries faced on the field. He likewise raised money and gave generously to this end. Finally, Tupper advanced the cause of missions without sacrificing the core of Southern Baptist doctrines. He deemed that rescinding appointments or removing missionaries was necessary because cooperative efforts require shared convictions. Tupper's legacy thus challenges us to be thankful to God for preparing us to serve even prior to our awareness of what such service will look like, to be mindful of how the whole body of Christ is gifted to serve in a variety of ways, to be intentional about combining God's sovereignty with human responsibility, and to be careful to guard that which has been entrusted to us in order that we too will be found faithful.

---

90   T. B. Ray, *Southern Baptist Foreign Missions* (Nashville: Sunday School Board, Southern Baptist Convention, 1910), 40–41.

THE R. J. WILLINGHAM ERA, 1893–1914

Mike Morris

ROBERT JOSIAH WILLINGHAM moved from the pastorate of First Baptist Church in Memphis, Tennessee, to the position of corresponding secretary of the FMB in August of 1893. In that year, FMB missionaries served in two general areas designated as "papal fields" (Italy, Mexico, Brazil) and "pagan fields" (Japan, China, Africa).[1] Because China, by far, contained the most FMB missionaries in 1893 (thirty-eight in

---

1 SBCA, 1894, 38–39.

August), and because Lottie Moon was there, Southern Baptists had directed much attention toward China.[2]

Despite crippling debt, Willingham saw the number of FMB missionaries increase from ninety-four to three hundred during his twenty-one years in office.[3] China continued to receive great emphasis during his tenure. The annual FMB report on May 13, 1914, listed 155 FMB missionaries in China (more than half the total number of missionaries).[4] The FMB began work in Argentina in 1903 and Uruguay in 1911.

After Willingham's death, other overseas categories showing increases during his twenty-one-year tenure were listed in a 1915 report to the convention: "native helpers" increased from eighty-six to 635; churches increased from seventy-five to 380; members increased from 2,923 to 30,000; baptisms increased from 383 to 5,252; and schools increased from sixteen to 339.[5] William Estep says, "Perhaps Willingham was at his best preaching on missions before a large audience."[6] Although Willingham had no overseas missionary experience, he used his preaching gift to motivate hearers to make greater efforts to support missionaries.

Willingham's enthusiasm for missions spread to his family. His son Calder was appointed by the FMB in 1902 to serve in Japan. Calder and his wife resigned in 1907 on account of her poor health. She died in 1910, but he remarried and returned to Japan in 1911.[7]

---

2   "Our Missionaries," *FMJ* 25, no. 1 (August 1893): i.
3   "The number of missionaries in the foreign fields was 94 when he became Secretary. Now there are 300 missionaries." William H. Smith, "The Passing of Dr. Willingham," *FMJ* 65, no. 6 (January 1915): 199. The number of missionaries changed during the interim period between Tupper and Willingham. The annual report of the FMB in 1915 said that there were ninety-two missionaries in May of 1893. FMBM, May 12, 1915. The *FMJ* in August of 1893 mentioned ninety-eight missionaries in "Compendium of Facts," *FMJ* 25, no. 1 (August 1893): 1.
4   FMBM, May 13, 1914.
5   SBCA, 1915, 124.
6   William R. Estep, *Whole Gospel Whole World: The Foreign Mission Board of the Southern Baptist Convention, 1845–1995* (Nashville: Broadman & Holman, 1994), 181.
7   FMBM, May 3, 1902; July 31, 1907; May 11, 1910; August 15, 1911.

Because of Willingham's bad health during the final year of his life, the FMB in March of 1914 changed his title from corresponding secretary to general secretary. In his new position, he would have "consultative and advisory relations with other secretaries and with all the departments of work, but shall not be held responsible for any of them."[8] At the same meeting, the FMB chose as home secretary J. F. Love, who became the leader of the FMB after Willingham's death. Willingham's daughter, Elizabeth, said that he was very happy "to know that Dr. Love had accepted the call to the Home Secretaryship. For many years he had known Dr. Love."[9]

METHODOLOGY CONTROVERSY

When FMB missionaries from America arrived in China, they needed to make an important decision about how to spend American money, which had immense buying power in China in that era.[10] Two options were possible. (1) Gradual self-support: After some Chinese nationals ("natives" in the parlance of that day) became Christians, the FMB missionaries could pay the Chinese nationals

---

8   FMBM, March 20, 1914.

9   Elizabeth Walton Willingham, *Life of Robert Josiah Willingham* (Nashville: Sunday School Board of the SBC, 1917), 266.

10 For instance, the FMB committee on China in 1907 recommended that "the Board grant the request of the members of the Laichow-fu station for an appropriation of $150.00 (gold) to be used in opening and maintaining a school for girls under the direction of Mrs. Lowe." FMBM, November 8, 1907. In 1911, the report of a special committee on a medical college in China was adopted, in which the FMB agreed "to contribute two thousand dollars ($2,000) gold, to be expended for the purchase of land, buildings and equipment to provide one member of the faculty and his residence and also agree to contribute for current expenses a sum not exceeding three hundred dollars ($300) gold, per annum." FMBM, February 9, 1911. Willingham's salary in 1893 was $2,500 per year. FMBM, July 23, 1893. In 1904, the salary of FMB missionaries was "$500 or $600 [per year] according to the countries in which they work." FMBM, March 15, 1904. In 1894, the FMB adopted the following policy: "Missionaries returning home on leave, as provided for in Section 6 and 7 shall be entitled to receive monthly, such sum as they may need for support and recuperation, provided sum shall not exceed $800 per annum for man and wife and the regular allowance for children, and $400 per annum for an unmarried missionary, and provided further that it shall not, without special action of the Board, be continued more than twelve months." FMBM, April 17, 1894.

to propagate the gospel and later try to gradually wean the Chinese nationals off the money coming from the missionaries, with the hope that the Chinese nationals would receive financial support from other Chinese people. (2) Immediate self-support: After some Chinese nationals became Christians, the FMB missionaries could encourage them to finance Chinese pastors and evangelists without using any money from the American missionaries.

The FMB missionaries in China disagreed about which option was best. The first option could seemingly produce results quickly. The second option often seemed slower, but the use of it led to better long-term results.[11] The IMB currently requires immediate self-support of nationals: "Dependency occurs when a local church requires resources from outside of its own members in order to carry out the core biblical functions of a church under normal conditions. Funding from foreign sources often comes from the best of motives and from generous hearts, but the unintended consequences can be harmful to church health and multiplication. Therefore, the IMB will not use funds to pay the salaries of pastors or to build church buildings, and we will not be conduits of funds from well-meaning churches and Christians in North America."[12]

---

11   Lottie Moon discussed the problems with the first church established in Tungchow, which was small after years of existence and whose pastor and assistants were paid with FMB money: "I regret to say that Woo shen sung's congregations are very small. . . . A 'self supporting church' sounds beautifully in Richmond, & reads prettily on paper, but to us who live in Tung Chow there is a spice of the ludicrous in the phrase when we see it applied to a church which receives from the Board its chapel, & its pastor's residence, & buildings for boys' school, & four hundred dollars for the support of a school, & a chapel in Chefoo, & salaries for three assistants (Messrs. Wang, Liang, & Sun, until recently paid assistants)—not to speak of the fact that a missionary & his family are also maintained in connection with that church. The church itself is pledged to pay $144.00 (greenbacks) a year: I do not know how many thousands the Board disburses annually for that church. A little modesty from a church which receives so much would be truly refreshing, especially when we remember that it commenced its independent existence a few years ago with the boast publicly uttered—'Now you will see what we Chinamen can do.' 'Now we have a church without foreigners'—and that last year it sent to the Board its defiant Declaration of Independence, asking 'What have you done for us in the past? What do you propose to do for us now?'" LML, March 24, 1876, no. 277.

12   *Foundations* (Richmond: IMB, 2018), 42.

The disagreement about whether to pay Chinese Christians to propagate the gospel was one of the factors that led to the Gospel Mission Movement, formed in 1892 and operative until 1910. This movement was controversial during this era when Willingham led the FMB. Regina Sullivan explained the seriousness of the situation among FMB missionaries in North China: "By the end of 1892, half of the missionaries at the North China station had resigned or been asked to do so. . . . A year later, as the controversy surrounding the newly named 'Gospel Mission' group reached its peak, Tupper's disappointment overcame him. At the SBC meeting in May 1893, he offered his resignation."[13]

Some of the Gospel Missioners eventually returned to the FMB, but in the meantime, the disagreement spread to America. Willingham's daughter said that "in certain sections of the country [America] many were found who sympathized with the Gospel Mission movement, and serious difficulties marred the co-operative fellowship which had formerly existed."[14] Willingham, according to his daughter, was "not in accord with the views of the 'Gospel Missioners.'"[15] As mentioned in the previous chapter, T. P. Crawford (1821–1902, leader of the Gospel Mission Movement) believed that FMB money should not be used to support national workers and that such a policy should be in place not only in China but also in every mission field. Crawford stressed the following tenets of his movement in 1902:

> The Gospel Mission Movement is sustained and propelled by the co-operation of three leading convictions which may be briefly expressed as follows: First—The gospel of

---

13 Regina Sullivan, *Lottie Moon: A Southern Baptist Missionary to China in History and Legend* (Baton Rouge, LA: Louisiana State University Press, 2011), 127–28.
14 Willingham, *Life of Robert Josiah Willingham*, 71.
15 She characterized the Gospel Missioners' belief in immediate, strict self-support as follows: "These men were opposed to the employment of natives as pastors, evangelists, or Bible women; also, to the appropriation of missionary money for native schools, as they believed that it was the missionary's duty merely to proclaim the gospel and through the native church to nurture the spiritual life of the convert." Willingham, *Life of Robert Josiah Willingham*, 71.

Christ as the power of God unto salvation, in every mission field unaccompanied by any kind of pecuniary inducement to the people; or in other words, through native self-support everywhere. Second—The churches of Christ should, as organized bodies, singly or in co-operating groups, do their own mission work without the intervention of any outside convention, association or Board. Third—Self-denying labours for Christ's sake, both by the churches at home and by the missionaries abroad.[16]

Before the Willingham era and despite hearing Crawford make his case for immediate and strict self-support, the FMB in 1885 advocated gradual self-support, the aforementioned philosophy that financial support received by nationals from foreign missionaries could be gradually reduced over time: "We clearly recognize Self-support as the consummation toward which all missionary operations shall tend."[17] Having served as interim corresponding secretary between Tupper and Willingham, H. H. Harris expressed the FMB's disagreement with (1) the Gospel Mission Movement's rejection of the "utility of a central board to select men," (2) its emphasis on preparing for the second coming rather than a slower approach of training converts and establishing churches, (3) its advocacy of complete freedom of missionary movement between cities or countries, (4) its criticism of other FMB missionaries, (5) its criticism of the use of mission money for schools, (6) its criticism of payment of FMB money to national workers, (7) its advocacy of the sacrifice of missionary lives when financial support fails, and (8) its strict requirement on all fields of identifying with the nationals (clothing, food, and houses).[18]

---

16   T. P. Crawford, *Evolution in My Mission Views or Growth of Gospel Mission Principles in My Own Mind*, ed. J. A. Scarboro (Fulton, KY: Scarboro, 1903), 24–25, quoted in Keith Eitel, *Paradigm Wars: The Southern Baptist Convention Faces the Third Millennium* (Oxford: Regnum, 2000), 46.

17   FMBM, November 6, 1885.

18   H. H. Harris, "Our Board and the 'Gospel Mission,'" *FMJ* 25, no. 2 (September 1893): 37–41.

After becoming editor of the *Foreign Mission Journal* in 1893, Willingham expressed agreement with Harris concerning the Gospel Mission Movement, and in 1909 (after almost sixteen years of service), Willingham expressed his continuing agreement with the principle of gradual self-support as opposed to immediate self-support.[19] Lottie Moon, however, supported Crawford's position on immediate self-support, although she did not agree with some of his other views.[20] By 1915, all FMB missionaries were required to sign a statement that they would encourage nationals to embrace self-support, but this statement did not specify whether the self-support would take effect immediately or gradually.[21]

Elizabeth Willingham also described the Gospel Missioners' belief that missionaries should "wear native dress, live in a native

---

19   "Dr. Harris' Article," *FMJ* 25, no. 3 (October 1893): 71; FMBM, August 6, 1909.

20   She said, "For our part of China, we see evil & only evil in the employment of paid native assistants." LML, July 10, 1886. Lottie had stated her same position ten years earlier: "I honestly believe, in common with other missionaries older & wiser than myself, that the curse of missions is foreign money. It corrupts the very foundation of all attempts to do good. . . . The policy of our mission has been to pay no one to preach the gospel. Every member of the church, male & female, is expected to preach as opportunity offers, whether in their home, visiting their neighbors, or journeying by the wayside. I think I may say truthfully that we have a live, working church. They preach because they love it, & esteem it an honor." LML, November 2, 1875, no. 61. She also expressed her loyalty to the Crawfords during an early year of her ministry in China: "If Mr. and Mrs. Crawford should decide it to be their duty to seek another field, the rest of our mission are a unit in the wish to be transferred with them, & this, not only from warm personal attachment to these dear friends with whom we have labored harmoniously & happily, but because we are unanimous in our views of mission policy." LML, March 24, 1876, no. 277. After the Crawfords left the FMB and moved away from Tungchow, however, Moon stayed in the FMB and in Tungchow.

21   The statement is recorded in the FMB minutes: "There are widely divergent views about how to cultivate self-support most rapidly. . . . Every missionary who has been sent out by our Board has been required to sign certain Articles of Agreement, one of which is as follows: 'Missionaries must encourage native Christians in self-support, as far as possible, especially in the education of their children, the payment of native teachers and preachers, the defraying of church expenses, and the aiding of poor saints. The self-support of native churches is an end which our missionaries should never lose sight of, and for the establishment of which they must constantly labor.'" FMBM, May 12, 1915.

house, and subsist on native food."[22] Dressing, living, and eating like nationals (without violating biblical standards) eventually became normal incarnational practices for missionaries, but those practices were considered strange at the time. Many missionaries did not understand particular aspects of biblical contextualization. Much earlier, Hudson Taylor had seen the need for incarnational clothing in China, and J. Herbert Kane said that Taylor's "decision to shave his head, grow a pigtail, and wear Chinese dress scandalized the foreign community."[23] Lottie Moon, who had a good working relationship with T. P. Crawford's wife, eventually wore Chinese clothes. In 1888, Moon asked for missionaries "ready to come down and live among the natives, to wear the Chinese dress and live in Chinese houses."[24]

Ethnocentrism, the belief that one's home culture is superior to all other cultures, was a problem for missionaries of this era. Western missionaries, intentionally or unintentionally, sometimes propagated both Western culture and the gospel. The nationals sometimes got the impression that becoming a Christian also meant adopting Western culture. Thus, an unnecessary barrier was placed between the nationals and Christ.

The debate concerning gradual versus immediate self-support raged among other evangelical missionaries during the same period. For example, John Nevius (1829–1893), a Presbyterian missionary in China, had seen the ill effects of foreign financial support of Chinese nationals. Nevius died at the beginning of the Willingham era, but his views were published, and they continued to influence missionaries after his death. In 1886, Nevius described the attitude of Chinese non-Christians when they saw that Chinese workers were receiving foreign funds when propagating the gospel: "The general opinion of the Chinaman as to the motive of one of his countrymen in propagating a foreign religion, is that

---

22   Willingham, *Life of Robert Josiah Willingham*, 71.
23   J. Herbert Kane, "The Legacy of J. Hudson Taylor," *International Bulletin of Missionary Research* 8, no. 2 (April 1984): 74.
24   LML, June 22, 1888, no. 435, published in *FMJ* 20, no. 3 (October 1888): 3.

it is a mercenary one."[25] The term "rice Christians" was used to describe nationals who pretended to be Christians so that they could receive material support from missionaries. The 1899 prefatory note to the third edition of John Nevius's book mentioned that from 1885 to 1899, "some Chinese missionaries have strongly argued against" his methods.[26] Thus, the debate about immediate self-support continued during the Willingham era.

Nevius pointed out the problems with the "Old System" of gradual self-support in contrast with the advantages of the "New System" of immediate self-support.[27] He noted the importance of precedents: "The Chinese are remarkable for their tendency to follow a fixed routine, and to be governed by precedents. If the first convert is soon employed, those who follow will expect to be also."[28] He stressed that new converts should stay in the situation in which they were called (1 Cor. 7:20, 24).[29] Nevius recommended itineration from a "fixed place of residence."[30] He began itinerating in the central part of Shantung Province around 1870, a few years before Lottie Moon arrived in China.[31] Nevius visited the area of Pingtu in 1870 and 1877, one of Moon's main areas of interest.[32]

Nevius traveled to Korea in 1890 and taught his methods to the early Protestant missionaries there for two weeks. His advice to the newly arrived missionaries to Korea was strictly followed. Important precedents were set, and a great period of Christian expansion eventually came to Korea as the young missionaries utilized the principle of immediate self-support from the inception of their

---

25   John L. Nevius, *The Planting and Development of Missionary Churches*, 4th ed. (Philadelphia: Presbyterian and Reformed, 1958), 17.

26   Nevius, *The Planting and Development of Missionary Churches*, 3.

27   Nevius, *The Planting and Development of Missionary Churches*, 7–29.

28   Nevius, *The Planting and Development of Missionary Churches*, 21.

29   Nevius, *The Planting and Development of Missionary Churches*, 19, 28.

30   Nevius, *The Planting and Development of Missionary Churches*, 78.

31   Nevius, *The Planting and Development of Missionary Churches*, 86.

32   Helen Nevius, *The Life of John Livingston Nevius* (New York: Fleming Revell, 1895), 285, 345.

work.[33] In China, however, the principle of gradual self-support was set early, and the principle of immediate self-support was difficult to implement after the precedent was set.

Lottie Moon had a good relationship with Nevius and his wife. Moon relayed some advice to Tupper sent by Nevius, and she recommended to Tupper that one of the articles written by Nevius be published in the *Foreign Mission Journal* of the FMB.[34] Moon and Nevius both served in Shantung Province, and Nevius had lived in Tungchow (1861–1863, 1869–1871), Moon's main city of residence after arriving in China in 1873.[35] On one occasion, she discussed a particular village with him when he passed through Tungchow (also spelled Tengchow).[36] Tungchow was also the Crawfords' main city of residence in China from 1863 to 1892.[37] In his dissertation about the Gospel Mission Movement, Adrian Lamkin says, "Crawford was influenced by two strong defenders of self-support, J. L. Nevius and C. H. Carpenter. . . . After 1863, he [Nevius] had almost daily contact with Crawford until he moved in 1871."[38]

---

33   Helen Nevius stated, "It was a marked event in my husband's life, which gave him great pleasure, both at the time and in the retrospect. Writing from Japan a few weeks later, he said: 'We had a delightful visit in Korea; and if the missionaries there were not benefited by our sojourn with them, it was not because they were not more than willing to profit by our suggestions and advice.'" Nevius, *The Life of John Livingston Nevius*, 447. Everett Hunt described the effect of the visit on the missionaries: "The two weeks of instruction Nevius gave the young Presbyterian missionaries in Korea in 1889 [sic] formed and focused their work. The Korea mission considered Nevius's suggestions so important that they adopted them as mission policy and gave all new missionaries a copy of his booklet, requiring them to pass an examination on it. . . . The greatest tribute to John L. Nevius is that the Nevius Plan is the most frequently cited factor in the outstanding growth of the Korean church." Everett Hunt, "The Legacy of John Livingston Nevius," *International Bulletin of Missionary Research* 15, no. 3 (July 1991): 123–24.

34   LML, December 24, 1877, no. 42; November 22, 1880, no. 5.

35   LML, March 24, 1876, no. 277. See also Nevius, *The Life of John Livingston Nevius*, 208, 247–48, 277, 291.

36   LML, October 3, 1887, no. 151, published in *FMJ* 19, no. 6 (January 1888): 2.

37   Mary Emily Wright, *The Missionary Work of the Southern Baptist Convention* (Philadelphia: American Baptist Publication Society, 1902), 115.

38   Adrian Lamkin, "The Gospel Mission Movement within the Southern Baptist Convention" (PhD diss., The Southern Baptist Seminary, 1980), 98.

The previous chapter explained that Crawford's *Churches to the Front!* caused a break between him and the FMB. James Spivey discusses B. H. Carroll's opposition to Crawford: "Carroll staunchly opposed Landmarkers like Crawford and Hayden because they threatened Baptist solidarity and the viability of organized missions."[39] In response to Spivey's comment about Carroll's opposition to Crawford and Hayden, Keith Eitel comments, "The latter was a Landmarker by choice; the former does not warrant the label in quite the same way."[40] Eitel continued, "It is safe to say that some of Crawford's ideas were compatible with Landmarkist ideology, but to conclude that he was an ardent advocate of the J. R. Graves type Landmarkism, goes beyond the evidence. Landmarkers, however, took advantage of the overlap with some of his ideas and used them for their own agendas."[41] Eitel also makes the point that "Crawford's primary publication evolved over nearly fifty years of his work in China."[42] Lamkin concludes that "when the Gospel Mission was begun in 1893, it was based on Crawford's experiences, and not upon Landmarkism."[43]

DOCTRINAL AND ECUMENICAL ISSUES

Doctrinal limits and ecumenism were other thorny issues affecting the FMB during this period. As yet, the Baptist Faith and Message did not exist. On May 13, 1914, in its annual report to the Southern Baptist Convention, the FMB position was clarified: "It is hardly necessary to say that the Foreign Mission Board will not enter upon any scheme, cooperative or otherwise, which in any way will compromise the principles of our denomination or will tend to impair denominational integrity."[44]

---

39   James Spivey, "Benajah Harvey Carroll," in *Theologians of the Baptist Tradition*, eds. Timothy George and David Dockery (Nashville: Broadman & Holman, 2001), 176.
40   Eitel, *Paradigm Wars*, 42.
41   Eitel, *Paradigm Wars*, 45.
42   Eitel, *Paradigm Wars*, 67.
43   Lamkin, "The Gospel Mission Movement within the Southern Baptist Convention," 209.
44   FMBM, May 13, 1914.

The FMB was willing to partner with Northern Baptists (American Baptist Missionary Union). In 1910, a union seminary was opened in Tokyo in cooperation with Northern Baptists. Due to the temporary absence of some faculty members, trustees of the seminary in 1913 arranged to have students "take certain studies under the teaching of the Presbyterian Seminary," and this action was temporarily allowed by the FMB, which stated that the studies were "along the line of undenominational and general subjects." The FMB emphasized, "We think it best that our brethren in Japan be assured that our Board is strongly of the opinion that no action should at any time be taken that would in any degree impair the fundamental fact that our seminary is and needs to remain strictly and clearly a Baptist institution pure and simple."[45] Because of the Northern Baptists' acceptance of alien immersion and cooperation with non-Baptist educational institutions, the Southern Baptists eventually withdrew from the Tokyo seminary in 1918.[46]

A union seminary had earlier been established in Shanghai, China, in 1906. Northern Baptists also partnered with Southern Baptists in that endeavor. The Northern Baptist report in 1907 noted that a Southern Baptist missionary served as president of the Shanghai institution and that students were involved in "prayer meetings or evangelistic services" on many evenings.[47]

Various doctrinal beliefs were challenged on the field. One missionary stated his reason for resigning: "If the Board requires me to believe that the Bible makes baptism a necessary prerequisite to taking the Lord's Supper, that I cannot believe."[48] Another missionary resigned because of his belief about the Sabbath.[49] Other

---

45 FMBM, July 26, 1913.

46 Eiko Kanamaru, "George Washington Bouldin and His Missionary Struggle with Southern Baptist Denominationalism in Japan: 1906–1933" (PhD diss., Baylor University, 1999), 151–56.

47 *Ninety-Third Annual Report of the American Baptist Missionary Union* (Boston: Louis Crosscup, 1907), 147–48.

48 FMBM, October 12, 1897.

49 FMBM, March 11, 1902.

doctrinal issues included "divine healing" and the "public speaking of women in mission work."[50]

RACISM, DISEASE, AND THE EFFECT ON AFRICA MISSIONS

The Willingham era at the FMB took place during the Jim Crow era in the South, where racial segregation was enforced. In 1892, the year before Willingham became corresponding secretary, Homer Plessy, a man of mixed race (one-eighth black), was arrested in New Orleans for refusing to leave a railway car designated for white passengers. In the infamous *Plessy v. Ferguson* ruling of 1896, the United States Supreme Court confirmed that the "separate but equal" policy was allowed for public facilities. Segregation thus became legally entrenched in the South. Some white members of SBC churches were arrogantly paternalistic; other Southern Baptists had a far worse attitude toward black people. Both groups adapted to the Southern culture in unbiblical ways.

During the Willingham era, the number of FMB missionaries in Africa did not change. In August of 1893, eleven FMB missionaries were listed for Africa in the *Foreign Mission Journal*, but five of them were in America "seeking restoration of health"; in 1914, eleven FMB missionaries were listed in the FMB annual report as being in Africa.[51] Racial attitudes, as well as disease, played a role in the low number of FMB missionaries in Africa. Disease adversely affected missionaries in many nations, but disease in Africa was particularly deadly to missionaries. In 1915, Scott Patterson, missionary to Nigeria, detailed the financial expenditures and cost in lives of FMB missionaries in Africa over decades:

> During these sixty-five years Southern Baptists, in obedience to Christ's command, have sent about sixty

---

50 FMBM, September 9, 1909.
51 "Compendium of Facts," *FMJ* 25, no. 1 (August 1893): 1; FMBM, May 13, 1914.

missionaries to the African field at a cost of about
$250,000.00. This includes traveling expenses, salaries
of missionaries, native workers, students, and boys'
support, and buildings and equipment. Of the sixty
missionaries some twenty-four have died on the field
or after leaving the field from the effects of the climate;
twenty-two have had to leave the field on account of ill
health due to the climate, and today we have about the
same number of missionaries on the field as in 1855.[52]

Some FMB board members favored the removal of all white missionaries from Africa. A degree of disagreement among board
members of the FMB concerning this possibility became evident
when a report by the Special Committee on Africa was debated
and tabled on May 2, 1898. The report suggested the substitution
of missionaries from a black Baptist group:

> After long and careful consideration, your Committee is
> persuaded that the work that is now being done in Africa is
> and has long been very costly in the lives of our missionar-
> ies; that it is non-progressive and unsatisfactory. This must
> necessarily be true as long as we have only two or three men
> on the field, each of whom on account of the climate, must
> return to this country every two or three years. To increase
> the number of white missionaries on the field is to open
> new graves where already many of our bravest men and
> women have fallen at the post of duty. . . . Your Committee
> therefore recommend: 1. That this Board express itself as
> willing to enter into such a plan of cooperation with the
> Board of Managers of the District Convention as shall
> have in view the ultimate transfer of our work in Africa to
> this body of colored Baptists. . . . 4. This Board reserves to

---

52   A. Scott Patterson, quoted in Samuel Pinnock, *The Romance of Missions in Nigeria*
(Richmond: FMB, 1917), 149.

itself the right to withdraw from this arrangement at the expiration of the three years, if they see clearly that the work in Africa is to suffer from the inability of our colored brethren to conduct such a work with judgment and vigor. In such an event, this Board is to retain full control of all its property on the field. If, on the other hand, they shall conduct the work wisely and well, this Board shall after the three years of cooperation withdraw from its field in Africa, thus turning over to the Board of Managers of the District Convention the Mission Stations and all property of this Board in Africa.[53]

The members of the special committee reflected the segregationist attitudes of their era.

The idea of removing white FMB missionaries from Africa had been evident at the beginning of Willingham's tenure; the 1893 committee report used offensive language, mentioning "the cultured Japanese and astute Chinaman" and "the most ignorant and barbarous African" in the same sentence.[54] At the end of Willingham's tenure, a report to the convention by the Home Mission Board's Department of Evangelism revealed a continuing problematic attitude in the SBC toward black people: "Social equality comes from the debasement of both races.... Except where all moral standards and ideals are obliterated, social equality in the South is impossible.... We are profoundly convinced from a providential standpoint—and

---

53   FMBM, May 2, 1898.
54   "The Committee on African Missions report: 1. That a letter from Brother T. A. Reid as to turning over our African Missions to our colored brethren opens up a question of much importance, but that the Committee is not prepared to make any recommendation in regard to it." FMBM, August 31, 1893. Earlier in the year, A. W. McGaha made the following statement to the convention: "The truth is, brethren, we are not spending men and means enough on pagan fields. These furnish the finest opportunity to show the world what the Gospel can do for fallen humanity—from the cultured Japanese and astute Chinaman to the most ignorant and barbarous African. We must send more laborers to these needy, and in some respects, promising fields. If we can't get enough suitable white men, who will dare say that suitable black men should not go to Africa?" McGaha, "Pagan Fields," SBCA, 1893, 25.

we believe in the hand of God working in all things—God let the Negroes come to this country to be Christianized that they might be the evangels of God to Africa."[55]

As a result of reported disease and such racially charged attitudes, not many candidates for FMB service were interested in serving in Africa. According to the FMB minutes of June 6, 1893, the Committee on New Missions and Missionaries reported that the "work in Africa seems greatly imperiled by the return of missionaries, actual and prospective, which seems to demand some vigorous action to secure missionaries to this field, there being very few who apply to go to the 'Dark Continent.'"[56]

Key figures in the SBC had some degree of positive concern for black people. Annie Armstrong, according to Bobbie Sorrill, "led in starting work with black women in Baltimore."[57] Armstrong helped black women in the National Baptist Convention organize for missions, and she spoke to the black women at their meetings in 1901 and 1905.[58] Armstrong showed some condescension when she wrote, "In a certain sense I agree with Brother Jasper that 'the world do move.'"[59]

During Willingham's 1907–1908 tour of FMB mission stations, he and his wife did not visit Africa.[60] Willingham's daughter, however, said that he "was always interested in the colored people" and that the black people "in Richmond recognized him as a warm friend."[61] She quoted the description of an incident involving Willingham in North Carolina when he witnessed to the black driver of his "hack."[62]

55   SBCA, 1914, 298.
56   FMBM, June 6, 1893.
57   Bobbie Sorrill, *Annie Armstrong: Dreamer in Action* (Nashville: Broadman, 1984), 122.
58   Sorrill, *Annie Armstrong*, 139, 181, 245.
59   Armstrong, letter to J. M. Frost, June 5, 1897, quoted in *Rescue the Perishing: Selected Correspondence of Annie Armstrong*, ed. Keith Harper (Macon, GA: Mercer University Press, 2004), 161.
60   Mrs. R. J. Willingham, "Visit to the Mission Fields," in Willingham, *Life of Robert Josiah Willingham*, 186.
61   Willingham, *Life of Robert Josiah Willingham*, 233.
62   Livingstone Johnston, quoted by Willingham, *Life of Robert Josiah Willingham*, 233–34.

Catherine Allen described Lottie Moon's attitude toward black people during Lottie's furlough of 1903–1904: "With her sister-in-law, she visited the Negro population around Crewe, providing food, clothing, teaching, and compassion.... Her racial views had escaped the thirty-year erosion which had occurred in the South between black and white. Her antebellum affection for blacks remained, with only a touch of condescension."[63] In a letter to Willingham, she gave evidence of that condescension, using the same phraseology as did Armstrong: "As our learned, colored brother, Jasper, remarked of the sun, so we may now say of Tengchow, 'It do move.'"[64]

LOTTIE MOON

In spite of her flaws, Charlotte Digges Moon (1840–1912) served with distinction in China during this period. Five months after her death, in its annual report to the convention, the FMB referred to her as "a queenly saint among missionaries" and described her work: "Her ministry in Shantung was principally to women and children, and the poor were her special charge. She devoted herself, her home, and nearly all of her salary to Christian social service. When overtaken by her last illness, she exclaimed: 'I have given all my money away and now I have nothing left.'"[65]

At the time when no male missionaries were in Pingtu, Catherine Allen described Moon as "unavoidably teaching men" and sending letters that "sought to shame American pastors for abdicating their duties to a woman."[66] Moon on one occasion was asked to read and explain the prodigal son passage to a mixed audience. She replied, "It is not the custom of the Ancient church that women preach to men."[67] In 1897, Moon said that two Presbyterian missionary men preached

---

63   Catherine Allen, *The New Lottie Moon Story*, 2nd ed. (Birmingham, AL: Woman's Missionary Union, [1980] 1997), 239.
64   LML, November 20, 1909, no. 113, published in *FMJ* 60, no. 8 (February 1910): 248.
65   FMBM, May 14, 1913.
66   Catherine Allen, "The Legacy of Lottie Moon," *International Bulletin of Missionary Research* 17 no. 4 (October 1993): 149.
67   LML, February 9, 1889, no. 124, published in *FMJ* 20, no. 10 (May 1889): 3.

for her at her church in Tungchow because no SBC men were available.[68] Later in 1897, a male FMB missionary regularly commuted there to function as the pastor.[69] She stated in her report to the 1897 SBC annual meeting that her work "includes men, women, schoolboys, girls and little children."[70] She avoided "preaching" in church worship services, but she was willing to talk to men in other formats.

Moon revealed the earlier work of Martha Crawford in Pingtu among men: "As I saw her last week instructing patiently for hours the men who eagerly gathered around her, my memory was haunted by the words of Scripture: 'That no man take thy crown.' It seemed to me that here was a woman doing the work of some young man among Southern Baptists in America who *ought* to be here. . . . Women are doing their own work and much of that which properly belongs to men."[71]

When the lone SBC male missionary serving in Shangtswang left for medical reasons, Moon, whose membership was at that church in 1888, said, "The direction of affairs falls to me. I shall be virtually the pastor."[72] She mentioned that in Säling she "taught women & girls in a small inner room, while the men & boys learned as best they could in the outer room which is used as a chapel";

---

68   LML, June 12, 1897, no. 184. She also mentioned that Presbyterians preached when
       T. P. Crawford was away from Tungchow. See LML, September 18, 1876, no. 251.
69   LML, October 2, 1897, no. 306.
70   SBCA, 1897, 58.
71   LML, May 25, 1888, no. 256, published in *FMJ* 20, no. 2 (September 1888): 2. Una
       Roberts Lawrence commented on the difference in views between Martha Craw-
       ford and Moon: "Mrs. Crawford had been in China so long that she had forgotten
       all the handicaps that interpretations of scripture had thrown around the oppor-
       tunities for women to teach the gospel, so she took the men in large classes. Miss
       Moon, true to the traditions of her Virginia upbringing, taught the women and
       girls only. . . . She had often had men to stand in her classes of women, but never
       before had she come face to face with the question of teaching a class of men.
       There was no man missionary nearer than Mr. Pruitt in Tengchow, and he could
       not come. . . . There was ample room for the men to sit back of her and with books
       in hand to study the scripture with the women who sat in front of her. She taught
       the women—if the men studied along with them, she was sure even Paul would
       not have objected!" Una Roberts Lawrence, *Lottie Moon* (Nashville: Sunday School
       Board of the SBC, 1927), 141–42.
72   LML, October 5, 1888, no. 49.

in the same letter, she said that the "movement in that region is growing, but a man is needed to push it."[73] Moon was willing to share the plan of salvation to a mixed audience.[74] In 1904, Moon said, "In general, I may say that I have never taught contrary to the usual views of Southern Baptists."[75] Allen said that Moon's struggles in Pingtu led her to write a letter in 1887 that led to the formation of the WMU in 1888 and the first Christmas offering.[76]

Moon was forced to evacuate her post during the Boxer Rebellion in 1900, and she did not think that she could return to Tungchow until after an extended period.[77] The missionaries' payments to national workers and the failure of the missionaries to adapt to the culture in biblically acceptable ways worsened the Boxer persecutions of missionaries and national Christians.[78] After spending almost a year in Japan, Moon returned to Tungchow in 1901. Before her 1903–1904 furlough, she needed to obtain American clothes because she had not had any for nine years.[79]

During her decades of service in China, Moon exhibited great endurance as she traveled to small communities away from her home city of Tungchow. At the annual meetings of the SBC, the number of villages and towns that she visited each year were often a

---

73 LML, January 8, 1889, no. 69.
74 LML, April 14, 1876, no. 120; September 6, 1898, no. 10. Catherine Allen mentioned the 1876 event in her biography. Allen, *The New Lottie Moon Story*, 108–9.
75 LML, November 14, 1904, no. 307.
76 Allen, "The Legacy of Lottie Moon," 150.
77 LML, July 17, 1900, no. 9.
78 Diana Preston described the situation: "Christian missionaries—fresh-faced and idealistic men and women from the American Midwest, bearded priests from Germany and France—came in search of souls. Often ignorant, dismissive, or contemptuous of the native culture, they and their aggressive proselytizing threatened the very fabric of Chinese family and village life. The Boxers despised their Chinese converts as traitors, 'rice Christians' who had sold themselves for a square meal. The Boxers' simmering resentment erupted across the northern provinces of Shantung, Shansi, and Chihli in the summer of 1900. Chanting mobs surrounded the mission stations and dragged out their terrorized occupants. Some they killed on the spot; others they took to Boxer temples to be slowly tortured to death. Tens of thousands of Chinese converts, Protestant and Catholic, were murdered." Diana Preston, *The Boxer Rebellion* (New York: Berkley, 2000), x.
79 Allen, *The New Lottie Moon Story*, 230.

part of China reports: 330 in 1881, 227 in 1883, 100 in 1884, 140 in 1895, 160 in 1896, 62 in 1897, 84 in 1898, 111 in 1899, 96 in 1900, 21 in 1902, and 22 in 1911.[80] Her work with schools in Tungchow also took much of her time, especially in her later years. Willingham recommended Lottie Moon as a speaker when she was in America. Concerning an upcoming conference, he wrote letters to two different women (Blount and Bernard) on May 15, 1903, describing Moon as "an earnest, excellent woman" (to Blount) and as "the best missionary whom you could secure for the work of which you speak in Asheville" (to Bernard).[81] While on furlough in America in 1903, she would speak only to women's groups.[82]

Some biographical accounts bear witness to Moon's declining mental state before her death in 1912. Una Roberts Lawrence described Moon as having "heaviness of heart," "depression," and "an uncontrollable sadness that swept all her bright spirit into a hopeless melancholia."[83] Catherine Allen said that Moon "dozed listlessly by day, tore her hair by night, and never ate"; she also mentioned Moon's "distress and terror" and "melancholia."[84] Regina Sullivan referenced Moon's "dementia," "paranoia," and "violent seizures."[85]

Before Willingham learned of her death, he expressed concern about her mental state in various letters in January of 1913. He said he had received a letter stating that she sometimes "gets violent, wishing to take her own life."[86] In a letter to Joshua Levering, a cousin of Annie Armstrong, Willingham explained, "Dr. Moon, a

---

80   SBCA, 1881, 1883, 1884, 1895, 1896, 1897, 1898, 1899, 1900, 1902, 1911.
81   Willingham to Blount, May 15, 1903, FMB Executive Correspondence, microfilm edition, copybook vol. 48, March 14–June 3, 1903, number 706, IMB Archives, Richmond, Virginia; Willingham to Bernard, May 15, 1903, FMB Executive Correspondence, microfilm edition, copybook vol. 48, March 14–June 3, 1903, number 714, IMB Archives, Richmond, Virginia.
82   Allen, The New Lottie Moon Story, 238.
83   Lawrence, Lottie Moon, 306–08.
84   Allen, The New Lottie Moon Story, 277, 285.
85   Sullivan, Lottie Moon, 152–53.
86   Willingham to Bryan, January 4, 1913, FMB Executive Correspondence, microfilm edition, copybook vol. 92, October 22, 1912–January 8, 1913, number 935, IMB Archives, Richmond, Virginia.

cousin of Miss Lottie Moon here, has arranged for her to be put, at least temporarily, in a sanitarium for nervous trouble, close to this city."[87] While on her way back to America, she died on Christmas Eve in 1912 in a ship in the harbor at Kobe, Japan.

ANNIE ARMSTRONG AND THE WMU

Annie Walker Armstrong (1850–1938) played a crucial role in support of the FMB during this period as she used her administrative skill to lead the WMU, which was first organized in 1888. She had not had a good relationship with Tupper, who had preceded Willingham as corresponding secretary of the FMB.[88] After an early misunderstanding with Willingham, she worked well with him for the remainder of her time as corresponding secretary of the WMU.[89]

The WMU raised a large percentage of the funds needed for the FMB during this era. According to Elizabeth Evans, by 1894, "Woman's Missionary Union was contributing between a fourth and a fifth of the Foreign Board's receipts."[90] In a WMU report that was part of the annual report of the FMB in 1908, Fannie Heck stated, "Truly, not even the most sanguine in 1888 would have believed that in 1908 the Union would give more money to Home and Foreign Missions than the whole Convention gave that year to these objects."[91] Some of the FMB's priorities could be ascertained by its specific suggestions to the WMU for funding. For the 1912–1913 church year, for instance, the FMB recommended that the WMU use the 1912 Christmas offering for "work in China," that "the Young Women Auxiliaries raise funds for supporting hospital work on foreign fields," that "the Sisters enlist the Royal Ambassadors in

---

87   Willingham to Levering, January 10, 1913, FMB Executive Correspondence, microfilm edition, copybook vol. 93, January 8, 1913–March 14, 1913, number 47, IMB Archives, Richmond, Virginia.
88   Sorrill, *Annie Armstrong*, 91–95.
89   Sorrill, *Annie Armstrong*, 111.
90   Elizabeth Evans, *Annie Armstrong* (Birmingham: WMU, 1963), 85. See also Willingham, *Life of Robert Josiah Willingham*, 152–53.
91   FMBM, May 14, 1908.

providing for the Boys' School at Toluca," and that "the Sunbeam Bands undertake the support of the kindergartens and schools for boys and girls in our various foreign fields."[92]

Armstrong offered her resignation as corresponding secretary in 1905 during a time of controversy about a training school for women in Louisville connected with Southern Seminary. In a 1900 letter to Willingham, Armstrong had said that she was in favor of a training school for women and that "it *must come*."[93] Armstrong, however, did not like the timing of the effort to establish the school, its location in Louisville, and the way the matter was handled. Her strong stand against the school led to a loss of support for her leadership among SBC women.

Although she offered her resignation in 1905, she was reelected. She continued to serve in her elected position until May of 1906. In a 1905 letter to Willingham, she stated that after she left her post in May of 1906, she would have nothing to do with SBC mission work.[94] Sorrill explained that Armstrong's reasons for opposing the school also included (1) concern about its financial cost, (2) fear that devotion to missions by women would possibly become diminished by the school, (3) opposition to women preaching, and (4) "political wire-pulling" used to create the school.[95] In 1918, Armstrong suggested that the annual Christmas offering be named for Lottie Moon, and her suggestion was accepted by the WMU. She died in 1938.

FMB MISSIONARY STRATEGIES AND METHODS

In 1911, the FMB made a statement about its methods: "As to methods of work used by the Foreign Mission Board, we designate them

---

92 FMBM, May 3, 1912.
93 Armstrong, letter to Willingham, February 27, 1900, quoted in Harper, *Rescue the Perishing*, 241. See also Sorrill, *Annie Armstrong* 214; Evans, *Annie Armstrong*, 164.
94 Armstrong, letter to Willingham, June 16, 1905, quoted in Harper, *Rescue the Perishing*, 306.
95 Sorrill, *Annie Armstrong*, 227–35. A "Woman's Missionary Training School" was developed in Texas, and it moved to Southwestern Baptist Theological Seminary in 1909. See J. M. Carroll, *A History of Texas Baptists* (Dallas: Baptist Standard, 1923), 986.

under the following heads: EVANGELISTIC, EDUCATIONAL, MEDICAL, PUBLISHING.[96] As mentioned earlier in this chapter, during the Willingham era, the number of schools increased from 16 to 339. The number of hospitals increased from none to eight, and "a number of printing plants" were financed by the FMB after having none at the beginning of the era.[97] Strategies and methods used by some representative FMB missionaries are described below.

In his dissertation, Daniel Lancaster explains the strategy used by the FMB missionary who helped establish the first Baptist church in Brazil: "Bagby also began to formulate his strategy for ministry: preaching in large cities, utilizing native helpers, establishing preaching stations, and eventually organizing churches and teaching institutions."[98] Lancaster continues, "Bagby organized the six churches of the Rio mission into the first Brazilian Baptist Association.... Self-support and evangelistic cooperation were the main topics discussed at the introductory meeting."[99]

Lottie Moon discussed her evangelistic strategy: "We need to make friends before we can hope to win converts."[100] In a letter ten years later, she explained in detail the need for building relationships, dealing with false worldviews, explaining the gospel, and following up with discipleship:

> The missionary comes in and settles down among the natives. His first object is to convince them that he is human and that he is their sincere friend. By patience and gentleness and unwearied love, he wins upon them until there begins to be a diversion in sentiment. . . . These heathen are not only without a knowledge of the gospel, but their minds are full of superstitions and false

96 FMBM, November 7, 1911.
97 SBCA, 1915, 124–25.
98 Daniel Lancaster, "In the Land of the Southern Cross: The Life and Ministry of William Buck and Anne Luther Bagby" (PhD diss., Southwestern Baptist Theological Seminary, 1995), 97–98.
99 Lancaster, "In the Land of the Southern Cross," 134.
100 LML, March 19, 1887, no. 123, published in *FMJ* 18, no. 11 (June 1887): 2.

notions. At every step, the missionary must remove error as he tries to teach the truth. . . . Then, when the Holy Spirit has converted that soul, how does it need guidance and instruction that it may walk worthy of the calling wherewith it has been called! Now let it be borne in mind that the case above presented is not a solitary one, but that it is fairly representative of every man, woman and child in a heathen community.[101]

Moon believed that form and meaning could not be separated. She condemned what today might be called a characteristic of an insider movement as she criticized a Chinese woman: "In kneeling outwardly to the dead, she pretended to herself that inwardly she kneeled to God."[102] As mentioned earlier, she affirmed self-support. She touted the construction in 1894 of a church building at Säling, near Pingtu, which was built by nationals and missionaries, not requiring any FMB funding.[103]

In Nigeria, FMB missionary Samuel Pinnock reflected the FMB priorities when he said that "the three chief methods of missionary effort are known as the evangelistic, educational and medical."[104] He utilized house-to-house visitation and special evangelistic services.[105] Nigerian evangelists were paid and supervised by FMB missionaries.[106] In 1917, only four Baptist churches out of thirty-one in Nigeria were both self-supporting and self-governing.[107]

---

101 LML, March 30, 1888, no. 433, published in *FMJ* 20, no. 1 (August 1888): 3.
102 LML, June 27, 1888, no. 283, published in *FMJ* 21, no. 2 (September 1889): 2.
103 LML, October 1, 1894, no. 53, published in *FMJ* 26, no. 6 (January 1895): 176; LML, May 1, 1907, no. 309.
104 Pinnock, *The Romance of Missions in Nigeria*, 133.
105 Pinnock, *The Romance of Missions in Nigeria*, 134–36.
106 Pinnock, *The Romance of Missions in Nigeria*, 136–38.
107 Pinnock, *The Romance of Missions in Nigeria*, 157–60.

CONCLUSION

Two statistics that were listed earlier stand out ominously during the Willingham era: the increase from 86 to 635 "native helpers" and the increase from 16 to 339 schools. The category "native helpers" referred to paid nationals.[108] In Willingham's report to the convention in 1913, he mentioned only ten overseas seminaries.[109] Thus, the vast majority of schools were for the education of children, teenagers, and college students.

Generally speaking, immediate self-support by the national workers (giving no American missionary money at any time to nationals for religious work) is superior to gradual self-support (gradually reducing money given by American missionaries to nationals). Once foreign money is paid to nationals, the gradual reduction of that money is difficult. In other words, once a precedent is set, a change in policy is painful to implement.

The immediate-self-support method taught by Nevius to the American missionaries in Korea was one of the factors leading to tremendous growth in churches there during the Willingham era. An opportunity was missed for starting Southern Baptist work in Korea during that propitious time. The FMB focused more on strengthening existing work than starting new work.

Concerning the emphasis on schools, a case can be made that literacy training is important so that nationals can read the Bible. Seminary training is also important so that national church leaders can refute false doctrine and understand how to lead churches properly. However, when salaried missionaries are heavily involved in teaching subjects such as arithmetic in a country where there

---

108 The education secretary for the FMB, T. B. Ray, described the work of the FMB in 1910: "On every field there is a regularly organized Mission. . . . Once a year the Mission meets and adopts an estimate of expenses for the coming twelve months, including salaries of the missionaries and of the native helpers and buildings and other equipment required." T. B. Ray, "Foreign Mission Board of the Southern Baptist Convention," in *Southern Baptist Foreign Missions*, ed. T. B. Ray (Nashville: Sunday School Board, 1910), 45.

109 Willingham, *Life of Robert Josiah Willingham*, 258–59.

is freedom to make disciples and plant churches openly, full-time missionaries should change roles and spend their time more profitably in evangelism and discipleship activities.

In 1893, Harris, the interim corresponding secretary, had argued for supporting schools for "secular instruction of the children of converts."[110] Secular instruction can take an enormous amount of time and money, and it can distract missionaries from more important tasks. For example, the FMB minutes from January 7, 1913, listed requests from the Committee on China for educational equipment (including land and buildings) for the North China Mission that totaled $85,000. The schools included in the request were an academy and a girls' school in Chefoo, an academy and a girls' school in Hwanghein, Bush Theological Seminary in Hwanghein, a kindergarten and a girls' school in Laichow, a girls' school in Pingtu, a girls' school in Tengchow, and the North China Baptist College.[111] The Committee for China also requested $116,000 for educational needs for the South China Mission, and the list included an academy, a seminary, and six boarding schools.[112] Donald McGavran explains that "in most parts of vast India, China, and many other lands, Christian schools have seldom led to substantial Christianization."[113] Obedience to the Great Commission should always be the primary task for evangelical missionaries.

Even though some FMB missionaries had flawed perspectives and methods, the work of the FMB was strengthened during the Willingham era. The financial resources of the FMB grew with the assistance of the WMU. Most importantly, nationals were saved, churches were planted, and leaders were trained. The sacrifices made by FMB missionaries were used by God in wonderful ways.

---

110 Harris, "Our Board and the 'Gospel Mission,'" 39.
111 FMBM, January 7, 1913.
112 FMBM, January 7, 1913.
113 Donald McGavran, *Effective Evangelism: A Theological Mandate* (Phillipsburg, NJ: Presbyterian and Reformed, 1988), 65.

HOPEFULNESS, EXPANSION, DISAPPOINTMENT, AND RETRENCHMENT

Paving the Way for the Next Generation of Southern Baptist Foreign Missions, 1915–1933

David S. Dockery

AS SEEN IN PREVIOUS CHAPTERS, James B. Taylor, Henry Tupper, and R. J. Willingham served as effective leaders for the strategic work of the FMB from 1846 to 1914. Taylor, the great patriarch of Southern Baptist missions, invested almost three decades in this important kingdom work until his death in 1871. Tupper advanced the effort for two decades, from 1872 to 1893. Willingham initiated an aggressive vision for Southern Baptist missions at the conclusion of the nineteenth century that resulted in its expanding reach into new countries. In addition, hospitals, schools, and publishing houses were established while making strides toward financial stability. When Willingham died in 1914, James Franklin Love, who had been serving as the FMB's home secretary, was elected in 1915 as its new leader. In this chapter, we will explore the work of Southern Baptist global missions from 1915 to 1933. Before doing so, it will be helpful to attempt to understand some aspects of the larger context for this time period, internationally, nationally, and denominationally. We will do so at this initial point in the chapter and then again before exploring the difficult days at the FMB when T. Bronson Ray was attempting to guide the work from 1928 to 1933.

THE CONTEXT: 1915–1928

National and International

Woodrow Wilson, who had previously served as president of Princeton University and governor of the state of New Jersey, was elected as the twenty-eighth president of the United States in 1912. His presidency, which began on March 4, 1913, ushered in a new progressive era. His years in the White House were greatly influenced by World War I and other international events.[1] During this period a sense of hopeful expectancy characterized the American scene. In 1915, the one millionth new Ford rolled off of the assembly line in Michigan as the first stop sign was being put in place in Detroit. People in Chicago celebrated the opening of a beautiful

---

1   See A. Scott Berg, *Wilson* (New York: Putnam's, 2013); John Milton Cooper Jr., *Woodrow Wilson: A Biography* (New York: Knopf, 2009); Barry Hankins, *Woodrow Wilson: Ruling Elder, Spiritual President* (Oxford: Oxford University Press, 2016); Anthony L. Chute, Nathan A. Finn, and Michael A. G. Haykin, *The Baptist Story: From English Sect to Global Movement* (Nashville: B&H Academic, 2015), 219–22; and Bill J. Leonard, *Baptist Ways* (Valley Forge, PA: Judson, 2003), 396–97.

new ballpark called Wrigley Field. Boston welcomed a new pitcher and slugger to the Red Sox named Babe Ruth, who hit his first home run in 1915. He would go on to hit 713 more as his name became synonymous with baseball. This sense of expectancy, which was evident across the nation, welcomed J. F. Love to his new role in Richmond, Virginia, the headquarters for Southern Baptist mission work. William R. Estep describes this period as one of "rising expectations."[2] The reality, however, pointed in more difficult and challenging directions.

The First World War was so momentous that many historians do not mark the conclusion of the nineteenth century until 1914, thus identifying August 4, 1914, the beginning date for the outbreak of the war, as the starting point of the twentieth century or the modern world.[3] A. T. Robertson, the brilliant scholar at The Southern Baptist Theological Seminary, declared, "The old world passed away when Belgium took her stand in front of the Kaiser's hosts. Modern history began on that date."[4] This war changed the world as people had known it. The Great War, as it was often called, brought about a cataclysmic clash that affected almost every continent.[5]

American Christianity

While an international war was taking place on the global scene, a fight for the soul of Christianity was taking place in America, particularly among Northern Baptists and Presbyterians. Many had predicted that the twentieth century would be "the Christian century." Indeed, historian William G. McLoughlin dared to say

---

2 William R. Estep, *Whole Gospel Whole World: The Foreign Mission Board of the Southern Baptist Convention, 1845–1995* (Nashville: Broadman & Holman, 1994), 187–216.

3 See Andrew Roberts, *A History of the English-Speaking Peoples Since 1900* (New York: Harper Collins, 2007), 87–135; Martin Gilbert, *A History of the Twentieth Century*, vol. 1, *1900–1933* (New York: William Marrow, 1997), 312–527.

4 A. T. Roberson, *The New Citizenship: The Christian Facing a New World Order* (New York: Revell, 1919), 8.

5 See Brian Stanley, *Christianity in the Twentieth Century: A World History* (Princeton, NJ: Princeton University Press, 2018), 12–35; Hew Strachan, *The First World War*, vol. 1 (Oxford: Oxford University Press, 2001).

that the story of American evangelicalism during the nineteenth century is the story of America itself, with its emphasis on rugged individualism, laissez-faire economic theory, the Protestant ethic regarding both work and morality, and the millennial hope in the Manifest Destiny.[6] By the end of the nineteenth century, however, that was all changing. Conservative Christians saw that the churches were losing their connection with the truth of the gospel message made clear in an inspired and authoritative Bible.[7]

As the twentieth century began, new movements were launched to revive, renew, correct, and sometimes even to separate from the established Protestant denominations, which conservatives viewed as growing in more worldly and more liberal directions. In the middle of the nineteenth century, evangelicalism was understood to be the equivalent of Protestantism. By the beginning of the twentieth century Protestantism was splintering over a host of issues such as Darwinism, naturalism, biblical criticism, and pragmatism, while struggling with expanding urbanization and industrialization.[8]

People looked for ways to nail down what seemed to be coming loose. Immigration had opened the door to pluralism, industrialization pulled people away from the farm to the factory, and urbanization changed the context from the pastures to pavements.[9] As the twentieth century began, the modernist-fundamentalist controversy moved publicly into full force. In 1910, the "five

---

6   William G. McLoughlin, introduction to *The American Evangelicals, 1800–1900*, ed. William G. McLoughlin (New York: Harper, 1968); also see David S. Dockery, "Evangelicalism: Past, Present, and Future," in *Trinity Journal*, n.s., 36 (2015): 3–21.

7   George M. Marsden, *Understanding Fundamentalism and Evangelicalism*, (Grand Rapids: Eerdmans, 1991), 7–61; Bill J. Leonard, "The Origin and Character of Fundamentalism," *Review and Expositor* 79 (1982): 5–17.

8   See Joel Carpenter, *Revive Us Again: The Reawakening of American Fundamentalism* (New York: Oxford University Press, 1997); Stewart Cole, *The History of Fundamentalism* (Hamden, CT: Archon, 1963); Norman Furniss, *The Fundamentalist Controversy, 1918–1931* (New Haven, CT: Yale University Press, 1954); Andrew Himes, *The Sword of the Lord* (Seattle: Chiara, 2011); and William B. Gatewood, *Controversy in the Twenties* (Nashville: Vanderbilt University Press, 1969).

9   See Walter B. Shurden, *Not a Silent People: Controversies That Have Shaped Southern Baptists* (Nashville: Broadman, 1972), 83–102.

fundamentals" were clarified by the Northern Presbyterians, reflecting on earlier versions spelled out by the Niagara prophecy conference. These five doctrinal tenets, which focused on the full inspiration and complete authority of Scripture, the virgin birth of Jesus Christ, the atoning death and resurrection of Christ, and the historical reality of the biblical miracles, were aimed at the primary challenges of liberalism. The publication of *The Fundamentals* in 1915, edited by R. A. Torrey, president of the Biblical Institute of Los Angeles, and funded by Lyman and Milton Stewart, included ninety well-reasoned, serious, calm, thoughtful, not shrill, and generally quite persuasive articles.[10] More than thirty of these articles dealt with the nature of Scripture. Authors represented a wide-ranging group of authors including three Southern Baptist contributors: E. Y. Mullins, president of Southern Seminary, wrote the article on Christian experience; J. J. Reeve and C. B. Williams, faculty members at Southwestern Seminary, penned the articles on biblical criticism and the doctrine of sin respectively. More than three million copies of the booklets were distributed at a cost of $200,000. What liberals labeled fundamentalism was actually a loose coalition of conservative Christian groups with various priorities representing different denominational traditions.

In 1919, however, fundamentalist leader William Bell Riley said the five fundamentals were not enough. He also wanted to stress separatism, dispensationalism, and lifestyle taboos, which continue to be distinguishing marks for some aspects of the fundamentalist movement nearly a century later.[11] At the prophecy conference held in Philadelphia from May 25 to June 1, 1919, and attended by six thousand participants, the World Christian Fundamentals Association was established.

---

10   R. A. Torrey, ed., *The Fundamentals*, 12 vols. (Los Angeles: Bible Institute of Los Angeles, 1915).

11   See William Vance Trollinger Jr., *God's Empire: William Bell Riley and Midwestern Fundamentalism* (Madison: University of Wisconsin Press, 1990); Timothy P. Weber, "William Bell Riley," in *Baptist Theologians*, eds. Timothy George and David S. Dockery (Nashville: Broadman, 1990), 351–65.

In 1922, Harry Emerson Fosdick, an ordained Baptist, preached his famous sermon at the First Presbyterian Church of New York City, "Shall the Fundamentalists Win? No!" Fosdick rejected the virgin birth of Christ as well as his substitutionary atonement. He similarly questioned the second coming of Christ while affirming biblical criticism and applauding new discoveries in evolutionary science. This famous sermon was published with the new title "The New Knowledge and the Christian Faith" and distributed as a booklet to thousands of ministers across the country.

Clarence Macartney, the pastor of the Arch Street Presbyterian Church in Philadelphia, provided an answer to Fosdick with his sermon "Shall Unbelief Win?" which similarly was published and widely distributed. Macartney contended that liberalism would lead to a Christianity without worship, without God, and without Jesus Christ.[12] In 1923, Princeton scholar J. Gresham Machen published *Christianity and Liberalism*, with the word *and* being key in the title, as Machen astutely treated the subject not as two forms of Christianity but as two different religions.[13]

In 1925 in the town of Dayton, in east Tennessee, the Scopes Trial gained the attention of the nation. Well-known political leader William Jennings Bryan served as the prosecution witness in the famous trial that convicted John T. Scopes, the high school biology teacher, for teaching evolution contrary to Tennessee's statute against doing so. The fundamentalists won the battle but seemingly lost the war.[14] John

---

12   See Gary Dorrien, *The Making of American Liberal Theology: Idealism, Realism, and Modernity* (Louisville: Westminster John Knox, 2003), 203–8; Martin Marty, *Modern American Religion*, vol. 2, *The Noise of Conflict, 1919–1941* (Chicago: University of Chicago Press, 1991); George Marsden, *Fundamentalism and American Culture: The Shaping of Twentieth-Century Fundamentalism* (New York: Oxford University Press, 1980); and Bill J. Leonard, *Baptists in America* (New York: Columbia University Press, 2005), 47–64.

13   J. Gresham Machen, *Christianity and Liberalism* (Grand Rapids: Eerdmans, 1987).

14   See Edward J. Larson, *Summer for the Gods: The Scopes Trial and America's Continuing Debate over Science and Religion* (New York: Basic Books, 1997); Lawrence W. Levine, *Defender of the Faith, Williams Jennings Bryan: The Last Decade 1915–1925*, 2nd ed. (New York: Oxford University Press, 1968); Michael Lienesch, *In the Beginning: Fundamentalism, the Scopes Trial, and the Making of the Antievolution Movement* (Chapel Hill: University of North Carolina Press, 2007).

Roach Straton, the well-known pastor of the Calvary Baptist Church in New York City, who had been educated at Mercer and at Southern Seminary, described how these issues made their way into Baptist life.[15] Regarding the relationship of science and Scripture, W. O. Carver, longtime professor of missions and world religions at Southern Seminary, suggested that Christians should not expect the Bible to contain an outline of scientific fields: geology, zoology, biology, botany, or other fields. The creation story, he maintained, was a work of art, which is theologically trustworthy but not scientifically accurate. Carver described Scripture in artistic terms that beckon interpretation since the Word of God does not become revelation until it becomes the experience of a person.[16]

While Carver pushed back against fundamentalism, he did not think of himself as a theological liberal, describing himself instead as one who presented moderating and mediating views on most things.[17] His openness to evolutionary theory pleased two Southern Seminary trustees: W. L. Poteat, president at Wake Forest University, who was one of the first Baptist leaders in the South to advocate publicly a form of Darwinism, as well as Samuel Brooks, president of Baylor University. Both were major leaders in Baptist life during this period.

DENOMINATIONAL

In 1925, at the same time the Scopes Trial was taking place in east Tennessee, Southern Baptists gathered on the other side of

---

15   See John Roach Straton, *Evolution versus Creation: Second in the Series of Funda-mentalist-Modernist Debates* (New York: Doran, 1924). Though Straton was not serving in a Southern Baptist congregation, he was not shy about offering his thoughts regarding happenings in both Southern and Northern Baptist settings.

16   W. O. Carver, "Characteristics of the Creation Story," *Western Recorder*, October 13, 1921; see also Robert V. Forehand, "A Study of Religion and Culture as Reflected in the Thought and Career of William Owen Carver" (ThD diss., The Southern Baptist Theological Seminary, 1972).

17   W. O. Carver, "Christianizing Evolution," *Review and Expositor* 23 (Winter 1926): 82–87; See John N. Jonsson, "W. O. Carver," in George and Dockery, *Baptist Theologians*, 384–99.

the state in Memphis at their annual convention. At this time, Southern Baptists for the first time in their eighty-year history adopted a full-orbed confession of faith. The confessional statement was a response to mounting concerns being articulated across the denominational context. It was an attempt to clarify Southern Baptist doctrinal commitments in the midst of the modernist-fundamentalist controversy that raged across the country in the early decades of the twentieth century, seeking to position Southern Baptists as neither modernist nor fundamentalist.

Baptist Faith and Message

The 1925 Baptist Faith and Message was largely a restatement of the 1833 New Hampshire Confession with minor revisions. The Southern Baptist Convention in 1925, however, chose to move beyond the realm of classic doctrinal affirmations not only by addressing the evolution question but also by making declarations regarding the importance of stewardship, cooperation, education, evangelism, mission, and social ministries.

The Southern Baptist Convention, by adopting the 1925 statement, placed itself in the great tradition of Nicaea, Chalcedon, the Reformers, and the Pietists on the doctrines of God, Christ, and salvation, while maintaining and articulating significant Baptist distinctives such as regenerate church membership, the priesthood of believers, congregational governance, believer's baptism, and the Lord's Supper. The work of putting together the 1925 statement was led by E. Y. Mullins along with L. R. Scarborough, the president at Southwestern Seminary; J. W. McGlothlin, president at Furman; and others.

The reports in the state Baptist papers at that time reveal that the adoption of the Baptist Faith and Message was seen as the major story coming out of the 1925 convention. Though the convention also approved the twelve-page report from the Committee on Future Programs to develop a general outline of plans for the next forward movement of Southern Baptists (which came to be known as the Cooperative Program),[18] it seemingly was only barely noticed because of the importance given to the Baptist Faith and Message. This marvelous plan, outlined in that twelve-page report, has been used of God in an amazing way to advance the collaborative work of Southern Baptists in this country and around the world since 1925.

The Cooperative Program
In 1919, two years after the establishment of the Executive Committee, Convention leaders proposed the Seventy-five Million Campaign, a five-year campaign to support the various mission agencies and ministries of the SBC. From these efforts, the Cooperative Program, under the leadership of M. E. Dodd, pastor of the First Baptist Church of Shreveport, Louisiana, was eventually adopted at the 1925 convention in Memphis.

The Cooperative Program is a cooperative partnership whereby churches across the Southern Baptist Convention combine financial gifts, given to and through state conventions, which are then passed on to support the work of national convention entities and agencies. These financial gifts are employed to send and support missionaries, equip pastors and church leaders, enable educational institutions, and address benevolent, social, ethical, and moral concerns.

The Cooperative Program became the glue for the Southern Baptist Convention and the vehicle to advance the work of Southern Baptist global missions. While the twentieth century did not become "the Christian century" as predicted, it in fact became the century of a much-divided and fragmented Christian movement in both Europe and the United States.[19] In the midst of these tensions, the Cooperative Program helped to promote a sense of pragmatic unity for Southern

---

18   See Albert McClellan, *The Executive Committee of the Southern Baptist Convention* (Nashville: Broadman, 1985), 453–70; Chad Owen Brand and David E. Hankins, *One Sacred Effort: The Cooperative Program of Southern Baptists* (Nashville: B&H, 2006).
19   See Stanley, *Christianity in the Twentieth Century*, 127–49.

Baptists in the 1920s.[20] In this context, J. Franklin Love was called to serve as the fourth leader and corresponding secretary of the FMB.

J. FRANKLIN LOVE AND THE FOREIGN MISSION BOARD (1915–1928)

Not only did R. J. Willingham pass away in 1914, but B. H. Carroll, founding president of Southwestern Seminary, died as well. Both were appropriately memorialized in the 1915 Convention Annual, but Willingham was given a glowing two-page tribute. During his tenure, Southern Baptists had truly become a missionary people.[21]

J. Franklin Love, who was born on July 14, 1859, was a graduate of Wake Forest College. He had served as pastor in North Carolina, Virginia, and Maryland before being named as state secretary of missions in Arkansas and then as assistant corresponding secretary of the Home Mission Board. With this experience he responded to the invitation to serve the FMB during the concluding period of the Willingham administration. With financial gifts increasing to missions, as reported by the Judson Centennial Committee, and with an enhanced awareness of the importance of missions for and among the churches within the Southern Baptist Convention, expectations for the coming years were quite high.[22]

Initially, during this period there were three secretaries for the FMB as reported by R. H. Pitt, editor of the *Religious Herald*, the state paper for Virginia Baptists. T. Bronson Ray and W. H. Smith also initially served together with Love, doing so, according to Pitt,

---

20 See David S. Dockery, "Convictional yet Cooperative: The Making of a Great Commission People," in *The Great Commission Resurgence: Fulfilling God's Mandate in Our Time*, eds. Chuck Lawless and Adam W. Greenway (Nashville: B&H, 2010), 387–400; also see, William H. Brackney, *Baptists in North America* (Malden, MA: Blackwell, 2006), 111–13, though as Brackney notes Southern Baptists had not yet reached the place of emphasizing efficiencies and ecclesiocratic practices like those in the American business sector; also William H. Brackney, *Baptist Life and Thought* (Valley Forge, PA: Judson, 1999).

21 See Estep, *Whole Gospel Whole World*, 184–89.

22 SBCA, 1915, 37–40, 125.

"without a particle of friction and in most loving cooperation."[23] As other observers have noted, the recommendation at the 1915 Houston Convention from the Efficiency Committee to amend the process for electing the FMB's corresponding secretary must have been greeted with unexpected shock. The FMB had been selecting its own leader since 1846. However, the motion to amend the process whereby there would only be one corresponding secretary for the Baptist Sunday School Board, the Home Mission Board, and the Foreign Mission Board, who would be elected by the convention and designated as the executive officer responsible to the boards of each entity as well as to the convention, passed overwhelmingly.[24] With this change, J. F. Love became the corresponding secretary with the responsibility to lead the foreign mission enterprise for Southern Baptists. His title was later changed to executive secretary.

The FMB gathered its members for meetings in May and June of 1915 to respond to the actions of the convention. In executive session the board affirmed the decision of the convention on June 16, 1915. The board members then clarified the roles of Smith and Ray, giving them basically the same duties as before while indicating that both men would now serve under Love's supervision.[25] Together with three geographical secretaries, a new leadership team had been put in place with J. Franklin Love, the best known of the six leadership team members, and probably the most experienced officer, now serving as the executive.

Love brought to this role not only years of pastoral and denominational support but also a keen mind and a prolific pen. With his

---

23 SBCA, 1915, 122–23.
24 SBCA, 1915, 43–65.
25 FMBM, May 17, 1915, and June 16, 1915. Love was paid approximately 10 percent more than Ray or Smith to distinguish his role as leader. In 1916, Smith resigned from his role after the Southern Baptist Convention asked the board to limit the number of associate secretaries to one. Smith graciously stepped away, leaving Ray as the sole associate to support Love's leadership. Obviously, the SBC still lacked a consistent understanding of governance at this point with management decisions for entities being made at the convention level. With the establishment of the Executive Committee in 1917, those dynamics began to move toward a more mature and effective understanding of order, organization, efficiency, and responsibility.

devout upbringing, he had become a convictional Baptist, authoring *The Appeal of the Baptist Program for Europe, Today's Supreme Challenge to America, The Mission of Our Nation, The Union Movement,* and *The Unique Message and Universal Mission of Christianity.*[26] He also had the support of Caroline, his wife, whom he had baptized after she read his work on a Baptist view of baptism. Love traveled more extensively than any of the previous FMB leaders, spending time in Europe, South America, and the British Isles. He died on May 3, 1928, after suffering a stroke. Key events during Love's tenure prefigured both of the decisions made at the Memphis convention in 1925: the adoption of the Baptist Faith and Message and the affirmation of the Cooperative Program. It is to those two initiatives that we now turn our attention.[27]

Confessional Convictions

Theologian Horton Davies described the twentieth century as the ecumenical century, a phrase he adopted in the title of volume 5 of his work *Worship and Theology in England: The Ecumenical Century, 1900–1965.*[28] While some trace such ecumenical initiatives to the historic 1910 missions conference in Edinburgh, Scotland, the reality is that this was primarily a missions conference and not an ecumenical gathering. In some ways, this event was the fulfillment of William Carey's dream for such a meeting a century earlier in Cape Town, South Africa.[29] Still, it must be admitted that

---

26 See Estep, *Whole Gospel Whole World,* 191–210; George Braxton Taylor, *Virginia Baptist Ministries,* Sixth Series, 1914–1934 (Lynchburg, VA: J. P. Bell, 1935), 272–73; E. C. Routh, "Love, James Franklin," in *Encyclopedia of Southern Baptists* (Nashville: Broadman, 1958), 2:809; Robert Nash, "Love, James Franklin (1859–1928)," in *Dictionary of Baptists in America,* ed. Bill J. Leonard (Downers Grove, IL: InterVarsity Press, 1994), 175.

27 See H. Leon McBeth, *The Baptist Heritage: Four Centuries of Baptist Heritage* (Nashville: Broadman, 1987), 638–39.

28 Horton Davies, *Worship and Theology in England,* vol. 5, *The Ecumenical Century, 1900–1965* (Princeton, NJ: Princeton University Press, 1965).

29 See Brian Stanley, *The World Missionary Conference, Edinburgh 1910* (Grand Rapids: Eerdmans, 2009). Robert Baker reported that E. C. Dargan, W. W. Barnes, and other Southern Baptists, functioning as fraternal representatives to the 1910 conference, responded positively to the idea of Southern Baptists participating with

without this conference there likely may not have been a World Council of Churches.

Shortly after the conclusion of World War I, conversations expanded regarding the need for all communions throughout the world to discuss matters of faith and order, which eventually took place at the 1927 Faith and Order Conference in Lausanne, Switzerland. In light of these developments and the initiatives related to the Interchurch World Movement, the FMB responded by putting together an important statement of faith to solidify orthodox Christian beliefs and faithful Baptist tenets,[30] a reaction not only to the ecumenical movement on the liberal side of things but also to the 1919 prophecy conference statement on the conservative side.

The 1920 confession of faith contained thirteen articles on Christian essentials as well as Baptist distinctives such as congregationalism, baptism, and the Lord's Supper. Missionaries were asked to affirm these commitments in addition to the statement on Christian union,

---

other evangelical denominations in this collaborative missionary effort. See Robert A. Baker, *The Southern Baptist Convention and Its People, 1607–1972* (Nashville: Broadman, 1974), 306. Also see John Mark Terry, Ebbie Smith, and Justice Anderson, *Missiology: World Mission* (Nashville: Broadman & Holman, 1998), 45.

30　See Baker, *The Southern Baptist Convention and Its People*, 304–6. Also, James Leo Garrett Jr., *Baptist Relations with Other Christians* (Valley Forge, PA: Judson, 1974). Northern Baptists responded much more positively to the Interchurch World Movement, which was a significant step toward a more fully developed ecumenism. See Thomas S. Kidd and Barry Hankins, *Baptists in America: A History* (Oxford: Oxford University Press, 2015) 172–82. This decision by both groups had implications for their understanding of the purposes and strategies for carrying out the work of global missions. Rather than strengthening and unifying the Christian church, the ecumenical movement wound up sacrificing significant doctrinal convictions and missionary activity associated with the movement that often dissolved into humanitarian programs rather than the proclamation of the gospel. Southern Baptists, with influence from J. F. Love, recognized that spiritual unity and cooperation can result in greater missional outreach than ecumenical organizational efforts. See Terry, Smith, and Anderson, *Missiology*, 45–46. In many ways, the trajectory articulated by Love served as an adumbration of more expanded and enhanced reflections on this important topic by other significant Baptist thinkers. See William R. Estep, *Baptist and Christian Unity* (Nashville: Broadman, 1962); Millard Erickson, *Christian Theology*, 2nd ed. (Grand Rapids: Baker, 1998), 1142–45; and James Leo Garrett Jr., *Systematic Theology: Biblical, Historical, and Evangelical* (Grand Rapids: Eerdmans, 1995), 2:623–24.

which had been approved by the board as well as the convention.[31]
While the SBC did not officially adopt its first statement of faith until
1925, the FMB statement continued a trajectory found among the
SBC seminaries. Southern Seminary had adopted the Abstract of
Principles at its founding in 1859. Southwestern Seminary had opted for the New Hampshire Confession at its founding in 1908. The
FMB statement served as an encouragement for the SBC to affirm its
own convention-wide statement in light of other movements in the
country and in the world, in addition to doctrinal concerns within
the Southern Baptist family. Love's heartfelt Baptist convictions were
clearly instrumental in this regard.

The Seventy-Five Million Campaign

During the first seven decades of the SBC, no unified strategy existed for the funding of global missions or any of the other shared
ministries across the convention. Most entities had agents, which
today would be called advancement officers, to represent the entities
to the churches, making appeals for support. Annual appeals were
also made at state convention meetings, at associational meetings,
and at special conferences or rallies. Occasionally, special campaigns had been implemented to raise money for the two mission
boards, such as the 1908 Apportionment Committee, which was
approved by the convention to work with state conventions in this
effort.[32] Timothy George notes that as early as 1859, only fourteen
years after the founding of the SBC and the year of the founding of
Southern Seminary, a general dissatisfaction with the agency system
was indicated, but no better plan had yet been formulated.[33] For
the next sixty years Southern Baptists explored various options to
find a better way to support the work of the mission boards and
the other entities.

---

31   SBCA, 1920, 197–99; Estep, *Whole Gospel Whole World*, 203–4.
32   See Albert McClellan, "Denominational and Distribution of Cooperative Program
     Money," *Baptist History and Heritage* 20 (April 1985): 14.
33   Timothy George, "The Southern Baptists Cooperative Program: Heritage and
     Challenge," *Baptist History and Heritage* 20 (January 1985): 5.

During the first morning session of the annual convention in 1919, SBC president J. B. Gambrell, building on the stirring convention sermon from M. E. Dodd, shared his prayer and desire for the convention "to adopt a program for work commensurate with the reasonable demands on us and to summon ourselves and our people to a new demonstration of the value of orthodoxy in free action."[34] In response, a Committee on the Financial Aspect of the Enlarged Program proposed that the convention, over the next five years, enter into a campaign to raise $75 million. George Truett, pastor of the First Baptist Church of Dallas, Texas, was appointed as chair of this new Campaign Commission, with L. R. Scarborough, president of Southwestern Seminary, serving as general director and I. J. Van Ness, president the Baptist Sunday School Board, serving as treasurer.[35]

Scarborough, who had chaired a major campaign to support Texas Baptist education in 1917, let people know that he believed the goal should be $100 million. He also thought the five-year period to be too long. The majority, however, thought the $75 million goal appropriate for the seventy-fifth anniversary of the convention. In 1920 Scarborough victoriously announced that Southern Baptists had exceeded the initial goal, with pledges totaling $92.6 million. A sense of triumphal hopefulness spread across the convention. It was, however, a short-lived feeling that would not be seen by the SBC again until after World War II.

Many pledges remained unfulfilled as difficult financial conditions swept across the South. Four years after the abundant pledge amount had been announced, it was made known in 1924 that only $58.6 million had been received, which was almost $34 million short of the pledged amount.[36] The FMB received $11,615,328, which

---

34 SBCA, 1919, 23.
35 See Jesse C. Fletcher, *The Southern Baptist Convention: A Sesquicentennial History* (Nashville: Broadman & Holman, 1994), 134–36.
36 SBCA, 1924, 32–35. See the helpful commentary provided by Kidd and Hankins, *Baptists in America*, 177–79. They note that Scarborough was given a one-year leave of absence from the seminary to lead the work. The total gifts fell quite short of the pledged amount. In anticipation of enlarged revenue streams, SBC agencies began borrowing money to expand their operations. Still, the sum raised represented a

was only about two-thirds of the amount they had anticipated. Unfortunately, all of the SBC entities had made plans and started new programs based on expectations associated with the amount of the pledges announced in 1920. No entity felt the sting from the shortfall, however, more than did the FMB. As Albert McClellan observes, "In some ways, Southern Baptists were worse off than before the campaign, for both state and SBC agencies had borrowed against the $92.6 million goal and were painfully in debt."[37] The Executive Committee of the Southern Baptist Convention, which had been established in 1917, devoted its energies for the next several years to addressing the financial challenges. What must be understood, in retrospect, is that the Seventy-Five Million Campaign created the context and sense of cooperation that paved the way for the adoption and development of the Cooperative Program.[38]

Based on the excitement connected with the 1920 announcement of more than $92 million pledged, the FMB projected a record budget amount of nearly $2.9 million for 1921, which included missionaries in fourteen fields across nine countries. The Love administration planned to send out one hundred new missionaries while increasing the amount in the emergency fund. Though the board had issued a "call to Southern Baptists," encouraging them to meet their pledges, they simultaneously adjusted to the reality that their revenue numbers were falling further and further behind. Still they hoped to increase the number of countries in which SBC missionaries were serving.[39]

---

significant increase in per capita giving over previous years. Southern Baptists had launched the campaign the same year that Northern Baptists had started their New World Movement, the goal of which was $100 million. The Disciples of Christ, Methodists, and Presbyterians had likewise launched campaign drives between 1913 and 1918, the largest of which was the Methodist Centenary fund at $115 million. Southern Baptists raised a higher percentage of their targeted goal than most other Protestant denominations. Baptisms also increased steadily, as did the number of students in Southern Baptist colleges. The $75 million campaign may have missed its target, but in shooting for the stars, Southern Baptists at least hit the moon.

37   McClellan, *The Executive Committee of the Southern Baptist Convention*, 64.
38   McClellan, *The Executive Committee of the Southern Baptist Convention*, 64–69.
39   See Estep, *Whole Gospel Whole World*, 203–7.

One of the few bright spots in the board's challenging financial picture came from the sale of a building that had been purchased with funds provided by the George W. Bottoms family of Texarkana, Arkansas. Apart from this wise and profitable transaction, the board found itself more and more needing to employ debt for regular operational purposes. The board also found itself needing to send more frequent and urgent calls for help to churches and state conventions. Estep summarizes the situation that the board faced at the conclusion of the five-year campaign:

> By 1925, the financial plight of the Foreign Mission Board and its consequences were frankly addressed in its report to the convention. After reviewing the impressive gains in baptisms and new churches on the mission fields during the five years of the Seventy-five Million Campaign, the committee bringing the report of the Board to the Convention in 1925 commented: It is not surprising, therefore, that the Foreign Mission Board is in a distressing dilemma. "We must either give more to Foreign Missions; do less Foreign Missions work, or continue to make debt. One thing is sure, we cannot continue as we are now going."[40]

Hopeful Markers

The 1925 *Annual of the Southern Baptist Convention* reported that these financial pressures were being experienced at the same time as when "responsiveness to our Foreign missionaries was never so gratifying. For example, during the five years of the campaign period there were 59,248 baptisms; 706 new churches established; 58,663 new members; an increase of 930 Sunday schools, with 49,400 new pupils."[41]

During these years, new missionaries were sent to Chile, Palestine, Romania, and Spain. The Lottie Moon Christmas Offering

---

40   Estep, *Whole Gospel Whole World*, 207
41   SBCA, 1925, 99.

remained stable with faithful gifts being employed each and every year to support the work. Another encouraging marker during this period came from the measurable increases in interest in mission service developed among Baptist college and seminary students. Major conferences to foster this student enthusiasm were held on the campuses of Southwestern Seminary in 1916 and Southern Seminary in 1917, with oversight provided by Charles Ball at Southwestern and W. O. Carver and Gaines Dobbins at Southern.[42] The Baptist Student Missionary Movement sparked an ongoing interest in missions resulting in additional conferences in Texas, South Carolina, and Kentucky in 1920. As a result of these well-attended conferences, Secretary Love observed that "the Lord is again visiting our schools and the hearts of young men and women are turning to missions fields."[43] The Baptist Sunday School Board, the Home Mission Board, and the WMU collaborated with the FMB to encourage future student work.[44] This shared effort led to the development of the Inter-Board Commission, which named Frank H. Leavell to serve as the first executive secretary of the new Baptist Student Union initiative.[45]

REFLECTIONS

There is certainly much for which to be grateful when reflecting on the solid leadership provided by J. Franklin Love from 1915 to 1928. His service on this earth came to an end on May 16, 1928, when the Lord called him home just weeks prior to the 1928 annual convention in Chattanooga, Tennessee. Love had carried heavy

---

42   Estep, *Whole Gospel Whole World*, 206.
43   See William Wright Barnes, *The Southern Baptist Convention* (repr., Charleston, SC: Nabu, 2011), 193–96. As we will see at the conclusion of the chapter, these stu-dent-movement conferences resulted in much fruit that would yield great blessings for Southern Baptist missions in future years.
44   SBCA, 1921, 205; Catherine Allen, *A Century to Celebrate: History of the Women's Missionary Union* (Birmingham, AL: WMU, 1987), 308–9.
45   See Baker, *The Southern Baptist Convention and Its People*, 299–300; Estep *Whole Gospel Whole World*, 207.

burdens related to the financial challenges during these years, and they affected his health. He had traveled frequently and widely as the board's ambassador. In addition, he carried on an admirable writing ministry. One additional challenge on top of the expanding debt load came when it was discovered in April 1927 that George Sanders, the FMB's treasurer, had swindled more than $100,000. This painful defalcation by the board's treasurer had to be reported at the 1927 meeting of the SBC.[46]

During Love's tenure the number of missionaries increased from 298 to 489, with representation expanding from nine fields to fifteen. Income more than doubled from $679,699 to $1,455,801. The same was true for baptisms: 5,190 to 12,542. The number of churches tripled, from 382 to 1,275, and preaching points grew in a similar fashion, expanding from 819 to 12,542.

His commitments to Baptist distinctives and Christian orthodoxy served all of Southern Baptists well during this period. He cautiously raised wise and insightful concerns regarding the perils of the Interchurch World Movement and related programs, even as those in the Northern Baptist Convention were choosing to move in a more ecumenical direction. At the same time Love supported the encouraging networks developed through the Baptist World Alliance, participating in one of the most important Baptist conferences ever held, in London in 1920.[47] As E. C. Routh noted, Love constantly "urged loyalty to Baptist principles and policy," doing so until the stress and burdens of the financial situation brought his life to an end.[48] The 1928 *Annual of the Southern Baptist Convention* records the tribute to Love from the committee on the Foreign Mission Board Report: "He was crushed by burdens that

---

46   SBCA, 1927, 161.
47   See J. D. Hughey, "Europe and the Middle East," in Baker J. Cauthen, et al., *Advance: A History of Southern Baptist Foreign Missions* (Nashville: Broadman, 1970), 194–95; also, Baker J. Cauthen and F. K. Means, *Advance to Bold Mission Thrust* (Nashville: Broadman 1980); also see F. Townley Lord, *Baptist World Fellowship: A Short History of the Baptist World Alliance* (Nashville: Broadman, 1955), 37–42.
48   Routh, "Love, James Franklin," 809. Allen, in *A Century to Celebrate*, 130, claims that "stress over the debt killed J. F. Love."

we should never have permitted to rest upon him. Truly, his name is to be inscribed on the roll of martyrs of whom the world was not worthy."[49] The report continues,

> Through his prolific pen and public addresses, he sounded in the ears of Southern Baptists a clarion call to worldwide evangelization. By his wise counsel in conference on the fields in the Orient, South America, Europe, and the Near East, he brought reassurance and renewed devotion to the missionaries. His unwavering faithfulness to gospel truths increased loyalty to them wherever he went. His zeal for the spread of the gospel was so unflagging that he pressed on without stint of time and physical strength until he lay exhausted and prone in death. We are bereft over the loss of our loved brother and mighty leader. Indeed, there is a prince and great man fallen this day in Israel.[50]

Larger Denominational Context

Taking a step back from a focus on the FMB, one recognizes the importance of seeing the Love administration not only within the particular SBC context of the time but also in the larger implication of those years for the twentieth-first-century SBC. During the second and third decades of the twentieth century, Southern Baptist life took significant steps toward denominational identity, maturity, and cooperation—steps that reflected Love's encouragement and involvement.

Southern Baptists witnessed the establishment of the Executive Committee in 1917, which as much as anything moved Southern Baptists toward a convention model of operation. Before this time, the central feature of the SBC was its annual meeting, which brought together a loosely knit collection of churches who were committed to Baptist polity and the Great Commission. Southern Baptists prior

---

49   SBCA, 1928, 51.
50   SBCA, 1928, 142.

to this time resembled some of the characteristics often associated with independent Baptists or certainly those groups that favored a societal model of ministry support.[51]

In 1918, the Baptist Bible Institute, which became New Orleans Baptist Seminary, was birthed. As has been previously noted, in 1925, when Southern Baptists gathered for their annual meeting in Memphis, Tennessee, a hallmark convention witnessed the adoption of the Cooperative Program, recommended by a committee led by M. E. Dodd, as well as the adoption of the Baptist Faith and Message as the first official confessional statement of the Southern Baptist Convention.[52] In the background of that first confessional statement were swirling issues related to doctrinal concerns, particularly at institutions like Baylor, Wake Forest, Mercer, and Furman, as well as an awareness of the fundamentalist reductionism represented at the 1919 prophecy conference in Philadelphia. E. Y. Mullins and L. R. Scarborough basically attempted to triangulate a position rejecting the Poteat brothers, who served as presidents at Wake Forest and Furman, and their liberal leanings, and the influence of fundamentalism, on the one side, and W. B. Riley, on the other side. They also kept an eye on the liberalism gaining a foothold in Northern Baptist life at the time through the growing influence of Shailer Matthews and Walter Rauschenbusch.

Both the Cooperative Program and the new confessional statement were influenced by the Seventy-Five Million Campaign and the development of the FMB's statement of faith. The reality is that developments in and related to the Love administration were instrumental in all of these things. There was an interrelatedness and interconnectedness associated with all of these initiatives that must not be missed. Those familiar with Southern Baptist history during

---

51   See Brand and Hankins, *One Sacred Effort*, 93; McClellan, *The Executive Committee of the Southern Baptist Convention*, 53–70.

52   See David S. Dockery, "Who Are Southern Baptists? Toward an Intergenerational Identity," in *The SBC and the 21st Century*, ed. Jason K. Allen, rev. ed. (Nashville: B&H, 2019), 79–93; David S. Dockery, *Southern Baptist Consensus and Renewal* (Nashville: B&H Academic, 2008), 41; and Fletcher, *The Southern Baptist Convention*, 140–46.

this period often know well the names and contributions of J. B. Gambrell, George Truett, E. Y. Mullins, A. T. Robertson, L. R. Scarborough, W. T. Conner, M. E. Dodd, and others. But it is impossible to understand and interpret these significant years in Baptist life without recognizing the sizable influence of J. Franklin Love. It may well be easier to see this influence from the vantage point of the early decades of the twenty-first century than it would have been from the second and third decades of the twentieth century. Love did not have the charismatic personality of R. J. Willingham, but Love helped to establish the denominational pattern for Southern Baptists, steering them away from nondenominational, interdenominational, and ecumenical patterns being encouraged in other circles. Love's appeal for additional funding in 1919 served as a catalyst for the Seventy-Five Million Campaign, leading to the development of the Cooperative Program, which God has used to fuel what has become the most important mission-sending organization in the world.

Love's courage and conviction to develop a statement of faith helped Southern Baptists remain doctrinally faithful rather than following other significant voices at the time like W. O. Carver, the longtime professor at Southern Seminary, who would have preferred a nonconfessional approach, which would have pointed in a more theologically progressive and ecumenical perspective.[53]

---

53 These thoughts were amplified in the 2018 Norton Lectures delivered at The Southern Baptist Theological Seminary (March 2018). Carver opposed the adoption of the 1925 Baptist Faith and Message, suggesting that it was a step toward Baptist creedalism. See comments in Carver's reviews of *The Church of the Spirit*, by Francis Greenwood Peabody, and *Chaos and Creed*, by James Priceman in *Review and Expositor* 22 (Summer 1925): 368–73. On page 1 of Gary Dorrien's important work *The Making of American Liberal Theology*, he claims that "the essential idea of liberal theology is that all claims to truth, in theology as well as in other disciplines, must be made on the basis of reason and experience, not by an appeal to external authority." While W. O. Carver may not have been a self-identified theological liberal, by his own statements, he certainly demonstrated a great appreciation for an openness to liberal thinkers and their methodological appeal to reason and experience. Carver, who served as professor of missions and world religions at Southern Seminary for more than four decades, seemed to have a special fondness for popular liberal leaders like Shailer Matthews at the University of Chicago and Harry Emerson Fosdick. See his positive

Love's thoughtful and careful administrative style also helped to solidify comity agreements in cooperation with Northern, British, and Canadian Baptists regarding the work in Europe that had lasting significance.[54]

In spite of the overwhelming financial challenges, Love's contribution was immense, not just for the FMB but for the larger work of the Southern Baptist Convention. While the financial pressures during the Love administration were intense, those pressures were compounded over the next five years as the Great Depression cast a dark shadow over the entire country and the work of the Southern Baptist Convention. It is to those years that we will soon turn our attention. Before doing so, we need to note the importance of 1928 for Southern Baptists. Not only was it the year in which Love was called home to glory, but it was also the year that the earthly life and ministry of E. Y. Mullins came to a conclusion.

1928: The Loss of Leadership in Southern Baptist Life

Just as a huge hole was created in Southern Baptist life in 1914 with the deaths of B. H. Carroll, founding president of Southwestern Seminary, and the missionary movement's leader, R. J. Willingham, so also in 1928 Southern Baptists lost two giants: J. Franklin Love and E. Y. Mullins. Love's influence was great, but the vast reach of Mullins as denominational statesman, civic leader, seminary president, educator, theologian, pastor, scholar, and author is nearly impossible to grasp. There was hardly any aspect of Southern Baptist life that he did not touch, having served as president of both the Southern Baptist Convention and the Baptist World Alliance.

---

reviews of their works in *Review Expositor* 22 (Summer 1925): 253–61, which can be contrasted with his negative review of J. Gresham Machen's *Christianity and Liberalism* in *Review and Expositor* 21 (Fall 1924): 344–49.

54 Robert Nash notes the importance of the place of missionary efforts in Europe as key to understanding Love's missionary philosophy (note Love's work *The Appeal of the Baptist Program for Europe* [1920]). See Nash, "Love, James Franklin," 175. For a broader picture of Baptist work in Europe, see Albert W. Wardin, ed., *Baptists around the World: A Comprehensive Handbook* (Nashville: Broadman & Holman, 1995), 177–286. Also, Estep's comments in *Whole Gospel Whole World*, 210.

Mullins, who was born on January 5, 1860, received his education at Texas A & M University and The Southern Baptist Theological Seminary. Following pastorates in Maryland and Massachusetts,
Mullins was called in 1899 to serve as the fourth president and
professor of theology at Southern. Mullins represented a paradig-
matic shift in Southern Baptist theology. Nowhere is this better
illustrated than in his 1917 publication, *The Christian Religion in
Its Doctrinal Expression*. Not only was his book used as a major
textbook at Southern and Southwestern Seminaries for decades,
but Mullins also powerfully influenced W. T. Conner, who served
as professor of theology at Southwestern for thirty-nine years.
Mullins's emphasis on the role of experience and his work on the
relationship between science and Scripture introduced new ways
of exploring theology and biblical interpretation.

Mullins remained very much in the mainstream of conservative Baptist thought during his decades of leadership, while
nevertheless engaging wide intellectual interests and theological
formulations. The release of his final major publication, *Christianity
at the Crossroads* (1924), testified to his unwillingness to embrace
fully the findings and the trajectories of historical-critical studies
of Scripture. Mullins affirmed the dynamic inspiration and full authority of Scripture in a manner reflective of the Northern Baptist
theologian A. H. Strong.

The most important development in the thought of Mullins can
be found in his emphasis on experience, which he borrowed from
the best of Pietism as well as the work of F. D. E. Schleiermacher,
the father of modern liberal theology. Though Mullins shifted the
discussion regarding theological method, he nevertheless contended that the Bible is fully reliable and authoritative.[55] He restated, in

---

55   See David S. Dockery, *Christian Scripture: An Evangelical Perspective on Inspiration,
     Authority and Interpretation* (Nashville: Broadman & Holman, 1995), 194–96. One
     could wish that Mullins's view of Scripture more closely mirrored Basil Manly Jr.
     Still, we give thanks that he did not move in the direction of Shailer Matthews or
     H. Wheeler Robinson. For differences in approaches, please see James Leo Garrett
     Jr., *Baptist Theology: A Four-Century Study* (Macon, GA: Mercer University Press,
     2009), 258–63, 350–54, 415–33, 550–54.

different ways, traditional Baptist tenets. Such an ongoing commitment was evident in one of his most visible and important addresses, delivered in 1923, "The Duties and Dangers of this Present Hour."[56] Mullins's leadership for the work of the 1925 Baptist Faith and Message was key, which was true for his numerous other denominational roles. His unequivocal commitments to the nature and authority of Scripture, the virgin birth, the sinless miracle-working life of Christ, his vicarious atonement, his resurrection, ascension, and second coming helped to steer Southern Baptists away from the pitfalls of both modernism and fundamentalism. Because missionary concern is rooted in what people believe and in their ongoing Christian experience, the theological commitments expressed by Mullins, particularly in "The Duties and Dangers of the Present Hour" and *Christianity at the Crossroads*, were important. Biblical convictions are the soil in which mission work grows, particularly for "people of the Book" like Southern Baptists. When Mullins died on November 23, 1928, Carver claimed that he was "the best-known Baptist in the world.[57] Not only did Southern Baptists lose two stellar leaders in 1928, but the financial conditions across the country were moving toward days of desperation.

THE GREAT DEPRESSION:
THE AMERICAN CONTEXT 1920–1933

The decade leading up to the Great Depression gave the American people reasons for optimism. The Eighteenth Amendment, to outlaw the production, transport, and sale of alcohol, was ratified

---

56   See Dockery, *Southern Baptist Consensus and Renewal*, 180–82.
57   See David S. Dockery, "Mullins, E. Y. (1860–1928)," in *The Encyclopedia of Christian Civilization*, ed. George Thomas Kurian (Malden, MA: Wiley-Blackwell, 2011), 3:1591–92; William E. Ellis, *"A Man of Books and a Man of the People": E. Y. Mullins and the Crisis of Moderate Southern Baptists Leadership*. (Macon, GA: Mercer University Press, 1985); Fisher Humphreys, "E. Y. Mullins," George and Dockery, *Baptist Theologians*, 330–50; David W. Bebbington, *Baptists through the Centuries: A History of a Global People* (Waco, TX: Baylor University Press, 2010), 258–60.

on January 16, 1919, after being adopted by thirty-six states.[58] The Nineteenth Amendment, giving women the right to vote, was ratified on August 18, 1919.[59] Warren G. Harding served as president of the United States from 1921 until his unexpected death in 1923.[60] Calvin Coolidge became the thirtieth president of the United States in 1923.[61] Herbert Hoover was elected as president in 1928.[62] A mere eight months after he took office, however, the stock market crashed and sent America into a spiraling depression.[63]

Economic challenges had existed across portions of the South throughout the decade of the 1920s. A nationwide financial downturn began in September of 1929, a day that became known as Black Tuesday. The worldwide gross domestic product fell by 15 percent between 1929 and 1932, bringing about the deepest, longest, and most widespread economic crisis of the twentieth century.[64] The impact on Southern Baptist life and Southern Baptist missions was devastating. Combined with the loss of stalwart leaders like Love and Mullins (as well as J. B. Gambrell [1921] and E. C. Dargan [1922] earlier in the decade), the years from 1928 to 1933 seemed almost overwhelming from a human perspective. In this context, the FMB reluctantly selected T. Bronson Ray as their next leader, but not without a complex, confusing, and circuitous search process.

---

58   Baptists of various stripes agreed that their consensus support for Prohibition was more important than concerns over evolution or any other contemporary issue of the time. See Ellis, "A Man of Books and a Man of the People," 209–15. The WMU joined these important efforts that shaped the ethos of Southern Baptists life for many decades thereafter. See Allen, A Century to Celebrate, 235–39.

59   Allen, A Century to Celebrate, 236–37.

60   See John W. Dean, Warren G. Harding (New York: Henry Holt, 2004).

61   See David Greenberg, Calvin Coolidge (New York: Henry Holt, 2006); Amity Shlaes, Coolidge (New York: Harper, 2013).

62   See William E. Leuchtenburg, Herbert Hoover (New York: Henry Holt, 2009).

63   See Amity Shlaes, The Forgotten Man: A New History of the Great Depression (New York: Harper, 2007); Jay Sexton, A Nation Forged by Crisis: A New American History (New York: Basic Books, 2018), 144–50. For a broader look at these matters within a global context, see Paul Johnson, Modern Times: The World from the Twenties to the Nineties (New York: Harper Perennial, 1991).

64   Shlaes, The Forgotten Man, 144–50.

T. BRONSON RAY AND THE FOREIGN MISSION BOARD (1928–1933)

T. Bronson Ray (1868–1934) grew up in Kentucky and received his education in the state. A graduate of Georgetown College and Southern Seminary, Ray was blessed with godly parents who had a heart for missions and missionaries. He served as pastor of the Immanuel Baptist Church in Nashville from 1898 to 1906. His influence was expanded in Tennessee with his service on the Baptist Sunday School Board and the Tennessee Baptist Board of Missions. Following eight years of pastoral ministry, Ray was invited in 1906 to serve as the first educational secretary for the FMB. In addition to the formative years in his home, Ray's keen interest in missions had been encouraged by his active involvement in the student volunteer movement during both his college and seminary years.

Energetic and creative, Ray envisioned a strategic role for mission study books. He served as editor and compiler of several books, including *Southern Baptist Foreign Missions*, *Only a Missionary*, *Brazilian Sketches*, *Southern Baptists in the Great Adventure*, and *The Highway of Mission Thought*. After one year he reported that eighty-four missions study classes had been formed.[65] By 1908, the number had increased to 517. His responsibilities also included editing the *Foreign Missions Journal*.

Ray served faithfully during the Willingham years, wearing multiple hats. He enthusiastically and successfully led Southern Baptists to reach their goal of $1,250,000 for the Judson centennial in 1912. In 1914, he was asked to serve as the FMB's foreign secretary; he was initially one of the three secretaries sharing leadership responsibilities with J. F. Love and W. H. Smith, following the death of Willingham. He continued to serve as foreign secretary throughout the years in which Love served as the FMB's leader until he was

---

65 See E. C. Routh, "Ray, T. Bronson," *Encyclopedia of Southern Baptists*, 2:1134; Estep, *Whole Gospel Whole World*, 210–12.

appointed associate secretary in 1927.[66] Upon the death of Love, who had been given the title of executive secretary prior to his death, Ray was invited to function as executive secretary, though he was not given the title while the board initiated a search for Love's successor, a search that was lengthy, frustrating, and dysfunctional.[67]

Estep chronicles well the years of 1928 and 1929, capturing the unexpected twists and turns of the search process. A committee was appointed to make a recommendation at the July 14–15 meeting in 1928 regarding the executive secretary role. Most expected the committee to look in Ray's direction. Instead, the committee asked for more time. In October, the committee approached S. B. Cousins, pastor of the Second Baptist Church in Richmond. Though he received a unanimous vote from the board, Cousins declined to serve.

The committee then successively turned to George Truett, J. B. Weatherspoon (faculty member at Southern Seminary), and J. W. McGlothlin (president at Furman). All three declined the invitation. The committee then went back once again to Cousins, Truett, and McGlothlin. As they had done previously, all three declined. Somewhat reluctantly, the board finally turned to Ray, inviting him on October 2, 1929, to serve as the executive secretary of the FMB. Sensing it was the Lord's will for him to serve in the role in which he had served as interim for seventeen months, he accepted the invitation. Less than four weeks later the stock market crashed.[68] In so many ways, Ray's brief tenure as the leader of the FMB is best understood as an addendum to the Love years, providing a sense of continuity for the FMB that connected the current work to both Willingham and Love.[69]

---

66   Routh, "Ray, T. Bronson," 1134; Estep, *Whole Gospel Whole World*, 210–12.

67   Estep, *Whole Gospel Whole World*, 211.

68   Estep, *Whole Gospel Whole World*, 211–12.

69   We need to remind ourselves that T. B. Ray was one of the four people, along with R. H. Pitt, W. H. Smith, and J. F. Love, to coauthor the moving tribute for R. J. Willingham at the time of his death in 1914. See Elizabeth Walton Willingham, *Life of Robert Josiah Willingham* (Nashville: Baptist Sunday School Board, 1917), 274–77. Ray served faithfully with the FMB for more than a quarter of a century with his time connecting the Willingham and Love years. Still, there is no mention of his name or

The Great Depression crippled the Southern economy. The FMB and other denominational ministries struggled until after World War II. Nearly one-fourth of the nation's banks closed. Similar reports came from business and industry. Farmers were forced to sell their farms, for they could find no markets for their produce. People were out of work; many lost their homes and their savings. It was an incredibly difficult time for churches across Southern Baptist life. Budgets were cut in half. Some estimated that more than one-fourth of church members were unemployed. Buildings received no upkeep, and pastors often served without compensation. Yet the people of God remained hopeful, trusting in the faithfulness of God and the good news of the gospel. Were it not for the heroic, determined, and sacrificial efforts of the WMU during these years, the FMB might not have survived.[70] Even with their well-founded hope, it was challenging for the churches, church leaders, the entities of the convention, and especially the FMB not to slide into a state of spiritual depression as well.[71] People were preoccupied with navigating ways to survive from week to week, causing their focus to turn inward rather than outward to the nations, which was reflected in the decline of gifts to the Lottie Moon offering.[72]

The revenue coming into the FMB for operations reached a ten-year low in 1929, and it continued to decline with each successive year from 1930 to 1933, reaching a low point in 1933 of $605,575, of which $65,000 was already designated for debt services.[73] Restructuring could not take place quickly enough to keep pace with the financial declines. Missionaries on the field were unable to get

---

his service in either Leonard's *Dictionary of Baptists in America* or William Brackney's *Historical Dictionary of the Baptists,* 2nd ed. (Lanham, MD: Scarecrow, 2009).

70   See Allen, *A Century to Celebrate,* 130–56; McClellan, *The Executive Committee of the Southern Baptist Convention,* 111–12; Crawley, *Global Mission,* 32.

71   See Robert T. Handy, "The American Religious Depression, 1925–1935," *Church History* 291 (March 1960): 3–16.

72   See Robert J. Hastings, *A Nickel's Worth of Skim Milk* (Carbondale, IL: Southern Illinois University Press, 1972), for a moving account of how one faithful Southern Baptist family struggled to survive those dreadful years.

73   See Estep, *Whole Gospel Whole World,* 213.

home, and missionary candidates could not be sent. Dozens of missionaries resigned, and few were appointed.[74] Concerns regarding Ray's leadership during this time of financial crisis were raised. As Eugene L. Hill observes, the FMB on March 13, 1930, six months after Ray's official appointment, elected E. Eugene Sallee, longtime missionary to China, to serve as home secretary in order to garner some much-needed assistance. Due to a serious heart attack that took him home to be with the Lord, Sallee only served one year.[75] Executive Secretary Ray had the difficult duty during these dark days to come to the Southern Baptist Convention each year and report the declining revenue, missionary losses, and administrative challenges.

Facing what appeared to be hopeless days, the board gathered again in October of 1931 to consider a change in leadership. It was obvious even in October of 1929 that Ray did not have the full confidence of the board. At this meeting the board reassigned Ray to the role of foreign secretary and declared a search for a new executive secretary. After one person had declined the invitation from the board, Charles E. Maddry, at the age of fifty-six, who had ample pastoral and denominational experience, and who had served as the executive secretary for the North Carolina Baptist Convention for more than a decade, was elected to serve as the next executive secretary of the FMB on October 1, 1932. Maddry's leadership will be the focus of the next chapter. Ray, who had reached the age of sixty-five, was named assistant executive secretary before being asked to retire in October of 1933. He died on January 15, 1934, less than three months after his involuntary retirement. At his retirement, to thank him for twenty-seven years of loyal service to the FMB, Ray was given the title of emeritus secretary, bringing to a conclusion one of the saddest chapters in the history of Southern Baptist missions.[76]

Solon B. Cousins provided an appropriate tribute, recognizing Ray's leadership for the Judson centennial, the launch of the mission

---

74   Estep, *Whole Gospel Whole World*, 213–16.
75   See Eugene L. Hill, "Administering Southern Baptist Foreign Missions," in Cauthen, et al., *Advance*, 25–76.
76   Hill, "Administering Southern Baptist Foreign Missions," 37–38.

study classes, the creation of additional important missions literature to connect the churches to work of global missions, and his faithful service to the FMB for more than a quarter of a century. In conclusion, Cousins noted,

> [Whether] one thinks of the books he wrote, or the campaign he directed, or the plans he inaugurated; whether one recalls his work as educational secretary, foreign secretary, associate secretary or executive secretary, one fact stands out transcendently above all that he did, and that was his devotion to Foreign Missions. To that cause he dedicated his life and in its service he died content. It was in keeping with the ruling purpose of his life that his last service should have been completion of a book telling the history of Southern Baptist Foreign Missions.[77]

In the introduction to the final volume on missions, W. O. Carver penned these words: "Through his twenty-seven years of service, Dr. T. B. Ray contributed to the missionary work of Southern Baptist in ways and in measure which could be known only to those who were intimately associated with the administration of the Board, and only by those who knew well enough the history and science of missions to enable them to appraise Dr. Ray's work."[78] While it was not possible to initiate work in any new countries or to start any new programs during Ray's years as executive secretary, his constancy, dependability, and loyalty to the work of Southern Baptist missions was commendable in almost every way. He served faithfully, wrote widely, and traveled to visit Southern Baptist missionaries in Europe, Brazil, Chile, Argentina, Mexico, Japan, and China during his many years of service with the FMB.[79]

---

77 SBCA, 1934, 160.
78 W. O. Carver, introduction to *Southern Baptists in the Great Adventure*, ed. T. B. Ray (Nashville: Baptist Sunday School Board, 1934), 6.
79 Routh, "Ray, T. Bronson," 1134.

FINAL REFLECTIONS

In 1792, William Carey, the British cobbler, exhorted a gathering of London ministers to "expect great things from God, and attempt great things for God." The Baptist Missionary Society was thereafter soon launched, setting into motion the modern missionary movement, which paved the way for thousands of missionaries to take the good news of Jesus Christ to the far corners of the earth. The various chapters in this book chronicle the story of Southern Baptist efforts to extend that work of making disciples of all the nations, which the SBC has attempted to do since its founding in 1845. This particular chapter in this unfolding story has focused on the work of Southern Baptist missions from 1915 to 1933, basically from World War I through the years of the Great Depression. These years were filled with initial hopefulness followed by much disappointment. The FMB made plans to extend its reach and expand its work following the victorious announcement in 1920 that pledges for the Seventy-Five Million Campaign had exceeded the goal by more than $17 million, only to watch the work of the board decline a dozen years later during the dark and downward days of the Great Depression. This chapter has chronicled these days by highlighting the events, actions, and decisions related to the leadership of J. Franklin Love (1915–1928) and T. Bronson Ray (1928–1933). The work of Southern Baptist missions has not taken place, and does not take place, in a vacuum; thus the extended commentary of related events during these years was necessary.

Stephen Neill has insightfully observed,

> Again and again in our survey we have seen Christianity not to be a European religion. But on the whole its attempts were far from successful. Whether we like it or not, it is the historic fact that the great expansion of Christianity coincided in time with the world-wide and explosive expansion of Europe that followed on the Renaissance; that the colonizing powers were the Christian

powers; that a whole variety of compromising relationships existed between missionaries and governments; and that in the main Christianity was carried forward on the wave of Western prestige and power.[80]

The World Missionary Conference at Edinburgh in 1910 was designed to turn the trajectory outward from Europe to the Majority World.[81] Following the events of World War I, however, as we have seen, Love once again prioritized SBC mission efforts in Europe, even while expanding the work in South America, the Middle East, and Asia.

Christianity in the early twentieth century, in both Europe and North America, faced a rapidly advancing liberalism, ecumenism, and secular ideologies that threatened to undermine its witness and integrity. Theologians and missiologists wrestled with the influence of Enlightenment and post-Enlightenment thought, which challenged the very heart of the Christian message, raising questions regarding biblical authority, Christian tradition, and the uniqueness of the gospel. Liberalism no longer understood Christianity as "the faith . . . once for all delivered to the saints" (Jude 3 ESV), but rather as our feelings about our dependence on God. Some spoke of the gospel as merely the highest point until now while others opined about the relative absoluteness of Christianity.[82]

These matters hit close to home for Southern Baptists during this period. American Christianity, particularly in the North, was engaged in a bitter fight over the truthfulness of Scripture and the meaning of the gospel. J. Franklin Love wisely led the FMB to adopt a statement of faith to solidify the Christian and Baptist convictions expected of Southern Baptist missionaries. Love recognized the need to push back against any understanding of universalism that asserted that all people will be saved irrespective of whether they hear and believe the gospel of Christ. As appealing as this proposal

---

80   Stephen Neill, *A History of Christian Missions*, 2nd ed. (London: Penguin, 1986), 414.
81   Neill, *A History of Christian Missions*, 415–17.
82   See Kirk R. MacGregor, *Contemporary Theology: An Introduction: Classical, Evangelical, Philosophical, and Global Perspectives* (Grand Rapids: Zondervan, 2019), 23–33.

may sound, it must be recognized that universalism dramatically undercuts the Christian message and the Christian mission. In many ways, this was the most important achievement at the FMB during this period.[83] The second was clearly the funding issues that paved the way for the development of the Cooperative Program, and the third may well have been the importance and encouragement given to the student movement.[84]

As Southern Baptists attempted to be faithful to the Christian mission and the Christian message, especially during the years of financial struggle, the unsung heroes could be found in the WMU. Estep notes that "the Women's Missionary Union became increasingly valuable to the Board in both the dissemination of missionary information and in raising funds for projects of the Board."[85] While many women championed the cause of missions across the SBC in the early decades of the twentieth century, no one did more to advance the mission cause than Fannie E. S. Heck, who served as

---

83   This effort was especially important given the implications of the thought of W. O. Carver, the leading missions thinker among Southern Baptists during the initial decades of the twentieth century. See Gregory A. Wills, *Southern Baptist Theological Seminary, 1859–2009)* (Oxford: Oxford University Press, 2009), 256–68. J. F. Love's timely work *The Union Movement* (1918) was pivotal. Here he proposed the importance of affirming a spirit of unity with all who acknowledge Christ as Savior and Lord while declining to cooperate with those who would compromise the essentials of the Christian faith. In doing so he sought to balance truth and love, theological conviction and personal grace, commitment and cooperation. In Love's words, "We need neither to throw away our convictions and personal courtesy nor our courtesy in order to be frank." For a recognition of the vital importance between theology and missions, see Timothy C. Tennent, *World Missions: A Trinitarian Missiology for the Twenty-First Century* (Grand Rapids: Kregel, 2010), and Harvey Conn, "Theological Systems," in the *Evangelical Dictionary of World Missions,* ed. Scott Moreau (Grand Rapids: Baker Academic, 2000), 947–49. For a further understanding of universalism, please see Michal J. McClymond, *The Devil's Redemption: A New History and Interpretation of Christian Universalism,* 2 vols. (Grand Rapids: Baker Academic, 2018). Also see the helpful contribution of Robin Hadaway, *A Survey of World Missions* (Nashville: B&H, 2020), 35–58.

84   See Estep, *Whole Gospel Whole World,* 206–7; also see J. Herbert Kane, *A Concise History of the Christian World Movement: A Panoramic View of Missions from Pentecost to the Present,* rev. ed. (Grand Rapids: Baker, 1982), 105, for a larger look at the student movement beyond the SBC.

85   Estep, *Whole Gospel Whole World,* 194–96.

president of the national WMU for fourteen years in addition to her service as president of the North Carolina WMU for nearly three decades. Without the ongoing support from the WMU, the financial issues at the FMB would have been even greater. In response to an appeal to the WMU in 1916, Love described the meeting as "the holiest hour we ever saw."[86] In the early 1930s, with the FMB sinking deeper and deeper during the Great Depression, the FMB declared that they would not have survived the summer of 1932 without the help of the WMU. The WMU labored responsibly and responsively to provide hope and encouragement for the work of Southern Baptist missions during those desperately dark days.[87]

Thanks to God's faithful provision and enabling providence, the FMB survived the daunting years of the Great Depression. The hopefulness a decade earlier had now turned to disappointment. Plans for expansion were put on hold during this time of decline and retrenchment. Love and Ray gave their best efforts, serving gallantly, giving their very lives for the cause in which they both so greatly believed.

During this period in 1925, a young man in Knoxville, Tennessee, made an unflinching commitment to full-time missionary service. Bill Wallace would become Southern Baptists' best-known medical missionary for his extraordinary labors in China, so much so that the story of "Bill Wallace of China" became a favorite to convey to boys and girls, as well as men and women, across Southern Baptist life for decades thereafter.[88] In 1921, one of the forty-seven candidates appointed for mission service with the FMB was a gifted young man who had just completed his preparation at Southern Seminary. Theron Rankin,[89] who was also appointed to China, would later be selected to provide leadership as the executive secretary of the FMB from 1945 to 1953. Eloise Glass, the daughter of missionaries to

---

86 Allen, *A Century to Celebrate*, 129–30.
87 Allen, *A Century to Celebrate*, 129–34.
88 See Jessie C. Fletcher, *Bill Wallace of China* (Nashville: Broadman, 1963).
89 See J. B. Weatherspoon, *M. Theron Rankin: Apostle of Advance* (Nashville: Broadman, 1958).

China, enrolled at Baylor University in 1927. She met another Baylor student named Baker James Cauthen in 1929. Following their days at Baylor, they attended Southwestern Seminary. Eloise had previously made a commitment to serve Christ as a missionary to China. As her friendship with Baker grew closer, she began to wonder if God might call him to mission service as well. Soon they were married by their professor, W. T. Conner, one of the two shaping theologians in Baptist life, along with E. Y. Mullins, during the first half of the twentieth century. Baker James Cauthen initially taught missions at Southwestern Seminary and then became secretary for Asia in 1946, before being elected to serve as the executive secretary for the FMB in 1954. Cauthen would serve with excellence as the visionary leader and as the SBC's "man for all nations" until 1979.[90] During his many years of leadership, the number of Southern Baptist missionaries increased from nine hundred to three thousand, and the number of countries in which Southern Baptists had representation expanded from thirty-two to ninety-five.

These are just three examples of missionary leaders who were remarkably influential in Southern Baptist life in the decades following the challenging years in the 1920s and 1930s. Clearly God was at work during these years, even the dark and disappointing ones, preparing a new generation through the excitement of the student movement and the faithful seeds sown by J. Franklin Love, T. Bronson Ray, W. H. Smith, W. Eugene Sallee, Fannie Heck, Minnie Kennedy James, Ethlene Boone Cox, and dozens of others. Indeed, the Lord used many during this time to prepare a new generation for "the furtherance of the gospel" "into all the world."[91]

---

90   Jesse C. Fletcher, *Baker James Cauthen: A Man for All Nations* (Nashville: Broadman, 1977).

91   See John D. Freeman, *Into All the World* (Nashville: Baptist Sunday School Board, 1935) and W. O. Carver, *The Furtherance of the Gospel* (Nashville: Baptist Sunday School Board, 1935). As can be seen from the footnotes, I have depended on a number of sources to write this chapter, none more so than William Estep's superb history of the FMB. I have found no better resource than *Whole Gospel Whole World*, especially for the years of 1915–1933. At many points my work follows closely Estep's account and interpretation of these important and challenging years.

WAR AND WITNESS

Southern Baptist Missions during the
Administration of Charles Maddry,
1933–1944

John Massey

W. **O. CARVER, FREQUENT CONTRIBUTOR** to *The Commission* and professor of world missions at The Southern Baptist Theological Seminary, observed in 1939, "No one needs to be told that the work of missions was conducted in a world of confusion and conflict. Both in the fields of operation and in the fields of support, the minds of men were largely occupied and preoccupied with affairs of politics, economics, industrial strife and in open warfare. . . . Truly it was not a world in which the progress of the Gospel could be taken for granted."[1] Charles Maddry led the FMB during a time of global conflict as described by Carver. He led Southern Baptists to remain faithful to the gospel in its missions endeavors at a time of world war and many global crises. He guided the FMB at a time of financial crisis to alleviate the organization's crippling debt burden. He also reorganized the missions agency according to business principles that would set the stage for Southern Baptists' greatest eras of global engagement, which came in subsequent administrations. Maddry's early life experiences, conversion and call to ministry, pastoral and denominational assignments, and education all played important roles in helping him survive and thrive in his time of leadership of the FMB as executive secretary.

Personal Life and Ministry of Charles Maddry

Charles Maddry (1876–1962) served as executive secretary of the FMB from 1933 to 1944. He was born the third of nine children (five girls and four boys) in a three-room log cabin on a North Carolina farm in Hillsboro on April 10, 1876, to William Alexander Maddry and Julia R. Sugg Maddry. In his autobiography Maddry describes an idyllic childhood that centered on working the family farm and attending the local school. At the age of eighteen Maddry decided to give up his studies and pursue the path of a subsistence farmer until a new teacher, J. P. Canaday, arrived in town and persuaded him to continue his studies. In his autobiography Maddry recollected, "I realize now, after sixty-years, that this seemingly casual meeting with a stranger on that winter morning was a crucial moment of my life. I was to discover that the six weeks spent under his instruction would mean more to me than all I had received in the haphazard years of school I had attended since I was five years of age."[2] Canaday recommended Maddry for entry into an exclusive

---

1   W. O. Carver, "Kingdom Facts and Factors," *TC* 2, no. 1 (March 1939): 70.
2   Charles E. Maddry, *An Autobiography* (Nashville: Broadman, 1955), 17.

preparatory school in Chapel Hill that would enable him later to attend the University of North Carolina. He remembered his time at the preparatory school:

> I walked three miles to the village every day, leaving my home about sunup or earlier, and cut wood until the bell rang for school at 9:00 o'clock. In the afternoon from 4:00 until 6:00 I cut wood again and then walked three miles to my home. I was a grown man, long and lank. I entered classes with boys and girls who were twelve and fourteen years of age. The first year I took subjects such as grammar, arithmetic, North Carolina History, United States History, physiology, and physics, often sitting up until midnight studying by the dim light of an oil lamp. My mother prepared my lunch of whatever happened to be at hand, and sometimes it was very poor and skimpy. I felt awkward and greatly humiliated to have to go into the classes of small boys and girls and start at the very bottom.[3]

He credited the teacher of the preparatory school, Sally Mae Wilson, with helping him succeed in his studies and improve his social graces. Maddry excelled at the university, especially in oratory, winning the Magnum Medal for Oratory in a prestigious speech contest held at the university.[4]

The saving light of Christ dawned on Maddry at eleven years of age, and a call to ministry later came in his teenage years. He recalled, "When I started to high school in the fall of 1896, the old longing to be a preacher came over afresh, but I kept the matter locked in my own heart and never breathed to anyone the turmoil and unrest of my soul over the momentous question of my life's calling and responsibility."[4] After receiving a bachelor's degree in philosophy from the University of North Carolina, Maddry

---

3   Maddry, *An Autobiography*, 19.
4   Maddry, *An Autobiography*, 27–28.

attended and completed his seminary studies at the only Southern
Baptist seminary at the time, The Southern Baptist Theological
Seminary in Louisville, Kentucky. Shortly thereafter, he married
Emma Parker, the first cousin-in-law of the well-known North
Carolina pastor Hight C. Moore, and started a family.[5]

Maddry served a number of churches as pastor in North Carolina. He went further afield in 1916 to become the pastor of the
University Baptist Church of Austin, Texas. Here he would expand
his contacts with Texas Baptists, including the popular Texas pastor
and Baptist statesman, J. B. Gambrell. More importantly, according
to Maddry's recollection, the move to the challenging Texas pastorate was one more step toward fulfilling his worldwide mission
aspirations. He recounted, "Through all the years, the growing
passion for world missions had dominated my life. In this move to
a new fellowship, I felt that God was leading me into greater open
doors for world service."[6]

Maddry's upbringing, education, pastoral experience, commitment to the cooperative work of Baptists, and denominational
service would uniquely prepare him to serve as the executive
secretary of the FMB. In late 1920, in his absence and without
his knowledge, the state convention of North Carolina Baptists
elected Charles Maddry on the first ballot to be the next secretary of the North Carolina State Baptist Convention. He served
as secretary during a decade when Southern Baptists launched
the Seventy-Five Million Campaign, celebrated a centennial of
Baptist work, and formed the Cooperative Program. The 1920s
were years of prosperity that expanded Baptist work, but the
decade also ended with the financial panic of the great stock
market crash of 1929. Once again Maddry credited his call to
world missions as the driving motive for accepting the position of convention secretary. He stated, "The one dominating
motive that had influenced my decision to accept the call of

---

5   Maddry, *An Autobiography*, 34.
6   Maddry, *An Autobiography*, 54.

North Carolina Baptists to come home and lead the missionary forces as general secretary of the convention at the close of 1920, was the missionary motive."[7]

Maddry's gifts as a denominational statesman and administrator did not go unrecognized by the SBC Executive Committee. On August 1, 1932, he began work in Nashville as the executive secretary of the Promotional Committee of the Southern Baptist Convention. His role was to promote the Cooperative Program among all Southern Baptists.[8] While serving the Executive Committee of the SBC, Maddry received a call informing him that he had been elected to serve as the next executive secretary of the FMB. Maddry was fifty-six years old. T. B. Ray had stepped down after just four years of service, and Charles Maddry began what would become a twelve-year tenure as executive secretary, beginning on January 2, 1933.[9] The progress of Southern Baptist missions under Maddry's tenure was marked by a denomination's commitment to bear witness to the gospel in spite of challenges to the advance of the gospel.

Global Challenges

Charles Maddry directed the work of the FMB from 1933 to 1944 as executive secretary during a time of global conflict, grinding poverty, and uncertainty. His administration spanned approximately the same amount of time as the presidency of Franklin D. Roosevelt. World War I had already devastated Europe, and the world was again on the brink of war. The Second Sino-Japanese War, of 1937 to 1945, was underway and threatened to destroy FMB work in China (and Japan), which other than Brazil represented the largest commitment of Southern Baptist mission resources at the time. Japanese forces occupied China for a time during the war, and some FMB missionaries were interned in Japanese prison

---

7 Maddry, *An Autobiography*, 67.
8 Maddry, *An Autobiography*, 69–70.
9 Maddry, *An Autobiography*, 72–73.

camps, including M. Theron Rankin, who would succeed Maddry as executive secretary of the FMB.

The Maddry administration also saw the rise of Adolf Hitler to political power in Germany, setting the stage for World War II. Maddry noted in his autobiography that during his visit to Berlin to attend the Baptist World Alliance, "President Hindenburg died, and Hitler came to power."[10] The editors of *The Commission* wrote in 1938 that "the rape of Austria by Hitler for sheer brutality and the utter disregard of all elemental and moral human rights, surpass in savage and ruthless abandon anything ever perpetrated by the Huns of nearly two thousand years ago. The guaranteed rights of racial, political, and religious minorities in Germany are totally disregarded."[11]

The Bolshevik Revolution in Russia had long since led to the suppression of evangelical Christian witness in Russia and the prevention of FMB access by the time of the Maddry administration. The editors of *The Commission* noted in 1938, "One of the supreme tragedies of Christian history, drawn out now through two decades of unspeakable madness and persecution, is the effort of the ruling despots in Russia to crush out all religion from the life of the people."[12] The FMB was aggressively making efforts to position mission stations near Russia for the day that Russia would once again be open to missionary work.

As executive secretary of the FMB, Maddry witnessed the bombing of Pearl Harbor on December 7, 1941, the "day that will live in infamy," while visiting FMB mission stations in Hawaii. Japan had already destroyed much of the FMB work in China and had now declared war on the United States. Maddry devoted an entire chapter in his autobiography to his experience as an eyewitness. Maddry recalled, "After hearing explosions I hastily made my way down two flights of steps leading to the hotel lobby. At the foot of

---

10   Maddry, *An Autobiography*, 87.
11   Editors, "Germany Has Learned Nothing," *TC* 1, no. 4 (July 1938): 155.
12   Editors, "Editorial Varieties," *TC* 1, no. 4 (July 1938): 156.

the stairs, I met the hotel manager. He was wringing his hands in an agony of hysteria, and calling out in a voice choked with sobs, 'Vacate your rooms at once. Come down to the ground floor. The hotel may be struck any minute. It's the real thing. It's the real thing.'"[13]

In addition to war, the Great Depression had begun in certain parts of the world in 1929 with the great stock market crash in the US and was making its devastating presence felt in America at the beginning of the Maddry administration. The Great Depression followed a time of relative prosperity for all Americans that led to a period of growth for Southern Baptists. The FMB, however, now faced crushing debt at the beginning of Maddry's administration. In these dire circumstances, Maddry provided stable and wise leadership that led to a significant reduction of missions debt and an organizational consolidation; this in turn led to the great eras of FMB expansion under the next two executive secretaries—M. Theron Rankin and Baker James Cauthen, respectively.

Budgetary Challenges
Jesse Ford, executive assistant, FMB, noted in 1939, well into the Maddry administration,

> The determining of the Foreign Mission Board's budget is a heart-breaking task. It is not the weeks of actual work that distress us, but the constant pull at our hearts as item after item has to be omitted in order to bring the budget within the limits prescribed by the Southern Baptist Convention. And what are those limits? The receipts of the previous year.
>
> As we went over the requests from the fields for 1940, everything except bare necessities was omitted. No advancement in the work; no additional help for over-burdened missionaries; not sufficient traveling funds to carry the missionaries into needy places. Just the most

---

13   Maddry, *An Autobiography*, 129.

acute needs and nothing more. Many such appeals as the following have had to be laid aside with aching hearts.[14]

At the beginning of his tenure as executive secretary, Maddry inherited budget cuts mandated by the SBC at its annual gathering in May 1932. The FMB report to the SBC in 1932 included these words: "Our debt is an awful burden. Southern Baptists, at the earliest date possible and in addition to what can be done out of our regular receipts, must put forth special effort to pay it off."[15] The SBC gave clear instructions to the FMB regarding its precarious financial situation to which the FMB responded in its meeting on February 9, 1933: "The Foreign Mission Board acting under clear and definite instructions given by the last session of the Convention, that the budget for 1933 must be made on the basis of only 88% of the cash receipts for Foreign Missions in the year 1932, was compelled to make severe and drastic reductions in the appropriations to all the mission fields."[16] The FMB retained thirty missionaries home on furlough because they did not have the money to send them back to the field. The FMB instructed those missionaries to find employment immediately as their support would end on December 31, 1933.[17] The *SBC Annual* struck optimistic notes despite the impact of the economic downturn: "The distressing decline in our receipts during the last two years has been discouraging, but this discouragement is dispelled quickly when we view the things done abroad. We may have a depression here in the homeland, but there comes to us evermore great expansion of heart with renewed determination to press forward when we hear of the marvelous triumphs of our work in other lands. Our missions are prospering wonderfully."[18]

At the beginning of the Maddry administration, in 1933 four Richmond banks held a note of more than $1 million.

---

14   Jesse Ford, "Cutting the Budget," *TC* 2, no. 12 (December 1939): 416.
15   SBCA, 1932, 156.
16   FMBM, February 9, 1933.
17   FMBM, January 12, 1933.
18   SBCA, 1932, 157.

Representatives from each of the banks called a meeting with the new executive secretary and president of the board to renegotiate the loan. The FMB budget for that year totaled $600,000. The bank asked for the $67,000 in interest on the loan and an additional $150,000 on the principal. The request of the bankers was met with shock and dismay. Had the banks persisted, Maddry informed them, the FMB would be put out of business. He said it would be tantamount to killing the goose that laid the golden egg. Maddry assured the bankers that Southern Baptists would rise to the occasion and pay the debts as it had done in the past. His assurance was enough for the bankers, who then requested that only the interest due on the loan be paid. Over two years the FMB had paid an additional $250,000 on the principal, owing in large part to the sale of a property in Rome that had almost doubled in value from the original purchase price with its sale to an insurance company. Mussolini nationalized this property within six months of the sale.[19]

In its 1943 report to the SBC, the FMB declared,

> One year ago we owed the banks of Richmond $114,500.00. On March 12, 1943, we paid the last cent of this indebtedness. On January 1, 1933, we owed four banks in Richmond the enormous sum of $1,110,000.00. We found, on our visits to the mission fields, that there were debts on the schools, colleges, publishing houses, seminaries, chapels, and missionary homes for which the Foreign Mission Board was liable, totaling $249,750.00. In ten years we have paid out in interest on money borrowed $265,893.56. The total paid out for debt service during these ten years is $1,625,643.56. Thanks be unto God who has made it possible for us to redeem the work of the Foreign Mission Board from the withering blight of debt. With God's help and the generous and sympathetic co-operation of Southern

---

19 Maddry, *An Autobiography*, 73–75.

Baptists we purpose to live within our income and stay out of debt![20]

In his final report to the FMB, Maddry claimed, "The Board has been freed of the crushing weight of debt that had greatly hindered and retarded the work for almost a generation. The endowment of the Board has increased in a most gratifying way."[21]

The Ecumenical Movement and Southern Baptist Missions

The Protestant missionary movement that began in the eighteenth century had created the phenomenon of world Christianity. The Edinburgh conference of 1910 recognized the shift from mission fields to the establishment of global Christian communities. Representatives from the global church were better represented in subsequent ecumenical meetings, which gave a visual display of the growth of global Christianity. Edinburgh gave birth to the ecumenical movement that led to the formation of the World Council of Churches, a global expression of what would later represent the more liberal theological side of confessing Christianity.

The reality of world Christianity immediately began to press the question as to how mission organizations were to conduct their work now that there were national partners to share the work of missions. Another set of questions also began to arise out of this setting of world Christianity: Should the new global Christian movement create unity in organization and doctrine in order to express a desired oneness in life, work, and witness? How should Southern Baptists fit into this emerging ecumenicity that increasingly represented more liberal theological beliefs and values, reflecting the theological shifts taking place in mainline denominations in the West? What parameters should Southern Baptist missionaries follow in seeking cooperation with other organizations to advance the Great Commission? The questions raised by the emerging

---

20   SBCA, 1943, 134.
21   FMBM, October 10, 1944, 3.

ecumenical movement had profound implications for Baptist work worldwide—questions that needed to be addressed by the SBC. One of the ways the SBC addressed the issue was to send a delegation to the 1938 International Missionary Conference in Tambaram, India, including Maddry as the executive secretary of the FMB.

1938 International Missionary Conference, Tambaram, India

W. O. Carver stated, "Our Secretary returns from Madras enthusiastic in his confidence that the strategy of Missions is following the lines of the New Testament, which in its turn is the expression and the record of the mind of Christ. Evangelism is to continue to be the central emphasis and the pervasive spirit of all the methods and undertakings of the men and the organizations that go forth into all the earth in the name of Jesus Christ."[22]

The Southern Baptist Convention selected Charles Maddry to be its delegate to the December 1938 conference of the International Missionary Conference (IMC) in Tambaram, Madras, India. The first meeting of the IMC was held in Jerusalem in 1928. The editors of *The Commission* in advance of the meeting called it "the greatest and most far-reaching gathering of Protestant Christianity since the days of the apostles."[23] The IMC was a continuation of the Edinburgh conference in 1910. Unlike the Edinburgh conference, the meeting in Madras would draw a greater representation of non-Western representatives; 464 delegates attended from seventy countries. The Madras meeting still reflected a concern for theological integrity and the preservation of the biblical gospel; subsequent meetings revealed an erosion of such theological concerns. The SBC was quick to offer expressions of confidence and practical cooperation to other like-minded institutions. It was as equally quick to raise concerns and dissociate from organizations that it deemed theologically liberal. The optimism expressed by Maddry over the Tambaram confidence was short-lived as subsequent meetings revealed

---

22   Carver, "Kingdom Facts and Factors," 102.
23   "The International Missionary Council," *TC* 1, no. 2 (March 1938): 49.

liberalizing trends in theology and reticence in world missions by participating groups.

The World Council of Churches

The FMB reflected the above concern in *The Commission*:

> There has grown up a widespread belief that the remedy for the ills of mankind is for all of the churches to unite into a world organization or federation of churches. Southern Baptists believe fully in the spiritual unity of all believers in Christ and we are willing to cooperate as far as possible with all others who love Christ and His cause. We do not believe organic church union is possible or desirable, and the Richmond Convention reaffirmed in unmistakable terms our wholehearted allegiance to the Word of God as the sole guide in all matters of faith and practice. We stand ready to unite with all believers in the world, on the solid rock of the Word of God; but beyond this we cannot go.[24]

W. O. Carver observed, "The pressing of the desire for organic union may very easily hinder the progress of the Gospel in its world mission, and may retard the growth of the sense of Christian unity which ought to pervade and must actuate all genuine and faithful followers of the Lord Jesus Christ. Church union is now the major objective of a number of men of wide influence and of eager leadership. Their efforts to utilize the missionary movement in the interest of organic union may easily hinder missions without promoting union."[25] Likewise, an editorial in the October 1939 edition of *The Commission* noted the rise of the World Council of Churches and the challenges that it posed to Southern Baptist missions:

---

24   Editors, "Unity versus Union," *TC* 1, no. 5 (September 1938): 190.
25   Carver, "Kingdom Facts and Factors," 71.

As the enlarging plans for the proposed interdenominational World Council of Churches are made public, we
are convinced that it is to be completely dominated by
the State Churches of Europe. The Church of England
and the Greek Orthodox Church of Rumania and other
southeastern European countries will, without doubt,
largely shape the policies and chart the course of the
new Council of Churches. Baptists, of course, stand for
everything in a spiritual sense that is absolutely contrary
to what these two powerful political State Churches stand
for. Southern Baptists may be reassured as to this whole
matter when they remember that George W. Truett is
Chairman, and Ellis Fuller is Secretary of the committee
appointed by the Southern Baptist Convention to report
to the next Convention on the acceptance or rejection of
the invitation extended to us to join this new movement
in religious power politics.[26]

J. H. Rushbrooke, longtime director of the Baptist World Alliance,
expressed the concerns of Southern Baptists in the July 1938 edition
of *The Commission* when he noted that an insistence on Christian
cooperation would lead to an expectation of conformity in organization and doctrine. He warned that joining such a world Christian
movement and organization would lead Baptists to cease being
Baptists. The insistence to conform would only lead to "ruin and
death to the cooperation which is attainable." He noted, "I repeat a
phrase to which Dr. Truett and I put our signatures, when addressing our brethren in India: 'Baptists cherish the three great words,
TRUTH, FREEDOM, UNITY; and *they rank them in that order*.'"[27]
The Baptist adherence to the set of beliefs that defined the Baptist
movement from the beginning took precedence over unity at all

---

26   Editorial, "The State Churches Will Dominate," *TC* 2, no. 10 (October 1939): 346–47.
27   R. H. Rushbrooke, "The Message of Baptists in the Present World Situation," *TC* 1,
     no. 4 (July 1938): 142.

costs. If Baptists had to advance the gospel with fewer global partners because of deep doctrinal division, then they were ready to do so.

The merging of the Life and Work Commission of Oxford and the Faith and Order Commission of Edinburgh in the budding World Council of Churches proved problematic for Southern Baptists on doctrinal and practical grounds. The SBC formed a special committee to formulate an official reply to the invitation extended to the SBC to join the World Council of Churches. The committee comprised the following members: George W. Truett (chairman), L. R. Scarborough, John R. Sampey, Charles Maddry, Ellis Fuller, A. J. Barton, E. Godbold, M. E. Dodd, W. R. White, David Gardner, Fred T. Brown, John H. Buchanan, and W. L. Ball. Their report to the SBC in 1940 was as follows:

> In a world which more and more seeks centralization of power in industry, in civil government, and in religion, we are sensible of the dangers of totalitarian trends which threaten the autonomy of all free churches. We wish to do nothing that will imperil the growing spirit of co-operation on the part of our churches in the work of giving the gospel of Christ, as we understand it, to all men everywhere. In the light of these considerations, we feel impelled to decline the invitation to membership in the World Council of Churches. . . .
>
> In justice to our own consciences, and on behalf of those who hold with us, we wish to express our conviction that Southern Baptists, along with other Baptist groups, should associate ourselves with our brethren of other denominations "in a fellowship of churches which accept our Lord Jesus Christ as God and Savior."[28]

Southern Baptists remained committed to the Baptist World Alliance, an institution they helped to found and fund. Truett, the

---

28   SBCA, 1940, 99.

famed Texas Baptist and pastor of the historic First Baptist Church of Dallas, Texas, served as president of the Baptist World Alliance during Maddry's tenure at the FMB. Maddry described Truett's last address to the Baptist World Alliance in Atlanta, Georgia:

> The address of the retiring president of the Baptist World Alliance, George W. Truett, before the recent session of the World Congress of Baptists in Atlanta was truly a masterpiece. It will go down in Baptist history as one of the greatest deliverances ever uttered by one of our leaders. He stated for Baptists of all time the great fundamentals of New Testament faith and practice with reference to soul liberty, the freedom of conscience, the separation of Church and State, and kindred doctrines that distinguish Baptists from all others. . . . Southern Baptists are justly proud of this great man. He stands out as the greatest leader among the twelve million Baptists in the world today. We praise God for such a leader in such a momentous hour in the history of the world.[29]

The FMB was also committed to cooperation with like-minded mission organizations in North America. Maddry would say in his final report to the FMB in 1944,

> We are happy to report an increasing spirit of good will and helpful cooperation with other religious groups in America. In 1934 the Board returned to active fellowship with the North American Foreign Missions Conference. This has led to an increasing sense of good will and helpful participation with brethren of other religious bodies in America. May we express the sincere hope that, while maintaining always our loyalty and devotion to our historic Baptist position and to the New Testament

---

29   Maddry, "A Magna Charta for Religious Liberty," *TC* 2, no. 10 (October 1939): 329.

principles that made us what we are, we enter into all phases of helpful and practical cooperation possible with other groups for spreading Christ's gospel to the nations.[30]

Southern Baptists were committed to theological and confessional integrity in their cooperation with other groups for the cause of missions. The authority of God's Word, the gospel of Christ as its central story, and a common confession of faith were three bases for cooperating with other Christian groups. The SBC decided on many occasions that theological integrity and maintaining historic Baptist distinctives were nonnegotiable in furthering the gospel among all nations. A certain set of evangelical theological beliefs guided missions cooperation with other Christian groups that ensured the preservation of the gospel and the integrity of local churches that FMB missionaries were instrumental in starting.

THE MANAGEMENT OF
SOUTHERN BAPTIST MISSIONS

Visiting Mission Stations

Modern modes of travel made it possible for the new FMB executive secretary to travel to all FMB work overseas. While touring the work in South America, Maddry made his first trip by sea and air with Southwestern Baptist Seminary president L. R. Scarborough. Maddry was committed to seeing the work firsthand, meeting missionaries and mission leaders, in order to make the best decisions possible as the executive secretary. He maintained, however, a commitment to allow missionaries on the field to have decision-making authority as it related to missions strategy, personnel issues, and budget. What Maddry began by way of extensive travel would become the norm for the following executive secretaries and later FMB/IMB presidents. He would say at the end of his tenure,

---

30 FMBM, October 10, 1944.

In 1934 the executive secretary began a systematic visitation of all the mission fields of our Board in the several lands where we have organized work. First, we visited the work in Europe, beginning with Spain and going on through Italy, Yugoslavia, Hungary, Rumania, and into Palestine and Syria in the Near East. Then, in 1935 we visited our work in Japan and China for six months. In 1936 we spent five months observing our work in Latin America. In 1938 we paid a visit to our Mission in Nigeria. The work there was established in 1850, and this was the first time that a secretary of the Board had ever gone to the Mission. We paid a return visit to our work in Italy in 1938 and 1939.[31]

The Department of Missionary Personnel

Reflective of the Maddry administration, the FMB gave careful attention to define further the call to missions and the qualifications of who could serve. Jesse Ford observed during the Maddry era of Southern Baptist missions:

What is the test which should be applied to determine the reality of a call to the foreign field? The first step is a complete surrender of one's self to the will of God, whether that be to go or to stay. God may call one to stay at home as well as to be abroad. The call to the foreign field must be a compelling, driving inner urge to win lives to Christ in lands where they have not yet had a chance to hear the story of salvation. This urge cannot be satisfied except by going. This yearning, impelling force must be born of prayer and grounded in love—love of God and love of man. As someone has said, "Do not be a missionary if you can possibly be anything else." As Paul said, "Woe is me if I preached not the Gospel." Only those should

---

31 FMBM, October 10, 1944, 3.

go who are willing to pay the price. Surely as Christians we should be called of God to whatever form of service we follow, but there are certain qualifications which need to be considered in connection with this "call" to foreign mission service. Let us look well into our motives and test them by the standard of Jesus Christ, who said, "He that would be great among you let him be your servant."[32]

J. W. Marshall stated, "The missionary is God's man, doing God's work, in God's way, in God's field, for God's glory. To be a missionary is to be engaged in the greatest work in the world; to be an ambassador for Christ is to be a successor to the Apostle Paul. A missionary is 'one sent on a mission.' He must be sent of God. Herein lies one of the greatest responsibilities of the Foreign Mission Board—to discover and appoint all whom God wants our board to send to some foreign field of service."[33]

In order to facilitate greater care in missionary recruitment, the FMB under Maddry's leadership established a Department of Missionary Personnel and a secretary to oversee the recruitment process. J. W. Marshall, the first secretary of the department of mission personnel, noted in 1944, "The responsibility of finding candidates and presenting them to the Foreign Mission Board rests with the Department of Missionary Personnel. All the work of this department is based upon the conviction that Jesus Christ is the Lord of the harvest. Few people have a task so delicate and difficult with such great and far-reaching importance as that of the Personnel Secretary of the Southern Baptist Foreign Mission Board."[34]

Marshall recounted the missionary fervor following World War I as Southern Baptists challenged young people to consider God's call on their life in light of the great needs and ministry opportunities that existed around the world. He acknowledged that enthusiasm

---

32   Jesse Ford, "The Missionary's Call," *TC* 1, no. 1 (January 1938): 27.
33   SBCA, 1944, 202.
34   SBCA, 1944, 204.

led many to serve internationally, but lack of adequate screening and preparation led many to return home prematurely. Marshall said in his 1944 report to the SBC, "Today, thousands of young people are offering themselves for foreign missionary service. This is encouraging, but at the same time the unfit must be carefully and prayerfully weeded out."[35] He emphasized that the needs were great in the postwar world. He observed, "The continued need for foreign missionaries is recognized by all who know conditions in countries around the world. The doors to some of our mission fields now are open wide; many new opportunities for evangelizing the world will come with the close of the war."[36] The FMB established the Office of Missionary Personnel in order to implement exacting standards for missionary recruits to meet the demands of a world without Christ.

Missionary Recruitment

Maddry mentioned the following in his final presidential report to the FMB in October 1944: "A new and more exacting standard of requirements for missionary appointees has been set up. We have now for several years exercised greater care in seeking out and bringing forward candidates for appointment as missionaries of this Board. The Foreign Mission Board of the Southern Baptist Convention has the worthy distinction of being the first mission board in America to employ a psychiatrist in the examination of missionary candidates."[37]

Maddry also noted, "Relying upon divine guidance we shall seek the very best advice and counsel of teachers, pastors, doctors, psychiatrists, and the secretaries, in our endeavor to select the highest type of missionary candidates for the future."[38] Marshall listed the following qualifications that the department of missions personnel utilized in assessing new candidates: spiritual, physical, intellectual, social, temperament, marriage and family, and practical. The spiritual requirements were as follows:

---

35   SBCA, 1944, 202.
36   SBCA, 1944, 202.
37   FMBM, October 10, 1944.
38   FMBM, October 13, 1943.

1. A vital and growing Christian experience.
2. A wholehearted devotion to the interpretation of Jesus' message to life today.
3. An unusual insight into Christianity and essential human nature.
4. A love for Christ that compels a sharing of faith and experience.
5. An ability to state clearly and convincingly the teachings of Christian faith.[39]

In addition to these spiritual qualifications, he said, "It is essential for missionaries to have Christ's attitude toward people of all other races. No volunteer who cannot love and share and work as an equal with his Negro friend in America, should ever go as a missionary to Africa, or to any other place."[40] Social qualifications are "tact, graciousness, poise, courtesy (especially in regard to manners and customs of the country to which he goes), and ability to maintain cordial relations with diplomatic and commercial communities."[41] The qualifications of temperament were described as follows: "Due again to the unusual difficulties and privations which may be incident to the missionary life, only men and women of unusual emotional and mental stability can be used. The importance of a cheerful and optimistic disposition, of an irrepressible sense of humor, of persistent energy, courage, and resourcefulness cannot be over-emphasized. The missionary must be mature emotionally, as well as in his judgment and common sense."[42]

Marshall did not address divorce and remarriage in the marital and family qualifications, only that the marriage "be healthy and stable," and that both spouses sense God's call for the task.[43] The

---

39 SBCA, 1944, 204.
40 SBCA, 1944, 204.
41 SBCA, 1944, 204.
42 SBCA, 1944, 204.
43 SBCA, 1944, 205.

Department of Missions Personnel also stipulated the need for practical experience before missionary appointment. Marshall noted,

> More and more the Board is requiring that the new missionaries, like the doctors, serve an internship in the homeland, thus allowing all the first personal and professional mistakes to be made among one's own people, who can more easily understand and make allowance for beginners, than can those of different backgrounds and cultures. At least one year of successful experience in work similar to that to which the missionary will be assigned is desirable and often required. Successful experience here is one of the best indications of success there. Actual experience in any kind of full-time salaried position is valuable preparation for missionary service.[44]

The most striking aspect of missionary qualifications was the age restriction. Marshall stated, "Missionaries should be between twenty-four and thirty-two years of age at the time of their appointment. Persons past thirty-two are likely to have difficulty in learning a new language and in making adjustments to a new environment."[45]

Missionary Preparation
The FMB established a high standard for missionary preparation and recruitment. Marshall stated, "Other things being equal, the higher the educational attainments, the more efficient is the missionary."[46] Recognizing the complexity of the task of cross-cultural missions demanded a complex approach to missionary preparation. Frank Means noted in 1944, "Contrary to an oft-expressed opinion, the task of training world missionaries is not exclusively

---

44   SBCA, 1944, 205.
45   SBCA, 1944, 203.
46   SBCA, 1944, 203.

the responsibility of theological seminaries and training schools. The educational and spiritual processes which eventuate in a well-equipped missionary are long and arduous. Formal missionary preparation is often superseded in importance by incidental, destiny-determining experiences and circumstances. A Christian home, the local church, the influence of Christian friends, and the varied life experiences of the candidate are real avenues of missionary preparation, even though they are somewhat intangible."[47] Means in no way diminished the importance of seminary training but magnified it. He continued,

> Each of our Southern Baptist seminaries maintains a chair of missions. The task of training world missionaries, however, is not committed exclusively to one department. The curricula of studies in Southern Baptist institutions are organized to assure a symmetrical training which embraces courses in all departments of theological training. Courses in Old Testament, New Testament, Greek, Hebrew, homiletics, evangelism, Church history, Christian doctrine, philosophy of religion, social ethics, religious education, and church music are fundamental parts of the missionary's training. They are as important to the missionary recruit as basic training for army privates and "boot camp" for naval recruits. The department of missions is one among many, and is not a "school of missionary training."
>
> A liberal elective system enables missionary candidates to pursue their specific interest in missions after the basic requirements of theological study have been met. Thus it becomes possible for the prospective missionary to intensify his study in certain directions. Whether he aspires to service at home or abroad, he must be well-grounded in missionary theory, missionary history, evangelism,

---

47   Frank K. Means, "Training World Missionaries," *TC* 7, no. 8 (September 1944): 7.

modern systems of thought, religious and social movements, contemporary history, the teachings of the Bible,
Christian ethics, and Baptist principles and practices.[48]

Means recognized that both seminary training and training on
the field are necessary to provide the missionary with the most
well-rounded preparation for missionary service. He observed that
"specialized study is highly desirable and vitally necessary, if the
missionary is to cope successfully with the problems peculiar to his
chosen field of work. There is a sense in which native traditions,
customs, and usages may be studied to best advantage on the mission field. But there is also a sense in which some of the problems
incident to a missionary career may be anticipated during the
period of theological training."[49] He suggested that missionaries in
training should pursue specialized study in the histories, cultures,
and religious systems of the people whom they are seeking to reach.
He observed, "Intelligent criticism is apt to be a sharper weapon
than unintelligent bigotry."[50]

Categories of Missionary Service

In 1944 Marshall listed four categories of missionary service: general
missionaries, medical missionaries, educational missionaries, and
technical missionaries. Marshall's report also lists the qualification
for each category as follows:

GENERAL MISSIONARIES. All missionaries are required to
have both college and theological degrees or the equivalent.

MEDICAL MISSIONARIES. In addition to the college
training the medical doctor is required to have an M.D.
degree from a Class A medical school, two years of

---

48   Means, "Training World Missionaries," 7.
49   Means, "Training World Missionaries," 7.
50   Means, "Training World Missionaries," 7.

internship, and at least one year of missionary training in a theological seminary or missionary training school approved by the Board. The missionary nurse should have a college or university degree, the R.N. degree, and a missionary training school or theological seminary degree. Experience, especially administrative, is desirable; and for some appointments courses in pedagogy are required.

EDUCATIONAL MISSIONARIES. Both college and theological seminary or missionary training school degrees are required. Graduate degrees in special fields—science music, sociology, education, and so forth—are desirable and often required/especially for those who will teach in mission colleges, universities, and seminaries.

TECHNICAL MISSIONARIES. In addition to the required college and seminary or missionary training school degrees, this missionary should have standard technical training in his specialty: agriculture, building, vocational training, printing, cinematography, and the like.[51]

The FMB sought to engage a broad range of gifted Southern Baptists in its efforts to reach the world with the gospel. The missiological approach to recruitment and deployment involved becoming aware of the needs that existed in the world, and where opportunities existed for engagement, the FMB deployed missionaries of all types of gifting, talents, and educational backgrounds to reach the lost with the gospel through meeting human needs in service of the gospel, evangelizing unbelievers, planting churches, strengthening churches, and training leaders. Regardless of the assignment, the FMB established stringent requirements for appointment and established a gospel priority to every assignment.

---

51   SBCA, 1944, 203.

MISSION REORGANIZATION

Maddry made the following observations about his reorganization of the FMB during his final report: "Early in our work with the Foreign Mission Board we realized that the administration of the world-wide program of foreign mission work, as carried on by Southern Baptists, was far beyond the ability and strength of any one man."[52] Up until this time individual mission stations directed the fieldwork of the FMB. In the larger countries FMB work was loosely connected. The time had come for a more structured approach to managing the FMB and in doing so set a precedent for subsequent executive secretaries and presidents of the FMB. Maddry set in motion principles of business management that would become more important to FMB leadership as the organization continued to experience an increase in field personnel from the hundreds to the thousands.

Maddry selected longtime missionary to China M. Theron Rankin as the regional secretary for China and Japan in 1935 after spending six months traveling in both countries. In 1936 missionary to Brazil W. C. Taylor became the regional secretary for Latin America. He was succeeded in 1941 by Everett Gill Jr. Former missionary to Africa George Sadler became the regional secretary for Europe, Africa, and the Near East.[53]

The growth of the FMB coincided with an emerging business model of management that demanded that the executive secretary employ modern methods of business management to give a sense of cohesion and efficiency to the work by centralizing management in the hands of regional secretaries. In time this would evolve into more of a centralized-management approach of the FMB/IMB from Richmond. The regional secretaries of Maddry's creation, however, remained on the field and did not interfere with the normal operations of the mission-station personnel, to whom was entrusted great latitude and authority over matters related to personnel, budget, and strategy.

---

52   FMBM, October 10, 1944. 3.
53   FMBM, October 10, 1944, 3.

MISSIONARY STRATEGY

At all levels of the FMB's work, a commitment to establish indigenous work with trained indigenous leadership permeated the organization's ethos and efforts. The FMB report to the 1943 SBC stated,

> The Board recognizes the fact that more and more the
> leadership in our foreign mission fields must be turned
> over to the native Christians. In the beginning our mis-
> sionaries were sent out to pagan lands to win converts
> and to establish churches. In this they were successful.
> Many of the native churches are today carrying on their
> work with no help from the Board. The very genius of our
> Baptist life demands that these churches be encouraged
> to organize their own district associations and national
> conventions, and carry forward their own program of
> evangelism and education. . . . The policy of the Foreign
> Mission Board in any country where we have an estab-
> lished work should be determined after conference with
> the Missions on the field and the native Baptist constitu-
> encies with which our Missions are associated. In a very
> real sense this policy must be the product of the joint
> thinking of the Board in Richmond, the missionaries on
> the field, and the native Christians.[54]

The FMB leadership realized that the Protestant missionary movement that had begun in earnest in the eighteenth century was
bearing fruit and creating global Christian communities and leaders
by the time of Maddry's administration. Southern Baptists were
committed to establishing self-sustaining work by turning the work
over to national leaders as soon as possible. The FMB was convinced
that the charge given to it by the SBC was to establish indigenous
Baptist churches after the pattern of the New Testament and assist

---

54   SBCA, 1943, 217.

those national-led Baptist churches to form Baptist associations and denominational structures that in some ways mirrored the Southern Baptist pattern. In the report the FMB encouraged national leaders to visit SBC churches to establish more understanding of the work and greater cooperation with national leaders. The FMB encouraged missionaries not only to establish churches but also to nurture the growth of churches as older brothers to younger brothers. "We will have achieved a major purpose on the Foreign Mission field when we have developed a self-supporting and self-directing native denomination."[55] Such lofty goals would have implications for the kind of missions candidates the FMB sought. The report continues, "It is therefore imperative that the missionary personnel of today and tomorrow should, in addition to other requirements, have an educational equipment, a breadth of vision, a sympathetic and cooperative attitude, which will enable them to desire and to promote this trend toward native independence, and to help the native churches to develop their Christian faith in keeping with the best of their own national culture and background."[56]

MISSIONARY FIELDS

During the time of the Maddry administration the work was divided into the following regions: Europe, Africa, the Near East, Latin America, and the Orient. The FMB, however, committed the bulk of its resources to Europe, Africa, China, and Brazil, which will be covered in this section.

Europe

In his autobiography Maddry expressed the following sentiment regarding FMB work in Europe: "There had been a growing feeling on the part of the supporting churches in the South and the

55   SBCA, 1943, 218.
56   SBCA, 1943, 218.

Board in Richmond that the time had fully come for the national churches in the several lands in Europe to assume a larger share in the support of their own pastors and in the organization of new work in the regions still unevangelized in their respective fields."[57] World War I had devastated Europe, but the time had come to challenge national Baptist work in more established fields to take over their own support. The FMB had paid pastors in strategic locations, such as Italy, where the work progressed slowly and where Baptist leaders were reluctant to give up the financial support that they had received from Richmond. Maddry and the FMB decided the time had come and proposed to the Baptist convention in Italy that they become self-supporting and that the property owned by the FMB be sold to help pay FMB debts. Not only was there a need for Baptist work in Europe to become self-supporting but also self-propagating.

Everett Gill, FMB European representative in Bucharest, Romania, noted of missionary strategy in Europe, "We do not attempt *direct* evangelism in these five countries, for two principal reasons: we cannot and we *should* not." He noted that direct evangelism is illegal, and it is the responsibility of nationals and not missionaries to evangelize their own people."[58] Gill further stated that "the best evangelism, therefore, can be done by the native brethren. It is a truism among students of missions that no nation or people was ever won by foreigners. Missionaries from abroad may, and usually do, begin such work, but the main winning must be by the native pastors and missionaries themselves."[59]

The FMB became even more committed to support the work in Europe through theological education. Gill noted that "the need of seminary and training-school work has been recognized from the first, for the young preachers and the young women."[60] Maddry said of the work in Yugoslavia, "The supreme need was for someone to

57   Maddry, *An Autobiography*, 79.
58   Everett Gill, "This Is Europe Calling," *TC* 1, no. 2 (March 1938): 45.
59   Gill, "This Is Europe Calling," 45.
60   Gill, "This Is Europe Calling," 45.

teach and train a native ministry. God has called and raised up a worthy and promising group of young men for ministry, but they were helpless without someone to teach them and guide them."[61]

The FMB leadership expressed a deep desire to evangelize Russia but realized that the time was not right. Gill expressed hope for future missions endeavors in Russia that had been closed to missionary work since the Communist Revolution. He noted, "All the while we turn our eyes and hearts, with prayers and expectation, toward Russia, now closed to gospel work. We are convinced that in time, by the grace of God, Russia will prove to be the greatest field for the Gospel of all the ages. That is, unless the former state-church does regain the upper hand, which thing no one expects."[62] Editors of *The Commission* magazine in 1938 expressed the same passion on the part of the FMB to evangelize Russia and a belief that one day God's providence would open the door to do so. They noted,

> One of the supreme tragedies of Christian history, drawn out now through two decades of unspeakable madness and persecution, is the effort of the ruling despots in Russia to crush out all religion from the life of the people. Of course, they will ultimately and utterly fail. The Russian people are deeply and profoundly religious, and one day all Russia will be wide open for the preaching of the Gospel. Against that day, Southern Baptists must be ready. . . . In Bessarabia, a Russian province until the close of the World War [I], we have already some 20,000 Baptists and more than 300 churches. The work is growing in a most marvelous and gratifying way. When the door swings open, we will be ready to cross the Dniester River, and march into European Russia with an army of trained preachers and evangelists.[63]

---

61 Maddry, *An Autobiography*, 88.
62 Gill, "This Is Europe Calling," 46.
63 Editorial, "Editorial Varieties," *TC* 1, no. 4 (July 1938): 156.

The FMB in Eastern Europe would become all the more important as a strategic launchpad for mission work in Russia. The time was not right under the Maddry administration, but when the Iron Curtain finally fell in 1989, the FMB was poised to take advantage of the opportunities that prior strategic geographical investments afforded to resume the work in Russia.

Africa

Maddry was passionately committed to Southern Baptist work in Africa, particularly in Nigeria, while recognizing the history of missions that preceded Southern Baptists' arrival on the continent. He wrote *Day Dawn in Yoruba Land* as an expression of his commitment to bringing the gospel resources of Southern Baptists to bear on the spiritual needs in Africa.[64] He acknowledged the trailblazing work of missionaries with African ancestry on the continent, such as Samuel Crowther, David George, Lott Carey, and Colin Teague. Maddry was the first executive secretary to visit the work in Africa, and he walked away from his trip with a deep impression of the needs of the people. He focused his reflections on the Yoruba people of Nigeria. Their physical and spiritual needs pressed on his mind. He identified the widespread practice of polygamy, divorce, lack of Christian-based education, and traditional African religions with their belief in one universal god, lesser deities, and ancestral spirits as obstacles that the preaching of the gospel must overcome.[65]

The FMB work in Africa during the Maddry administration was plagued by the perils of war. Global conflict stalled the return of field personnel to their assignments in Nigeria, creating a massive burden for the few that remained on the field. The war also hindered the flow of communication from missionaries to Southern Baptists, rendering it difficult for later historians to piece together details of FMB work in later years. In the FMB report to the 1944 SBC, George Sadler noted, "Upon Africa, the Dark Continent, the

---

64   Charles E. Maddry, *Day Dawn in Yoruba Land* (Nashville: Broadman, 1939).
65   Maddry, *Day Dawn in Yoruba Land*, 11–30.

present world conflict has turned the spotlight of publicity, and that land of vast wealth and unlimited resources is gaining its merited recognition among the nations. But that same conflict has imposed handicaps upon the missionary work, creating great difficulty in regard to the transportation of missionaries, and maintenance of communication."[66] Despite the challenges, the FMB remained resolute to bring the light of the gospel to Africa and establish the work in Nigeria on a firm foundation.

Sadler described the work in Africa as primarily centered on Nigeria with sixty missionaries under appointment in Nigeria alone. By 1943 thirty-two of these missionaries were in the States on extended leave due to the war, while twenty-eight remained on the field. The FMB in Nigeria comprised ten mission stations, with Ogbomosho as the largest station, where the FMB established a hospital, leper colony, home for orphans, and the Baptist seminary that still exists today. Sadler reported that the FMB had assigned "over a dozen missionaries" to serve this station. "The other stations were in Iwo, Abeokuta, Lagos (the port city), Shaki, Benin City, Port Harcourt, Igede, Ede, Oyo."[67] Missionaries and national workers worked from these stations to "carry on their three-fold ministry of preaching, teaching, and healing."[68] Sadler continued, "From these centers work is carried to remote areas, the missionaries and native pastors traveling by auto or on foot, by canoe or motor launch. Holding services in the crude mud churches, teaching in the schools, conducting classes among the women, treating the sick at a roadside clinic."[69]

In 1939 Maddry reflected on Southern Baptist missions in Africa, noting,

> Eighty-nine years ago Southern Baptists sent the first missionary to Nigeria. Since that time 119 choice young

---

66   SBCA, 1944, 209.
67   SBCA, 1944, 209.
68   SBCA, 1944, 209.
69   SBCA, 1944, 209.

men and women out of our churches have "followed in His train" as missionaries to dark Africa. It has been a costly undertaking. A total of seventeen have died while in the service of the Board, and ten of these sleep in the soil of Africa or beneath the waves of the Atlantic. Many others came back broken and incapacitated for life because of the fearful toll of African disease and climate. Trying to give the gospel to "every creature" in Nigeria has been a costly business. Jesus said that "except a grain of wheat fall into the ground and die, it abideth alone; but if it die, it bringeth forth much fruit."[70]

China

Maddry toured the work in the Orient for seven months—a feat no other FMB executive secretary was able to accomplish. Maddry noted in his autobiography that China made two indelible impressions on him upon his arrival: "the crowds, the countless thousands crowding roadways, streets, and shops . . . [and] the sight of the throngs of ragged, hungry, hopeless beggars."[71] The work in China was among the most strategic, along with Brazil, and represented the largest commitment of Southern Baptist resources in the missionary task. The work in China faced the challenge of the Sino-Japanese War during the Maddry administration and the resulting widespread displacement of FMB missionaries. By the end of Maddry's tenure as executive secretary, the FMB experienced the loss of life, resources, and access to the country. Not until the reopening of China in the post-Mao era were missionaries able to reengage this strategic country with the gospel. In the meantime, the scattering of FMB missionaries into Southeast Asia under the following administration of M. Theron Rankin led to the establishment of Baptist work among the Chinese diaspora that constituted a sizeable minority in many Southeast Asian nations.

---

70   Maddry, *Day Dawn in Yoruba Land*, 209.
71   Maddry, *An Autobiography*, 97.

Rankin, FMB secretary of the Orient, reported to the SBC in 1944, "Four-fifths of the missionary work conducted by the Foreign Mission Board in the Orient now lies behind Japanese lines. But military and political divisions form no barriers to the Spirit of God. Behind the lines of war, God is working today. We have abundant evidence of this in the Orient."[72] China was the scene of heroic missionary work in the face of war, social upheaval, and political change. The advance of the Japanese drove many missionaries away from their fields of service while others remained behind to serve, risking their lives to fulfill their calling and keep vital ministries going during the conflict. The FMB policy during the Japanese occupation in China was expressed by E. B. Willingham:

> In areas of special danger we deem wise the evacuation of mothers with children, of those whose health is too uncertain for the hardships which threaten and of those whose furloughs are shortly due and whose services can be spared. In all such cases we leave the decision to the discretion of the mission, after due consultation with the Chinese convention. In urgent messages Chinese Christian leaders state that they covet the fellowship of all able-bodied missionaries in this crisis. We authorize the continued service of such missionaries as freely elect to remain and whose remaining is approved by their respective missions acting after consultation with the Chinese convention concerned. Those who withdraw and those who elect to stay are alike assured of our sympathy and support.[73]

War would not deter missionaries in China from carrying out their work. Willingham expressed the intention and belief of the FMB that times of crisis are laced with opportunities for gospel

---

72   SBCA, 1944, 211.
73   E. B. Willingham, "Southern Baptists Pledge Support," *TC* 1, no. 1 (January 1938): 4.

proclamation to both Chinese and Japanese. He commented, "We are servants of a Master for whom seeming disaster is the door to larger opportunity. The proclamation of the gospel must go on. It is the Word of God to suffering, distraught humanity. To witness to that gospel now in every land with renewed devotion is a call to all the followers of Jesus Christ."[74]

In his report to the SBC in 1943, Maddry spoke of the direct impact of the war on missionaries in China and Japan. He noted, "On the twenty-fifth of August, 1942, after weary months of tedious negotiations through the medium of the Swiss Government, the following missionaries from Japan and China, having been exchanged in Portuguese East Africa, were landed in New York from the Swedish S.S. *Gripsholm*."[75] Of the thirty-six missionaries who had been repatriated from China and Japan, the following names were included: C. L Culpepper, M. Theron Rankin, and Bertha Smith. The report also listed the seven who were still interned in a Japanese prison in Manila and the thirty-five missionaries who remained in occupied China. Maddry continued, "In Macao, four of our loyal workers are 'suffering hardships as good soldiers of Christ Jesus.' Lacking adequate food, unable to secure the actual necessities of life, tortured by cases of starvation and suffering which they are powerless to relieve, the following noble missionaries are doing their utmost: Miss Lora Clement, Miss Leonora Scarlett, and Rev. and Mrs. J. L. Galloway."[76]

The war years were devastating for the work in China, devastation from which the FMB/IMB has never recovered. Maddry spoke of the devastation when he reflected,

> The losses of our Board in China and Europe have been enormous. We estimate that the Japanese invaders have looted and destroyed not less than one million dollars'

---

74 Willingham, "Southern Baptists Pledge Support," 4.
75 SBCA, 1943, 135.
76 SBCA, 1943, 136.

worth of the Board's property in China. All of the mission work of Southern Baptists in that country has been overrun and devastated by the wasting war that has been raging in China for more than seven years. Our eight hospitals, our schools, colleges, seminaries, chapels, and missionary houses have been stripped and, in many cases, completely destroyed. Our more than two hundred missionaries laboring in China have been robbed of all of their personal and household goods, including libraries, pianos, and automobiles. The missionaries alone have lost a hundred and fifty thousand dollars' worth of personal effects.[77]

The work in China was as diverse as the landscape. Until Maddry consolidated the FMB work in China under M. Theron Rankin as secretary for the Orient, the work in China was divided into north China, south China, the interior, and central China. Missionaries served as evangelists, church planters, theological educators, Christian educators in schools and universities, medical missionaries, and various other compassion ministries. All were committed to the goal of reaching China and her many people groups with the gospel of Jesus Christ. The one common element in all of the work was the advance of the gospel as the priority of missionaries and a commitment to the starting of Baptist churches; Southern Baptist missionaries were in sync with their denominational ethos and ecclesiology. FMB strategies were diverse in China, but core elements remained the same—the preaching of the gospel, gospel-prioritized human-needs ministries, the starting of Baptist churches, publications in the vernacular language, and the training of church leaders.

Southern Baptists established key institutions in China that demonstrated a concern for the long-term transformation of Chinese society with the gospel of Christ. The University of Shanghai was one such institution. Maddry believed that this university was one of the greatest tools of evangelism in all FMB work in China.

---

77 FMBM, October 1944, 6.

Graves Theological Seminary was another key institution that reflected the FMB commitment to the training of national leadership. Stout Memorial Hospital also played a significant role in advancing the gospel in China by meeting the physical needs of the Chinese people while also disseminating the gospel to the patients under its care. Dr. Bill Wallace served in this hospital. The North Gate Baptist Church in Shanghai provided strategic support to the work of the FMB in China in a variety of ways. The church was formed in the home of J. L. and Henrietta Shuck, Baptist missionary pioneers in China, and it became a launchpad of missionary efforts across China.

The beginning of the expulsion of FMB missionaries from China during the second Sino-Japanese War began during the Maddry administration, though the full missionary exodus did not occur until Rankin's administration during the second Chinese civil war, when the Communist insurgency took control of China. Maddry observed two significant developments regarding the work in China immediately after his administration. He wrote in his autobiography, "The Communists have shut us out of China for a season, but God is still at work behind the Bamboo Curtain, and multitudes of Chinese Baptists remain faithful."[78] He later concluded, "Our missionaries formerly working in China have been deployed to other areas in the Orient where millions of Chinese and other people may be reached, Formosa [Taiwan], Philippines, Korea, Thailand, Malaya, and Indonesia."[79]

Brazil

Maddry reflected on his first trip to South America by noting, "In May, 1936, the Foreign Mission Board authorized the Executive Secretary to visit our missions in South America and to select a Baptist leader to accompany him on an inspection tour of our work in the lands of South America. I selected Dr. L. R. Scarborough, president of the Southwestern Baptist Theological Seminary at Fort Worth, to go with me. He and Mrs. Scarborough made the trip at

---

78 Maddry, *An Autobiography*, 101.
79 Maddry, *An Autobiography*, 107.

their own expense."

The work in Brazil, particularly, was quite advanced by the time of the Maddry administration. The work had begun in 1881 with the arrival of the Rev. and Mrs. W. B. Bagby of Texas. R. S. Jones, reflecting on the beginning of the Baptist work in Brazil, noted, "In 1881 the Foreign Mission Board opened work in Brazil, the fourth country to be entered by missionaries of the Southern Baptist Convention. Rev. and Mrs. W. B. Bagby were appointed as the first missionaries to this country. In 1882 Rev. and Mrs. Z. C. Taylor were sent to join the Bagbys. Dr. and Mrs. Bagby are still living. All that has been accomplished for the Kingdom in South America has been done during the lifetime of our first missionaries."[80]

Maddry not only encountered "a glorious company of devoted and courageous missionaries" but also "found that the [Brazilian] Convention [was] ready to assume a larger part than ever before in the plans for the support of the work."[81] He concluded, "The seed-sowing of fifty years on the part of the North American Foreign Mission Board was beginning to pay rich dividends in the promise of national churches to assume a larger share in the evangelization of their own people."[82]

Maddry's goal of challenging Brazilian Baptists to assume more support for the work in Brazil in no way diminished his view that Brazil was still in need of new FMB missionaries.

In July 1938 R. S. Jones noted,

> The needs of Brazil are almost beyond description. The country, larger than the United States, is divided into twenty states. These states are much larger than the States of the United States of North America. Five are larger than Texas. In eight of these states there is no missionary. When Dr. J. F. Love, former Secretary of the Foreign Mission Board, was in Brazil in 1922, there were five states

---

80   R. Jones, "Brazilian Briefs," *TC* 1, no. 4 (July 1938): 156–57.
81   Maddry, *An Autobiography*, 110.
82   Maddry, *An Autobiography*, 110.

without missionaries. The need for a missionary couple for each of these five states was called to his attention as the greatest need. He promised that the Board would meet it at the earliest possible moment by sending these five couples. However, when Dr. Charles E. Maddry visited Brazil in 1937, he found the need still unmet and the missionary group depleted until instead of five there were now eight states without missionaries. This need must be met. Will you make it possible?

Dr. Maddry, writing back to the office from Brazil, said, "We must have these eight couples. If we could have them, we could win Brazil to Christ in this generation to the extent that America is Christian." God grant that we may lift up our eyes and see this whitest of all fields unto harvest![83]

From the beginning, the missionaries to Brazil engaged missionary work in this predominantly Catholic country with the three-self principle in mind. Evangelism, church planting, and the training of leaders were all top priorities that characterized FMB strategy in Brazil. By 1938 FMB missionaries had established two seminaries—one at Recife in the north and one at Rio de Janeiro in the south—along with two training centers for women in the same locations. Jones noted, "The work of the missionary is unique, in that the missionary who best succeeds works himself out of a job. Brethren John Shepard, H. H. Muirhead, A. B. Langston, S. L. Watson, W. C. Taylor and others have given many years of service, training Baptist leaders in the colleges and seminaries in Rio and Recife. Their work was done so effectively that today many of the positions formerly necessarily held by missionaries are ably filled by Brazilians."[84] Jones continued,

All of the great city churches in Brazil have as pastors Brazilians trained in our colleges and seminaries.

---

83   Jones, "Brazilian Briefs," 156–57.
84   Jones, "Brazilian Briefs," 150.

You will doubtless agree that the missionaries mentioned above succeeded in the largest possible way when they trained leaders who could fill the places they had held, and thereby worked themselves out of a job. This is the highest ideal a missionary can have. This type of success gives the missionary a larger place of influence and service. The Brazilian, more than ever, feels his need of the counsel and moral support of the missionary, and he cannot succeed without him. However, fewer missionaries will be needed in the future for administrative work and they will be free for pioneer evangelistic work in the vast unoccupied areas.[85]

The FMB Brazil mission and its Brazilian Baptist partners were committed to the establishment of schools and colleges. Jones reported in 1938 that eleven colleges and schools existed, serving primary grades through junior college in order "to evangelize and train workers."[86] FMB missionaries and their national partners also established a Home Mission Board and a Foreign Mission Board. The HMB directed the efforts of Brazilian Baptists to expand the work at home and bring the gospel to the interior. The HMB also directed gospel outreach to 1.5 million Indians, living and working in Brazil. The FMB established missionary work in Portugal and Portuguese-speaking Africa. Jones referred to the Brazilian FMB work in Africa as the "great grandchild of the Foreign Mission Board of Southern Baptists."[87]

In 1939 William Bagby, the great statesman and founder of the work in Brazil, passed away. He left behind a heritage of Christian leadership and missionary work that has not been forgotten by Brazilian Baptists. He was survived by his wife, Mrs. Bagby, who was an effective missionary in her own right. The Bagbys had five

---

85   Jones, "Brazilian Briefs," 150.
86   Jones, "Brazilian Briefs," 150.
87   Jones, "Brazilian Briefs," 150.

children, all of whom served as missionaries—four in Brazil and
one in Argentina.

Bagby arrived in Brazil in 1881. Within his first three years he
started two churches. The very first Baptist church in Brazil was
founded in Bahia, and later he established the First Baptist Church
in the capital, Rio de Janeiro. The night before his arrival in Rio,
he said, "After a voyage of forty-eight days from Baltimore we are
anchored tonight in the quiet waters of Rio. It is the most beautiful
scene my eyes have ever beheld. Pen cannot picture the loveliness of
these encircling mountains, clad to the top with luxuriant verdure,
and dotted with villas and chapels. . . . Oh, may God grant that his
truth, as it is in Jesus, shall fill this land from north to south, and
from the Atlantic to the Andes."[88] The editors of *The Commission*,
reflecting on his legacy in Brazil, said of him,

> Dr. Bagby was a great gospel preacher and an untiring
> evangelist. He was gifted in the art of training and orga-
> nizing his converts. The churches which he started grew
> and multiplied in a marvelous way, and today, in the
> fellowship of the Brazilian National Convention we have
> over six hundred churches with more than fifty thou-
> sand members. There are five colleges, two theological
> seminaries, two missionary training schools for women,
> a publishing house, a Baptist paper, and Home and For-
> eign Mission Boards, that are giving the Gospel to the
> unevangelized areas of Brazil and sending missionaries
> to the homeland of Portugal. There are numerous high
> schools, primary and industrial schools, and many other
> institutions and agencies conducted by the Baptists of
> Brazil—all of which began fifty-eight years ago, when
> W. B. Bagby of Texas and Anne Luther of Missouri heard
> and answered God's call to Brazil.[89]

---

88   SBCA, 1940, 185.
89   Editorial, "A Great Missionary Pioneer Has Fallen," *TC* 2, no. 10 (October 1939): 347.

In June 1939 Rev. E. A. Nelson, the "Apostle to the Amazon," died. The FMB would report that nine other missionaries in Brazil died in the same year. The FMB report to the June 1940 SBC in Baltimore, Maryland, included the following:

> On June 15, 1939, Rev. E. A. Nelson, known throughout Brazil as the Apostle of the Amazon, passed to his reward. He labored nearly fifty years in Brazil and forty-two years with the Foreign Mission Board. He came home on a furlough long deferred in November, 1936, and on January 1, 1938, was placed on the emeritus list. He was restless and unhappy in the homeland. His heart was in Brazil and on the pension of an emeritus missionary he went back to the Amazon Valley alone, leaving in Oklahoma with the children and grandchildren Mrs. Nelson, his aged and devoted companion of fifty years in Amazonia. Only in eternity will we know the full extent and magnitude of the spiritual and eternal investments made by this great and Christ-like soul in the vast reaches of Amazonia. In rapid succession, then, throughout the year came the cables announcing the homegoing of nine other devoted souls who gave a full measure of service and devotion to Christ, even unto death.[90]

LEADERSHIP CONTRIBUTIONS

Maddry reflected in his autobiography,

> I finished all my visits to all the mission fields of our Board with the trip to the newly-established Hawaiian Mission in December, 1941. I was tired when I went out to Honolulu. I came back home completely exhausted, nervous, and sleepless, the burden of the work in the

---

homeland, the continuous travel in foreign lands, the effort to pay off the crushing debt on the Board, together with the heavy responsibility of the administration of the affairs of the Board at home and abroad, had undermined my health. I knew I was headed for the scrap heap unless some way was found for complete rest. This was impossible as long as I remained Executive Secretary.[91]

According to the last report that Maddry gave to the messengers of the SBC in 1944, the FMB employed 484 missionaries serving across the world. Brazil and China contained the largest share of FMB missionaries.[92] Maddry's contributions were many, and each was significant to the future of the FMB/IMB. Maddry oversaw the move of FMB headquarters to its current location on Monument Avenue in Richmond, Virginia. He helped eliminate FMB debt. He recognized that the FMB needed an organizational structure that would divide the responsibilities of oversight among regional secretaries without sacrificing the local mission structures that empowered missionaries to be the primary decision makers regarding missionary work in their respective areas. Maddry was the first executive secretary to travel extensively and visit FMB work firsthand. His denominational statesmanship helped pull Southern Baptists together in dire economic and theological times to support the Cooperative Program for the global advancement of the gospel. His administration resisted the pull of the ecumenical movement that liberalized theology and called for a moratorium on missions. Rather than heeding the call to retreat from aggressive missiological engagement, he intensified it. Charles Maddry, for all of the aforementioned reasons, helped set the stage for a period of great missiological advance for Southern Baptists that would begin with his successor, M. Theron Rankin.

---

91   Maddry, *An Autobiography*, 137.
92   SBCA, 1944, 263.

LEADING THROUGH HISTORY'S SEAMS
Milledge Theron Rankin, 1894–1953

Keith E. Eitel

A TAILOR CUTS CLOTH FROM A PATTERN to fit together suits of clothes. Where the pieces fit, there is a seam line. In parallel, history splices together, and the point of pivotal change is a seam—one piece touching the other, and something new emerging. Similar historical patterns from the former may continue onto the incipient seam pattern, but the form, meaning, and function of the new piece make things noticeably different. Timothy C. Tennent states that in this way people in particular times and places are "living on the seam of history." As pertains to Christian things, he continues, "It is a special opportunity to live during a period in history when you can witness firsthand one of these great cultural and geographic transmissions of the gospel."[1] This chapter analyzes selected elements of Milledge Theron Rankin's (1894–1953) life, leadership, and significance as one of the Southern Baptist Convention's Foreign Mission Board executive secretaries. He lived on three distinct seams of twentieth-century history, led Southern Baptists in their international mission efforts during two of the three, and began to do so into the third only to die as it began.

LIFE'S JOURNEYS: THREE SEAMS OF HISTORY

Sectional strife between the North and the South over the institution of slavery brewed throughout the United States long before the formation of the SBC, but nationwide, Baptists in America had tentatively coexisted since 1814. A climactic breach came over whether slaveowners could serve as missionaries under the auspices of the Triennial Convention (the Baptist union that existed from 1814 to 1845). The latter arose out of the efforts of Luther Rice to unite Baptists in the cause of international missionary activity.[2] The new alignment of churches in the South became the SBC. The preamble of the convention declares its purpose: "A plan for eliciting, combining and directing the energies of the whole denomination in one sacred effort, for the propagation of the gospel."[3]

The convention exists today, still engaged in that founding purpose. The Foreign Mission Board (since 1997 known as the International Mission Board)[4] is herein termed FMB or IMB as

---

1   Timothy C. Tennent, *Theology in the Context of World Christianity: How the Global Church Is Influencing the Way We Think about and Discuss Theology* (Grand Rapids: Zondervan, 2007), 6.

2   William R. Estep, *Whole Gospel Whole World: The Foreign Mission Board of the Southern Baptist Convention, 1845–1995* (Nashville: Broadman & Holman, 1994), 34–35.

3   Estep, *Whole Gospel Whole World*, 49.

4   Keith E. Eitel, *Paradigm Wars: The Southern Baptist International Mission Board Faces the Third Millennium*, Regnum Studies in Mission (Oxford: Regnum, 2000), 114–15.

pertains to dates discussed. Rankin was the first field missionary selected to assume leadership of the FMB in the then nearly full century of the board's existence.

Beginnings

Milledge Whitfield Rankin (1852–1925) and Emma Croxton Rankin (1868–1938) had seven children. Milledge Rankin was born in 1894 as the fourth child in the family. Rankin grew up in a pastor's home, and spiritual influences came early in his life. He professed Christ as savior well before his adult years. An austere financial upbringing shaped his life, values, and character. It created stamina that would hold him in good stead for the things he encountered in later life.[5]

Rankin began his tertiary education at Furman University in South Carolina but encountered financial difficulties and suspended his studies there to work for funds to continue his education. During the years of working and saving for further studies, he came under the influence of the pastor and congregation of the First Baptist Church in Durham, North Carolina. When ready to finish his university degree, he transferred to Wake Forest College (now University) and graduated in 1918.[6]

Elsewhere in the world, war raged. Since 1914 Germany and the Allied forces had fought to a standstill; in 1917 the United States entered the war and tipped the balance of forces in favor of the Allies. Radical changes followed and formed the world that Rankin entered for his missionary career. In November 1918 the war ended. Rankin began as a missionary during this first pivotal seam of twentieth-century history, as the world restructured in the war's aftermath. That very fall semester, Rankin enrolled in The Southern Baptist Theological Seminary in Kentucky. Perhaps the realities and challenges of a new world order piqued Rankin's sense of life's trajectory and

---

5   Estep, *Whole Gospel Whole World*, 252–53.
6   Estep, *Whole Gospel Whole World*, 252–53; and J. B. Weatherspoon, *M. Theron Rankin: Apostle of Advance* (Nashville: Broadman, 1958), 8–10.

defined his calling to be a missionary. This was the first cataclysmic seam of history that Rankin witnessed, and he journeyed into the mission field shortly after World War I when a new order ensued. Other, more local factors influenced him as well. The seminary community had days of emphasis to promote awareness of the biblical, theological, and historical foundations for missions as God's means of bringing to fruition a universal offer of redemption in the world. These days were designed to convict and mobilize young leaders to engage in missionary activities.

Another of life's intersections came during his seminary days. He met Valeria Green, the daughter of China missionaries, fell in love with her, and recognized God's call on both their lives to marry and to serve in China. Valeria graduated in 1920 and journeyed on to China. A year later, Rankin followed after he graduated from the seminary with a master of theology degree. However, both dedicated their lives to missions in China independently but simultaneously during the same campus emphasis when the seminary hosted a missionary speaker from China. Their lives thus merged onto the same path.[7]

Embers of the Student Volunteer Movement still burned in the aftermath of the European war; this further motivated the surviving generation to go to the edge of where spiritually lost lives are lived out and to carry the gospel to them. Southern Baptists had seen the need to evolve and expand their overall missionary presence. Hence, they initiated a convention-wide effort to raise $75 million to fund the whole program of cooperation among Southern Baptists, inclusive of other facets of the SBC's ministries. In the early 1920s the campaign began. By 1925 it seemed to be a failed project as it fell far short of the planned and ambitious funding aim. However, the concept proved doable if budgets and expenditures did not overreach the goals. This funding process now is called the Cooperative Program of the Convention.[8]

---

7   Weatherspoon, *M. Theron Rankin*, 11–13.
8   Jesse C. Fletcher, *The Southern Baptist Convention: A Sesquicentennial History* (Nashville: Broadman & Holman, 1994), 133–34.

In 1921, riding on this wave of excitement and hope, the FMB "appointed forty-seven candidates in a single day."[9] Rankin was one of them and headed out to serve in Canton, China.

A Novice China Missionary: 1921–1927

Rankin's first years in China were busy, fulfilling, and frustrating.[10] He spent most of the first year diligently engaged in language studies. He knew this was the key to cultural understanding and communication of the gospel to the people. In the early stages, he grew frustrated because it seemed a bookish endeavor exclusively. This field frustration is a common issue even in modern field settings where language studies are separated from learning about the culture through social engagement with the people. As his language ability grew, cultural engagement became more exciting and fulfilling.

In that era, there was a south China mission. It was an association of Southern Baptist missionaries working in various roles throughout southern China. Rankin observed those meetings. As a novice, he did not sense he should do much but listen and learn. The sessions were an odd blend of fraternal spirit and fellowship, with intense debates over policies and practices. Rankin grew disillusioned by this. As one biographer said of Rankin's conclusions regarding this event, "Individuality had difficulty in finding common ground with the community. Here was something with which he would have to live, but only as an evident fact that pained him."[11] Rankin's manner led him to decide always to hear others out before finally forming his own conclusions regarding leadership and policies or practices.

After learning the language well enough to engage the work, turbulent times began in China. The end of dynastic governance had happened before he entered China. Social unrest grew with the

---

9   Weatherspoon, *M. Theron Rankin*, 14.
10 Weatherspoon, *M. Theron Rankin*, 14. The outline for significant phases of Rankin's life and work follows the chronology provided by Weatherspoon, Rankin's chief biographer.
11 Weatherspoon, *M. Theron Rankin*, 20.

competitive leaders stepping forward to lead the nation's teeming millions. Nationalistic tendencies were at odds with communist ideologies that were rampant in the 1920s. Rankin realized that the only way effectively to counter these tendencies was through biblically teaching national believers and leaders. The mission formed the Graves Theological Seminary, and Rankin was one of the first faculty members. Later, though reluctantly, he assumed the presidential role but eagerly sought indigenous leadership. One of the core values Rankin developed was the need for indigenizing all the functions of the mission whenever and wherever possible at the earliest moment. As he later wrote of this subject, he said this attitude should prevail in all missionary work: "It is inevitable that, as these churches develop and grow, the relationship of the foreign missionary to them changes. We are but forerunners for them. They must increase, we must decrease. The hope of evangelization of their people lies within themselves and not within foreign missionaries. Neither as individuals, nor through the denominations that send us to work with them, can we exercise authority or 'lord it over them.' We must insist that their responsibility is to God and that he is their only authority."[12]

Academics Again: 1927–1928

First-term missionaries come back to school with focal questions learned out of the mix of cross-cultural experiences. In Rankin's case, he returned to The Southern Baptist Theological Seminary to pursue a doctorate in theology.[13] As he was departing China, there was a move to form a united front of all Christian faiths, and thereby formation of an ecumenical council for China developed. The advantages and disadvantages of this move pressed in on his thinking and were the

---

12 Milledge Theron Rankin, "New and Old in Missions in the Orient," *Review and Expositor* 40, no. 4 (1943): 444.
13 See his doctoral dissertation. M. Theron Rankin, "A Critical Examination of The National Christian Council of China" (PhD diss., Southern Baptist Theological Seminary, 1928). Also see Richard Edward Bray, "An Examination of the Life and Ministry of M. Theron Rankin" (PhD diss., New Orleans Baptist Theological Seminary, 1994). The latter is mostly written as an assessment of Rankin's dissertation.

subjects to which he turned his attention when pursuing further studies. Under the tutelage of W. O. Carver (1868–1954) at Southern Seminary, he took up the study of a movement evolving out of the Edinburgh world missionary conference in 1910. Rankin developed his dissertation thesis as a critique of the National Christian Council of China. It proved to be a test case for evaluating the global trends toward ecumenism, and it was beneficial for him in that stage of life as well as later as the executive secretary leading the FMB as a global mission agency.[14] An analysis of his dissertation as an expression of his missiological and ecumenical convictions will appear later. J. B. Weatherspoon records insights into Rankin's aims and motivation for doing this research: "I have attempted to make this examination from a non-partisan point of view. I have had no theory concerning the Council to prove. . . . In the constitution of the National Council, there was no statement of theological or ecclesiological tenets. It presented the Christian groups in China a statement of aims proposed and a method of procedure."[15] Though formed as a voluntary association for the unification of all streams of church life in China, the organization drifted swiftly to use its collective force of influence to merge all elements into a unified church structure that has proved to diminish core beliefs of individual denominational entities and make doctrine unimportant.[16]

Years of Travail: 1928–1935

While the Treaty of Versailles may have formally ended World War I, it did not settle the turbulence of the era. Regional skirmishes ensued. Russia was still settling down after a bloody revolution, Germany's colonies were carved up and apportioned to the Allied

---

14 Weatherspoon, *M. Theron Rankin*, 34–35.

15 Weatherspoon, *M. Theron Rankin*, 37–38.

16 For an assessment of this erroneous policy on a global scale that was ingrained in the belief system of the National Christian Council of China at a more recent point in history, see David J. Hesselgrave, "Will We Correct the Edinburgh Error? Future Mission in Historical Perspective," *Southwestern Journal of Theology* 49, no. 2 (2007): 121–49. Hesselgrave provides the long-term effects of this foundational policy decision.

powers, Hitler was on the rise in Germany, and communism surfaced strongly in China while a simmering civil war boiled over in sectarian parts of the country. Rankin and the other missionaries of southern China continued with the work to evangelize and train Chinese nationals for the work of the ministry. Rankin resumed his role at Graves Theological Seminary. The turmoil in China took a toll on the student population in the seminary. There were divided opinions among students and Chinese faculty as well. Battles for the future of China spilled over into the ministry population and created strife among churches.

Seminary enrollment declined steadily, and by 1929 the financial crisis throughout the world crippled the economy in America as well as gifts to the SBC's mission work. Such dismal circumstances affected the morale of missionaries in general and specifically that of Rankin. In these circumstances, he turned inward and grew depressed as he questioned the work as a whole.

He worked through it with encouragement from the FMB leadership at home. They advised him not to close the seminary but to restructure it and to move forward toward more autonomy for the Chinese leaders by incorporating them into the ruling board for the seminary. However, there was a flaw in the design, and Rankin tried to mitigate it. Though the nationals brought their views and opinions to the table when the seminary board met, they had no control over the budgets or policies, which were still in the hands of the FMB and the missionaries. Indigenous progress stalled. Through Rankin's leadership, a proposal created a new reality. The FMB ceased controlling the school in 1933. The local association of Chinese churches was to assume control, and if they wanted any FMB personnel to assist, then they were happy to ask for it but without the types of foreign control formerly imposed on them.

Rankin's leadership skills were noted back in the US, and leadership of the FMB invited him to assume the role of secretary for the Orient, the first such regional position created. Eventually, this meant he would need to relocate to the US to advise and lead out in the affairs of that region. More turmoil, however, was on the horizon.

Global Upheaval: 1940–1944

A second seam of twentieth-century history, through which Rankin led out in advancing missionary causes, was the war in Asia that commenced from the time of the Japanese invasion of China in 1937. The scope of the war grew and became global by 1939, and by 1941 it encompassed most of Asia, Europe, and colonial areas. Rankin was serving the various FMB missions in Asia, and he was trying to deal with the issues arising from encroachments and forced integration of all churches in Japan under one entity without international influences or funding.

As sometimes happens in times of violence, an invading army trapped some missionaries. In December of 1941, the Japanese invaded Hong Kong. Rankin and five others were hiding in an apartment initially unnoticed by the Japanese.[17]

Eventually, all American expatriates lived out their internment in Hong Kong's Stanley Prison. They were approximately three hundred in number. By July 1942 Rankin and the others were released in a prisoner exchange worked out between Japanese and American officials. Life in the prison was spartan at best. The prisoners were in charge of their care, and food was sparse. The organization of their self-governance was of utmost importance to lessen the horror of war and imprisonment.

Leading On: 1945–1953

The financial collapse on Wall Street in 1929 led to a decline in giving for obvious reasons and in turn crippled the budgets of several agencies within the SBC.[18] The FMB was no exception. In 1933, during the height of the financial crisis, C. E. Maddry assumed the executive secretary's role with the sole objective of recovering from the board's bankruptcy. Slowly the country improved and giving

---

17 Weatherspoon lists the other five missionaries trapped by the invasion. They were "the Cecil Wards, Miss Flora Dodson, Miss Orris Pender, and Oz Quick." Weatherspoon, *M. Theron Rankin*, 93.

18 Weatherspoon, *M. Theron Rankin*, 93. Except where otherwise noted, this segment follows closely the emphases set forth by Weatherspoon's sixth and seventh chapters.

came back to normal levels; but implementing austerity programs within the board's operations required Maddry's steadfast priority of purpose in holding the organization together during the storm. For twelve years Maddry led the board as it recovered financially. In 1945 the SBC would be one hundred years old. This event seemed a pivotal time for a new beginning. He announced his retirement to the board, and a search committee was formed. After a season of prayer, the committee members took a secret ballot and unanimously nominated Rankin to become the first field missionary ever elevated to lead the whole organization. In January 1945 Rankin assumed the role.

Rankin's brief but effective tenure as the executive secretary bore many personal characteristics that were reflected in his administrative policies and procedures, his ability to read world trends in the aftermath of the most destructive war in human history, and his ability to see ways through the mire of devastation and lead on to a new advance. Rankin honed his skills for teamwork and consensus building while in China as a young missionary. Now that he was seasoned and mature, these skills proved essential in leading the FMB through the social storms after World War II. He emphasized complete transparency and saw his viewpoint as one among many. He invited contrary views to help the team make the best collective decisions. Rankin was self-secure enough to avoid personal petty prejudices and to encourage the same in others.

Additionally, building up financial reserves while at the same time trying to push toward an advance in the work was a delicate task that involved many critical decisions. During the financial crash and the economic depression, there had been little funding to evacuate missionaries from war-torn zones. Under Rankin's leadership, the FMB set aside reserves to avoid such circumstances in the future.

Rankin had an uncanny ability to read the signs of the times. He could see the present in the context of the past and set forth clear directions for the future steps the FMB should take in light of global affairs. The most evident of such realities was the horror of devastation in both Asia and Europe after World War II. Rankin challenged the SBC to rally to the causes of aiding in the humanitarian crisis created by the ravages of war. Rankin expressed his opinion regarding these circumstances in an editorial: "With the direst need around the world that we have ever known and the most significant open doors of opportunity we have ever had before us, it will be inexpressibly tragic if we stand still at such a time in the life of the world as this."[19]

As critical as relief aid was throughout the world, Rankin did not sense that it was the only thing with which the FMB should be concerned. In the aftermath of bombed-out European rubble, the fractured hearts and crippled faith of believers and unbelievers alike were noticeable. The crisis created an open door to aid in the time of both physical and spiritual needs. As was his usual inclination, he wanted to spur the FMB's work toward an advance in evangelism, church planting, and training of leadership on a worldwide scale. Rankin aimed to shore up work that existed before the war and enter new places that were now in such need. All of this was happening at the early stages of national realignment. Centuries-old colonial empires were breaking up throughout Africa, Asia, and in parts of Latin America. They were spawning new nation-states.

In 1910, the Edinburgh conference pointed evangelical Christianity toward interfaith cooperation that had ripple effects throughout the individual fields of missionary work. Those influences were also affecting the FMB's work around the world. As seen earlier, Rankin grew disenchanted with the vision for organic integration of Christian bodies in China that trended toward a single-church union that would undermine unique or individual denominational doctrinal values and convictions. World War II interrupted these trends, but postwar they resumed

---

19 M. Theron Rankin, "Shall Southern Baptists Peg Our Program of Foreign Missions," *Biblical Recorder*, November 5, 1947, 5. See also other publications wherein his urgent appeal appeared: Rankin, "Southern Baptists and Foreign Missions," *Biblical Recorder*, October 24, 1945, 14; and Rankin, "Relief Supplies Desperately Needed," *Biblical Recorder*, November 7, 1945, 6.

with renewed vigor. Rankin wanted to cooperate in a limited sense with other Christians. As noted by Baptist historian William R. Estep, Rankin's attitude was to say, "While we welcome the opportunity of working together, there are limits beyond which we cannot go."[20] Rankin's tenure and legacy as the executive secretary of the FMB, though short-lived, was marked by his administrative skills, his understanding of missionary roles in the midst of radically changing global affairs, and the FMB's advance through the social storms.

One of Rankin's first duties as the executive secretary of the FMB was to work with Maddry for a smooth transition between their administrations and to ramp up the planning and execution for the centennial celebration of the SBC's founding and simultaneously the first one hundred years of the FMB's existence. Initially, this was set to take place in May 1945. However, SBC executive committee officials received notice from US government and military officials to postpone the annual meeting of the SBC: "The war effort denied Southern Baptists their planned centennial celebration in 1945. Due to a government ban on large group meetings, they canceled their annual session once again. . . . It was finally celebrated in Miami, Florida, in 1946."[21]

A substantive document commemorating the FMB's celebration had been prepared for 1945 and later presented to the SBC in session in 1946. It delved into the history and the then-current circumstances of the board in the context of the world at large, and it projected new directions for a new century. Maddry contributed an introductory piece, and as Rankin was transitioning to the

---

20   William R. Estep, "Course-Changing Events in the History of the Foreign Mission Board, SBC, 1845–1994," *Baptist History and Heritage* 29, no. 4 (1994): 10. As evidence of Rankin's open-minded yet cautious observer role in ecumenical affairs, he attended the formation of a missions conference for North America and chaired the committee working on concerns for religious liberty throughout the world's mission fields. See "Report of the Fifty-Sixth Annual Meeting of the Conference of Foreign Mission Boards in Canada and in the United States," January 10, 1950, 134.

21   Fletcher, *The Southern Baptist Convention*, 175.

executive role, he supervised the construction of the remaining document. It is a treasury of missiological conviction and vision. While many subjects are covered, one stands out. It pertained to the convictions the document stated regarding racial attitudes. The report presented this statement in the section regarding missionary personnel selection authored by the secretary in charge of that function: "The Foreign Mission Board will appoint only those who give evidence of a Divine call to foreign mission service. Missionaries need to have Christ's attitude toward people of all other races. No volunteer who cannot love and share and work as an equal with any member of the human race should ever go as a missionary to people of other lands."[22] Given the historic sensitivities regarding race in the founding and development of the SBC, this was a bold statement for a better future. In the era when the report was generated, race relations were still tenuous throughout the United States, but they were especially so in the Southern states. It is an accolade to Rankin's legacy that as the editor of the report, he made sure to include this section.

As the postwar world realigned and revolutions begun before the war continued to unfold, especially in China, missionaries were affected along with their work. A significant challenge during Rankin's administration was the case of William L. Wallace (1908–1951). Wallace was a medical doctor serving at the Stout Memorial Hospital in Wuchow, China. He was a single missionary devoted to the care of his patients through both the Japanese attacks during World War II and the Communist revolution in the aftermath of the war. Wallace opted to stay in Wuchow, and Communist soldiers eventually imprisoned him in December 1950. They tortured him, and he was found dead on February 10, 1951. According to Everley Hayes, the nurse recounting the story claimed his body showed signs of being beaten to death.[23] This scenario became the official

---

22 "One Hundredth Annual Report: Foreign Mission Board," in *Thanking God and Taking Courage* (FMB Minutes Access # 2736, 1945), n.p. The personnel secretary was J. W. Marshall.

23 Estep, *Whole Gospel Whole World*, 280–83.

rendering of his death by the FMB.[24]

Considerable confusion surrounded the details of the way Wallace died while in custody. According to the official version, he looked beaten to death by the Communist authorities. However, in a series of reports to the FMB and Rankin from the US State Department, differing accounts unfolded. Hayes rendered a lengthy report to State Department officials. In the report, she stated that the Communist officials gave her conflicting statements. One version was that Wallace shot himself, and the other account was that he hung himself. When she retrieved the body, the visible indications were that he did not look like someone who had hung himself. The ligatures around the neck seemed fabricated. However, before she could remove the body for burial preparation, she was required to sign a statement concurring with the officials that he committed suicide by hanging:

> On the morning of February 11, 1951, a letter was sent from the police department to the hospital asking them to inform me that Dr. Wallace had hanged himself on February 10 and to ask me to come over and confirm the fact. . . . We were shown the body and the marks on the neck, but before we were allowed to move the body, we were required to sign a statement that he had hanged himself. . . . We were escorted by a military guard of four soldiers from the prison to the grave. This guard stood by and watched until the last spade of dirt was thrown into the grave. There was no way to make a private examination of the body in the hospital. . . . Because of the presence of the soldiers that was no opportunity for a burial service.[25]

---

24 For the official FMB version see Jesse C. Fletcher, *Bill Wallace of China* (Nashville: Broadman, 1963).

25 Letter from Walter P. McConaughy, American Consul General Hong Kong, "To the Foreign Mission Board of the Southern Baptist Convention Regarding Transmission of Statement by Miss Everley Hayes in Regard to the Death of Dr. W. L. Wallace," August 28, 1951.

Confusion regarding his death lingered as indicated by the life insurance company's inquiry to the State Department attempting to
clarify things. The policy could not pay out until it was definitively
clear as to whether he committed suicide.[26] Rankin was the FMB's
negotiator throughout this unfolding and heroic drama.

By midyear of 1953, Rankin learned of his health condition
while preparing for a journey to South America on FMB business.
The physician examining him thought he seemed in good health
but did wish to do some blood tests. The news came back that it was
leukemia. On June 27, 1953, Rankin passed into the final symbolic
seam of history for every person, life after death.[27]

CONCLUDING ASSESSMENT

The analogy of a seam in history draws into comparison two distinct
realities, the connection of cloths with the flow of time and human
events. Rankin lived on three critical seams of history during the
twentieth century: World War I, World War II, and the emerging
Cold War. Each prior reality was passing, and global affairs pushed
forward to a new pattern of historical sequence. Leadership by those
with keen insight and, in the realm of missions, clarity of conviction
mingled with seasoned experience proved essential during such
tumultuous times. Rankin rose to such challenges and led the FMB
through those waters of crisis at various levels of authority. During
phase one, he was a novice missionary learning through patient trial
and error how mission work is enacted on the grassroots level. As
phase two came to the forefront, Rankin led in both regional and
global levels of decision-making for the FMB and, thereby, for the
SBC as a whole.

Finally, the clouds of Cold War realities challenged him as the
world's powers squared off and a tense balance ensued after World

---

26 Reginald Damerell, "Letter from New York Life Insurance Company to the State
Department Regarding the Death of Dr. William L. Wallace," October 29, 1951.
27 The notice of Rankin's passing is recorded here among other places. "The Church
Roll," *The Christian Century*, July 29, 1953.

War II. It changed the political face of nations and influenced the way that missionaries could or would function primarily in the postcolonial era. Rankin seemed to be able to glean the critical lessons of the past and apply them to the emerging future in each transitional period. He was, as Weatherspoon says, the "Apostle of Advance."[28]

---

28 Weatherspoon, *M. Theron Rankin.*

8

ADVANCING A WORLDWIDE WITNESS

Baker James Cauthen, 1954–1979

Thomas Nettles

THE REPORT OF THE FMB for 1980 began with these words: "This past year's foreign mission effort was accomplished in the midst of shocking human suffering, devastating inflation, political turmoil, resurgent religions, militant secularism, and indescribable moral decay. These create the environment for missions every year. Next year will be no different."[1] The report was presented by Keith Parks as a

---

1   SBCA, 1980, 85.

summary of world conditions in the final year of the leadership of Baker James Cauthen.

Twenty-six years earlier, in 1954, in the last report prior to the initiation of Cauthen's tenure, George Sadler reported, "Years ago we used to sing: How long must they wait for the Good News?" He surmised that many who are tired of waiting "have turned to Mohammedanism and Catholicism and Communism. And now, for the time being, at least, they are beyond the reach of our message." Others, however, still within reach, "constitute a mandate to Southern Baptists."[2]

The way of the world is relentless; human sinfulness is pervasive; false religion abounds; and opposition to gospel truth, given the fears and corrupting powers of this dark age, is universal. Parks's words are true: "Next year will be no different." Though each aspect of the condition of the world described seems shocking, discouraging, and depressing, it has never been any other way since the expulsion of Adam and Eve from Eden. It has never been kinder and gentler. Baker James Cauthen had experienced it and would lead the FMB in such an age.

A PHILOSOPHY TO PENETRATE THE DARKNESS

M. Theron Rankin, just a few weeks before his death from leukemia, set forth a clear philosophy of missionary work as distributed within the framework of a variety of ministries. Work was being done in thirty-two countries where 879 missionaries served. Though the report included relevant statistics, Rankin pointed out that the real task of the missionary focused on training. Though missionaries are active in their efforts to "lead people to a personal faith in Christ Jesus as Lord and Saviour," their more substantial long-term goal is to "develop a strong, well trained, indigenous Christian constituency" who call and train their own pastors through their own agencies and institutions.[3]

---

2   SBCA, 1954, 105.
3   SBCA, 1953, 102–3.

This also was the final year, 1953, that Cauthen reported to the convention as secretary to the Orient. He described the sobering, and threatening, reality of communism. He referred both to the tragedy and the glory of Christian work in China. "Large numbers of Christian workers endured long months of bitter imprisonment" with ever-increasing pressure against Christian work. "Persecution is not direct," but Christians "must face charges that they are spies for Western powers" unfriendly toward the Communist government. Christianity is the real threat, but "the charges are usually on the basis of some political pretext." Systematic policy to deconstruct Christian witness and institutions brought them so "firmly under the grip of the government that they have lost their Christian usefulness."[4] The University of Shanghai now functioned as a government school for workers. Many theological seminaries were forced to close.

The last report that Cauthen himself gave as executive secretary (1979) reflected the dramatic growth of Southern Baptist foreign missions. New programs had been initiated for both shorter-term missions and large numbers of volunteer missions projects. Cauthen reported that appointments reached a new high in 1978 for the third straight year, totaling 350 for all categories (compared to eighty-four in 1952), an increase of 25 percent over 1977. This increase included thirty reappointments and 181 new career missionaries, a number that exceeded career appointments in 1977 by 40 percent and exceeded by 5 percent the highest previous year (1963). Also appointed were thirty-six missionary associates, ninety-five journeymen, and eight special-project medical workers. The net missionary personnel gain for the year was 130, the largest net gain since 1966. By the close of 1978, the missionary staff totaled 2,906, including 224 missionary associates, 183 journeymen, and twelve special-project medical workers. The board also arranged for 2,866 persons to participate in volunteer involvement projects overseas in 1978. These statistics reflect new types of missionaries that did not exist in 1953.

---

4 SBCA, 1953, 154–55.

At the end of 1978 Southern Baptist foreign missionaries were assigned to ninety-four countries and territories. Bolivia, Haiti, Mauritius, and St. Martin had been added. Baptist churches with which the FMB had cooperative relationships grew from 8,533 churches and 1,071,922 members to 10,449 churches and 1,214,699 members and reported 94,543 baptisms. The report also indicated how Southern Baptist missionaries had been instrumental in helping organize and participate in massive evangelistic campaigns in several countries, including full involvement with the Billy Graham Evangelistic Association in Singapore and the campaign of Luis Palau in Ecuador.

This report also showed that, from the standpoint of trouble spots in the world, tribulation, tensions, and challenges had not diminished, although their locations had shifted. China had changed as Teng Hsiao-ping began promoting modern economic development, relaxed some internal pressures, and made overtures to the outside world. The United States announced formal recognition of the Peking government and broke a long-standing defense treaty with Taiwan. The implications of this development, both for the people of mainland China and Taiwan, were unpredictable. In Southeast Asia, however, Vietnam and Cambodia were involved in intense and brutal conflict. Refugees from both countries marched onto the world conscience. These refugees included many Chinese people, who "caught the world's attention as pathetic 'boat people,' often preyed upon and denied refuge." The Camp David Accord had taken place but was of uncertain implementation. Opposition to the shah of Iran had reached dangerous proportions. The government of Afghanistan was overthrown in a "pro-Soviet coup." Fighting continued in Lebanon, and the "Palestinian issue showed no sign of solution." Conflict throughout southern Africa yielded the possibility of radical and dictatorial governments, as well as in Zaire, Uganda, and Ethiopia. Cuban forces were a factor in these revolutionary developments.

Having been initiated into missionary work in the midst of a time of spiritual power and of intense worldly turmoil, Cauthen was well-attuned to the dialectical rhythm of both these realities in a fallen world in which God is redeeming sinners.[5]

BAKER JAMES CAUTHEN

The increase of the missionary force and the kinds of mission activities emerged from the Advance program that Rankin had initiated and reflected the growth of Southern Baptists. At the same time, such steady and impressive growth, in human terms, would not have occurred apart from the energetic work of Cauthen and his unceasing call for more funds and more people to execute the Great Commission. In the January 1954 edition of *The Commission*, Frank Means introduced Cauthen to Southern Baptists with "Meet the New Secretary." Acknowledging that "he carries responsibilities which no man should be asked to bear alone, and which Cauthen himself would be unwilling to undertake without a complete reliance upon the Lord," Means gave a summary of how "divine providence has been at work in remarkable ways to prepare him for leadership in our world mission program."[6]

Born in Huntsville, Texas, on December 20, 1909, Cauthen moved with his family to Lufkin, Texas, soon after that. Under the encouragement and godly influence of his parents, Cauthen professed faith in Christ at six years of age and at eight sensed that God wanted him in gospel ministry. At age seventeen he entered Stephen F. Austin State Teachers' College and also began to serve as pastor of a rural church near Nacogdoches. After graduating from Stephen F. Austin, Cauthen continued study at Baylor University, where he received an MA in 1930. He moved to Fort Worth where he received his ThM degree and began serving as pastor of

---

5 SBCA, 1979, 86–90.

6 Frank Means, "Meet the New Secretary," *TC* 17, no. 1 (January 1954): 2. Most of this specific biographical material is taken from this source. The reader also should refer to Jesse Fletcher, *Baker James Cauthen: A Man for All Nations* (Nashville: Broadman, 1977). See also *TC* 42, no. 10 (October 1979): 1–40; the issue is titled "The Cauthen Years." See also Baker James Cauthen, et al. *Advance: A History of Southern Baptist Foreign Missions* (Nashville: Broadman, 1970), 58–76.

Polytechnic Baptist Church seven months before graduation. He had known Eloise Glass, the daughter of missionaries to China, at Baylor, making her appearance at Southwestern Seminary a matter of more interest to him. Their college acquaintance fostered a mutually respectful friendship, gave rise to deep admiration, and finally to a commitment to marry. They were married in the seminary chapel on May 20, 1934, immediately after Eloise had received her degree. Cauthen continued in ThD work, completed the degree in 1936, and was asked to continue academic work in the seminary as a professor of missions. He accepted the position while continuing his calling as full-time pastor at Polytechnic. The feverish pace that these two positions determined for him accustomed him to long hours of work, planning for multiple tasks simultaneously, and a crunching economy in time distribution. His students were victims of his personal energy with stiff requirements in the missions classes and consistent probing of conscience concerning the massive imbalance of gospel preaching between the southern United States and many countries with extremely sparse or no gospel witness.

While serving in these capacities, with Eloise pursuing her calling as a busy pastor's wife, the Cauthens had two children—Carolyn, born in 1937; and Ralph, born a year later. They committed themselves to pray about receiving the challenge for mission work that Cauthen so often placed before his classes. In 1939, Baker James and Eloise appeared before the board for appointment. He described their careful pattern of prayer and thought that culminated in this sense of call: "During the past year we became so unmistakably impressed that God was urging us to go to China that we came to believe that we would be untrue to the call of God if we did not offer ourselves for that service. For many months we made it a matter of prayer, and the conviction grew with such intensity that we felt assured it was the voice of God. We, accordingly, have taken this step and rejoice in God's leadership."[7] Later Cauthen recalled, "My wife and I were appointed as missionaries in April 1939 and were

---

7   Baker James Cauthen, quoted in Means, "Meet the New Secretary," 3.

presented to the Southern Baptist Convention meeting in Oklahoma City in May of that year, along with nine other newly appointed
missionaries. I had the privilege of addressing the convention for a
few minutes. It was my first time to say anything from the platform
of the Southern Baptist Convention."[8]

When they arrived in China, the country was under attack
by Japanese forces. Within weeks they were in the sound of war,
a constant companion for their years in China. His observations
concerning the extremity of the needs, both physical and spiritual,
of the people combined with his lack of facility in the language
led to some convicting impressions about missionary labors. He
mentioned first the extreme poverty that "beggars description."
He saw one family seeking to sell their baby in exchange for food.
Second, he saw the appalling spiritual ignorance and need. One
person asked him if Jesus was an American. Third, he had seen
the power of the gospel to give "life, hope, and transformation."
Fourth, Cauthen noted the "wide open door for evangelism."[9] That
observation taught him to press for laborers while there was time,
for such doors could be closed rapidly.

The helplessness in the face of these challenges when he was
forced to remain silent gave him sympathy with missionary recruits
and a determination to establish means for language facility more
rapidly and thoroughly. At the end of his first year, Cauthen was
preaching in Chinese. He maintained a heavy schedule in churches
and in schools. In a series of evangelistic meetings in Shanghai, he
reported, "All together there have been about seven hundred people to make public profession of faith in Christ as their Saviour."[10]

Eventually, the war drove Cauthen to Kweilin in southwest
China, the capital of Kwangsi Province and an important center of
Baptist work. The situation did not allow his family to accompany
him. They were sent to the Philippines for a time. When they were

---

8   Baker James Cauthen, "Final Year," *TC* 42, no. 1 (January 1979): 47.
9   Cauthen, quoted in Means, "Meet the New Secretary," 3.
10 Cauthen, quoted in Means, "Meet the New Secretary," 30.

reunited, the war was also reaching Kweilin, and frequent trips to a bomb shelter became a part of their lives. In addition, Ralph was stricken with polio and Carolyn had an extended bout with a debilitating fever. Mrs. Cauthen became critically ill. These experiences made Cauthen aware not only of the trials and dangers often undertaken in missionary life but also of the great blessing of home life. He observed, "The sharpness of these separations is blunted, however, by the fact that God shows missionaries through these times of loneliness the great treasure he has given them in their home life so that when there are occasions of uninterrupted home life they become seasons of blessedness which refresh the soul."[11]

China always was on the mind of Cauthen. In 1962 he wrote an article for *The Commission* titled "Lest We Forget" that recounted Southern Baptist work in China from its beginning to the events of fall 1948 through spring 1949, when "the communist armies marched victoriously from the north to the south, and China came under the power of the hammer and the sickle." The expulsion of the last missionary occurred in 1951 after the death of missionary physician William Wallace, who had been imprisoned by the Communists for fifty-three days. He recounted the actions of the government toward Christian churches including the "Three-Self Committee" and its virtual prohibition of preaching anything distinctively Christian in these government-recognized churches. Cauthen showed why he felt so deeply about the missionary efforts in general and the years of Chinese work in particular.[12]

He had confidence that the living Christ would not forsake them. "Chinese Christians," Cauthen pointed out, "have shown themselves willing to follow Christ even to the point of dying for him." Both the Boxer uprising and the Pacific war produced striking examples of this. He viewed them as skillful in adapting to difficult circumstances and surviving under adverse conditions without compromising basic truth. Those who were not able to endure

11   Cauthen, quoted in Means, "Meet the New Secretary," 30.
12   Baker James Cauthen, "Lest We Forget," *TC* 25, no. 1 (January 1962): 19–20.

grieved those who maintained loyalty to Christ. Chinese pastors and other Christian leaders endured imprisonment, long periods of brainwashing, public humiliation, personal suffering, and family disruption. Cauthen was confident that when we "see our Chinese Christian friends before the great, white throne, we will hear many wonderful reports of suffering in Christ's name and following him without thought of self."[13]

In 1946, upon Rankin's election as executive secretary, Cauthen was appointed as secretary to the Orient, succeeding Rankin in that position. With Rankin's agreement, the Cauthens sought to live on the field in Shanghai. Cauthen was grateful for that understanding, for it gave him firsthand knowledge of all the permutations that challenged the missionary effort in Asia. In that year, he wrote, "There is more hunger in the Orient today than has been experienced in all modern times. War, drought, flood, disrupted communications, pests, storm, hoarding by pitiless men—all have combined to bring the Orient into hunger."[14] These postwar conditions called on Southern Baptists to make special efforts to help relieve these people from possible starvation, but much more from the pervasive spiritual destitution. Consistent demand for his presence in Richmond as part of a team of administrators made a move there necessary. He could have access to a larger amount of information concerning the new areas into which Southern Baptists were entering.

Within a year of the move back to Richmond, Rankin had died. George Sadler told Cauthen that his name had been put forth as executive secretary. He and Eloise considered requesting the board not to consider their names at all, but "throughout the entire experience," Cauthen testified, "there came repeatedly convictions that we should leave the matter in the hands of God."[15]

Upon Cauthen's election, the acting executive secretary, George Sadler, spoke of the transition from Rankin to Cauthen. He observed

---

13 Cauthen, "Lest We Forget," 20.
14 Baker J. Cauthen, et al., *Now Is the Day* (Nashville: Broadman, 1946), 20.
15 Baker James Cauthen, "Twenty-Five Years," *TC* 41, no. 12 (December 1978): 37. See also FMBM, October 13–14, 1953, 100–101.

that Rankin, "as completely as any man we have known," embodied the spirit of foreign missions. While his death constituted "a
grievous blow," when it was known that Rankin's illness was likely
to be fatal, the minds of many began to turn toward Cauthen. He
had been Rankin's successor as secretary to the Orient, and a large
number of individuals were of the opinion that he was the person
who should succeed him as executive secretary. On October 14,
members of the board acted in accordance with what appeared
to be the will of the majority of Southern Baptists, and Cauthen
became the eighth executive secretary of the FMB.

Cauthen responded, "Inasmuch as we have sought to leave our
own hearts completely in the hands of God for his direction, we
can feel nothing else except a call of duty at this time." In asking for
their continual prayer and undergirding as he had sensed during his
fourteen years of service to this point, Cauthen confessed, "If it were
a matter of considering whether we are worthy or capable of such a
responsibility, we would not in the least consider it. But there is an
assurance that, if God is directing, he will give his enabling grace."[16]

When Keith Parks succeeded Cauthen, he made note of Cauthen's passion and drive as abiding influences in the philosophy of
missions at the FMB. Parks highlighted Cauthen's "leadership and
dynamic proclaiming of foreign missions" as a challenge and inspiration to Southern Baptists. Particularly he noted "his prayerful,
Bible-saturated, single-minded devotion to Christ and his world
mission" to drive the denomination to world involvement. In spite of
his physical absence, Parks believed that "his influence will continue
to be felt" for the "basic philosophy and primary purpose that Baker
James Cauthen declared with such force will remain the operating
principles of this agency." Of special interest, he observed, "The
pattern he followed in adapting to changing circumstances will be
expanding in light of present realities."[17]

---

16   Cauthen, "Twenty-Five Years," 37.
17   SBCA, 1980, 85.

CALLING OUT THE CALLED

As seen in the 1976 recommendations for Bold Mission Thrust, a consistent theme of Cauthen in his challenges to the churches and in his personal ministry was the duty to "call out the called" and make sure their means of support was available. The report that year referred to that task in four contexts. "That the Convention call upon all our churches, state conventions, institutions, and Southern Baptist Convention agencies to unite in a viable and dynamic program for calling out the called." Educational institutions should challenge students to answer, "'Here am I, send me,' if they feel called to the mission field." All encampments and assemblies should conduct services "for calling out the called." Pastors should lead their churches to have an annual life commitment "for calling out the called."[18]

In the FMB report at the SBC in 1956, Cauthen placed the call to world missions squarely on the shoulders of each local church. "The Scriptures clearly teach that each New Testament church has world responsibilities. Making disciples of all nations is not a labor to be undertaken at our option or convenience. It is the mission given to us by our sovereign Lord."[19]

In his first editorial for *The Commission*, Cauthen wrote about the need for more than money. After showing the overwhelming monetary commitment needed as missionaries were assigned to different fields of service, Cauthen turned his attention to the call of the missionary. "With all my soul," he emphasized, "I believe the thing that would electrify Southern Baptists into a dynamic world undertaking far beyond anything yet anticipated would be the challenge of hundreds or even thousands of our choicest young people laying themselves without hesitation on the altar to go anywhere in the world to devote their lives to the service of Christ." He asked younger pastors, already well trained in both the theory and practice of Christian ministry, to consider going to the mission field.

---

18   SBCA, 1976, 55.
19   SBCA, 1956, 111.

He quoted missionary Keith Falconer: "While vast continents are shrouded in almost utter darkness and hundreds of millions suffer the horrors of heathenism and of Islam, the burden of proof lies upon you to show that the circumstances in which God has placed you were meant by him to keep you out of the mission field." Every student enrolled in a theological seminary, Cauthen added, should ask himself, "Why shouldn't I go?" With transportation so rapid that any place in the world is brought to the doorstep, "Would it not be right to offer yourself to the Lord to go where the darkness is deepest?" Those studying for other careers should look to the possibility of "a call to a higher task." Each church should pray that the Lord would call its finest young people to the mission field. If only one young person from each of the 29,496 churches cooperating with the convention were to respond to God's call, "what a vast army of volunteers would be available!" This would challenge Southern Baptists to "heights of stewardship." Parents should offer their children to the Lord and "beseech him to call them to the mission field if it be his will."[20] "In the face of a world tottering on the brink of chaos, we hear the ringing, unmistakable words of our Lord's Great Commission."[21]

In an article titled "Basic Requirement for World Missions," Cauthen again placed the responsibility on each Southern Baptist to justify his or her not going to the mission field. "The fact that millions in darkness have never heard the name of Christ puts the burden of proof on staying to light another candle where many already are burning." He explained the great variety of gifts put into use by the multiplicity of opportunities for ministry on the mission field. He continued Rankin's emphasis on "developing indigenous Christianity in the lands they serve." The indigenous work, however, still needed the supplemental support, both financially and personally, from more stable and affluent sending organizations. "I am certain that if young people could read the letters appealing

---

20   Baker James Cauthen, "More Than Money," *TC* 17, no. 4 (April 1954): 9.
21   Baker James Cauthen, "More Than Money," 26.

for missionaries which come to my desk from Indonesia, Malaya, Thailand, the Philippines, Formosa, and Korea their hearts would respond." None should hesitate because there are "enough missionaries" or for their fear that they would not be appointed.[22] If such a thing is in one's heart, "it is your duty to respond."[23]

Along with the need for increased personnel, the commensurate need for financial support found consistent expression from Cauthen. In the convention report for 1955, Cauthen noted, "Throughout 1954 the conviction that Southern Baptists must greatly enlarge our world ministry continued to deepen." He reported that the Cooperative Program and the Lottie Moon Christmas Offering had put more resources into the hand of the mission board than in any previous year of its history. Volunteers from college, seminary, and adult professions indicated that "by midsummer of 1955 we will have appointed more missionaries than were appointed in all of 1954." But the financial support, in Cauthen's opinion, was not near the potential of the convention. For all causes, Southern Baptists gave more than $300,000,000 in 1954. If only five cents on the dollar were to make it to the support of missions, the board would have $15,000,000, and $30,000,000 at a tithe of the total. He believed that in response to "immeasurable world need," Southern Baptists could make such a commitment. This commitment would bless every church in the convention and strengthen every cause. "It would enable Southern Baptists to grow in sacrificial spirit and power. It would make possible our sending the Light to many areas we have not reached." The reality, however, was that "it was necessary to cut out $300,000.00 from the requests made by the missions for current work" and fell two million below urgently needed expansion in several areas. Dedication of life would mean dedication of material things. He called, therefore, the churches to serious prayer and labor to see one of their number appointed

---

22   Baker James Cauthen, "Basic Requirement for World Missions," *TC* 17, no. 5 (May 1954): 9.

23   Baker James Cauthen, "Basic Requirement for World Missions," inside back cover.

to foreign missions. Should that happen, a flood of 29,899 people would "volunteer to take the Light into the darkness." He emphasized the vision of Rankin to have 1,750 missionaries abroad at the earliest possible time.[24]

In 1961, the board reported, "At the beginning of 1961 there were 1,480 missionaries under appointment for service in forty-five countries." They stated that the objective by the close of 1964 was to have a minimum of two thousand missionaries. In 1962, the report showed encouraging progress. The 1961 final total showed 1,548 missionaries under appointment for service in forty-seven countries. During the entire history of the FMB since it was established in 1845, a total of 2,820 missionaries had been appointed. "It is quite remarkable," the report noted, "that more than one-half of these missionaries are serving today." Around 183 emeritus missionaries still lived, who by their prayers and testimony reinforced the world task.

By 1963, the Advance program had been accomplished. Cauthen, in a piece titled "What Next?," described the original Advance program as something that "seemed fantastic. It would call for an outlay of $20,000,000 a year and triple the number of missionaries sent by Southern Baptists." The Advance program made high demands of persons who had borne special responsibilities, but the goal was accomplished. By the end of 1963, 1,800 missionaries represented Southern Baptists in fifty-three countries, reinforced by more than $20,000,000 made possible through the Cooperative Program and the Lottie Moon Christmas Offering. Cauthen then advocated that further advance must follow and continue to expand the stewardship of the gospel.[25]

In 1970, Cauthen edited a history of the FMB. Cauthen kept up the familiar sense of urgency by asserting that "one of the chief objects of prayer should be for the calling out of laborers to the

---

24   SBCA, 1955. 110.
25   Baker James Cauthen, "What Next?," *TC* 26, no. 9 (October 1963): 9. See also
      SBCA, 1964, 121.

Lord's harvest." Each church should pray that "from its own congregation there would go forth at least one foreign missionary." In
addition, he made sure that ringing in the ears of Southern Baptists
would be the repetitive chorus of support through the Cooperative
Program and the Lottie Moon Christmas Offering. He called for
increasing percentages given to foreign missions at every level of
Southern Baptist life.[26]

Also, in 1970, Cauthen wrote an article titled "Warning Lights"
in *The Commission*. Though he detected no immediate crisis, he
emphasized that the number of missionary volunteers had fallen
from 261 in 1969 to just a few more than 200 for 1970, and that
every level of convention must be addressed to help Baptists develop
an urgency about "Christ's expectations for sharing the gospel of
redemption on a world scale now." The second warning light was
financial. Increased personnel meant increased expenditure and a
decreasing percentage of budget money for support of programs
and construction of needed facilities. The answer, of course, was
not to cease emphasizing the need for missionaries but to give
more heartily. Cauthen expressed his confidence that "Southern
Baptists will not be prepared to see a slowdown in foreign missions
occasioned either by a dropping off in the number of missionary
volunteers or by a decline in financial support."[27]

In 1973, twenty years after his first editorial, Cauthen continued
with his consistent call to the churches to look conscientiously at
their church budgets in light of the pressing international need. He
cited comparative statistics for several years from 1948 through
1972. He reported, "Gifts made by Baptists in the churches in 1972

---

26   Cauthen, *Advance*, 304. Other writers were Jesse Fletcher, Winston Crawley, Cor-
      nell Goerner, J. D. Hughey, and Frank Means. It was published for the 125th year of
      both the SBC and the Foreign Mission Board. Cauthen described the work briefly
      as "not a definitive history written primarily for scholars, nor is it a collection of
      popular missionary stories." Rather it was for "well-informed members of church-
      es." It intended to "set forth the story of this enterprise as it has progressed across
      the years, with something of the joy, and sorrow, victory and defeat, faith and aspi-
      ration which lie at its heart" (1–2).
27   Baker James Cauthen, "Warning Lights," *TC* 33, no. 7 (July 1970): 21.

totaled $1,023,146,829, but gifts received by the Foreign Mission Board through the Cooperative Program, the Lottie Moon Offering, and special designated gifts combined reached a total of $35,439,524—less than 4 cents of each Baptist dollar." Over 50 percent of that was given through the Lottie Moon Christmas Offering. "This means that Southern Baptists utilized more than 96 cents of each Baptist dollar in our own country and less than 4 cents to share the gospel of Jesus with the rest of the world."[28] Each year, he added, immediate needs on the field fall short between $4 million and $7 million. Writing in September, he knew that churches were soon preparing budgets for the next year, and he hoped that his report would encourage them to designate a greater percentage to the Cooperative Program.

The September issue of *The Commission* included major research and promotion articles on the Cooperative Program. Other writers—Hal Wingo, Drew Gunnels, and Winston Crawley—echoed Cauthen's concern that local churches and state conventions absorbed an increasing percentage of total gifts. Crawley closed his article with a serious admonition. "But surely Southern Baptists should be able to agree on and dedicate themselves to the purpose of world evangelization and to the basic concept of base and outreach. This would mean a determination, by individuals, pastors, churches, and conventions, that as resources keep growing, an ever-larger portion will move onward toward the reaching of the whole world."[29]

Among the early editorials by Cauthen, one was titled "More Missionaries Are Needed—Now."[30] He wrote about the wide variety of skills needed on the mission field: preaching, publishing, medical work, theological education, bookkeeping skills, and secretarial expertise. All of these kinds of gifts and skills could be used efficiently and productively on the mission field.

---

28 Baker James Cauthen, "Money for Missions," *TC* 36, no. 8 (August 1973): 24.
29 Winston Crawley, "Needed: A Clear Distinction," *TC* 36, no. 9 (September 1973): 14.
30 Baker James Cauthen, "More Missionaries Are Needed—Now," *TC* 17, no. 6 (June 1954): 8–9.

In particular, Cauthen could speak from personal experience, "there is a distinctive thrill about preaching on the mission field. One often finds himself preaching to those who have never heard the name of Jesus or have had only slight touch with the gospel." He also emphasized the work of missionary women in several places where no male missionaries had been appointed. They were efficient in Bible study sessions but were solicitous of missionary couples for a preacher. It was not just numbers that Cauthen was after. "A small group of God-called, well-trained, thoroughly committed servants of Christ can accomplish far more than a larger number without these necessary qualities." The FMB continued to look for high standards in missionary appointments. "Amid these standards the most important, aside from a personal experience of grace, is a positive conviction of divine mandate. Only that kind of missionary has the staying quality so urgently necessary."[31]

A VARIETY OF PROGRAMS

One answer to this multiplicity of needs was given in the introduction of two shorter-term programs. These programs were designed to provide specialized help in critical times and additional personnel for certain initiatives.

Missionary Associates
On October 11, 1961, the personnel committee recommended to the board the employment of missionary associates to meet a limited number of urgent, specific requests for specialized personnel. They would do basic missionary work without the long-term involvement assumed by a regular missionary. They were employed, not appointed, and their work was limited to one term, or upon recommendation, a second term. *The Commission* reported, "This program is but one of many ways in which the Board is seeking to develop a more flexible approach to missionary outreach. In it

---

31   Cauthen, "More Missionaries Are Needed—Now," inside back cover.

the Board is taking advantage of an opportunity to waive certain requirements to secure persons with unique experience and unusual ability for specific tasks." Audrey Dyer of Minnesota was the first missionary associate. She was a well-trained nurse with excellent experience, both overseas and in the United States. She filled a need at the Ire Baptist Welfare Center in Nigeria.[32]

In only a slight nuance of that program, *The Commission* announced that the personnel department was seeking ten "qualified nurses for employment on a contract basis for two years in order to meet critical needs for missionary nurses." After two years of service, both the Board's and their obligations would end.[33]

Journeyman Program

The missionary Journeyman program was begun to enlist college graduates under twenty-seven years of age to work two years overseas with career missionaries.[34] This program constituted the condition on which Jesse Fletcher agreed to become secretary for missionary personnel. He accepted the position in November 1963. By the summer of 1964, Fletcher, along with others, had designed the program. The first group of forty-six journeymen was set apart at First Baptist Church, Richmond, Virginia, on August 10, 1965. The program was received well by the churches and the missionaries on the field, and it became a source of new appointees when many who served that program returned to the field under full appointment.

Fletcher replaced Elmer West Jr. in the position of secretary. West was returning to the local church as a pastor but still maintained strong convictions about the relation between these shorter-term programs and the full appointee. He had been instrumental in establishing the missionary associate program. In departing, he warned against any tendency to increase numbers by lowering requirements. To lower standards "to accommodate desires of earnest brethren

---

32   Elmer West, "Missionary Associates Meeting Special Needs," *TC* 26, no. 5 (May 1963): 15.
33   "Foreign Mission News," *TC* 26, no. 9 (October 1963): 29.
34   "News," *TC* 33, no. 6 (June 1970): 40.

whose zeal is more evident than knowledge regarding long-range missionary task of evangelism and church development" would "invite ultimate defeat of an effective gospel witness even though the immediate results might indicate great success. . . . Mediocrity is never more apparent than in an overseas setting." He asked questions about long-term evangelism and observed, "Our brethren are confused as to what the main thrust of missions should be in our day." Adding a bit more opinion that showed not only his conviction about the purpose of missions but also his concern that confusion was present, he emphasized, "The compelling need will always be for the person who will plant his life among God's creatures in another land to learn their language and learn their ways. There is no substitute for the hard core of missionaries who have committed themselves to the long pull."[35]

Fletcher agreed. Though these additions made possible involvement of people in projects that did not involve career commitment, the career missionary still stood as the "keystone for world strategy." Ten years into his work as director of the Missions Support Division, Fletcher argued that "the crossing into another culture, the learning of another language, the breaching of barriers cannot be attempted, much less accomplished by anything short of a career missionary." Though many Christian denominations had diminished the category of career missionary, and other observers hurled cruel caricatures—"Missionaries are part and parcel of a white imperialism"—Southern Baptists had increased their number of career missionaries. Also, they handled the criticism with wry humor, devoted and wise strategy, and a policy of indigeneity in perceived outcome. Fletcher insisted that the career missionary has been "deeply sensitive to deculturating the gospel and doggedly determined to let the word of freedom inherent in the gospel develop apart from anybody's politics or economics." Fletcher was convinced that the call to career missions would saturate a person's spirit with sufficient challenge for his devotion to Christ, his natural talents,

---

35   Elmer West, "Foreign Mission News," *TC* 26, no. 9 (October 1963): 28.

his spiritual gifts, and his sense of enduring discipleship to last beyond a lifetime. "The challenge of career missions is increasingly life size. The multiskilled, multilingual, internationally life-styled career missionary is coming to constitute a hard corps of professionalism around which the church's overseas ministry is expanding. In pockets of pain, ignorance, and darkness, the career missionary in other lands is caught up in a spiritual battle eliciting all of his potential—something few people back at home ever experience."[36]

To show that the Journeyman program provided well-qualified, experienced, and committed missionaries to the lifetime corps, *The Commission* would sometimes highlight the work done by journeymen who had continued for special extended work or as career missionaries. Doug Kellum began as a journeyman in Vietnam from 1972 to 1974. He continued working with Vietnamese refugees in Arkansas in 1975 and then went to Thailand to work with Cambodian and Vietnamese refugees there beginning February 1976. In addition to some hard manual labor, Kellum turned the mail-call routine into an evangelistic opportunity by giving a devotional talk and distributing Bibles before issuing the mail. *The Commission* reported, "By the end of 1977 more than 150 persons had been baptized, and 25 others were awaiting baptism." The growing Christian presence among the ethnic groups put an end to the frequent fighting that had formerly prevailed.[37]

Troubles within the Convention

Conflicts that arose within the convention did not have a major impact on the functioning of the FMB during the Cauthen years. In fact, the presence of that agency in its central concerns for evangelism and Great Commission commitment was a major stabilizing factor in what could otherwise have been disruptive. When it appeared that theological tension might threaten denominational unity and thus interrupt the increased flow of revenue, Cauthen would issue

---

36   Jessie Fletcher, "Keystone for World Strategy," *TC* 36, no. 10 (October 1973): 2–3.
37   "A Loving Hand to Survivors," *TC* 41, no. 4 (April 1978): 12–13.

cautionary words encouraging love and unity. The race issue in the early 1960s in the nation at large and the South in particular had a disturbing impact on the fields in which Southern Baptists served. The combination of racial tension and doctrinal division probably prompted Elmer West Jr. to his observations made at his departure from the board in 1963. He indicated that "these are days of peril and pain for Christians in America and Southern Baptists in particular." Probably indicating his discomfort with increasing theological diversity, the irresolution of the convention in solving these ongoing tensions, and the turmoil over vicious racist activity among Baptists in the South, West said, "All is not well with us. We have paid dearly for some of our successes. We are prone to panic and look for scapegoats. Our shouted panaceas have a hollow ring. Many times we are afraid to talk to each other within the context of Christian love and trust. We pass our resolutions and pray, but we are tempted to run for the exits and avoid the revolution which surrounds us. Even foreign missions may be an escape for some people. God forbid!"[38]

Elliott Controversy

The first doctrinal confrontation during these years centered on Ralph Elliott, an Old Testament professor at Midwestern Baptist Theological Seminary, and his method of employing the discipline of higher criticism in the interpretation of the Bible. It surfaced in 1959, when some students protested the views of biblical truthfulness expressed by Ralph Elliott in his interpretation of Genesis. Trustees were able to contain the brewing controversy for a short time. It became convention-wide, however, when in 1961 Broadman Press published his book *The Message of Genesis*. Elliott's interpretive method allowed him to deny the real historical credibility of some events of Genesis while seeking to distill the overall doctrinal message from the text.[39]

---

38 Elmer West, "Foreign Mission News," *TC* 26, no. 9 (October 1963): 29.
39 Ralph Elliott, *The Message of Genesis* (Nashville: Broadman, 1961).

Though efforts were made to keep the issue isolated to the seminary, Ramsey Pollard, pastor of Bellevue Baptist Church and president of the SBC in 1960, referred to this brewing controversy. Engaging this isolated tempest at Midwestern, Pollard stated, "Southern Baptists need a purity of purpose and a purity of doctrine. It does matter what you believe." Salvation was an intensely doctrinal issue; a wrong message, wrong theology, could have tragic eternal consequences. Salvation by sacraments and good works is not the same as salvation by faith alone in Jesus Christ. Some had become "so tolerant and wishy-washy in our doctrine that we are insipid and impotent." Without mentioning names or places, Pollard observed, "We hear in this day and time from some of our educators a great deal about academic freedom. Well, I am in favor of academic freedom, but I don't want a man or a woman in our Baptist colleges, universities, and seminaries who feels that he or she has the right to teach that the Word of God is not true." Baptist money should not go to any institution or professor who intimates "that the miracles in the Word of God are not true." He only knew of one place where such was being done, and he intended to go "to the president of that institution and to the board of trustees." To any person who denied the miraculous in God's dealing with his people he gave this message—"get out of our seminaries! Get out of our churches!"[40]

After the publication of the book in 1961, the controversy became so agitated that the convention in 1962 passed a resolution affirming the entire Bible as the "authoritative, authentic, infallible, Word of God" and opposing theories that undermined the Bible's "historical accuracy." Trustees were asked to "remedy situations" that threatened this historic position. Broadman made an administrative decision to withdraw the book from publication. In October 1962, Elliott was dismissed, not for his theology or his method of interpretation, but for "insubordination," a refusal to consent to trustee instruction that he not seek another publisher for his book.

---

40   SBCA, 1960, 79.

The episode led to a call for a revision of the Baptist Faith and Message. This revision was presented to the convention in 1963. Herschel Hobbs, president of the convention that year and chair of the committee to revise the confession, preached. He looked at crises in the world such as the atomic threat, the communist threat, and the threat of overpopulation. Within the convention, one of the tensions was the production of the confession of faith. The process, Hobbs claimed, "has demonstrated that brethren of Christian conviction and love can work together." He said that the twenty-four persons on the committee agreed "without a single serious theological difference." The six seminaries studied the statement "without voicing an objection to its theological concepts." Now, instead of using such theological muscles to bash one another's heads, "we should be using them to lift toward God a world which writhes in the throes of sin and death." In light of that, Hobbs gave a strong call for "an unprecedented program of world missions." Still, the field is the world, and it seemed that communists were taking such a vision more seriously than Christians. Communism could not be defeated with guns and bullets but only by the gospel of Christ. "The missionary strategy of two decades ago will not suffice in this hour." He then called for a variety of approaches of which the mission boards, publishing houses, and Radio and Television Commission were all aware. "Such an enlarged concept of missions must utilize a greater variety of the skills of men and women." He then asked, "Will the children of light in their generation be wiser than the children of this world? Upon this answer may well rest the future of the world for the next thousand years, if Jesus delays His return."[41]

Because others were speaking with such force to the relation between the theological tension and the cause of missions, the FMB made few statements about either the Elliott controversy or the adoption of the new confession. They were, however, very concerned about the intense racial issues that burned during the early sixties.

---

41   SBCA, 1963, 93–94.

Racial Turmoil

In 1962, *The Commission* carried an article by Ebb C. Smith, missionary to Indonesia, about the brutal racism that caused distress around the globe. He described the Muslim concept of enslavement to Allah, *Ummat*, as that which destroyed any sense of segregation, prejudice, or racial superiority and made them claim Islam as the religion of all men. Because of the racial tensions rampant in the United States, South Africa, and other European-based cultures, they viewed "Christianity [as the religion] of white men only." Smith, however, saw the cross of Christ as a far superior motivation for racial unity but lamented that its implications had been practiced so scarcely in some cultures. He applied these observations to the task of missions: "World events seem at times to bear out such a mistaken idea because some Christians in practice fail to implement the mandate of the cross in relation to race—and the Christian world mission task staggers beneath the weight of inconsistency."[42]

In 1963 Cauthen wrote "This We Could Do." In light of escalating racial tension in the United States and particularly in the South, he observed that many "are not aware of how greatly these tensions affect the witness of God's servants abroad and our possibility of maximum service in this new day of world evangelization." One could have learned this truth quickly simply by thumbing through the pages of *The Commission*, but Cauthen reminded the Baptists of the South, "A great portion of our mission work is among nonwhite peoples of the world, to whom all matters concerning race are extremely delicate." He had received much information from the fields concerning "the bearing of racial disturbances upon the witness they seek to give." One highly competent missionary had commented that "nothing has ever occurred to so tarnish the image of America," adding, "The best of our columnists, not to speak of the worst, are literally tearing us to pieces." Cauthen advocated steps toward remedying this sad circumstance. He recommended that churches "make it clear

---

42   Ebb Smith, "Acceptance of *All* Men," *TC* 25, no. 2 (February 1962): 16.

that all people—regardless of race, nationality, wealth, poverty, or station in life—are welcome to worship in our churches." After some observations about the post-Civil War and twentieth-century development of separate congregations for whites and blacks, Cauthen advocated that clearly annunciated public policy should be stated of openness in the churches to persons of all races and nationalities. "This is something Southern Baptists could do. It is something nobody can do for us. It would have long-range value for world evangelization. We might discover that our total witness for Christ in a world of desperate need would take on new power and significance."[43]

This same issue of *The Commission* carried a notice that 160 missionaries on furlough signed a resolution that read: "That we go on record as grateful to God for every earnest effort currently being put forth in Southern Baptist life in the interest of progress and justice to improve race relations in our homeland, and that we pledge anew our fervent prayers that the day may soon come when tensions will be resolved on the basis of God's love and concern for all people everywhere, regardless of racial origin."[44]

In July, Brooks Hays, a former president of the SBC (1958 and 1959) and a White House special assistant to President Kennedy, spoke to the FMB and thirty-two missionary candidates about the necessity of achieving "Christian justice and Christian brotherhood in its highest and truest sense in our beloved Southland." Having visited Sierra Leone, Liberia, and Nigeria, he unofficially surveyed the job of Christian missions and concluded that the task at home was the improvement of race relations and demonstration of Christian love and brotherhood. As he looked at the potential good that could be done by these candidates, he said, "If we fail in

---

43   Baker James Cauthen, "This We Could Do," *TC* 26, no. 6 (June 1963): 15. Interestingly, in 2019, the Southern Baptist Executive Committee inserted into the terms of fellowship in the Southern Baptist Convention this requirement: "The Convention will only deem a church to be in friendly cooperation with the Convention . . . which . . . does not act to affirm, approve, or endorse discriminatory behavior on the basis of ethnicity." SBC Bulletin, Tuesday June 11, 2019, 4.

44   "Foreign Mission News," *TC* 26, no. 6 (June 1963): 31.

this matter of brotherhood at home we are going to frustrate them at every point."[45]

In September 1963, *The Commission* carried an article by Daniel R. White titled "Racial Prejudice: A Factor in Christian Missions." He had preached this earlier in an associational meeting in Louisiana, and it was edited for publication. His points were, "Christianity Is Not Exclusive," "Attitudes in the U. S. Are Handicaps," "Race Solution Would Aid Missions," and "Prejudices Hinder [the] Cause of Christ." In writing about the phenomenon of white flight, the author remarked, "Can we say to people around us, 'Because you are not white, we have no message for you?'" He also observed that "American prestige shot to a new high when the Supreme Court ruling against segregation in public schools was announced. It dropped to a new low when Southerners began to speak against the ruling. Baptist leaders must take a stand against this matter or else we must pull down our missionary banners and admit that we do not mean business in winning our world."[46] Hawaiian Baptists also noted the disturbing effect that racism in the South had on attempts to evangelize. In December, *The Commission* carried a news article that the assassination of President Kennedy was electrifying in Africa. His emphasis on civil rights made some think that a white supremacist had killed him. Had this actually been the case, "our missionaries in several African countries would have found it difficult to continue at their work." This observation reflected the fact that "any outbreak of racial violence anywhere in the United States might have disastrous effects on our work overseas."[47]

The Broadman Commentary Controversy

The failure to deal decisively with the relation of higher criticism to pervasive biblical truthfulness gave rise to another controversy over the Bible. Broadman Press began publishing its "largest

---

45   "Foreign Mission News," *TC* 26, no. 7 (July 1963): 29.
46   Daniel White, "Racial Prejudice: A Factor in Christian Missions," *TC* 26, no. 8 (September 1963): 7–9.
47   "Foreign Mission News," *TC* 26, no. 11 (December 1963): 13.

publishing venture in the history of Broadman Press."[48] The original volume 1, published in 1969, included a commentary on Genesis by G. Henton Davies, a British Baptist scholar, that took the same approach to Genesis as had Ralph Elliott. In addition, the general editor, Clifton Allen, had written an introductory article titled "The Book of the Christian Faith," in which he not only denied but severely criticized "verbal inspiration" because a "careful reading and examination of the Scriptures discloses some obvious contradictions or discrepancies . . . quite sufficient to raise a problem as to the validity of verbal inspiration."[49]

In light of these and other problems, Gwin T. Turner, a pastor from California, moved that "because the new *The Broadman Bible Commentary* is out of keeping with the beliefs of the vast majority of Southern Baptist pastors and people this Convention request the Sunday School Board to withdraw Volume 1 from further distribution and that it be rewritten with due consideration of the conservative viewpoint."[50] When the item came to a vote, the motion passed 5,394 to 2,170.[51]

Publicity about Turner's intent to call attention to the issue of theological problems with the commentary had circulated before the convention. Cauthen sought to defuse the possible negative effects this could have on the unity of the convention around missions in a June editorial in *The Commission*. Recalling the emotion of a Falls Creek assembly singing "I Have Decided to Follow Jesus," Cauthen emphasized that "there must be no turning back from our determined purpose to share the gospel of Jesus Christ with all the world." We must not be sidetracked, turned into bypaths with "divergent matters." Because "nothing should cause us to turn aside from our major purpose" of going to the world with the gospel, "We must let nothing divide us." Our unity depends on being able to discern the difference

---

48 *The Broadman Bible Commentary*, rev. ed. (Nashville: Broadman, 1973), vol. 1, inside of front dust jacket.

49 Davies, *Broadman Bible Commentary*, 1:7.

50 SBCA, 1970, 63.

51 SBCA, 1970, 78.

between bedrock convictions and opinions. "If we let opinions take on the driving force of conviction, we will lose our way in endless entanglements and confusion." Cauthen said that "our words should become more gentle, carefully chosen, and appreciative."[52]

Though Chauncey R. Daley, editor of the *Western Recorder*, was no theological ally of W. A. Criswell, he represented the overriding desire for unity in programmatic matters above doctrinal conformity when he made a statement of gratitude to Criswell. "His powerful personality and spiritual magnitude have been the most calming force in the Convention." Apart from his manner of presiding, "this Convention would have been complete pandemonium."[53] One sees the continuation of this concept of denominational as opposed to doctrinal unity in the presidential address of Carl Bates in 1972. He gave a pretty typical response to this conservative movement in pitting confessional theology against the need for conscientious missionary and evangelistic involvement. He eschewed "power structures" that sought uniformity. "Our churches," Bates reiterated, "have steadfastly refused to forfeit one whit of their freedom to interpret the Holy Scriptures for themselves in exchange for any creed or creed-like statement devised thus far."[54]

Committee of Fifteen

In 1974, the convention ordered a major strategic study of future work for the convention, including long-term plans for the FMB. This recommendation came from a "Committee of Fifteen," ten pastors and five laymen who had been appointed by the Executive Committee of the SBC.[55] They were to study the operations of all the convention agencies and make recommendations for more efficient operation per their assignment from the convention.

---

52   Baker James Cauthen, "No Turning Back," *TC* 33, no. 6 (June 1970): 34.
53   SBCA, 1970, 82.
54   SBCA, 1972, 93
55   For a summary of the work of this committee, especially in relation to the FMB, see William R. Estep, *Whole Gospel Whole World: The Foreign Mission Board of the Southern Baptist Convention, 1845–1995* (Nashville: Broadman & Holman, 1994), 312–15.

When the particular suggestions for the FMB were released to the Baptist Press in January 1974, the administration of the board took strong exception to the suggestions, their implications, and the implied shift in the assignment structure. They felt that the suggestions that had arisen from a meeting of the Committee of Fifteen with the administrative staff of the FMB had "established priority concerns by selection not so designated by the study."[56] The committee suggested in recommendation 20, "We think that the development calls for a major review of existent strategy and a bold new development of guidelines for new strategies. These should be developed by a knowledgeable and broad based sympathetic committee as soon as possible."[57]

Though emotional fireworks popped, and strong exception was taken to both content and method of the committee, Cauthen felt that the major problem came from the infringement on the normal protocol for SBC agencies in channeling plans through the boards of trustees and the resident staff. This was an unwarranted, unconstitutional overreach by the Executive Committee of the SBC, and in Cauthen's studied opinion, the assigned duties and authority had been usurped. These strong objections and challenges to the report led to a significant alteration of its impetus. The change called for a "total Convention mission strategy" involving all the mission agencies, the WMU, the Brotherhood, and the Executive Committee. It was to "involve all appropriate agencies in developing a challenge to Southern Baptists to help meet world needs in the final quarter of this century." A final report presented in 1976 issued a call to all churches, individuals, and other institutions to join the bold initiative.

Meanwhile, after the first flurry of confrontations, the FMB positioned itself as already engaged in the restudy of strategy. In October

---

56 Estep, *Whole Gospel Whole World*, 313, citing a letter from Jesse Fletcher to the Executive Committee.

57 *The Report of the Study Committee of Fifteen to the Executive Committee of the Southern Baptist Convention* (Nashville: The Executive Committee of the Southern Baptist Convention, 1974), 107, cited in Estep, *Whole Gospel Whole World*, 314.

1974, Cauthen wrote, "The foreign Mission board is engaged in a far-reaching study of plans for the future. Escalating world-wide needs make imperative a careful review of all existing plans and earnest seeking for God's guidance toward whatever bold new plans may be helpful in sharing Christ with the whole world."[58] Winston Crawley, director of the board's overseas division, followed up with an article ("For the Greatest Yield") that began, "Everyone uses strategy." Explaining that mission teams on the field always strategize, he noted the urgency for a constant review of plans. Rapid population growth, challenges from other worldviews, and more development of technology in transportation and communication made a constant review necessary. The existing strategy included widespread cooperation between the churches, the board, the missionaries, and the churches on the field. Second, the strategy was decentralized by each mission adapting to particular circumstances general principles set by the board. Indigenous strength was a central principle as well as a "comprehensive" use of various ministries. Flexibility was the final principle. Crawley expressed his hope that church members would avoid "well-worn stereotypes in the thinking about missions" and that it would result in "more sympathetic understanding of the work missionaries are doing and the problems they face and help church members to pray more effectively for missions."[59]

In 1976, Cauthen reported to the convention the immense amount of planning, consulting, and evaluating that had been done throughout 1975 and the comprehensive and sweeping nature of the involvement. This intense study included "dialogues with denominational leadership groups, a consultation involving 300 people from all over the world, and recommendation from missionaries in 82 countries about strategy for the next 25 years." Again he emphasized his perennial call for personnel and financial support: "It is fully anticipated that Southern Baptists will respond to a new thrust in mission

58   Baker James Cauthen, "An Open Invitation," *TC* 37, no. 10 (October 1974): inside front cover.
59   Winston Crawley, "For the Greatest Yield," *TC* 37, no. 10 (October 1974): inside front cover, 1.

advance both by increased giving through the Cooperative Program and the Lottie Moon Christmas Offering and by earnest prayer that the Lord of the harvest may thrust laborers into his harvest."[60]

In that year, the convention received a final report from the Committee of Fifteen. This report began the convention-wide impetus called "Bold Mission Thrust." Article 1 set the stage: "That the Convention set as its primary missions challenge that every person in the world shall have the opportunity to hear the gospel of Christ in the next 25 years, and that in the presentation of this message, the biblical faith be magnified so that all men, women, and children can understand the claim Jesus Christ has on their lives." It called on all churches and convention agencies to promote and magnify "the biblical concepts of missions, the importance of missions education, and the power inherent in the interdependence and cooperation of the churches." The two mission boards were requested "to undertake seriously the creative addition of new patterns for work that will help accomplish the objective." A strong doctrine of stewardship was encouraged for the individual, for the churches toward the Cooperative Program, and for the state conventions toward the national convention. In the mandate for comprehensive inter-agency cooperation in this program, Cauthen's concern that the entire thrust recognize "the leadership responsibility of the two boards" was embraced. Article 15, as already mentioned, emphasized that special emphasis be given convention-wide to the stewardship of "calling out the called."[61]

TRANSPARENT REPORTING TO THE CONVENTION

The FMB sought month by month and year by year to present to Southern Baptists an accounting of the full sweep of missionary work. The annual convention report and the monthly publication of *The Commission* provided the platform.

---

60   SBCA, 1976, 98.
61   SBCA, 1976, 54–55.

Under the general heading of "Program Report" in the SBCA each year, the report of the FMB included details about missionary support, evangelism and church development, schools and student work, publication, medical work, and benevolent ministries. The Missionary Support Division gave information on personnel, missionary education, promotion, and furlough. Management Services included information on the business side of the entire enterprise.

The Commission provided a constant source of information about all things missions. New appointees, veteran career missionaries, the variety of types of missionary outreach, month-by-month news, insight into the difficulties as well as the rewards of missionary life, and a constant probe into the consciences of Southern Baptists to engage their lives more seriously with foreign missions filled its pages. The challenges before missionaries were not sugarcoated but were laid out in their stark reality. Displacement from familiar surroundings, adjustment to a different culture, learning a language, separation from friends and family, loss of loved ones, quick evacuation in case of highly unstable political conditions, quick movement from one assignment to another, the slow beginnings of a lifetime commitment that produces a feeling of irrelevance and uselessness—all these were discussed frankly in *The Commission*. All of this was made bearable, according to Carl Whirley, by "the absolute lordship of Jesus Christ and . . . our utter subjection to Christ based on his redeeming work for us."[62]

Southern Baptists were kept abreast of ongoing labors, the creativity required by unexpected challenges, and the tragic loss of life. In 1954, the first year of Cauthen's secretaryship, Everett Gill reported to the board that the new regime in Colombia issued decrees "prohibiting Protestant work in eighteen so-called 'mission' territories, many of which are inhabited by Indians, and (2) by a more recent decree prohibiting non-Catholics from engaging in religious activities outside of their own churches."[63]

62   Carl Whirley, "The Servant Role," *TC* 36, no. 10 (October 1973): 17.
63   "Briefly," *TC* 17, no. 4 (April 1954): 8.

The conflict in Korea was prominent in the minds of Southern Baptist missionaries to that area. Ione Gray informed Southern Baptists about the overwhelming stream of orphans caused by the brutality of the conflict. These difficult circumstances had given the Baptist churches of Korea an "indomitable faith and courage" strong enough "to shake the Christians of America out of their lethargy." Gray considered her visit to Korea "about the most disturbing experience of my life." All of the refugees from the North had heartrending stories. One Baptist deacon, chosen by his family as the one person who could escape, left a wife and three children. He had heard from them most recently two years before when they were "living in caves seeking to evade the communists."[64] The writer closed the article by pointing to the glaring responsibility created by the stark difference of situations. "I have never been hungry, I have never really been cold. No bombs have ever been dropped on my home and my family. But this accident, which made me a spectator on the sidelines of misery, disease, pain, suffering, and starvation, also gave me the responsibility of sharing what I have with the people of Korea. I can no more escape my responsibility than they can escape from their land of tragedy."[65]

From the 1974 Program Report, one can see quickly how complex and difficult the task is in coordinating missionary strategy on a global scale. The Yom Kippur War had occurred with all the residual complications between the US and Russia as well as Israel and the Arab powers. Watergate was an all-consuming concern in the United States with the international implications brought on by that political turmoil—the devaluation of the dollar, the energy shortage, the oil embargo, and the Vietnam truce agreement, which brought home troops and prisoners of war but left fighting still present in Vietnam and Cambodia. Uganda posed a major problem of political unrest with foreigners "gradually being squeezed out."

---

64   Ione Gray, "Lunchtime in Korea," *TC* 17, no. 5 (May 1954): 4–5.
65   Gray, "Lunchtime in Korea," 5.

Chile saw the expulsion of the Marxist government and the rule of the military established. The Bahamas became independent; Peron returned to power in Argentina after eighteen years of exile.[66]

As in every year of the report, 1974 included statistics that would allow Southern Baptists to give at least a numerical measure of the work being done. The Department of Missionary Personnel reported missionaries under appointment as 2,538, including the appointment of 229 new missionaries. They served in seventy-seven foreign fields. Those newly appointed missionaries included 124 career missionaries, fourteen missionary associates, seventy-five missionary journeymen, three special-project medical workers, and thirteen reappointments. Of the total number of missionaries, career missionaries stood at 2,226 while the auxiliary programs added 312—including 172 associates, 137 journeymen, and three special-project workers. One hundred ninety-eight losses were registered during the year. The largest number of losses during the year was due to resignations, a total of 119.

Among the career missionaries, the men averaged 31 and the women 30 years of age, while the average family had two children. Missionary associates averaged 55 and 49 for men and women respectively. Journeymen averaged 23 years of age. The appointees came from thirty states and all six Southern Baptist seminaries. Twenty-three percent of the new missionaries were seminary gradu-ates. The new missionaries were assigned to twenty-eight categories of work, including fifty-one for general evangelism, twenty-eight for secondary teaching, thirty-six for youth and student work, eight for theological education, six as business managers, twelve as music missionaries, and eleven as nurses.[67]

In 1972, missionary nurse Mavis Pate was killed by Arab com-mandos when they ambushed a car in which she was traveling from Gaza to Israel. Her mother, Mrs. J. H. (Mattie) Oden, wrote a poem in remembrance of her daughter. The fourth of five stanzas said,

---

66   SBCA, 1974, 116.
67   SBCA, 1974, 125.

Thus, our parting daily loses
Something of its bitter pain,
And while learning this hard lesson
My great loss becomes my gain,
For the touch of grief will render
My wild nature more serene,
Give to life, one aspiration,
A new trust in the unseen.[68]

The 1974 Program for Missionary Support included the following information: "Tragedies in the missionary ranks during the year included the murder of Gladys Hopewell and the death of Clyde Jowers by automobile accident."[69] In 1978, this report mentioned that the killing of missionary Archie Dunaway led to the relocation of some Rhodesian missionaries. *The Commission* for August and September filled in the details of the tragic event and of the long-term persevering missionary service of Dunaway. He was stabbed to death by four bayonet thrusts by a band of nationalist guerillas on June 15 in Sanyati hospital. His body was found the next day after a thirteen-hour search. Dunaway served as a maintenance supervisor at the hospital and as an area evangelist. Mrs. Dunaway was a missionary nurse and directed a school for midwives.

In another 1978 SBC report item, we learn that "Southern Baptist missionaries were able to return to Ethiopia, but only on a limited basis." That brief statement would include the work of missionary Sam Cannata, a surgeon of outstanding ability. His work in Rhodesia, appointed in 1957, had resulted in an eye infection by which he lost his sight in one eye. When work in Ethiopia was opened, Sam Cannata requested a transfer there in 1968. He flew to remote villages, conducted medical clinics for hundreds who had no access to such care, and used these occasions to bring "the good news of Jesus Christ to those in need." Cauthen included an

---

68   Mattie Oden, "My Mavis," *TC* 36, no. 10 (October 1973): 21.
69   SBCA, 1974, 11.

editorial about a book Cannata had written titled *Truth on Trial.* It chronicled the arrest of the Cannata family in Ethiopia in 1978. The family was released after questioning, but the physician himself continued under arrest for fifteen days. Cauthen called the book a "thrilling narrative that leaves the reader spiritually blessed and strengthened . . . an intimate portrayal of the deep pain and suffering which must be endured, but also of the victory that comes by faith and the reality of God's action in response to prayer." Cauthen thanked God for "his wonderful deliverance of the Cannatas through this hard experience."[70]

The reports of the courageous and continued witness of missionaries in Uganda during the reign of terror by Idi Amin were certainly and justifiably designed to impress Southern Baptists with the quality and God-sustained witness of their missionaries. Web Carroll chronicled some of these in "Turn About in Uganda."[71] Such troubles on an international scale prompted a cartoon in *The Commission* that depicted two area secretaries talking with each other, with one responding, "This fellow wanted to work in a country not in turmoil. I told him Utopia isn't one of our fields."[72] In this edition Cauthen wrote the article "Missions without Missionaries." His opening sentence stated the stark reality of the world's political hostility to the Christian gospel. "A look at the world map indicates a grim fact: there are many places where, due to policies of the government in power, it is impossible for missionaries to go: China, North Korea, Manchuria, Vietnam, Laos, Cambodia, Burma, Mozambique, Angola, and many others could be added to the list."[73] Cauthen said that closed doors did not eliminate our obligation to find ways to get the gospel to people. He discussed a variety of ways that witness still could be possible: "We can pray. God rules in all the world, and he has power to change circumstances which at any moment

---

70   Baker James Cauthen, "Truth on Trial," *TC* 41, no. 10 (October 1978): 37.
71   Web Carroll, "Turnabout in Uganda," *TC* 42, no. 12 (December 1979): 10–13.
72   "Out of Commission," *TC* 41, no. 9 (September 1978): 36.
73   Baker James Cauthen, "Missions without Missionaries," *TC* 41, no. 9 (September 1978): 37.

may appear hopeless." People can often be engaged through radio, publications, brief visits, invitations from nationals, distribution of Bibles, and hospitality situations among local believers. He also reminded his readers that "it is easier to close doors than open them." Sometimes small mistakes "can close doors of opportunity for a long time." The rapidity with which political regimes can change and the ease with which countries could consequently be closed to missionaries made the FMB establish a policy of "non-political involvement." The SBC in 1978 under the influence of the Christian Life Commission adopted a Declaration of Human Rights. It called human rights a "major moral issue" of our time and said that Southern Baptists should be committed to "political action on behalf of human rights at home and abroad, responsibly involving ourselves as God's salt, God's light, and God's leaven in the whole political process." "That's easy to say," Jane Robison responded. She described the galling complexity of understanding political movements in a country in relation to the churches and the missionary. The apolitical stance frequently is highly difficult to maintain, for political issues quickly devolve into moral issues. After giving examples of how Southern Baptist missionaries had helped ameliorate situations in a variety of countries, Robison cited Winston Crawley, who explained, "The point tends to be political when the missionary takes a public stance that identifies him with a group that is in opposition to another group. And it is not appropriate for a guest in a country to take sides in political controversies." Aware of the inextricable connection between Christian preaching and the advocacy of moral righteousness, Kenneth Park said, "There's speaking against, and then there's agitating." One has to "make a fine distinction between the two." Robison closed her article with the summary that drove the missionary policy: "While other groups are working to change the laws, Southern Baptist missionaries are working to change the hearts of the people. Human rights will never be a reality without Christ."[74]

---

74   Jane Robison (quoting Winston Crawley and Kenneth Park), "The Missionary and Human Rights: Walking the Tightrope of Dilemma," *TC* 41, no. 9 (September 1978): 16–19.

IRREPRESSIBLE COMMITMENT

"Suffering may be great. Death may have to be faced. But always underneath are the everlasting arms." So wrote Baker James Cauthen in July 1979.[75] In spite of the demonstrable reality of the dire circumstances—financial challenges, political turmoil, war, missionary martyrdoms—that challenged mission work every year, Baker James Cauthen manifested irrepressible enthusiasm for the work every year of his twenty-six years of service. "I lay down this task," he wrote in his last editorial for *The Commission*, "with a heart full of love for the Foreign Mission Board and for the great Baptist family of which it is a part." He assured his readers that with the same devotion and expectation to which he so often called them, "My wife and I turn our faces toward the future with high expectation of our Lord's continuous leadership and with readiness to follow him in doing his bidding wherever he leads to the end of our days."[76] One can sense his infectious spirit in his closing statement in the last report to the Southern Baptist Convention made under his administration.

On October 14, 1953, the Foreign Mission Board entrusted to me the responsibility of being its executive director. I had previously served eight years as secretary for the Orient and six years as missionary to China along with my family. On December 20, 1979, I will reach age 70 and will retire at the end of that month after more than forty years with the Foreign Mission Board and a total of fifty-three years of preaching the glorious gospel of redemption. What a privilege it is to serve the Lord Jesus! His promises are sure under all circumstances. His leadership is clear and his grace is sufficient. The best part of life is to do his will. To him be all the praise,

---

75   Baker James Cauthen, "The Everlasting Arms," *TC* 42, no. 7 (July 1979): 47.
76   Baker James Cauthen, "In God's Hands," *TC* 42, no. 12 (December 1979): 46.

honor, and glory. How we thank God for Southern Baptists! They have prayed, laid their lives upon the altar, and provided support for worldwide labor through the Cooperative Program, the Lottie Moon and Annie Armstrong offerings, and gifts for relief. They have welcomed missionaries into their churches and have gone to the ends of the earth to assist them in witnessing and ministry. Words could never express sufficient gratitude for missionaries who have followed Christ across the world. They have faithfully preached the Word, planted and nurtured churches, trained Christian workers, and reached out loving hands to comfort the distressed. They have braved crises, dangers, economic turbulence, and wars. They are trees of righteousness planted throughout the earth. Nearly 3,000 of them now serve in 94 countries. We praise God for the members and staff of the Foreign Mission Board. Through all these years our hearts have been united in love, prayer, confidence, and commitment to Christ. They are true yoke-fellows in the service of our Saviour. Southern Baptists are poised for the greatest missionary undertaking in all history. Who can measure what God may do if we faithfully follow him in the tremendous challenge of Bold Mission Thrust? My wife and I come to this time with absolute confidence in the mandate of our Master upon which rests the whole missionary enterprise. If we had ten thousand lives, we would gladly give them in this blessed cause.[77]

---

77   SBCA, 1979, 86.

THE ADMINISTRATION OF KEITH PARKS, 1980–1992

John Mark Terry and Micah Fries

I**N AUGUST OF 1979** the trustees of the Foreign Mission Board
elected R. Keith Parks as the executive director of the FMB
(title later changed to president). He served in that position
for the next thirteen years. During his tenure the FMB experienced significant changes; but perhaps more significantly, his tenure also saw significant turmoil related to the Conservative Resurgence within the broader Southern Baptist Convention. This
larger struggle ultimately resulted in Parks's departure not only
from the FMB but also from the SBC. His tenure can be measured
with a number of significant milestones. These include the introduction of the concept of unreached peoples, the establishment

of the Eloise and Baker James Cauthen International Learning Center, the creation of the Global Strategy Group, the creation of Cooperative Services International (CSI), the establishment of the nonresidential missionary program, and the establishment of the International Service Corps. Parks retired from service with the IMB in October of 1992.[1]

PARKS'S BACKGROUND

Perhaps no leader of the Foreign Mission Board took office with better preparation than Keith Parks. He grew up in Texas and Arkansas, a child of parents who loved him but lacked financial resources. This was due, in part, to a childhood illness that Parks faced, and the accompanying medical bills, and because of the Great Depression, which began just two years after his birth. Parks professed faith in Christ as a nine-year-old boy. He remembers well what God did in his heart that day: "When I was in the Junior Sunday school department, our pastor gave a simple gospel message with an invitation in our General Assembly. I had been in Sunday school all of my life. I had the information. But that morning the Holy Spirit convicted me that I was a sinner and Jesus would save me if I would ask him. I did—and he did! Reexamination of this experience through the years has confirmed its authenticity."[2] Parks grew up in a Southern Baptist church, but he recounted that he, surprisingly, had almost no exposure to missions, even though it was central to the SBC. It was after graduation from college, at North Texas State College (now the University of North Texas), that God made him aware of missions and then called him to serve as a missionary:

> After graduating from the University of North Texas, I was part of the second group of BSU summer

1   International Mission Board Timeline, https://www.imb.org/175.
2   "Keith Parks: 'Missionary Is Still My Dominant DNA,'" *Baptist Standard*, January 31, 2018, https://www.baptiststandard.com/opinion/profiles/keith-parks-missionary-still-dominant-dna.

missionaries. Four of us went to San Andres Island off the coast of Colombia. Some who had never heard about Jesus accepted him as Savior. I did not know there were people like that in the world. I came back to enter Southwestern Seminary wishing that I could go tell them, but, assuming missionaries were holy and virtually perfect (a concept soon corrected), I knew that I did not qualify. However, the tug toward those who had never heard continued. Dr. Jack McGorman preached at Mission Day Chapel. Dr. Cal Guy extended the invitation. I felt I should respond. But I was afraid that I would make a public decision and then would not follow through. Finally, I said to the Lord, "I am going to start toward the aisle. If this is not right, stop me." As I moved my foot toward the aisle, a warmth flowed through my body, an assurance filled my heart and I practically ran to the front. That decision is as relevant today as it was then.[3]

Parks met and fell in love with Helen Jean Bond at a Baptist Student Union state convention, although they did not marry until later, while he studied at Southwestern Baptist Theological Seminary. They married just two years before they first left for the mission field. The FMB assigned them to serve at the Indonesia Baptist Seminary. Later, Parks served in national and regional leadership for the FMB, before returning to the headquarters in Richmond to serve as vice president in charge of the Mission Support Division. In that role he supervised the departments of personnel, missions education, denominational relations, and communication.[4]

---

3   "Keith Parks: 'Missionary Is Still My Dominant DNA.'"
4   Jeff Brawner, "An Evaluation of the Ten Universal Elements of David Garrison's Church Planting Movement Theory as Employed by the International Mission Board of the Southern Baptist Convention" (PhD diss., Mid-America Baptist Theological Seminary, 2008), 43.

PARKS'S ELECTION TO LEAD
THE FOREIGN MISSION BOARD

Parks's election as executive director (president) of the FMB was not a surprise to anyone who paid close attention to the board and to the broader SBC. Parks gradually assumed increasing responsibility over the years and had achieved respect and stature inside the FMB. His personal character, as well as his leadership ability, were obvious. The trustees of the FMB elected him unanimously in 1980, and his election was applauded by all who knew him. In his dissertation, Alben Gaston describes his election in nearly glowing terms: "Parks was eminently qualified after stints in Indonesia (1954–68), as Secretary for Southeast Asia (1968–75), and Mission Support Division Director (1975–79). In Indonesia he enacted creative approaches and initiated 'far-reaching changes in the board's operation' during his presidency. He campaigned for restoring previous CP [i.e., Cooperative Program] percentages to reverse sagging FMB receipts and created a Development Office to bolster funding. Parks surmised only increased funding could advance Bold Mission Thrust beyond impressive theory status."[5] This election was lauded by nearly everyone within the FMB and SBC; but it was not long before the decision to make him president became less popular, and he found himself in significant conflict with the same trustee board that had unanimously elected him just a few years before. However, at the time of his election, he was affirmed, and he moved quickly to establish himself as president and to point the FMB toward what he believed were the highest priorities.

---

5   Alben H. Gaston, "An Examination of Selected Features of the 1995–2000 Covenant of Cooperation between the International Mission Board (SBC) and Global Focus" (PhD, diss., Mid-America Baptist Theological Seminary, 2004), 79.

PARKS'S ADMINISTRATION OF
THE FOREIGN MISSION BOARD

Parks's tenure at the helm of the FMB demonstrated a passion for those who had not yet heard and believed the gospel. He also communicated an optimistic vision for the FMB's future: "You and I are privileged by God to live in a time when there are more people, in more places of the world, ready to respond to the gospel than at any time in all human history. Not all people are responsive, but from all parts of the world more and more people are responding, will respond, and would respond if they had a chance."[6] This optimism and emphasis challenged the way that the FMB fulfilled its task. Parks believed the FMB needed to change its strategy in order to accomplish effectively its mission. Parks's new emphasis centered on unreached peoples. The focus on unreached people groups was a new concept to Southern Baptists and other missions organizations. Gary Baldridge, in his short biography of Parks, describes Parks's passion and strategy as not only groundbreaking but also demonstrably influential in ways that few others have been: "[Parks] had contributed as much to the gospel's penetration into so-called 'closed' countries as any missions leader in the twentieth century."[7] This development was not just the introduction of a new strategy, but, more surprisingly, Parks's leadership led to the development of the first defined strategy in the history of the IMB—at least a strategy identified as such.

Before his tenure as president, Parks also helped to establish the previously mentioned Bold Mission Thrust (BMT) program. As it became apparent that the organization needed a new direction, SBC leaders formed a committee to review the FMB's plans and strategies. This committee set goals for Southern Baptists' missions and evangelism. The goals became "Bold Mission Thrust 1976–2000."

---

6 R. Keith Parks, "Commitment to God's World Plan," Potpourri, *Contempo*, September 1991, 22.

7 Gary Baldridge, *Keith Parks: Breaking Barriers and Opening Frontiers* (Macon, GA: Smyth & Helwys, 1999), 1.

BMT was a monumental leap for the FMB since, until that time, there had never been a written strategy. Winston Crawley explained that in 1974, at the request of the SBC's Historical Commission, Jesse C. Fletcher (then director of the Mission Support Division of the FMB) reviewed minutes of the board from 1845 to report on the development of "Foreign Mission Board strategy." He found that it was not until 1965 that the board first "officially spoke to the word strategy."[8]

When the SBC approved BMT, it also specified goals for the FMB. Some of those new goals to be accomplished by the year 2000 were to preach the gospel to all the people in the world, have five thousand missionaries under appointment, establish work in at least 125 countries, send ten thousand lay volunteers per year by the year 2000, and see a tenfold multiplication in churches and baptisms overseas. Parks now had definite goals and a focused strategy.[9] That the FMB would operate for 120 years without a strategy seems foreign to our modern understanding of corporate life; but, as Keith Whitfield and Nathan Finn point out, the concept of institutional strategy is something of a modern concept that was intuitive prior to the time it appeared in the FMB's corporate culture.[10]

In keeping with Parks's desire for the unreached to have access to the gospel, he affirmed BMT, and it animated his strategic efforts.[11] This large goal was the kind of motivation that served Parks well. As William Estep states,

> Although he stated at the time of his installation that he intended to walk in the steps of his predecessor, he did that and much more. Immediately, Bold Mission Thrust became his "game plan." He also began to make certain

---

8   Brawner, "An Evaluation of the Ten Universal Elements," 45.

9   Brawner, "An Evaluation of the Ten Universal Elements," 45.

10 Nathan Finn and Keith Whitfield, personal conversation with Micah Fries, November 10, 2018.

11 R. Bruce Carlton and E. Coye Still III, *Strategy Coordinator: Changing the Course of Southern Baptist Missions* (Eugene, OR: Wipf & Stock, 2011), 1–2.

changes that revealed that he was his own man. Southern Baptists soon learned that they not only had a Bold Mission Thrust plan but also a bold missions leader at the helm of the FMB. Keith Parks was perhaps the most knowledgeable missiologist ever to direct the energies of Southern Baptists' foreign mission effort.[12]

One could hardly overstate how significant the BMT campaign was to Parks's theory of mission engagement. Almost every change that Parks instituted at the FMB could be traced back, at some level, to BMT. Although later questions arose about Parks's theology and commitments, in the end Parks maintained that his frustration with the Conservative Resurgence centered on what he believed were distractions from BMT and the fulfillment of the missionary task that arose as a result of the existing tension that emanated from the Conservative Resurgence.

PARKS'S GUIDING PRINCIPLES

Early in his service as the leader of the FMB, Parks spoke to the FMB trustees and explained the principles that guided him and the FMB.

1. A biblical basis of all we do.
2. Our primary purpose is evangelism that results in churches.
3. The incarnational approach which emphasizes the career missionary.
4. The priesthood of believers, meaning every Baptist is a witness and through volunteer opportunities can be involved personally in missions.
5. The indigenous principle which means that churches which are established are "home grown" or "natural" in their environment.

---

12 William R. Estep, "Course-Changing Events in the History of the Foreign Mission Board, SBC, 1845–1994," *Baptist History and Heritage* 29, no. 4 (1994): 5–13.

6. A comprehensive approach, indicating that we do not focus on one single issue or use one single method but try
to express the total scope of ministry to which Southern
Baptists are committed.
7. The responsibility of communicating what is happening on
the mission field back to Southern Baptists.

All of these strands are interwoven to form one mission fabric.
We cannot tear one out without weakening the total.[13]

Parks repeated this list of principles to the trustees several times
during his tenure.

PARKS'S INNOVATIONS

Eventually, Parks looked back on BMT and the strategies that were
initially implemented at the FMB, and he determined they were
insufficient for the fulfillment of the BMT vision. This retrospective
view ultimately led him to the focus on unreached peoples, the implementation of nonresidential missionaries, and the development
of the Cooperative Services International strategy. Parks stated, "In
1985, we looked at a map of the world and realized our 'bold' plans
to reach the world did not include over half the world's countries
which were closed to traditional missionaries and included the
vast majority of those unreached with the gospel. We joined with
others to try to adjust mission approaches to change that reality."[14]
Although the quote reveals Parks's modesty, his willingness to make
what seemed at the time a risky, and somewhat controversial, shift
with the FMB proved to set a bold precedent. Other mission boards
and organizations followed the FMB's example. This shift, arguably,

---

13   William R. Estep, *Whole Gospel Whole World: The Foreign Mission Board of the Southern Baptist Convention, 1845–1995* (Nashville: Broadman & Holman, 1994), 341.
14   William O'Brien and Keith Parks, "Why Is 24:14 Different Than Previous Efforts?,"
Mission Frontiers, January 1, 2018, https://www.missionfrontiers.org/issue/article/
why-is-2414-different-than-previous-efforts.

has reframed the way most North American missions organizations go about their task.

This kind of risk-taking seems appropriate for the leadership of a mission board, but it was not, and is not, necessarily a hallmark of Baptist decision-making. Parks, however, did not fear creativity and innovation. His willingness to push the boundaries of accepted missionary practice was revealed in the early years of his service on the field in Indonesia and all the way through his leadership as president of the FMB. By looking back at his early years in Indonesia, we get a glimpse of the kind of flexible and creative risk-taking that Parks embraced if he thought the strategic shift might advance the gospel among unreached peoples. Estep, in his history of the IMB, makes the same case:

> Before becoming FMB president, Parks had given considerable attention to developing indigenous churches in Indonesia. He was convinced that the traditional duplication of institutional life of denominations in the States was not "getting the job done." So, he led the mission to foster more indigenous methods of evangelism, church life, and theological education. Parks's objective was to promote evangelism that results in New Testament churches. Since he felt that Southern Baptist missionaries should be primarily "church planters," he led the board to develop programs of consultation and networking with the mission boards of "Great Commission" Christians.[15]

Another creative idea that Parks had was to hire David Barrett, an Anglican who was doing innovative research, identifying unreached people groups. Parks hired Barrett as a consultant with the IMB, and he worked with FMB researchers and leaders to identify the unreached people groups and to develop strategies to evangelize

---

15   Estep, "Course-Changing Events in the History of the Foreign Mission Board," 5–13.

them. Barrett was the creator of the *World Christian Encyclopedia*. David Garrison, who was one of the foremost innovators and developers of IMB strategy, particularly under the tenure of Jerry Rankin, worked closely with Barrett and believed Barrett to be one of the primary reasons why the IMB was able to evangelize so many unreached peoples. Upon Barrett's death, Garrison reflected on Barrett's influence on missions in general and on the IMB, specifically.

> More than any other man, David Barrett showed us what the whole world looked like through the lens of the Great Commission. He showed us how God viewed the world, and particularly the unfinished task. David Barrett defined for us, for all of us, the boundaries of the ends of the earth, what he called "World A." Once we saw the tragic plight of more than a billion unreached, unengaged souls, we set out for them with a passion. When David Barrett came to the Foreign Mission Board as a consultant in 1985, less than 3 percent of our mission force was deployed to this last frontier. Today, as a result of Barrett's prophetic push, more than 80 percent of the people groups our missionaries serve among are unreached.[16]

As stated earlier, Parks's tenure was marked by innovation that influenced the mission-sending world broadly beyond the FMB. It is arguable that the greatest source, or motivation, of that innovation and change in emphasis and strategy came as a result of Barrett's research and his advocacy for World A. Barrett's research, combined with Parks's platform, enabled the shift that would ultimately occur. As Baldridge observes, "Parks had in Barrett the new practical concept and the database, and in the FMB the financial and human resources necessary for a massive shift toward the most neglected

---

16 "Missions Researcher David Barrett Dies," BP, August 8, 2011, http://www.bpnews. net/35901/missions-researcher-david-barrett-dies.

peoples on earth. Most important of all, Parks championed the strategy that would open the doors through which many Great Commission people could walk."[17]

This change in emphasis in strategy was not just a change in thematic approach but actually featured significant changes in the way the FMB functioned. Parks established a new leadership paradigm that employed Barrett's research in order to develop strategies to enable the field personnel to identify and evangelize these unreached World A people. As Estep states,

> He was convinced that the board, particularly, should think in global terms. In order to bring to its attention the needs of the whole world, he led the board to form a "think tank" made up of the vice presidents, designated the "Global Strategy Group." David Barrett, a world-renowned missiologist, was employed as a consultant for the board in developing a global approach. One result of this new approach was to recognize the need to develop a means of getting the gospel into numerous countries behind closed doors. The result was the nonresidential program in which missionaries would enter closed countries on tourist visas for short periods of time and attempt to establish cell groups of Christians that would eventually form themselves into churches. By 1993, such missionaries were serving in twenty-nine countries.[18]

As Estep points out, not only did this think tank produce strategies for reaching World A, but they also developed the concept of nonresidential missionaries, which has become a common strategy for missionary-sending agencies today. This nonresidential strategy

---

17 Baldridge, *Keith Parks*, 4.
18 Estep, "Course-Changing Events in the History of the Foreign Mission Board," 5–13.

was necessary to access most of World A, because most of World A was located in countries where missionaries could not reside. This required innovative thinking to develop creative access approaches. The concept of a nonresidential missionary was a stark departure from the country-focused, mission-station approach that had prevailed throughout the FMB's history. It allowed missionaries to reside outside of the country they were tasked with reaching. The missionaries utilized creative methodologies to gain access to the country and engage those within the country, traveling in and out of the country on brief trips. The FMB has produced its own historical record, and it includes the following description of the evolution of the nonresidential missionary strategy:

> The convergence of various factors within the evangelical Christian community created a ripe environment for the development of the nonresidential missionary (NRM) paradigm. Aware of and influenced by all these events taking place, leaders at the Foreign Mission Board (FMB) of the Southern Baptist Convention (SBC), earnestly desiring to have a truly global strategy deployed the first NRM in 1987. The NRM concept was the brainchild of David Barrett, who in 1985, contracted with the Board to base his World Evangelization Research Center at its headquarters in Richmond, Virginia. Although Barrett conceived the idea of a nonresidential missionary approach to the world's unreached peoples, he did not have the resources needed to implement this novel missionary concept. However, the partnership between Barrett and the FMB created the fertile environment that allowed this innovative paradigm to emerge.[19]

---

19   Bruce R. Carlton, "An Analysis of the Impact of the Non-residential/Strategy Co-ordinator's Role in Southern Baptist Missiology" (ThD diss., University of South Africa, 2006), 35.

The nonresidential missionary paradigm proved valuable not only because it allowed the mission board to access creatively people who had previously been unreachable but also because it was the forerunner for the Cooperative Services International unit within the FMB.[20]

In 1985 Parks introduced another innovation: Cooperative Services International. Parks and his administrators, especially Lewis Myers, developed CSI in order to respond to opportunities in restricted access countries, especially China and Muslim countries. These nations refused to grant visas to missionaries. One of the early projects was to send English teachers to Communist China. As CSI evolved, it became the department in the FMB that focused on unreached peoples all over the world, but especially in World A. Eventually, Jerry Rankin, during his presidency, recast the whole IMB in the image of CSI, shifting the IMB's approach to engaging unreached peoples.[21]

Parks also changed the way the FMB trained its new missionaries. When he assumed leadership of the FMB, he expressed dissatisfaction with the Missionary Orientation Center, which was located in Callaway Gardens, a golf resort in southern Georgia. For fourteen years the FMB rented a cluster of guest cabins during the tourist off-season and conducted two orientation sessions for new missionaries each year—one in the fall and one in the winter. Parks believed that sending new missionaries to a golf resort communicated an incorrect image and placed the missionaries in a location that distracted them from their training. Parks chose Sam James, formerly a missionary to Vietnam, to design a missionary orientation center and to develop a revised program of training. The trustees approved both, and they resolved to build the new center with special donations. Harwood and Louise Cochrane donated 238 acres near Richmond, and the FMB staff

---

20   FMBM, April 7, 1997.
21   Keith E. Eitel, *Paradigm Wars: The Southern Baptist International Mission Board Faces the Third Millennium* (Oxford: Regnum, 2000), 114.

raised $12 million to construct the Missionary Learning Center, which opened in 1984.[22]

In 1987 Parks called for a reorganization of the FMB staff and administration. A key aspect of that reorganization was the creation of the Global Strategy Group. The Global Strategy Group included the newly elected vice presidents for the regions of the world, as well as Cooperative Services International. Parks intended for this group to develop international strategies that would accelerate world evangelization. One of the first decisions of the group was to propose the nationalization of FMB institutions overseas. Like Parks, they questioned the effectiveness of institutions—like hospitals, seminaries, and schools—to accomplish the FMB's main tasks of evangelism and church planting. The group hoped to reassign missionaries from those institutions to church-planting efforts.[23]

Another decision by the Global Strategy Group provoked a strong backlash among FMB missionaries. This was the so-called "70/30 Plan." The Group called for 70 percent of the missionaries to devote at least 50 percent of their time to personal evangelism. Many missionaries protested this plan. They believed the plan discounted the value of their institutional ministries, while other missionaries insisted that multiplying disciples and national leaders would be more effective. Nevertheless, the 70/30 Plan was implemented, and that action prompted the resignations of many missionaries who served in institutions.[24]

While Parks was innovative and creative, there were some areas where he still tended to approach missions more traditionally. One of those areas was the distinction between long-tenured career missionaries and short-term as well as volunteer missionaries. This specific aspect of his missiology is likely one of the more significant distinctions between Parks and his successor, Jerry Rankin, who would capitalize on both short-term and volunteer personnel, and

---

22 Estep, *Whole Gospel Whole World*, 347.
23 Estep, *Whole Gospel Whole World*, 355.
24 Estep, *Whole Gospel Whole World*, 356.

would see both areas grow exponentially under his service. Parks, however, placed a premium on the long-term career missionary. He believed that the incarnational nature of the gospel and missions demanded that missions be done by long-term workers. He displayed this in Indonesia, where he emphasized increased indigeneity in church planting, evangelism, and leadership training. He clearly embraced an embodied presence on the mission field. Parks and his family were embedded in the culture, taking on the characteristics of the culture around them. This led to his insistence on the priority of career missionaries. Flint Miller references Parks's affinity for the career missionary:

> Though other mission groups tend toward short-term or volunteer workers, we place emphasis on the career missionary. God in His wisdom determined to reveal the fullness of truth by wrapping humanity around deity and walking among us (John 1:14). The true essence of the nature, person and purpose of God is revealed perfectly in the God-man Jesus Christ. We affirm the perfection and uniqueness of the incarnation in Christ, but we also find many Scriptures underscoring this principle of incarnation. This causes us to reaffirm the importance of Christians embodying the gospel in any community. There must be those who go to learn a language and culture, to suffer, weep and rejoice with the people in order to help them understand about God by seeing the good works of Christians living among them.[25]

Parks argued that the incarnational service of longer-tenured career personnel was a reflection of the character of Jesus. This theological priority makes it unsurprising that he insisted on career service

---

25 Flint Miller, "'Mixed Messages': A Study of Southern Baptist Missionaries in East Asia and Their Attempt to Interpret and Apply the Concept of Ministering Incarnationally" (DMiss diss., Asbury Theological Seminary, 1996), 59.

as a priority for the FMB. This was obviously more important, in Parks's mind, than mere pragmatic concerns.

One of the most popular changes that Parks made at the FMB was the development of a position dedicated to promoting prayer for the missionaries and the world. To this position he first appointed Catherine Walker, a recently retired FMB missionary who had served in Indonesia and who was much loved by those who knew her.[26] This appointment demonstrated a commitment to elevate the importance of prayer, but also to remind the personnel on the field that Parks believed in the power of prayer. At the time of Walker's death, Parks reflected on her life in an interview with the Baptist Press and discussed not only what she meant to him but also how she had almost single-handedly reshaped the way that Southern Baptists thought about unreached peoples:

> "She came to be a trusted adviser to us, and one of the strongest spiritual influences in our lives," Parks recalled. "I told her that [the prayer strategy job] was a very simple assignment: All she had to do was to get specific prayer requests from the missionaries, share the requests with Southern Baptists, find out how God answered the requests and inform those who had prayed. I feel she set a model that has been a blessing all over the world to those who sent requests as well as those who prayed for them," Parks said. "She was instrumental in initiating prayer for unreached people groups, which at the time were unknown to most Christians. It was amazing how groups like the Kurds and Kazaks suddenly became well known. Only the Lord knows the full extent and impact of her life. We know that she was very special to us."[27]

---

26 Carlton, "An Analysis of the Impact of the Non-residential Strategy," 73.
27 Erich Bridges, "Catherine Walker, 100, Missions Prayer Pioneer, Dies," BP, January 11, 2016, http://www.bpnews.net/46120/catherine-walker-100-missions-prayer-pioneer-dies.

Walker's commitment to prayer, but even more specifically, her efforts to enlist prayer support for unreached peoples, speaks well of Parks's leadership and to the success of the dissemination of the vision that Parks had for the FMB, across the whole organization. Walker was living out this new commitment that the FMB had embraced. Walker's personal, spiritual walk was significant enough that she cast a long shadow over those with whom she worked.

Another hallmark of Parks's missiology was his belief in evangelism that results in churches. He clearly prioritized the multiplication of disciples and churches. He embraced the strategy of the Church Growth Movement with its emphasis on church planting. This strategy motivated Parks to make church planting the FMB's primary task. Justice Anderson explains how Parks's emphasis on local church planting, which indicates the centrality of the local church, was a concept that was becoming accepted across the evangelical spectrum:

> Southern Baptists have added necessary dimensions to their theology of evangelism, largely as a contribution of the Donald McGavran Church Growth School. David Bosch describes it as the shift from "*conversio gentilium*" to "*plantatio ecclesiae.*" In short, it is what Keith Parks means when he says, "evangelism which results in churches," and he would add, "which know how to reproduce themselves." Church planting has become, almost to an extreme, the *sine qua non* of home and foreign mission work. It reflects a return to the importance of the local congregation in all Christian circles—the ecclesial base communities of Catholicism and the new emphasis of the para-church societies—and an evidence of the universal impact of the Church Growth School.[28]

---

28   Justice C. Anderson, "Changing Patterns of World Mission Work," *Baptist History and Heritage* 27, no. 3 (1992): 19.

Clearly, Parks's emphasis on church planting led to its widespread adoption in international missions and North American missions. Parks's concern reflects the classic indigenous missions strategy (the three-self movement), first articulated by Henry Venn and Rufus Anderson and later affirmed by Donald McGavran. This, along with his emphasis on incarnational missions, reflects Parks's theological convictions that influenced some of his more traditional missiological views.

Parks further established himself as an innovator in the area of partnership missions. His commitment to partnership led to agreements with other Great Commission Christians outside of the SBC family. Parks believed in collaborative missions. This is not just a Parks commitment, though this was a widely held belief among Southern Baptists. This was certainly true for those leading the SBC's domestic and global mission boards. In an article on SBC missions, Estep evaluates the mission board's commitment to partnership mission:

> Well-planned programs which are integrated with existing work and performed in concert with local leadership are preferred to the more short-term projects which might suffer from inadequate follow-up. However, this opinion is not in any sense intended to discredit projects which often meet immediate and critical needs, such as projects of disaster relief. From the HMB and a stateside perspective. Ervin E. Hastey stated the case well: "It is my opinion that this method [partnership missions] represents one of the most effective ways to do mission work. It links a strong Baptist state convention with a developing convention and through this linkage both human and material resources can be provided and shared." From a FMB and an international perspective, R. Keith Parks, FMB president, said that partnership in missions is most productive when there is "coordination through the Foreign Mission Board," "careful advance planning," "full

consultation," "adequate preparation," "sharing in both directions," and "funding beyond existing commitments." The ultimate principle involved, as Parks well expressed it, is that we are in partnership not only with each other but with God.[29]

Positively, it could be said that Parks was a quintessential Baptist, looking for collaborative mission at every opportunity. Conversely, there was the appearance of control by the FMB, as it desired all Southern Baptist global work to be conducted through itself. Nevertheless, this commitment does reflect a historic Baptist commitment to working together to accomplish the mission of God. As Parks said, this belief was ultimately theological and not pragmatic. Partnership with each other is a reflection of partnership with God. This partnership with each other is merely a reflection of God's triune nature and God's activity with humanity. Parks's desire to collaborate in missions, combined with his passion for seeing those who are unreached gain access to the gospel, led him to a fresh willingness to partner with other believers and organizations outside of the SBC and the FMB. Parks's efforts to lead in this area were replicated and built on by the presidents who followed him, but his presidency marked a new day in this regard. In his dissertation on this specific topic, David Rogers identifies Parks's efforts here as thoroughly different from those leaders who had come before him: "Though Baker J. Cauthen during his tenure as FMB Executive Secretary (1953–1979) commended friendly relationships between Southern Baptist missionaries and those of other denominations on the field, the 1979 election of R. Keith Parks as Executive Director signaled a new day for the FMB with regard to interdenominational cooperation."[30]

---

29   Francis M. DuBose, "Local Church and State Convention Partnerships in Missions," *Baptist History and Heritage* 26, no. 1 (Jan 1991): 25.

30   David Rogers, "A Critical Analysis of the History of Southern Baptist Approaches to Interdenominational Cooperation in International Missions" (PhD diss., Southeastern Baptist Theological Seminary, 2015), 211.

Parks's effort to partner broadly was unusual because the FMB had a global reputation as being aloof from other missions agencies. This increased commitment to partnership prompted the FMB to clarify what these partnerships would look like, affirming the importance of each group's maintaining their theological positions and affirming that the FMB would continue to remain distinctively Baptist. From Parks's perspective, however, this initiative was advantageous as it enabled increasing numbers of people to gain access to the gospel and provided for the better collection of global data. The enhanced research helped strategic planning and alleviated the danger of duplication of efforts overseas. Barrett, himself not a Southern Baptist, addressed the excitement of this possibility in 1987, as he cited Parks's explanation of what these increased partnerships would look like:

> Some 200 groups have made contact with your Foreign Mission Board searching for ways of mutually strengthening each other in the task of evangelizing the world.... We are taking initiatives in convening other Great Commission Christians to network with them in order to witness to all people more effectively and more quickly. Each group will maintain its own identity and integrity while maximizing all our efforts to share the gospel more rapidly and more productively with everyone. We must break out of being consumed with ourselves and become more concerned about the souls of a world. We must link hearts, hands and minds with the Christians of this world if we are going to tell everyone about Jesus Christ.[31]

This commitment has now become commonplace, but it was surprising in the 1980s when Parks pioneered it. Crawley, in his history of

---

31   R. Keith Parks's Address at SBC Annual Meeting 1987, cited in David B. Barrett, "Forecasting the Future in World Mission: Some Future Faces of Missions," *Missiology* 15, no. 4 (1987): 443.

SBC mission work, described the manner in which the FMB functioned as an almost matter-of-fact reality: "Southern Baptist mission work is carried on in the context of the larger Christian family and in cordial relationship and increasing correlation with the work of other denominations."[32] Other organizations had functioned this way for years, but the FMB had not. The leadership Parks displayed in this matter has become common practice among Southern Baptists.

KEITH PARKS AND THE CONSERVATIVE RESURGENCE

Parks's tenure, while significant and influential in many ways, was marked to an even greater degree by the controversy that ended in his resignation. Parks served during the early years of what has become known as the Conservative Resurgence. This reform movement in the SBC began in the 1970s and continued through the 1990s. This reform of both theology and authority centered on a certain perspective of the Bible; *inerrancy* was the key word. When the conservative faction gained ascendancy, one's view on inerrancy determined whether a person could occupy a leadership position in the SBC. Parks was cautious at the beginning, and he was able to remain somewhat free from the controversy that affected the heads of so many other SBC agencies. Early on he identified himself as a conservative. Those around him also affirmed him as a conservative. He said, "Never once was I accused of not believing the Bible or having liberal theology or of practicing poor missiology."[33] However, there were signs that he was not as conservative as some would prefer. His reticence with respect to the word *inerrancy* was chief among the issues that troubled conservatives. As Baldridge writes, "He would not attribute any characteristics to the Bible other than those its writers used to describe it. 'The word inerrancy is never

---

32 Winston Crawley, *Global Mission: An Interpretation of Southern Baptist Foreign Missions* (Nashville: Broadman, 1985), 227.

33 Baldridge, *Keith Parks*, 54–55.

used in the Bible,' he noted repeatedly."[34] His hesitancy was seen as a worthy conviction by his supporters, but it was seen as a reason for suspicion by some conservatives.

Parks showed evidence, at times, of affirming the theological convictions of the conservative faction within the SBC. For example, in 1988 a missionary, Michael Willett, was dismissed by the FMB over concerns about his theology. After questioning it was determined that Willett did not necessarily believe in all of the miracles as recorded in Scripture, and he favored the ordination of women. These positions prompted the FMB to dismiss Willett from his service. In an article published by the *Washington Post*, Parks defended the decision based on theological grounds: "[Keith] Parks ascribed Willett's dismissal to his 'doctrinal ambiguity,' particularly about Jesus' miracles."[35] Parks's position here resonated with conservatives. However, many of the less conservative Southern Baptists argued that Parks's reaction was pragmatic—that he had been placed in a situation where he had no other alternative. Parks "was put in an impossible situation," commented Harold Songer, veteran New Testament scholar at The Southern Baptist Theological Seminary. "He was Custer in Indian country."[36] This view of Parks's theology displayed confusion and the tense state of the trustee board that governed the FMB and to whom Parks was accountable.

Parks's theology, at least so far as soteriology was concerned, seemed to be consistent with a more traditional (non-Calvinist) Southern Baptist position. Jeremy Darden writes, "Parks's Traditionalist views, combined with his concern for lost people who lived in countries that had no gospel access, drove him to extend missions into these places."[37] This traditional Southern Baptist soteriology,

---

34 Baldridge, *Keith Parks*, 55.
35 George W. Cornell, "Southern Baptist Missionary Denounced, Fired for Beliefs," *Washington Post*, August 13, 1988, https://www.washingtonpost.com/archive/local/1988/08/13/southern-baptist-missionary-denounced-fired-for-beliefs/77d6c000-ac15-4b0e-923d-e6ad931a3468/?utm_term=.62b8cffa18df.
36 Cornell, "Southern Baptist Missionary Denounced, Fired for Beliefs."
37 Jeremy S. Darden, "An Evaluation of Calvinism's Effect on Southern Baptist Missions and Evangelism" (PhD diss., Mid-America Baptist Theological Seminary, 2016), 95.

as Jeremy argues in his dissertation, fueled Parks's desire to see the gospel go to the nations. It also seemed to ignite Parks's passion for creativity and innovation with respect to his missiology.

Parks's service with the FMB came to an unceremonious conclusion due to his disagreements over theology and practice with the leaders of the Conservative Resurgence. This tension began early on in his tenure, but many attempts were made to continue to work together. As early as 1982, Jimmy Draper, then president of the SBC, sought to affirm Parks's leadership, saying, "I want first of all to express how deeply I appreciate and believe in Keith Parks. Keith would tell you that one of the first letters he received after taking this position was one from me expressing confidence and prayers."[38] Attempts like this, from both sides of the controversy, appear to have been heartfelt and well-intended.

Finally, though, there occurred a breakdown in Parks's relations with the FMB trustees. This breakdown involved several issues. One of the first arose during the 1982 SBC annual meeting. A supporter of the conservative faction introduced a resolution affirming the nation of Israel. This motion moved beyond simply supporting Israel; it endorsed governmental action to affirm Israel. This resolution troubled some FMB missionaries and Parks as well. He believed this resolution might spark a backlash against FMB missionaries in the Middle East. In her thesis on the topic, Melanie Trexler describes the explosive nature of the debate:

> The most significant destabilizing factor came in the form of Resolution 4, a proposed SBC statement in favor of Israel that circulated at the annual Convention meeting in June 1982. SBC fundamentalists, who adhered to a strict, literalistic biblical interpretation and affirmed dispensational premillennialism, supported Resolution 4. In addition to "strong" support for the Israeli state, Resolution 4 urged that the United States government

---

38 Estep. *Whole Gospel Whole World*, 366.

to "publicly and privately assure Israel and her enemies of such support." The resolution sparked heated debate among conference delegates. President of the Foreign Mission Board R. Keith Parks adamantly opposed it, arguing the lives of SBC missionaries in the Middle East could be endangered if it passed. SBC minister Norris W. Sydnor, who presented the resolution to the delegates gathered at the annual Convention, countered Parks's claim and argued the SBC could not "compromise on the Scripture on this issue or any issue when the Word of God is involved . . . we must stand 'unashamedly and fearlessly' for Israel's survival and prosperity."[39]

Those who disagreed with Parks and favored the resolution insisted that to reject the resolution on the grounds of protecting missionaries would be a denial of the content of Scripture. Those who, like Parks, took issue with that position suggested that this specific resolution was not clearly scriptural but was, instead, based on a specific eschatological interpretation and should be avoided as it could cause serious danger. Those who supported the resolution tended to be both very conservative and premillennial. They also were increasing in number on the FMB's board of trustees and were, therefore, Parks's superiors in FMB governance. This disagreement led to increased tension between Parks and the FMB trustees.

A second issue involved a European FMB seminary located in Rüschlikon, Switzerland. In a news report written at the time, Bill Leonard attempted to outline the main form of the struggle about Rüschlikon.

Last fall trustees recommended that the FMB withdraw some $365,000 already budgeted for the Baptist Theological Seminary in Ruschlikon, Switzerland. The trustees

---

39 Melanie Elizabeth Trexler, "Evangelizing Arabs: Baptists and Muslims in Lebanon, 1895–2011" (PhD diss., Georgetown University, 2014), 217–18.

had relinquished control of that school to the European Baptist Federation over two years ago but agreed to continue funding for a few more years. In defending the withdrawal of funds, trustees cited the expense of maintaining a school in Switzerland, its small student body (approximately 48 students) and the school's failure to hire more conservative faculty. Some were disturbed that the seminary invited E. Glenn Hinson, longtime faculty member at Southern Baptist Theological Seminary in Louisville, to be a visiting professor at Ruschlikon for the fall 1991 semester. Indeed, several trustees seemed ready to label Hinson a heretic without a hearing or benefit of due process from the mission board or his own seminary. One declared that the appointment of Hinson, whom he called "a liberal of the liberals," demonstrated the European seminary's insensitivity to conservative concerns. (Hinson has since resigned from Southern to take a position at the moderates' independent Baptist Theological Seminary at Richmond, Virginia. With his departure and the recent departure of Lloyd Allen, SBTS has lost all four members of its church history department within one year.) Not all conservatives agreed, however. William Hancock, the FMB's conservative chairman, warned that withdrawing funds was the wrong response at the wrong time. Hancock may prove to be correct, since the affair has renewed controversy throughout both the SBC and the European Baptist community. After the FMB trustees in December voted to uphold their decision, Keith Parker and Isam Ballenger, longtime executives with the FMB, resigned in protest. Their statements infuriated many board members who criticized FMB executive director Keith Parks for providing the pair with a forum in which to express their dissent. Parks's own career seemed in jeopardy, and in late March he announced that he would retire in October. He had sought a two-year term with the board, but the trustees would only offer a year-by-year contract.[40]

Leonard has stated well the nature of the issue, as well as the ultimate resolution—namely, that Parks would resign, effective the same year, 1992. Those who supported defunding the seminary were confident in their decision because of their belief that theological compromises were occurring. Parks, and those who disagreed with the decision, disagreed for a number of reasons. Parks argued against the decision because it denied the fundamental rule of indigeneity. He suggested that the withdrawal of funds demonstrated a belief that only those who functioned in agreement with the SBC at large were capable of being partners. Also, some Southern Baptists did not view Hinson's theological positions as problematic. Then, there were those like William Hancock, the chairman of the trustees for the IMB, who believed the timing was poor and there was a need to fulfill the FMB's financial commitment to the school. Nonetheless, those who desired to withdraw funding prevailed because they constituted a majority of the FMB's trustees. This action by the trustees caused Isam Ballenger, the vice president for Europe and the Middle East, and Keith Parker, the area director for Europe, to resign their positions.[41]

The result of this controversy was that Parks submitted his resignation in April, to take effect in October. Stan Hastey states, "Once the working majority was achieved, however, the pressure on President R. Keith Parks and other administrators became more and more intense. Finally, in May 1992 and following repeated threats to his continued tenure, Parks announced his retirement, effective October 31, 1992, citing irreconcilable philosophical differences with his directors."[42] This action surprised many because he had

---

40   Bill J. Leonard, "Splintering Continues for Southern Baptists," *The Christian Century* 109, no. 11 (1992): 326.
41   Estep, *Whole Gospel Whole World*, 362.
42   Stan Hastey, "The Southern Baptist Convention, 1979–1993: What Happened and Why?," *Baptist History and Heritage* 28, no. 4 (October 1993): 22.

already come to an agreement with the trustees to resign three years later, in 1995. Parks advanced his resignation date because he believed he could not continue to work with the trustees.

Parks relates a story about a powerful experience at an FMB retreat that was led by Henry Blackaby. The retreat included both FMB administrators and trustees. After having what he describes as a mountaintop experience, Parks shares how God made it clear that he should resign: "As he [Blackaby] was in some directed prayer time he was talking about death to self and raising the question what we were holding onto that we ought to surrender to the Lord. It became clear to me, in that moment, that the one thing I was holding onto was my role as president of this organization. And it also became clear that the trustees were not going to affirm my leadership."[43] For Parks this decision was a combination of spirituality and pragmatism. He believed that God had moved in his heart and compelled him in this direction, but he also recognized that it was likely necessary because of the intractable nature of his relationship with the trustees. There was not much hope at this point for the trustee relationship to be repaired.

One of the reasons for this ongoing tension was the disagreement between Parks and the leaders of the Conservative Resurgence about the unifying factor in SBC life. Parks argued that it was missions that united the convention, while many conservatives argued for doctrine as the source of the SBC's unity. In an interview with Phil Hopkins, Parks explained how he argued this issue with Adrian Rogers and how he ultimately came to realize that this would not change among the Conservative Resurgence leaders:

> Early on I would argue with Adrian Rogers about that [basis for unity in the SBC] and he'd say no, "the theme that has held us together is not missions, but doctrine." Well, historically I don't think that's accurate because

---

43   R. Keith Parks interview by William R. Estep, June 19, 1992, cited in Estep, *Whole Gospel Whole World*, 365.

historically the SBC is composed of people with varying theological perspectives.... My assessment is that they're [conservatives in the SBC] from an independent Baptist viewpoint where conventions are built around doctrine [sic] than from the heritage that we as Southern Baptists have had that the convention is built around missions. And so after arguing with Adrian several times, I finally came to realize that for him and I think for Paige [Patterson] and for others the unifying element ought to be a unifying perspective of theology . . . according to the Scripture, the Living Word is more important than the written word . . . it's a mistake in my estimation to elevate Scripture above Christ.[44]

Parks, of course, contended that those who hold this view about doctrine are not, in fact, Southern Baptists in heritage but are, instead, more like independent Baptists. This proved to be a chasm too big to span, and as the leaders of the Conservative Resurgence gained authority within the SBC, Parks knew that the time had come for him to leave not only the FMB but also the SBC ultimately.

After Parks's resignation, he was offered the opportunity to join the newly formed Cooperative Baptist Fellowship as the director of its new missions agency. Parks quickly accepted the opportunity and set about building a missions agency from the ground up in the image that he had attempted at the FMB. In something of a surprise decision, the trustees of the FMB strongly affirmed Jerry Rankin as the successor to Parks. This was remarkable because some of the trustees who were strong leaders in the Conservative Resurgence, chief among them Paul Pressler, opposed Rankin's nomination.

---

44   R. Keith Parks, interview by Phil Hopkins, April 4, 2000, Oral History, Southeastern Baptist Theological Seminary, Wake Forest, NC.

CONCLUSION

The tenure of Keith Parks included both positive and negative elements. He began his service as president with great fanfare and optimism, but he ended his administration in controversy and frustration. While it is true that he disagreed with the leaders of the conservative faction in the SBC, it is also undeniable that Parks led the FMB to innovate in many respects. His innovations affected both the FMB and many other North American missions agencies. Parks deserves to be remembered as a pioneer in missiology, an innovator who assisted the IMB in becoming what it is today. However, it is also fair to remember Parks as someone who resisted what the SBC is today in regard to theology.

THE JERRY RANKIN ERA, 1993–2010

Robin Dale Hadaway

THE TRUSTEES OF THE FMB elected Jerry A. Rankin as president on June 14, 1993. Although the initial vote tallied fifty-nine in favor of Rankin's election and fourteen opposed, Judge Paul Pressler, one of those in opposition and a major leader in the SBC Conservative Resurgence, offered a motion in the interest of unity to make the election unanimous.[1] Although the new president hailed from the domination's geographical

---

1   William R. Estep, *Whole Gospel Whole World: The Foreign Mission Board of the Southern Baptist Convention, 1845–1995* (Nashville: Broadman & Holman, 1994), 377–78.

heartland and experienced a conventional Southern Baptist upbringing, his presidency would prove to be far from traditional. Rankin's theology, missiology, and practice would challenge,
stretch, and lead Southern Baptists in heretofore new directions.

Due to the conflict the FMB trustees had experienced with
the moderate-conservative Parks administration, the presidential
search committee encountered difficulty finding a candidate with
missionary experience, administrative-leadership capability, and
conservative theological credentials.[2] After an eight-month search
during which one candidate declined the position, the committee
turned to missionary Rankin, the area director for South Asia and
the Pacific, to become president. Although personally theologically
conservative,[3] Rankin would prove to be a maverick in other areas.

When Rankin began his presidency in 1993, the FMB employed
3,978 missionaries in 129 countries, excluding thirty other countries where Cooperative Services International[4] (CSI) missionaries
lived.[5] When Rankin retired in 2010, missionaries were no longer
assigned to geographical countries but to people groups within
those nations. The number of countries where missionaries resided
increased somewhat, but the emphasis was no longer on geography;
rather, it had shifted to ethnicity. Officially, the missionary headcount reached a peak during the Rankin era of 5,656 missionaries
in 160 countries, engaging 1,198 people groups.[6]

---

2   Keith Parks was personally theologically conservative, but, like many denomina-
    tional leaders of his day, tolerated a certain degree of moderate to liberal mission-
    aries and institutions on the field. Parks attempted to be fair to both sides. To his
    credit, he offered me a staff position in the home office in 1990 even after I identi-
    fied myself as a strong proponent of the Conservative Resurgence.

3   Jerry Rankin, interview with Micah Fries, May 18, 2018, in Micah Fries, "The Per-
    sonal Life of Jerry Rankin: Influences, Challenges, and the Forces That Shaped His
    Leadership" (unpublished paper, May 31, 2018), 5.

4   Cooperative Services International was a program started during the Parks era to
    do mission work in closed or limited-access countries where missionaries could
    not obtain missionary visas or were not allowed to do normal missionary work. Be-
    ginning small, it grew to become one of the administrative areas within the FMB.

5   Estep, *Whole Gospel Whole World*, 377.

6   Scott Peterson, email to author, November, 6, 2018.

PERSONAL LIFE

Born in Tupelo, Mississippi, in 1942, Jerry Rankin grew up in Clinton, Mississippi. He and his wife Bobbye retired to the same home where Jerry was raised. Jerry's father wanted his children, especially his sons, to appreciate the value of farm life. Every morning and each afternoon, before and after school, Rankin performed tedious farm chores, including feeding the pigs and milking the cows. Rankin reports chafing under these duties but performing them as a dutiful son.[7] As a boy of ten years of age Rankin accepted Christ as his Savior and Lord at a Billy Graham crusade in nearby Jackson, Mississippi. The joy of this experience birthed in the young man a burning desire that everyone in the world should come to know Jesus Christ. This experience led Jerry into a lifelong conviction that he expresses in this way: "I think that everybody ought to realize if they are called to salvation, they're called to missions."[8]

Although the Baptist institution was located less than a mile from his home, Rankin moved into the dormitory of Mississippi College to become fully immersed in college life. At the school, Rankin was elected president of the Baptist Student Union. Acting on his growing commitment to missions, Rankin spent two summers on evangelistic ventures to New England and the Philippines. These summer ministry experiences confirmed Rankin's call to missions. Upon graduation from Mississippi College in the spring of 1964, he enrolled at Southwestern Baptist Theological Seminary in Fort Worth, Texas, the following year. While in college, Rankin served as the pastor of Sadler Baptist Church and in other ministry positions. A year after graduating from seminary in 1969, the Rankins were appointed as career missionaries to Indonesia by the FMB.[9]

Rankin married the former Bobbye Simons of Mobile, Alabama, shortly after her graduation from Mississippi College in

---

7 Jerry Rankin, interview with the author, October 11, 2018, Clinton, Mississippi.
8 Jerry Rankin, in Fries, "Personal Life of Jerry Rankin," 1–2.
9 Estep, *Whole Gospel Whole World*, 379.

1966. Although there is much debate about the identity of the best
mission board president, there is little doubt that Bobbye Rankin
was the preeminent president's spouse to serve in that position.
She never met a stranger and always knew everyone's names and
those of their children. Since the IMB missions force consists of
more than 50 percent women, the wife of the president possesses
a crucial function as a role model, encourager, and counselor for
female missionaries. As the "first spouse," Bobbye served without
peer. The Rankins raised two children, Lori and Russell, on the
mission field. As missionaries serving four hours from the nearest
missionaries, Jerry would watch the couple's small children one
day a week so that Bobbye could have a ministry to Indonesian
women. Additionally, Jerry participated in the homeschooling of
their children to assist his wife.[10]

While a student at Southwestern Baptist Theological Seminary,
Rankin reports being influenced by missions professor Calvin Guy.
According to Rankin, Guy introduced him to the missiology of Roland Allen and Donald McGavran. Roland Allen's *The Spontaneous
Expansion of the Church* instilled in the aspiring missionary the idea
of indigenous principles. Additionally, the Church Growth theories
of McGavran convinced Rankin about the priority church planting
should have in missions.[11] These seminary influencers would greatly
influence Rankin's missiology and practice in the future.

Arriving in Indonesia in 1970, Jerry and Bobbye Rankin attended language school at Bandung on the island of Java. During their
first ten years on the field, Rankin served as a general evangelist
and church planter. This experience was followed by almost five
years as the associate to the area director and then six years as the
area director for South Asia and the Pacific.[12]

The family's first assignment was difficult. The Rankins were
assigned to the city of Jember, Indonesia, and worked with a Muslim

10   Jerry Rankin, interview with the author, October 11, 2018, Clinton, Mississippi.
11   Jerry Rankin, interview with the author, October 11, 2018, Clinton, Mississippi.
12   Estep, *Whole Gospel Whole World*, 380. As area director, Rankin gave oversight to
      more than five hundred missionaries in fourteen countries from Pakistan to Fiji.

people group called the Madurese. Rankin found these inhabitants not particularly responsive to the gospel, and said that although he was "frustrated and despondent" with the lack of interest in the gospel by these Muslims, the experience brought him closer to the Lord, causing him to fall on his face before God in prayer. Additionally, he began a practice of fasting each week, punctuated by occasional fasts of three days in length. Rankin's lifelong interest and participation in spiritual warfare date from this period. After fasting and prayer, Jerry reports discovering a reservoir of power to confront the spiritual powers of darkness in the places where he served.[13]

Election as President

Rankin's election as president on June 14, 1993 was surrounded in controversy. During the weeks preceding the election, rumors surfaced that he was a charismatic.[14] Rankin describes the experience that led to these reports in an interview with Micah Fries:

> In the midst of this kind of emerging charismatic movement and seeing things develop and happen and trying to distinguish this, the real thing that just, the straw that broke the camel's back was an experience of translating a message in tongues. It was in Singapore, one of our oldest, biggest, historic churches, Queensland Baptist Church. The pastor said, "We are moving in a new dimension of spiritual life and things are happening in our church. I want you to come and preach and help our people understand how this is not contrary to what it means to be Baptist." I went into the service. It was a wonderful worship experience. I just sensed God's presence in an unusual way through the worship. And the worship leader stopped at a point in the service and said, "If God has given a message to anyone from our church, a word of

---

13   Jerry Rankin, interview with the author, October 11, 2018, Clinton, Mississippi.
14   Estep, *Whole Gospel Whole World*, 378.

Scripture, an exhortation, we want to invite you to share that with the congregation at this time." Someone else quoted a Scripture, someone else pronounced a blessing, an encouragement. And then from the back, I heard this message in tongues. I'd been in full gospel meetings with my brothers in the States and had witnessed some of these kinds of experiences. I was somewhat skeptical about the reality of it. I was sitting up on the front row and when he spoke, I was hearing it in English, exactly what he was saying. There was no question about it. My knees go weak. I got breathless. I thought, "This is not happening." Of course, I understood I was being given the interpretation but I thought, "I'm a missionary. I'm a Baptist. I'm an Area Director." This is just God's way of blessing me, of affirming the message I'm going to speak. Then the worship leader said, "If God has given an interpretation to anyone, we'll hear that now." And in that instance, there was no option but to be obedient to what God had chosen to do in my life. I've thought about that several times. It's never happened since. Never happened before. But why did God do that? Whether or not I'm right or not, I came to two conclusions. One, I had been preaching and telling everyone spiritual gifts are valid. I'm not a cessationist. They are valid. So, one, I think God was just going to check me out. Do I really believe it's valid and He was going to give me a chance to find out? The second thing, I think He knew what was coming in the future to become president of the IMB, and He was testing me to see if I would be obedient to what He was doing in my life no matter what the cost was. Losing my career, leadership position, my reputation, yet I would still be obedient to what He chose to do in my life. Micah, I am convinced I would have never become president of the IMB, which is kind of counterintuitive because a lot of people say, "How did you become president having done this?" But I think it was a test of obedience, seeking the power of God and His message. So that was probably a watershed of how God worked in my life in experience and walking in obedience and so forth.[15]

In an interview in the Rankin home, Jerry related to me the same story. Rankin said his interpretation of tongues only occurred this one time but acknowledges having a "private prayer language" that he exercises during his devotions. Rankin also stated that God speaks to him (not audibly) and confessed, "I'm somewhat of a mystic."[16] Despite occurrences that can only be described as unusual for a Southern Baptist leader in 1993, Rankin was elected president of the FMB with 78 percent of the trustee vote.

The Early Years of the Rankin Presidency

Although theologically conservative, William Estep says Jerry Rankin was not a "party man,"[17] and he refused to walk in lockstep with either the convention conservatives or the moderates. Rankin made several moves that demonstrated this tendency. First, in an action that dismayed theological moderates, he broke precedent by joining Grove Avenue Baptist Church, the flagship congregation of the conservatives of Virginia, rather than the First Baptist Church of Richmond, which was aligned with the Baptist General Convention of Virginia. After the FMB moved to Richmond, Virginia, every FMB president had joined the First Baptist Church, now identified with Cooperative Baptist Fellowship and the moderate wing of the SBC. Rankin said that when in Richmond while serving as an area director, he attended the church where he felt the most comfortable—Grove Avenue Baptist Church. Rankin denies having any other motive and was surprised anyone would question his motives for such a personal and spiritual decision such as church membership when it had nothing to do with convention politics.[18]

---

15 Jerry Rankin, in Fries, "Personal Life of Jerry Rankin," 9–10.

16 Jerry Rankin, interview with the author, October 11, 2018, Clinton, Mississippi.

17 Estep, *Whole Gospel Whole World*, 380.

18 Jerry Rankin, interview with the author, October 11, 2018, Clinton, Mississippi.

On the other hand, Rankin offended the conservative leadership of the SBC by seeking rapprochement with the WMU.[19] He visited their headquarters in Birmingham, Alabama, to assure them of his backing of their mission—supporting the global SBC outreach effort. WMU leaders at the time, however, were not in sympathy with the conservative direction of the convention, especially in regard to its leaders. Jerry desired to bring all Southern Baptists together under the banner of the FMB. Rankin states that threading the needle between the conservatives and moderates in the SBC represented one of the greatest challenges of his presidency.[20] He explains, "While I did try to thread the needle and bring moderate churches on board to missionary support, it was clear I had no toleration for their liberal doctrine (growing out of not being inerrantists) and lack of cooperation as Southern Baptists, even refusing to accept designated financial support from CBF [Cooperative Baptist Fellowship] churches."[21]

As Rankin began his new administration, he moved quickly to streamline the organization. He inherited an entity called the Global Strategy Group (GSG) at the top of the organization. The GSG consisted primarily of regional vice presidents, one for each of major geographical regions of the world. These included vice presidents for Asia; Africa; the Americas; Europe, the Middle East, and North Africa; and Cooperative Services International (CSI), the only non-geographical region. Each of these vice presidents supervised one or more of the ten area directors. Rankin had previously worked for the vice president for Asia as one of the Asia area directors. The area directors, although residing on the mission field most of the year, participated as members of the GSG when they were in the States. Within a few months of moving to Richmond, Rankin disbanded the GSG to decentralize the organization and empower field leadership. Don Kammerdiener reports that Rankin said it represented

19 Estep, *Whole Gospel Whole World*, 380.
20 Jerry Rankin, interview with the author, October 11, 2018, Clinton, Mississippi.
21 Jerry Rankin, email to the author, June 18, 2019.

an unneeded layer of administration. Three of the GSG members retired while three others accepted other positions in the home office. From 1993 until 1997 Rankin supervised an overseas organization that experienced turmoil on the field. "Turf" battles between the geographical areas and CSI fueled much of the conflict. For instance, prior to Rankin's ascension as president, one nonresidential missionary couple received an assignment to a people group that spanned the countries of Eritrea, Egypt, and Sudan. Egypt lay in the North Africa and Middle East area while Eritrea and Sudan rested in the eastern and southern Africa area. Neither area had placed missionaries where this people group resided. Despite this fact, the area directors objected to the couple living in their respective areas as either residential or itinerant missionaries. Therefore, this CSI couple moved to one of the three countries where no IMB personnel lived. This scenario repeated itself all over the world. The conflict escalated to the point that four years into Rankin's presidency, the Senior Executive Team (SET)—Rankin, the overseas vice president Avery Willis, and the executive vice president Don Kammerdiener—decided to disband CSI as part of "New Directions," in part to end intraorganizational conflict.

New Directions (1997)

New Directions began on July 1, 1997, with the expansion of ten geographical areas with ten area directors (ADs) into fourteen regions with as many regional leaders (RL).[22] The administration announced the restructuring at a spring trustee meeting. Subsequently, Rankin and trustee leaders conducted interviews for the RL positions. Three of the ADs were retained while the remainder of the new leadership was chosen from lower field administration or directly from the field. Four of the fourteen RLs came from the ranks of CSI, as CSI was subsumed as part of

---

22 Deryl Ray Davis, "Paradigm Shift in Missions: A History of Jerry A. Rankin's Leadership to Embrace Southern Baptist Churches in the Great Commission Task" (DMin diss., Columbia International University, 2011), 107.

New Directions. One of the stated purposes of New Directions was to distribute and diffuse CSI methodology and concepts and, most importantly, administration, throughout the larger organization.[23]

Rankin states,

> In early 1997, SET was meeting, praying, and discussing about how rapidly the world was changing, how God was moving and where we ought to be as a global mission agency when we entered the new millennium in three years, and how to get there. Seeing the effectiveness of CSI in engaging closed countries and unreached people groups, we needed to eliminate the schism and seek ways to incorporate the ethos and vision into our traditional missions. (2) We needed to eliminate the bureaucratic local mission structure that diverted so much mission personnel, time and energy and stifled new visions and initiatives. (3) We needed to make a radical shift from 90% of our work being in open countries, basically supporting established work of national convention partners, to evangelizing the lost and unreached parts of the world.[24]

The CSI configuration featured direct supervision of all field personnel. The former CSI structure included an area director, two associate area directors, four field coordinators, strategy coordinators, and finally field missionaries. Every person reported to a supervisor, and each missionary composed dated goals and objectives and filed monthly reports. On the other hand, the traditional area structure, although headed by area directors and associate area directors, at the mission level functioned through elected mission administrators, committees, and democratic business meetings, complete with *Robert's Rules of Order*. Within six months

---

23   Fries, "Personal Life of Jerry Rankin," 11–12, 20.
24   Jerry Rankin, email to the author, June 18, 2019.

of the start of New Directions, all of the RLs had abolished the latter and instituted a structure mirroring the former. In the new mission structure, each missionary would have a supervisor. The democratic structure of the mission gave way to more of a business model, which ensured more accountability. This new model was a tremendous change. For more than 150 years missionaries had operated more or less independently. During the Rankin administration, however, field personnel began to be directed from the home office through trustee-elected or Richmond-appointed field administrators.[25] This shift in mission administration marks one of the major accomplishments of the Rankin era.

Another feature of CSI that was adopted in the new structure was the assignment of personnel to ethnolinguistic people groups as opposed to geographical countries.[26] Each CSI missionary was sent to a particular people group which might span the boundaries of several countries. The traditional areas, on the other hand, assigned their personnel to specific nations. Initiated during the Parks administration, this focus on people groups exponentially expanded during the Rankin era. Over the next several years, all field personnel assignments, except those with business, financial, member care, or personnel-services duties, would be linked to people groups rather than countries. This linkage was in keeping with the vision statement of the Rankin years that stated, "We will lead Southern Baptists to be on mission with God to bring all peoples of the world to saving faith in Jesus Christ."

A third feature of CSI's enduring heritage involves an emphasis on strategic vision and innovation. Whereas the ADs were usually chosen for their administrative gifting, CSI leadership leaned more toward strategy, entrepreneurship, and flexibility. Rankin says that

---

25 ADs were instituted during the Cauthen administration, but they did not directly supervise missionaries. ADs approved budgets and personnel requests and suggested strategies, but personnel, supervision, and operating decisions were conducted by committees and administrators elected by democratically organized missions within their respective countries.

26 Davis, "Paradigm Shift in Missions," 109.

their goal was "to reorganize into regions that were compatible geographically, culturally and strategically and represented relative similar numbers of missionary units. We sought leaders who were visionary and demonstrated strategic thinking rather than leaders who basically managed personnel, finances and policies."[27] Rankin's decision to disband both the traditional areas and CSI and meld them into a more vibrant organization would prove to be one of the enduring legacies of the Rankin years. He attempted to combine the best of both structures. The old area system offered stability whereas the CSI structure allowed for greater flexibility and accountability.

The year 1997 brought not so much a new direction to the FMB (soon to become the IMB in the year 2000) as a new focus on engaging the world's unreached people groups. A new field leadership, chosen by Rankin himself, coupled with a military or business-style command structure allowed him to more quickly engage the world's remaining ethnicities and control costs at the same time. At the field level, CSI was organized into teams led by strategy coordinators (formerly known as nonresidential missionaries or NRMs). Within the next few years, the entire IMB structure would reflect CSI's team-based business model, featuring top-down administration and supervision rather than the democratically organized mission configurations of the past.

Despite popular belief, Rankin did not dictate to his regional leaders either the strategy or the structure for their regions. He only asked the RLs to devise tactics to reach all of the unreached people groups and population segments in their areas. Many field missionaries considered New Directions as "Richmond dictated," but Rankin considered the new structure to be "field-based" because the RLs resided overseas with the rank-and-file missionaries. This dichotomy of understanding would persist until the majority of the missionaries on the field had been appointed under the new system. For these reasons, New Directions stands as one of the pivotal events in recent IMB history.

---

27   Davis, "Paradigm Shift in Missions," 109.

Baptist Faith and Message 2000 (BF&M 2000)

The Southern Baptist Convention at its annual meeting in the year 2000 updated the denomination's 1963 doctrinal statement. Some within the conservative leadership of the SBC harbored doubts about the orthodoxy of many of the denomination's employees, including their missionaries. Soon a movement surfaced that asked for all denominational ministry-related employees to sign the BF&M 2000. At first, Jerry Rankin and the IMB resisted these demands. Later, however, under pressure from forces in the denomination, he and the trustees reversed course, believing the move was necessary to restore confidence in the orthodoxy of missionaries. As the leader of the organization, Rankin enthusiastically took the lead in asking missionaries to affirm the BF&M 2000.

Some missionaries resisted, declaring they had endorsed the 1963 Baptist Faith and Message in good faith and should not be asked to affirm an updated version of a document they had already approved when they were appointed. They said that neither their beliefs nor practices had changed, and they resented having their theology questioned. Others countered that if the missionaries' beliefs were orthodox, they should have no problem with affirming a simple, updated doctrinal statement. Rankin prevailed, but the victory came at a cost of about seventy-five missionaries either resigning or retiring rather than affirming the new statement, including one RL and his wife. During this process, Rankin asked each RL to meet personally with every missionary who was hesitant to sign the BF&M 2000. With 99.9 percent of all missionaries signing the BF&M 2000, questions about the doctrinal orthodoxy of Southern Baptist international missionaries faded away.

IMB Connecting (2009)

Early on, Jerry Rankin noticed a trend toward personalization in missions. Although the concept of partnership missions began during the Cauthen administration, it was greatly expanded during the Parks years.[28] The Rankin presidency, however, transformed short-term missions (STMs) into one of the major pillars of IMB strategy. Rankin saw that relatively cheap airfares, increased constituency affluence, and the new generation's desire to partake in missions would give birth to a new global movement of participatory missions.[29] Heretofore, churches were asked to donate to the denomination's vehicle (the Cooperative Program) to support mission causes. Now church members were challenged to both support missions financially and travel overseas themselves.

When missionaries journeyed by ocean vessel, it was impractical for individual church members to participate in STMs. After World War II, George Verver, the founder of Operation Mobilization (OM), changed the course of missions by establishing the first STM-sending agency. A few years later, individual Southern Baptists founded independent STM organizations, mirroring the OM model. The IMB followed suit, establishing and then expanding the Partnership Mission Department. This ministry connected Southern Baptist churches, independent mission entities, and individuals with FMB missionaries to plant churches, build chapels, and participate in human-needs ministries.

Although partnership missions had been part of the two previous administrations, both Cauthen and Parks prioritized the career missionary role, relegating the former to more of an ancillary task. Rankin, however, decided the IMB should also become a prominent STM mission society while retaining its career missionary-sending function. Furthermore, under Rankin, the IMB would increasingly become a connection point between SBC churches and overseas churches and missionaries. Missionaries would function as "stackpoles"—connecting and facilitating multiple ministries both locally and abroad. The new emphasis resulted in the change of the IMB logo to "IMB Connecting." This philosophical change acknowledged that the task of foreign missions was beyond what 5,500 missionaries

---

28   Estep, *Whole Gospel Whole World*, 352–53.
29   Davis, "Paradigm Shift in Missions," 33–34.

could perform. It would take other mission agencies, churches, and individuals to join with IMB missionaries to fulfill the Great Commission mandate. Rankin says, "It is not the responsibility of the International Mission Board to do missions on behalf of Southern Baptists. The Great Commission was given to every church, every believer, association and denominational entity. Our responsibility is to mobilize, train, and facilitate every Southern Baptist being obedient and involved in fulfilling the Great Commissions."[30]

Not everyone agreed with Rankin. Detractors said that by encouraging churches to participate in partnership missions, resources were being drawn away from the Southern Baptist financial support plan—the Cooperative Program. Instead of giving to the Cooperative Program and other SBC mission causes, churches might withhold funds to support their own mission trips. Rankin countered that Southern Baptist churches were going to be involved in personalized missions either with the IMB or without it. Whereas Rankin desired to catch the STM wave and personalize missions for every church, critics felt Rankin helped cause some of the problems and then solved them in his own way. Other detractors pointed to the missiological difficulties inherent in the STM paradigm. Critics charged that some volunteers showered nationals with resources, abrogating the indigenous principles Rankin himself espoused. On the other hand, Rankin believed that better training for STMs would solve such problems and represented a better alternative than discouraging volunteers from fulfilling their Great Commission tasks.

The official change of the IMB logo in 2009 to IMB Connecting would prove to be a pivotal point in IMB history. At this juncture, the agency moved from being primarily a mission-sending entity to embracing a joint focus of mobilizing local churches and sending out missionaries.[31] This required a change of mindset in the home office and on the field, a transformation that is one of the accomplishments of the Rankin era.

---

30   Jerry Rankin, email to the author, June 18, 2019.
31   Davis, "Paradigm Shift in Missions," 1.

Church Planting Movements

Soon after the beginning of New Directions, the IMB published a small booklet titled *Church Planting Movements*, authored by the new strategy associate vice president David Garrison.[32] The church planting movement (CPM) would become the driving philosophy behind church planting at the IMB. CPM theory actually constitutes a restatement of the "three-self" indigenous missiology of Henry Venn of the nineteenth century. In his groundbreaking work, Venn theorized that churches planted overseas should be self-governing, self-propagating, and self-supporting. Wilbert Shenk writes, "Venn and his American contemporary Rufus Anderson (1797–1880) sought to clarify the main goal of mission and the most effective means of realizing it. The concept of the indigenous church emerged as the central construct of mission theory. A church was judged to be indigenous when it was self-propagating, self-financing, and self-governing. Venn developed his theory of mission in a series of pamphlets and policy statements written in the years 1846 to 1865."[33]

Garrison says that CPM theory is not so much a methodology as observations about what transpires when healthy, indigenous churches are planted. Garrison writes, "A Church Planting Movement is *a rapid multiplication of indigenous churches planting churches that sweeps through a people group or population segment.* There's a lot more we could add to this definition, but this one captures its essence. You'll note that this definition describes what *is* happening in Church Planting Movements rather than *pre*scribing what *could* or *should* happen."[34] Some practitioners trying to implement CPM theory as a method attempted to replicate the church planting results in other, less responsive parts of the world. Since a CPM simply describes what happened in a given area, not prescribing what they should do, this proved frustrating to many missionaries.

---

32   David Garrison, *Church Planting Movements: How God Is Redeeming a Lost World* (Midlothian, VA: WIGTake Resources, 2004).
33   Wilbert R. Shenk, "Venn, Henry," in *Biographical Dictionary of Christian Missions*, ed. Gerald H. Anderson (New York: Macmillan, 1998), 698.
34   Garrison, *Church Planting Movements*, 21 (emphasis original).

Taking a cue from Roland Allen's 1932 *The Spontaneous Expansion of the Church*, CPM missiology adds rapidity to the church planting equation. Garrison comments concerning the rapid pace of starting the new congregations he desires: "'How rapid is rapid?' you may ask. Perhaps the best answer is, 'Faster than you think possible.' Though the rate varies from place to place, Church Planting Movements always outstrip the population growth as they race toward reaching the entire people group. Once you've viewed a few of the case studies, you'll begin to get the idea."[35] One reason rapidity in church planting would become popular in IMB circles is that results would come about faster and the overwhelming task of church planting could be carried out with greater dispatch. The other reason has to do with theology.

Many CPM advocates believe, as Allen suggests, that when God is at work, results come swiftly. Indeed, when critics suggested that rapid church planting prevents in-depth discipleship, Rankin was sympathetic but countered that rapid church growth is God's work and cannot be criticized.[36] The nebulous nature of the CPM definition and the theory's insistence on rapidity caused uncertainty among the missionary force as to how to recognize, facilitate, and nurture CPMs. The CPM concept is used by many people, but CPMs themselves have proved to be elusive in practice.

Jerry Rankin's Theological Orientation
Rankin resists theological categorization and would not subscribe to any of the following descriptors 100 percent. That being said, each of these systems can be observed to some extent in Rankin's thinking.

End-Times Eschatology
Throughout Rankin's career as president, he was accused of believing that reaching every people group with the gospel would usher in the second coming of Jesus Christ. Although Rankin

---

35   Garrison, *Church Planting Movements*, 21–22.
36   Fries, "Personal Life of Jerry Rankin," 18.

disagreed with this analysis, often during his messages over the years, he referenced Revelation 5:9, juxtaposing it with Matthew 24:14. These verses read as follows:

> And they sang a new song, saying, "Worthy are You to take the book and to break its seals; for you were slain, and purchased for God with Your blood men from every tribe and tongue and people and nation." (Rev. 5:9 NASB)

> This gospel of the kingdom shall be preached in the whole world as a testimony to all the nations, and then the end will come. (Matt. 24:14 NASB)

To proponents of end-times eschatology these verses seem to teach that when someone from every people group believes in the gospel, Christ will return. The implication is that when missionaries reach individuals from every people group, the second coming of Jesus Christ will be hastened. Critics saw this as advocating the view that humankind could influence God's prophetic timetable through human action. Rankin denies holding this view, but detractors say that he continued to advocate for this line of thought.[37]

Mysticism

A self-described mystic, Rankin nonetheless refuses the label of charismatic Christian. He believes the miraculous gifts of the Holy Spirit continue today but does not consider himself a neo-Pentecostal.[38] Even though Rankin practices a "private prayer language," he does not consider this to be "speaking in tongues." Rankin's support of the contemporary practice of the "sign gifts"—including the raising of the dead and other dramatic miracles—trouble many traditional Southern Baptists. Furthermore, his embrace of

---

37   Micah Fries, "Church Planting Movements: The Missiology and Methodology of the New Directions Strategy of the International Mission Board, 1997–2010" (unpublished paper, February 22, 2018), 12–13.
38   Fries, "Personal Life of Jerry Rankin."

the spiritual territory normally reserved for the charismatic movement caused some division within the missionary ranks during his tenure. Indeed, CPM methodology, the favored theory during the Rankin years, teaches that miraculous signs *always* accompany indigenous church planting movements.[39] Rankin's denial of being a charismatic, while at the same time endorsing some of the movement's theology and practice, caused some dissonance during his administration.

Calvinism

When asked if he was a Calvinist, Rankin said, "I have an appreciation for Reformed Theology,"[40] but he did not indicate he subscribed wholeheartedly to Calvinism. Although comfortable with some of the results-oriented church growth theories of Donald McGavran that were introduced to him during his seminary days by Cal Guy, Rankin's missiology leans more toward the "glory of God" perspective of the Reformed leader and pastor John Piper. For previous generations, the primary motivation for missionaries preaching the gospel was "to seek and to save that which was lost." Generally, Reformed thinkers like Piper believe the church has been given the task of missions primarily to glorify God. Rankin agrees with this concept. Furthermore, Rankin sees access to the gospel as more important than attempting to populate heaven with as many people as possible. For him, this access to the good news for every person on earth trumps church growth strategies and methods.

The Rankin Administration

Like any leader, Rankin possessed his own unique style. Rankin could be gracious, affable, and approachable with both friends and new acquaintances. Although many administrators offer lip service to an open-door policy, in reality their subordinates do not

---

39   Curtis Sergeant, William Smith, and Susan Smith, *Characteristics of a CPM*, quoted in Fries, "Church Planting Movements," 26.

40   Jerry Rankin, interview with the author, October 11, 2018, Clinton, Mississippi.

feel welcome without an appointment. Rankin's open-door policy
was real. When this author needed to speak with Rankin, he was
always able to visit with him on a moment's notice.

Despite these strengths, as a leader he could be a loner. Rankin
leaned not toward consensus but rather often made decisions inter-
nally without much outside input and without preparing his staff
in advance.[41] In some ways, it was a strength because after praying
and fasting over a decision, he was convinced it was from God.
This belief gave Rankin the fortitude to persevere in the face of
much opposition. Sometimes Rankin's decision-making process,
however, represented a weakness. Occasionally his decisions totally
surprised his subordinates. This reaction would startle and perplex
Rankin and require much effort to create sufficient buy-in before
going forward. Rankin cared about how people perceived his decisions, but this attitude did not stop him from making unpopular
rulings. Even if opposed by close advisors and confidants, Rankin
rarely reversed himself.

Concerning perceptions of Rankin, there was little middle
ground. Many saw him as a spiritual leader possessing genuine
charisma. Others viewed him as somewhat aloof and arbitrary. All
agreed he was a hardworking president. Nevertheless, Rankin was
an agent who brought significant change at the IMB, and much of
it was positive.

The Last Frontier

Closely associated with unreached peoples, the "Last Frontier"
concept emphasizes engaging the final people groups on the earth
with the gospel. Rankin says, "I'm disappointed that we continue
to give so much attention to maintaining and nurturing established
work where the gospel is readily accessible; we prefer the gratifying harvest fields where we can bolster our egos with impressive
statistics while millions of Achenese, Sri Lankans, Maldivians and

---

41   Davis, "Paradigm Shift in Missions," 106, 114.

Thais are swept into hell, untouched by the gospel."[42] Although these people groups are unreached, Rankin believes that with personnel assigned to them they could well turn responsive to the gospel. He terms these unreached peoples "neglected harvest fields."[43] Rankin calls this new area to be reached the Last Frontier of the Great Commission.[44]

When New Directions began in 1997, a dual focus of harvest and unreached was announced by the FMB. This concentration slowly changed, however, to more of a single focus to evangelize the Last Frontier. In 1997, the four administrative areas in the Americas totaled more than twelve hundred missionaries. By the end of Rankin's tenure in 2010, the Americas had been reduced to one region with less than four hundred missionaries in all of Latin America. A similar downsizing of the missionary force occurred in sub-Saharan Africa. Of course, morale suffered among missionary personnel who remained in the so-called reached parts of the world.

In the first years of the new millennium, the newly named IMB led the charge of mission agencies into the Last Frontier. With its larger size and greater budget, the IMB was able to move personnel and appoint new missionaries to more remote and less responsive areas. This new paradigm was research driven.

In 1997 the Global Research Department (GRD) of the FMB utilized a 20 percent threshold to determine when a people group or population segment attained the ability to reach themselves. Research by David Sills showed that the 20 percent benchmark was arbitrary. Sills says, "Initially, missionaries were working with the figure of 20 percent evangelical as sufficient to consider a group reached; this was based on a sociological axiom that if 20 percent of a population accepts a new idea, the adopters can perpetuate and propagate it within the group without outside help. Missiologists made the application that if a group was at least 20 percent

---

42   Jerry Rankin, *Empowering Kingdom Growth to the Ends of the Earth: Churches Fulfilling the Great Commission* (Richmond, VA: International Mission Board, 2005), 6.
43   Fries, "Personal Life of Jerry Rankin," 24.
44   Jerry Rankin, quoted in Fries, "Church Planting Movements," 20.

evangelical this group could continue the work of evangelism without the help of outside missionaries, thus freeing the missionaries to move on."[45] Some leaders at the US Center for World Missions determined that 20 percent was "too high," citing one study that implies that when 20 percent of a people adhere to a view they can sway the majority.[46] These principles lowered the threshold for "reachedness" from 20 percent to 2 percent. Patrick Johnstone writes, "The original Joshua Project editorial committee selected the criteria less than 2% evangelical Christian and less than 5% Christian adherents. While these percentage figures are somewhat arbitrary, there are some that suggest that the percentage of a population needed to be influenced to impact the whole group is 2%."[47] Mission leaders arbitrarily chose the lower figure as the benchmark to decide when a group was adequately reached and when a people group or population segment could be exited.

By 1998 the new leaders in the IMB GRD reduced the figure to 12 percent. Within a few years, the IMB and many other mission groups were using 2 percent as the threshold to differentiate between unreached and when a population could reach itself. While the Last Frontier must be joined, statistics were gradually employed to distance missionaries from portions of the world above the 2 percent evangelical benchmark, portions that were normally the more receptive fields. Rankin claims that his personal opinion "is that 10% would be considered 'reached' and represent the capacity of local believers to engage the remainder of a people group, but that

---

45   M. David Sills, *Reaching and Teaching* (Chicago: Moody, 2010), 108.

46   Concerning this 20 percent threshold, Mark Terry and J. D. Payne write in *Developing a Strategy for Missions: A Biblical, Historical, and Cultural Introduction* (Grand Rapids: Baker Academic, 2013), 188, "In his renowned work *Diffusion of Innovations* (2003) [Everett M.] Rogers explains that when a new idea, product, or concept is introduced into a society, the spread, or diffusion of that knowledge occurs rapidly and throughout the society when 10 to 20 percent of the population has embraced it. Although Rogers's initial work was conducted in the field of agriculture, missiologists in the 1970s and 1980s applied his finding to the dissemination of the Gospel across and people group."

47   Patrick Johnstone, in Sills, *Reaching and Teaching*, 109.

did not justify diminishing or eliminating missionary personnel."[48] Although missionary personnel may not have been diminished or eliminated during the Rankin era, this was the net result due to the IMB allowing natural attrition to shift personnel resources from the "reached" part of the world to the "unreached" areas. Rankin asserts that "the 2% criteria simply distinguished the unreached from the unengaged. . . . Below 2% were still basically unengaged and therefore represented a priority of deploying personnel."[49] Since there were so many people groups to engage within people groups less than 2 percent reached, most IMB personnel were sent to ethnicities below the 2 percent threshold well before any of the people groups ever reached 10 percent.

The debate revolves around what is involved in the missionary task. The question concerns whether missions is primarily a pioneering effort to reach the Last Frontier or whether the "teaching all things" is also key. During the Rankin era, the former gradually supplanted the latter.

Partnering with Great Commission Christians

One of the hallmarks of the Rankin era involved partnering not only with fellow Baptists in STMs but also with compatible mission groups within the broader evangelical community. Formerly, due to its size, and to some extent its provincialism, the FMB seldom worked with other mission agencies. CSI began to change this because often part of a strategy coordinator's plan involved partnering with other mission groups. Missionaries did not associate with incompatible mission groups, but they often formed alliances with parachurch groups and evangelical mission agencies.

To forestall criticism as well as theological problems, IMB leaders developed five levels of approved partnerships for their missionaries as they related to other agencies. The IMB Relationships: Levels, Goals and Guidelines document states the following:

---

48   Jerry Rankin, email to the author, June 18, 2019.
49   Jerry Rankin, email to the author, June 18, 2019.

IMB missionaries relate to non-IMB entities at different levels depending on their goals and needs. These relationships range from expedient to eternal in their significance. The deeper the level, the greater the significance.

Level One:
Goal: Entry to the target population (e.g. tourism, business, education, etc.)
Guiding Principle: Suitability to target population

Level Two:
Goal: Prayer for the population, ministry to felt needs for purpose of pre-evangelism
Guiding Principle: Response to spiritual & physical needs

Level Three:
Goal: Evangelism & Scripture distribution
Guiding Principle: Commitment to biblical evangelism

Level Four:
Goal: New Testament church (i.e., Baptist or baptistic)
Guiding Principle: Commitment to planting New Testament churches

Level Five:
Goals: Ministerial training, theological education, ordination, deploying missionaries, etc.
Guiding Principle: Doctrinal purity[50]

Although IMB missionaries benefited from partnering with evangelical entities such as Wycliffe Bible Translators, Campus Crusade for Christ (now CRU), Operation Mobilization (OM),

---

50   Office of Overseas Operations, *Something New under the Sun: New Directions at the International Mission Board, SBC* (Richmond, VA: IMB, 1999), 36.

and Missionary Aviation Fellowship (MAF), sometimes the partnerships were questionable. For instance, when I served in the CSI area of the FMB (a year before Rankin was elected president) I learned that not all missionaries shared the same understanding of acceptable level 1 partnerships. I attended a meeting with about fifteen IMB personnel along with a representative of the Eastern Orthodox Church. The discussion centered on how IMB missionaries might facilitate the entry of Orthodox missionaries into portions of the Muslim world. I stated after the representative had departed that I did not feel comfortable bringing "error" to my people group.

Rankin did not desire to cooperate with other mission groups to achieve ecumenical unity but rather to marshal more resources, both material and personnel, to achieve the task of world evangelism. Rankin said, "Cooperation and unity is not an end in itself. Cooperating with others is a utilitarian approach to accomplish a mutual objective."[51] Overall, the IMB was able to influence positively other mission agencies by engaging with them. On one occasion the regional leaders of the IMB met with their counterparts of the Wycliffe Bible Translators. Such cooperation went a long way toward achieving a more unified evangelical approach to missions.

Statistical Growth

The Rankin era saw many new countries, people groups, and population segments become engaged by IMB missionaries and Baptist partners. Statistically, IMB missionaries and missions reported sharp gains during the Rankin era. According to the 2010 SBC Convention Annual, the IMB saw an increase in its missionary force from 4,000 missionaries in 142 countries in 1993, to more than 5,500 missionaries working with 1,190 people groups in 2008.[52] The book also states that IMB missionaries and their

---

51 Jerry Rankin, cited in "A Critical Analysis of the History of Southern Baptist Approaches to International Cooperation in International Missions" (unpublished paper, 2015), 220, quoted in Fries, "Church Planting Movements," 9.

52 SBCA, 2010.

national Baptist partners "saw a dramatic increase in the number of new church starts and baptisms, from about 2,000 churches and more than 260,000 baptisms in 1993, to about 27,000 new churches and more than 565,000 baptisms in 2008."[53] These statistical increases represent astounding growth. The increases are probably a direct result of IMB missionaries redoubling their efforts in evangelism and church starting. Some of these increases occurred because missionaries were freed administratively to pursue new strategies that resulted in posting great numbers.

NEW METHODS

Training 4 Trainers (T4T)

Ying and Grace Kai, although serving as Clinical Pastoral Education hospital chaplains in East Asia, accepted the call to become church planters as part of New Directions. Beginning in 2000, the Kais reported 906 new plants with over 10,000 new believers. By the ninth year, these churches reportedly numbered 158,993 with 1,718,143 baptisms.[54] The T4T method asks each new member or trainer to enlist five nonbelieving friends and share Christ with them. The leader welcomes the prospects into his home, shares his Christian testimony, and hopefully leads them to faith in Jesus. The "trainer" and his group of five new believers become a new unit. The disciples instruct the five new members to share their testimonies with five others who in turn do the same.

During the following week, the trainer's five new members have theoretically led five nonbelievers to the Lord, who have begun their own small assemblies. The first trainer leads his disciples through a six-week training plan. At the same time, his disciples and their devotees direct new converts through the training material and evangelize others. As the T4T movement grows, the new converts

53   SBCA, 2010.
54   Steve Smith with Ying Kai, *T4T, A Discipleship ReRevolution: The Story behind the World's Fastest Growing Church Planting Movement and How It Can Happen in Your Community* (Monument, CO: WIGTake Resources, 2011), 21.

are one week behind their trainers and one week ahead of their own disciples.[55] Sometimes these new congregations with week-old believers are called churches while at other times they are referred to as Bible studies. A number of years ago, I asked Ying Kai the following question during a training session in Asia: "How many people actually follow instructions and witness to their friends?" Kai replied, "About one in five." This 20 percent success rate has led to amazing results.

Steve Smith contends that rapid church planting is appropriate. He says that in places where a majority of the Christians are new, the young believers have to become the church leaders or there will be no leaders at all.[56] The T4T method stresses the importance of every T4T member sharing their faith and discipling others to do the same. Detractors counter that placing very new Christians in positions of leadership is problematic. Additionally, most of the new T4T congregations resemble Bible studies rather than churches. Sometimes proponents call the T4T groups churches before they meet the biblical requirements for becoming a church.

Nonetheless, T4T was exported as one of the primary methods favored in IMB regions throughout the world during the Rankin administration. Hailed as the strategy that would work all over the globe, the method was even brought to the United States and introduced to Baptist state conventions and associations. Results outside of Asian society, however, have been mixed. T4T seems to work in cultures that respect tradition and authority and less well in more individualistic societies.

The Camel Method

Developed in South Asia, the "Camel method" is a gospel-bridging methodology that uses a Christian interpretation of the Qur'an to evangelize Muslims. Kevin Greeson developed the method while watching Muslim converts win Muslims to Christ. He writes,

---

55   Ying Kai, *Trainers: Establishing Successful Trainers,* 2nd ed. (Hong Kong: Ocean, 2005), 5–6.

56   Smith with Kai, *T4T,* 257, 266.

It soon became clear to us that the shortest bridge available was found in 13 verses of *surah al-Imran*, chapter 3 of the Qur'an, which spoke of *Isa al-Masih* (Jesus Christ). This passage declared that Jesus would be born of a virgin; that He would do miracles; that He would be a sign to the whole world; that Allah would cause Him to die and raise Him again to heaven. To help us remember the key points in the chapter we used the acronym C-A-M-E-L.[57] These letters brought to mind the chapter's key teaching that Isa's mother, Mary, was **C**hosen to give birth to Isa; that **A**ngels announced the good news to her; that Isa would do **M**iracles, and that He knew the way to **E**ternal **L**ife. In this way, the Camel method was born.[58]

This technique cites Mary, Jesus's mother, during the initial steps of the Camel acronym (C-A). This can be confusing because the Qur'an replaces the Holy Spirit with Christ's mother in the Trinity.[59] Furthermore, the third step of the Camel method (M) attributes the miracles in the apocryphal Gospel of Thomas[60] to Jesus. The final step in the Camel acronym signifies "eternal life" (E-L). The Camel method cites sura 3:45[61] as the Qur'anic verse that points to Christ's

---

57 Kevin Greeson in *The Camel* (Arkadelphia, AR: WIGTake Resources, 2007), 16, claims "missionaries didn't invent the Camel method. It is the method we learned from Muslim-background believers." Westerners most likely influenced the development of the C-A-M-E-L acronym because the Arabic transliteration of camel would be *jimel*. The Arabic-script version would be written from right to left without vowels, Semitic style (L-M-J).

58 Greeson, *The Camel*, 41–42.

59 The Qur'an views the Trinity as Father, Son, and Mary. See, George W. Braswell, *Islam: Its Prophet, Peoples, Politics, and Power* (Nashville: Broadman & Holman, 1996), 251.

60 Greeson, in *The Camel*, 105, quotes Qur'an sura 3:49 in support of Jesus performing miracles. "And (make him) an apostle to the children of Israel: That I have come to you with a sign from your Lord, that I determine for you out of dust like the form of a bird, then I breathe into it and it becomes a bird with Allah's permission, and I heal the blind and leprous and bring the dead to life with Allah's permission."

61 Greeson, in *The Camel*, 105–6, quotes from sura 3:54–55 as the Qur'anic verse that Jesus is the way to eternal life: "And they planned and Allah (also) planned, and Allah is the best of planners. And when Allah said: O Isa, *I am going to terminate the period*

resurrection, although Muslims disagree with the interpretation.[62] Detractors both inside and outside the IMB have criticized such contextualized models. Sam Schlorff advocates a more direct strategy: "The focus is on what Mohammad understood the terms to mean and how his original hearers would have understood him. In practical terms, this means that Qur'anic language may not be interpreted in terms of what one might think similar biblical language might have meant. It cannot be filled with Christian content."[63]

Pioneer Evangelism

As a missionary in Brazil in 1989, Thomas Wade Akins developed pioneer evangelism to start churches using laymen rather than ordained clergy.[64] This approach uses inductive Bible studies in the homes of lost people to evangelize them and start churches. Instead of selecting Christian homes for the new church starts, this method seeks unaffiliated individuals who are willing to host a weekly group.

The sequence begins with Bible lessons taught by the church planter during weeks one through six. Most who attend all the introductory sessions will usually come to faith in Christ. The next six weeks consist of further discipleship lessons. The pioneer evangelist relinquishes leadership of the new church to someone within the congregation. Although developed in Brazil, this method has flourished all over the world. The distinctive feature of this approach is that the pioneer evangelist does not convene the group in either his own home or the home of another Christian. These

---

of your stay (on earth) and cause you to ascend unto Me and purify you of those who disbelieve and make those who follow you above those who disbelieve to the day of resurrection; then to Me shall be your return, so I will decide between you concerning that in which you differed" (italics added for emphasis). Again, Greeson does not give a source of the interpretation (translation) of the Qur'anic sura (verse).

62   Greeson, The Camel, 118, 127, 138.
63   Greeson, The Camel, 133.
64   Thomas Wade Akins, Pioneer Evangelism: Growing Churches and Planting New Ones That Are Self-Supporting Using New Testament Methods (Rio de Janeiro: Junta de Missões Nacionais, Convenção Batista Brasileira, 1999), 17.

congregations are planted among unbelievers so that their friends are secure attending.

Baptist Global Response

Another innovation during the Rankin years was the establishment of Baptist Global Response (BGR). Formed in 2005, BGR replaced the Human Needs Department of the IMB with an independent agency that receives funds from Southern Baptist human needs offerings in addition to other sources donated by individuals and churches. Unofficially affiliated with the IMB, BGR has a separate board of directors but is operated and supervised by IMB missionaries. BGR allows Southern Baptists through the IMB to extend their reach beyond evangelistic mission work to relief and development. Operating in over one hundred countries, BGR strives to minister in Jesus's name in disaster-relief emergency situations. Rankin says about the establishment of BGR, "We were often forbidden to be engaged in responding to natural disasters around the world as well as other humanitarian projects in closed countries since the IMB would exploit the situation to proselytize. With the resources of Southern Baptists and a global network of personnel we needed to create a separate legal entity that was not identified as 'missionary.'"[65]

Rankin did not specifically endorse any of these methods but encouraged regional leadership and missionaries to innovate to reach the nations for Christ. "Whatever it takes—WIGTAKE" (for "Whatever It's Going to Take") became one of the refrains in the Rankin era.

CONCLUSION

The Rankin years featured a time of rapid expansion in Southern Baptist missions. The IMB saw great statistical growth in the number of personnel, budgets, baptisms, and new churches. In terms of the number of missionaries and financial support, the Rankin era represents the high-water mark in the expansion of the IMB. When

---

65   Jerry Rankin, email to the author, June 14, 2018.

Rankin's term began in 1992, the FMB was engaging 584 people groups in 147 countries. By the time Rankin announced his retirement, the IMB was engaging 1,198 people groups in 160 countries.[66] The financial crisis in the US economy in late 2008 caused a drop in all charitable giving, and the IMB proved no exception. Although the Rankin years ended with the IMB on sound financial footing, Rankin's successors sold unneeded overseas properties, drew from reserves, and allowed attrition to reduce the number of missionaries to balance the budgets after 2009. Ten years after Rankin's retirement, the IMB missionary force stood at just over 4,200, a drop of almost 25 percent.

During a time of denominational reorganization, the FMB of 1845 became the IMB in the year 2000. New administrative structures and innovative strategies were also instituted. A few of the new approaches proved controversial with constituencies, and the administrative changes brought some turmoil within the organization. Rankin carried out major field reorganizations twice during his seventeen years as president. Many of these changes proved successful, while a few were less so. Throughout a period of advancement in missions and often tumultuous change, however, the rank-and-file missionaries continued to evangelize and disciple new converts and push toward the evangelization of the nations. Rankin contends that he was only a vessel used by the Lord and that the credit for any achievements during his tenure should go to Christ. Rankin believed the administrative changes were necessary to focus field personnel more on the evangelistic task and less on mission administration. Detractors, however, believed the reorganizations increased the administrative burdens on field personnel rather than reducing them. Concerning strategy, Rankin allowed field missionaries to develop innovative approaches unhindered by red tape. If some missionaries went too far, then the regional or affinity group administrations were expected to step in to correct aberrant doctrines or faulty practices.

---

66   Scott Peterson, Office of Global Research, IMB, email to the author, June 11, 2019.

The Rankin years were marked by on-and-off conflict between the president and his trustees. By the end of his tenure, however, Rankin had settled into a good working relationship with this body. Upon his retirement in 2009, Rankin received the title of president emeritus. He continued his work with lectures at the IMB International Learning Center and teaching for Mississippi College and Columbia International University (CIU). At CIU Rankin directed the Zwemer Institute for Muslim Studies. The Rankin era at the International Mission Board was a time of unprecedented mission growth, missionary advance, and expansion.

THE TOM ELLIFF YEARS AT THE INTERNATIONAL MISSION BOARD, 2011–2014

Robin Dale Hadaway

O N FEBRUARY 16, 2011, the trustees of the IMB unanimously elected Thomas D. Elliff as president.[1] Elliff succeeded Jerry Rankin, who had retired the previous year. When IMB trustee chairman Jimmy Prichard called Elliff about his interest in the position, Tom's wife Jeannie had only recently

---

1   Eric Bridges, "Elliff Elected Unanimously to Lead the International Mission Board," BP, February 16, 2011, http://www.bpnews.net/34848/elliff-elected-unanimously-to-lead-intl-mission-board.

completed her last chemotherapy treatment for cancer. Elliff promised to go before the Lord and see whether God would give him a vision for the position. After a month of prayer and fasting, he agreed to serve, saying, "God painted a picture on the wall of my heart and a vision of what we could do."[2]

PREPARATION

A third-generation pastor and a fourth-generation Oklahoman, Elliff was born on February 11, 1944, in Paris, Texas, just across the border from Oklahoma. When he was in the third grade, his father accepted a call to Bethany Baptist Church in Kansas City, Missouri. It was there, slightly more than a year after his conversion, that Tom first heard the missionary testimony of Martha Gilliland, an FMB medical missionary to Nigeria. After completing high school, Elliff enrolled at Ouachita Baptist University in Arkadelphia, Arkansas. Upon graduation in 1966, he married the former Jeannie Thomas. Following a year and a half of graduate school as a teaching fellow at Ouachita, Elliff enrolled as a student at Southwestern Baptist Theological Seminary in Fort Worth, Texas, graduating in 1971. The following year, he accepted a call as pastor of the Eastwood Baptist Church in Tulsa, Oklahoma.[3]

After nine years of leading this vibrant and growing church, Tom and Jeannie perceived the leading of the Lord to become foreign missionaries. This occurred following a week at Glorieta Baptist Assembly, where former FMB president Baker James Cauthen delivered his final message at a missionary appointment service and the new president, Keith Parks, was elected. Concerning their call to missions, Elliff says, "Missions is not as much about having a burden as it is about being obedient."[4] Following God's direction, the Elliff family completed FMB missionary orientation at Callaway

---

2   Tom Elliff, interview with the author, May 13, 2019, Oklahoma City, Oklahoma.
3   "Bio: Tom Elliff," BP, February 17, 2011, http://www.bpnews.net/34667/bio-tom-ell.
4   Tom Elliff, interview with the author, May 13, 2019, Oklahoma City, Oklahoma.

Gardens, Georgia, in the fall of 1981, arriving in Zimbabwe during the month of January the following year. In the fall of 1982, the Elliffs' oldest daughter, Beth, was severely injured in an automobile accident. By July of 1983, the Elliff family decided their daughter was not making sufficient progress in her recovery, so they returned to the States, resigning from missionary service.

After pastoring Applewood Baptist Church in Lakewood, Colorado, from 1983 to 1985, Elliff moved to the First Baptist Church of Del City, Oklahoma, to serve as pastor for the next twenty years. In 2005, Rankin tapped Elliff to serve as the senior vice president for spiritual nurture–church relations of the IMB. During this time, Elliff focused on shoring up the doctrinal preparation of IMB missionaries journeying to the field. In 2009, Elliff resigned from the IMB to devote his time fully to Living in the Word Publications, a writing and speaking ministry focused on spiritual awakening that he had founded four years earlier.

PRESIDENCY

Elliff had been offered the IMB presidency earlier in 1991. He declined, however, saying that the Lord would not give him a release to change the focus of his ministry. Elliff says, "I've never sought a position in my life. I never considered myself as part of a movement. I'm really not a 'political guy.'"[5] Twenty years later with a second chance, Elliff responded affirmatively to the trustee presidential search committee's plea to lead the IMB. While Elliff claims he was the least qualified person to come into this role, his service as a vice president provided for him the genesis of a vision about the future of the IMB. Now as the president he could implement the vision he believed God had given him.

Elliff asserts that he began his presidency with the intention of fulfilling the following objectives. These goals represent part of the vision this new president conceptualized as he began his new role.

---

5   Tom Elliff, interview with the author, May 13, 2019, Oklahoma City, Oklahoma.

Adherence to a Single Vision

As IMB president, Elliff desired to coalesce the whole organization around one vision. To this end, Elliff conducted random visits around the Richmond headquarters, dispensing five-dollar bills to the staff members who could quote the IMB vision statement from memory. The vision stated, "Our vision is a multitude from every people, tribe, nation and language knowing and worshipping the Lord Jesus Christ." Elliff was convinced that if the entire organization adhered to this vision, the other major objectives could be accomplished.

Emphasis on Doctrinal Integrity

As one of the leaders of the Conservative Resurgence in the SBC, doctrine was especially important to the new president. While serving as an IMB vice president, Elliff taught many of the doctrinal courses for new missionaries at the International Learning Center. The pretests and posttests he administered to the prospective missionaries for thirteen consecutive Field Personnel Orientation (FPO) classes convinced him candidates were "all over the map" doctrinally. Elliff said that the results of these tests surprised him, and he was determined to correct the deficiency. He determined to make doctrinal purity a hallmark of his presidency.

Prioritizing Prayer

Elliff believed that because the IMB purported to be a spiritual organization, it should be an entity that bathed its operations in prayer. In an early effort in this direction, he invited people to join him in a prayer room he had added to his office area. Adhering to his principle of prioritizing prayer, he then shifted Overseas Vice President Gordon Fort into a newly created vice presidency for prayer and spiritual nurture. This move established the first ever denomination-wide school of prayer and raised the profile of the Office of Prayer within the IMB. While all Baptist leaders support the idea of increasing prayer in principle, in practice the concept often receives short shrift. This is not true of Elliff. Of his thirteen books, three of them explore the subject of prayer. These volumes include *A Passion for Prayer*,[6] *Praying for Others*,[7] and *The Pathway to God's Presence*.[8] By emphasizing prayer, Elliff raised the spiritual temperature within the Richmond office.

Local Church Adoption of People Groups

At the outset of his presidency, Elliff decided to introduce a new program to bring more local churches to the table and more individuals participating in international missions. At his first SBC annual meeting, in 2011, Elliff challenged each SBC church to adopt a specific unreached people group—not just for prayer, but to develop a unique strategy for their church to personally reach the adopted unreached people group with the gospel. He called the new initiative "Embrace." More than twelve hundred churches officially signed on to be involved in this more participative format of missions. The IMB Global Research Department reports the following statistics at the beginning and end of Elliff's tenure:

> IMB People Group Engagement:
> January 2011: 845 people groups in 144 countries
> August 2014: 907 people groups in 137 countries

> SBC People Group Engagement (engagement by churches, groups of churches, or associations):
> January 2011: 79 people groups in 18 countries
> August 2014: 144 people groups in 40 countries[9]

IMB Connecting

Although initiated during the Rankin administration, the IMB Connecting concept was greatly expanded during the Elliff presidency. Whereas the Embrace program connects churches with unreached

---

6   Thomas D. Elliff, *A Passion for Prayer: Experiencing Deeper Intimacy with God* (Fort Washington, PA: CLC, 2010).
7   Thomas D. Elliff, *Praying for Others* (Nashville: Broadman, 1979).
8   Thomas D. Elliff, *The Pathway to God's Presence* (Fort Washington, PA: CLC, 2014).
9   Scott Peterson, IMB Department of Global Research, email to the author, June 11, 2019.

people groups, the IMB Connecting initiative links IMB missionaries with specific Southern Baptist churches. Elliff initiated a plan during his years according to which no missionary could leave for the field without first having a joint meeting where local church staff and IMB staff representatives were present with the missionary. The sending church agreed to commit itself to undergird the missionary in prayer, faithful giving, and by agreeing to participate in the missionary's ministry. This program resulted in missionaries and churches being more connected with one another in the mission task.

Financial Stability

The great financial downturn of the final months of 2008 greatly and negatively affected all charitable giving in the United States. Despite the opinion of many to the contrary, the IMB was always financially "in the black." It remained solvent by not spending its full budget each year and by drawing modestly on funds set aside as financial reserves. Elliff's strategy to combat the financial crisis was threefold.

1. *Allow Attrition.* Elliff continued the practice of his predecessor to reduce the missionary force by normal attrition. Instead of appointing new missionaries to replace those who retired, died in service, or resigned for various reasons, many positions were left unfilled. The goal was to reduce the IMB force by about 10 percent. Since almost 75 percent of the IMB annual budget is personnel-related, it was thought that such reductions could balance the books until the US economy recovered. Although attrition significantly helped in this regard, it did not fix the problem. Attrition caused the following drop in numbers during Elliff's tenure. When Elliff began in 2011 the IMB counted 5,014 missionaries. Upon his retirement, the missionary headcount stood at 4,832.

2. *Promote Stewardship.* As the US economy continued to decline at the beginning of the century's second decade, Elliff

and others on the IMB staff asked SBC churches and individuals to increase their giving to the Cooperative Program and the Lottie Moon Christmas Offering. Although both offerings reported gains, the amounts were not sufficiently large to solve all of the IMB's financial problems without additional measures.

3. *Sell Properties.* As a 175-year-old organization operating across the world, the IMB possesses a tremendous amount of real estate around the globe. When the IMB shifted to a "Last Frontier" and "unreached people group" philosophy during the Rankin era, many properties in South America, sub-Saharan Africa, and some in Asia became redundant. Many properties were put up for sale and the proceeds designated to fund the daily operations of the organization. Some criticized this move, saying that sometimes real estate had to be repurchased or space rented when new personnel came to the field. IMB staff members countered that unused properties deteriorate rapidly in the tropics, making it wise to sell unneeded housing before upkeep costs escalate.

Build Morale

The Rankin era of missions featured both tumultuous change and strategic advance. Elliff came into the president's role, however, as a pastor with a shepherd's heart. His default mode was to proceed with care and concern for the feelings of his missionaries and staff. Concerning this approach, Elliff states, "You want people to feel better about themselves and their role."[10] To punctuate this shift in style, Elliff would often stand at the entrance of the Richmond headquarters offices and personally welcome employees into the building. He prioritized the IMB's weekly chapel hour and dined as often as possible in the learning center lunchroom with missionaries and IMB employees. He also instituted periodic spiritual

---

10   Tom Elliff, interview with the author, May 13, 2019, Oklahoma City, Oklahoma.

life retreats for all home office staff members. When asked about how he operated as IMB president, Elliff responded by describing himself as the pastor of the organization.[11]

Missions Advocacy
One of the reasons Elliff was chosen as president of the IMB was due to his strong preaching ability. Elliff determined to be out among Southern Baptists, preaching in as many churches, associations, state conventions, colleges, and seminaries as possible. Elliff's strong ties to the local church, his role as past president of the SBC, and his many other denominational relationships made him an ideal advocate for Southern Baptist missions and a bridge-builder within the denomination.

Emphasis on Southern Baptist "Ownership"
Because Elliff became IMB president in his late sixties, he viewed the role from the standpoint of a Baptist statesman rather than from the vantage point of a chief executive officer. Elliff saw the IMB as God's organization and a stewardship to him from Southern Baptists. Part of this perspective came from his many years of pastoring Southern Baptist churches. He desired for Southern Baptists to feel the IMB was uniquely *their* mission board. Therefore, Elliff emphasized that Southern Baptists *owned* the IMB.

ACHIEVEMENTS

Although Elliff was only in office for three and a half years, a number of his accomplishments are notable.

The Macedonia Project
To mobilize people to the field more quickly, Elliff and IMB staff members initiated the Macedonia Project (MP). The MP allowed missionary units to jump-start their appointment process through

---

11   Tom Elliff, interview with the author, May 13, 2019, Oklahoma City, Oklahoma.

online seminary education. Often, candidates are called to missions from secular occupations or minister in parts of the country where they do not have the opportunity to attend seminary classes to obtain the educational credentials to be appointed as IMB missionaries. The MP enables individuals to serve on the mission field while simultaneously taking online seminary classes. The IMB provides a 50 percent scholarship for the missionary while the seminary where the student is taking classes provides the remaining 50 percent of the scholarship. This allows missionaries in the MP to receive free seminary education while serving on the field. By the time the missionary unit returns to the States after their first term, they have completed the requirements for their forty-five-semester-hour master of theological studies degree or its equivalent. The program has been so successful that it continues today.

A Reemphasis on Theological Education

Elliff's experience of teaching missionary orientation classes during his vice presidency convinced him of the need to strengthen theological education, not only among IMB missionaries, but also for the board's national partners overseas. For this reason, he established a new vice president position to fill this requirement. Chuck Lawless of Southern Seminary was asked to serve in this position. Additionally, theological consultant missionaries were added to each geographical affinity to assist national churches and conventions to strengthen and expand the theological education footprint in their areas. These missionaries also recruited stateside colleges and seminaries to assist missionaries on the field in training their nationals. Furthermore, seminary-professor missionaries were appointed to teach on the faculties of educational institutions abroad. Elliff's advocacy on behalf of theological education represented a significant shift of emphasis at the IMB from the Rankin years.

The Establishment of the Office of Prayer

As has been already been stated, Elliff raised the visibility of prayer at the IMB by elevating the Office of Prayer to a higher prominence than ever before. Keith Parks originally established the prayer office, inviting Elliff to come to Richmond for its dedication and conduct a prayer seminar for the staff. The Office of Prayer continued as a mid-level department under Parks's successor Jerry Rankin. Elliff, however, established the new school of prayer under Gordon Fort's leadership, installing him as senior vice president. This move spotlighted prayer within the IMB.

Promoting Harmony and Stability

As a pastor with a shepherd's heart, Tom Elliff sensed that the organization needed a breather from the periodic reorganizations and frequent revisions of strategies of the recent past. The Elliff presidency emphasized the affirmation of individuals among both field missionaries and home office staff. Although supportive of the Rankin presidency's policies and its unprecedented expansion, Elliff's emphasis was different. He believed individuals would work best under caring, inspirational leadership. Elliff chose the best people he could find to place in positions of prominence and allowed them to do their work.

HALLMARKS OF THE ELLIFF ERA

Personal Evangelism

Personal soul-winning marks Elliff's life. This emphasis overflows with the result that Elliff inspires others to emulate his example. In an organization whose purpose involves evangelism and church planting, its leader needs to model these traits. Elliff shares Christ with others frequently and in retirement hosts evangelistic events in his home. Additionally, Elliff wrote a helpful book titled *What Should I Say to My Friend?*[12] In this treatise, which he wrote while serving as an IMB vice president, Elliff shares how one might witness to a lost person on the mission field. The book is written like

---

12 Thomas D. Elliff, *What Should I Say to My Friend?* (Richmond, VA: International Mission Board, 2009).

a novel. Elliff walks the prospective missionary through both the doctrinal issues and methods necessary for missionaries to share Christ overseas. A passion for evangelism and missions lies at the heart of Tom Elliff's ministry.

Emphasis on Spirituality

Spirituality is a difficult quality to quantify. By any reckoning, however, Tom Elliff fits this category. Prominent IMB emeritus missionary Wade Akins told me, "Tom Elliff truly is a man of God." Indeed, Elliff's ministry has been marked by an emphasis on spiritual renewal, prayer, and personal revival. Elliff sees spirituality as essential for men and women to serve in the ministry, especially in missionary roles. Elliff's tenure was marked by an intentional emphasis on increasing the spirituality at the IMB and beyond.

An Affirmational Leadership Style

When asked about how he led his affinity-group strategists (formerly called regional leaders or area directors) in regard to mission strategy, he replied, "They are wonderful, capable people who know how to do their jobs. They know what to do. I would not want to tell them what to do."[13] Elliff saw his job as more empowering his leaders rather than dictating their actions. He cast the broad vision, leaving strategy formulation to the experts. One former IMB vice president told me how Elliff came alongside him during a family crisis, offering support like a pastor. Elliff excelled in the affirmational and spiritual leadership of his direct reports but did not supervise them in the traditional sense.

Some people criticized Elliff's lack of knowledge regarding specific mission methods and field strategies. He conceded his lack of knowledge in this area and therefore depended on his affinity group strategists and overseas leadership team. After encouraging Gordon Fort to lead the prayer office, Elliff invited John Brady to join the leadership team as vice president for overseas operations

---

13   Tom Elliff, interview with the author, May 13, 2019, Oklahoma City, Oklahoma.

and mobilization. Elliff trusted Brady, an accomplished missiologist, to give direction to field strategies. If a theological problem developed within the field strategy, Elliff would become involved. Otherwise, he preferred to allow the experts to oversee the strategy issues overseas. Due to this preference, some believed Elliff was too much of a hands-off manager. Elliff counters by saying that when good leaders are chosen from the outset and empowered to do their jobs, the organization is better served that way than with stifling micromanagement.

CONCLUSION

Although he had declined the IMB presidency once in the early 1990s, Elliff received an unsolicited second opportunity to lead the organization almost twenty years later. Although he served on the field for less than three years, his brief taste of career missions gave him a unique perspective never before seen in an IMB president. Here was someone from the nucleus of the denomination's leadership who had also served as a rank-and-file missionary. This distinctive vantage point allowed him to calm the waters during a turbulent time at the IMB and refocus the organization. Elliff had no intention of being such a short-term president, but when his wife's cancer returned, he felt it was necessary to resign as IMB president after three and a half years of service in the position. His tenure was brief, but his impact was great. His upbeat, affable and calming personality restored joy and contentment to IMB missionaries and staff alike. This tranquil interlude would be brief, however, as a new president would take the growing financial crisis at the IMB head-on. Elliff retired on August 27, 2014, and the search for a new president began again.

THE IMB FACES THE TWENTY-FIRST CENTURY

Paul Akin

ELEVEN BILLION IS THE PROJECTED world population at the end of the twenty-first century.[1] A population forecast of that magnitude has enormous implications for the IMB. Yet this population forecast serves as a reminder that Southern Baptists and the IMB have always faced arduous challenges. As the IMB faces the twenty-first century, it once again finds itself facing considerable obstacles such as economic volatility, global pandemics like the coronavirus, and cyberwarfare.

---

1 Jo. M. Martins, Fei Guo, and David A. Swanson, *Global Population in Transition* (Cham, Switzerland: Springer International, 2018), 26–28.

Throughout its 175-year history, the IMB has repeatedly faced tremendous challenges and threats to its very existence. Some of the most critical challenges have been financial or economic in nature. On at least three different occasions, the IMB has faced economic challenges that have considerably threatened the long-term viability of the organization. The economic and financial challenges that emerged from the American Civil War, the Great Depression, and the Great Recession provide helpful context for the IMB as it faces the twenty-first century.

First, more than a decade after its formation in 1845, the American Civil War (1861–1865) almost ruined the mission efforts of Southern Baptists. The flow of funds to and from Richmond for the sake of missions almost dried up completely during this time. At the conclusion of the Civil War, the IMB found itself in substantial debt and with less than two dollars in its bank account.[2] Due largely to the leadership and efforts of J. B. Taylor, the IMB survived the Civil War and pressed onward in its mission efforts in Asia and Africa at that time.

Second, the Great Depression (1929–1939) also had a very damaging and almost fatal effect on the IMB. The earlier Seventy-Five Million Campaign and postwar economic growth had greatly increased optimism among Southern Baptists regarding global missions. William R. Estep writes, "Expectations were high now that funds would match the volunteers for missionary service. Both the Foreign Mission Board and the Home Mission Board planned to expand their operations in unprecedented fashion."[3] However, the amount of money pledged during the Seventy-Five Million Campaign differed drastically from what was actually contributed by Southern Baptists. The lower-than-anticipated giving during the campaign in 1925, along with an internal embezzlement scandal in 1927 and the Great Depression in 1929, devastated the financial

---

2   William R. Estep, *Whole Gospel Whole World: The Foreign Mission Board of the Southern Baptist Convention, 1845–1995* (Nashville: Broadman and Holman, 1994), 99.

3   Estep, *Whole Gospel Whole World*, 202.

sustainability of the board. Retrenchment became the strategy in order for the organization and mission to survive during this second major financial crisis.[4]

Third, the Great Recession (2007–2009) had, and a decade later continues to have, a considerable impact on the IMB and other faith-based organizations. John Dickerson in evaluating the substantial impact of the Great Recession on Christian churches and organizations writes,

> The church's overall numbers are shrinking. Its primary fuel—donations—is drying up and disappearing. And its political fervor is driving the movement from within. In addition to these internal crises, the outside host culture is quietly but quickly turning antagonistic and hostile towards evangelicals. . . . Around the globe, cultures are changing faster and with more complexity than ever before. . . . As George Friedman writes in his forecast, *The Next 100 Years*, "It is simply that the things that appear to be so permanent and dominant at any given moment in history can change with stunning rapidity. Eras come and go."[5]

One cannot disregard or ignore the remarkable impact of the Great Recession on Southern Baptist work in North America and around the world. For the IMB and SBC, the Great Recession, combined with other realties, resulted in a decreased budget,[6] a gradual decline

---

4   Estep, *Whole Gospel Whole World*, 208–13.

5   John S. Dickerson, *The Great Evangelical Recession* (Grand Rapids: Baker Books, 2013), 12–13.

6   In 2010, the IMB overall budget was $317.6 million (Erich Bridges, "International Mission Board Return on Investment: Souls," BP, December 1, 2010, https://www.baptistpress.com/resource-library/sbc-life-articles/international-mission-board-return-on-investment-souls). In 2018, the IMB overall budget was $264.4 million (Julie McGowan, "2017–18 LMCO Totals Nearly $159 Million," imb.org, October 5, 2018, https://www.imb.org/2018/10/05/lmco-nears-159-million). In less than a decade the overall budget of the IMB has been decreased by more than $50 million, or roughly 20 percent.

in membership across the denomination,[7] and an overall reduced missionary force around the world.[8] In some ways, the Great Recession was the catalyst that forced the IMB to transition from an established twentieth-century approach, reset, and develop a twenty-first-century strategy. A changing world and changing dynamics often require a new perspective and an innovative approach, and those realities inevitably necessitate a change in strategy. Change is precisely what has characterized the IMB over the last decade.

NEW REALITIES NECESSITATE NEW LEADERSHIP

In the aftermath of the Great Recession, the IMB was positioned for a season of change. Tom Elliff, who had faithfully served the IMB for several years as president, communicated to trustees in early 2014 that he was ready to retire and encouraged the trustees to begin an active search for his successor. Elliff had done an admirable job leading the IMB since March of 2011 but due to his age and stage in life determined that a new leader was needed for the future. Therefore, IMB trustees recognized that change was essential for the long-term sustainability and viability of the organization.

IMB trustees made a bold and deliberate hire to succeed Elliff as president of the IMB.[9] After much discussion, debate, and political maneuvering across the SBC, the board of trustees on August 27, 2014, elected David Platt to be the next president of the IMB. Platt had served for eight years (2006–2014) as the senior pastor at the Church at Brook Hills in Birmingham, Alabama. At the time of his election, Platt, thirty-six, was the youngest president ever chosen

---

7   Travis Loller, "Southern Baptists See 12th Year of Declining Membership," *Religion News Service*, March 24, 2019, https://religionnews.com/2019/05/24/southern-baptists-see-12th-year-of-declining-membership.

8   In November 2010, the IMB reported 5,110 missionaries. At the end of November 2019, IMB reported 3,656 missionaries. That is a reduction of more than 1,450 missionaries in less than a decade.

9   David Uth describes the search process here: "Transcript: David Platt Press Conference," BP, August 29, 2014, http://www.bpnews.net/43260/transcript-david-platt-press-conference.

in the history of the IMB. Elliff was seventy. The hiring of Platt was a monumental development in the SBC and created a substantial reaction from across the denomination.

Platt's election as president was somewhat controversial across the convention.[10] Some disliked his record of giving to the Cooperative Program, others complained about his theology, and some opposed Platt because of his youth or the fact that he had never served overseas as a missionary. Regardless of the contrary responses, IMB trustees made a clear statement about the need for new leadership to help stabilize and reset the organization and position it for the future. While there were certainly some dissenting voices, the overwhelming majority of IMB trustees and Southern Baptists were thrilled with the hiring of Platt.[11] There was palpable excitement in Richmond at the IMB's headquarters and across the denomination at the news of Platt's election.

In an era of economic turmoil, financial decline, and denominational stagnancy, the election of Platt brought a fresh sense of hope for Southern Baptists and for the future of the IMB. In fact, IMB missionaries were perhaps the most excited constituency concerning the election of Platt, and it was the missionaries that Platt himself was most excited to lead and to encourage. In God's providence, Platt would have the unique opportunity of meeting face-to-face with the top two hundred IMB field leaders soon after his election. A collaborative meeting of IMB field leaders from all over the globe had already been planned to take place in Asia in the fall of 2014. This meeting would provide Platt with the rare opportunity of meeting, listening to, learning from, and getting to share his heart and desires with the top echelon of IMB leadership.

---

10   Bart Barber, "Why David Platt Should Not Be the Next IMB President," *Praisegod Barebones*, August 25, 2014, http://praisegodbarebones.blogspot.com/2014/08/why-david-platt-should-not-be-next-imb.html.

11   Ronnie Floyd, Kevin Ezell, Fred Luter Jr., Russell Moore, and others all publicly supported and celebrated Platt as the new president of the IMB. See Diana Chandler, "SBC Leaders Affirm Platt as IMB's Leader," BP, August 27, 2014, http://www.bpnews.net/43239/sbc-leaders-affirm-platt-as-imbs-leader.

PLATT'S VISION

At this strategic gathering in Asia in the fall of 2014, Platt immediately took the opportunity to cast a vision for the future. He spoke boldly to a room full of IMB leaders in Asia about what would later become known as his "five desires" for the IMB. These five desires were to mark his leadership and drive everything that the organization would do under his watch. He communicated the following:

> I am amazed when I consider the magnitude of what God in his grace has created in the International Mission Board. To see an organization with over 170 years of mission history in the past is extraordinarily humbling, and then to see more than 50,000 congregations joined together in the present specifically for the spread of the gospel to people who have never heard it is truly breathtaking. Moreover, it practically defies imagination to realize that the International Mission Board exists alongside a North American Mission Board, six of the largest seminaries in the world, a publishing house dedicated to producing gospel-centered, mission-focused resources, an Ethics and Religious Liberty Commission confronting the key cultural issues of our day, and a network of state conventions and regional associations all aimed at serving and supporting local churches on mission. Without question, what God has created not just in the International Mission Board, but altogether in the Southern Baptist Convention, is absolutely remarkable. So how can the International Mission Board (IMB) steward the trust that God has so clearly given to us and the churches we serve in the future?[12]

---

12   David Platt, "The Future of the IMB and Our Collaborative Great Commission Work," in *The SBC and the 21st Century*, ed. Jason K. Allen (Nashville: B&H Academic, 2016), 169.

After acknowledging the scale and stewardship of his new role, Platt outlined his five desires for the IMB through several talks over the course of three days.

Exalting Christ

Foundational to anything and everything at the IMB, Platt believed that the goal of exalting Christ was to be supreme. He argued, "In order for the IMB to be faithful to the collaborative task entrusted to it by Southern Baptist churches it represents, Jesus must be the center of everything the IMB does."[13] For Platt, the starting point in an effort to exalt Christ was uncompromising confidence in the Word of God. He urged those in the room to acknowledge that "the Bible must serve as the authority for *what* the IMB believes and *how* the IMB operates. . . . Leaders and strategists across the IMB must start in God's Word, on our knees, reading, digesting, observing, seeing, learning, and letting the Word drive every facet of our work."[14] In summarizing this first desire, Platt concluded by stating, "All those associated with the IMB must want the glory of Christ more than life itself. For everyone associated with the IMB, missions must not be our life. Instead, Christ must be our life, and missions must be the overflow of lives that exist to exalt him."[15]

Mobilizing Christians

In an effort to exalt Christ among the nations, Platt also believed that it was essential to mobilize Christians for the nations. He declared, "With more than 2.8 billion people in the world who still lack access to the gospel, the IMB cannot settle for anything less than aggressive calls for all Christians to pray passionately, give sacrificially, and go intentionally for the glory of Christ among all peoples."[16] Citing the example of the Moravians in missions history, Platt asked this room of leaders to consider what God might do if

---

13   Platt, "The Future of the IMB and Our Collaborative Great Commission Work," 170.
14   Platt, "The Future of the IMB and Our Collaborative Great Commission Work," 170.
15   Platt, "The Future of the IMB and Our Collaborative Great Commission Work," 171.
16   Platt, "The Future of the IMB and Our Collaborative Great Commission Work," 172.

Southern Baptists began praying fervently, giving generously, and going intentionally out of the overflow of their desire and passion to see Christ glorified among the nations. Platt believed that if the IMB really wanted to see God move and work in a fresh way, more energy and effort needed to be spent intentionally mobilizing Christians at home and abroad.

Serving the Church
One of the convictions central to Platt's missiology is the understanding that the local church is God's chosen agent for the accomplishment of the Great Commission. Platt noted, "Christ's commission is not going to be completed primarily by individuals, conventions, or even by missions organizations like the IMB, but by local churches that are making disciples and multiplying churches."[17] Platt shared his concern that missions organizations, if they are not careful and aware, can usurp the responsibility of the local church in global missions. He underscored the need for coordinated cooperation and collaboration by churches to accomplish this task. He summarized his perspective by stating, "The IMB exists to partner with more than 50,000 Antiochs (Acts 13) across the Southern Baptist Convention: churches of all sizes worshipping, fasting, and praying, leading to those churches sending and shepherding missionaries for the spread of the gospel all over the world."[18] The IMB laboring to serve and work alongside the church was a critical conviction and desire for Platt as he led the IMB.

Facilitate Church Planting
If the local church is God's chosen agent for the accomplishment of the Great Commission, then the planting and establishing of the church among unreached people and places is paramount for IMB strategy. The IMB is a leader in church planting around the

---

17   Platt, "The Future of the IMB and Our Collaborative Great Commission Work," 173–74.
18   Platt, "The Future of the IMB and Our Collaborative Great Commission Work," 174.

world. Platt desired for that to remain true and only increase in scope. If the IMB was going to excel in any one facet of mission strategy, it would be facilitating church planting around the world for the glory of God.

Playing Our Part

Last, in all the talk about strategy and desires, Platt acknowledged that one day this mission would be complete. The vision of Revelation 5 and 7 would be realized, and there will be a multitude around the throne from every nation, tribe, people, and language praising the Lamb of God. Therefore, IMB leaders and missionaries needed to discern wisely the unique part God was leading them to play in the completion of Christ's mission. Platt remarked, "In the days to come, the IMB must continually look at the opportunities before us, the resources available to us, and the wisest ways possible to steward those opportunities and resources in obedience to him."[19] In concluding, he recalled the decision facing the Israelites at Kadesh Barnea (Num. 13–14) to obey the Lord and play their part or to cower away in fear. He remarked that the IMB, like the Israelites in Kadesh Barnea, had a choice to make—retreat or engage. He closed by stating that the IMB could retreat and embrace cultural Christianity, "or we can decide that Jesus is worth more than this. We can recognize that he has created us, saved us, and called us for a much greater purpose than anything this world could ever offer."[20]

The meeting in Asia concluded with substantial excitement and anticipation for the future. The five desires were a compelling, fresh, and uniting vision for the IMB. The vision centered on Christ, his Word, and his plan to rescue and redeem a lost world through the mission of his church. It was exciting for the IMB to consider the role that they might play in that mission.

---

19   Platt, "The Future of the IMB and Our Collaborative Great Commission Work," 179.
20   Platt, "The Future of the IMB and Our Collaborative Great Commission Work," 180.

TEAM FORMATION

Often when new leaders are brought in to inspire and implement change, they will seek to build their own team and bring in people with fresh eyes and a fresh perspective. But before making any new hires, Platt wisely retained the services of Clyde Meador. Meador, sixty-nine at the time, had served as the executive vice president (EVP) of the IMB since 2003. Platt shared with Baptist Press, "I want and need the kind of biblical, missiological, experiential, and personal wisdom that exists in Clyde Meador."[21] Meador would continue to serve on the IMB executive team as executive advisor to the president.

Less than three months after electing Platt, IMB trustees voted to approve Sebastian Traeger to be the new EVP at the IMB. Traeger, like Platt, did not have any previous overseas missionary experience; however, he was an elder at Capitol Hill Baptist Church and had some history working with smaller Christian organizations. His primary expertise was in business startups and consulting prior to coming to the IMB. The hire of Traeger, a graduate of Princeton University, was somewhat controversial to some inside and outside the IMB due to his lack of vocational ministry experience and seemingly busi-ness-first mindset. Nevertheless, IMB trustees voted and approved Traeger to serve in this capacity alongside Platt.

At the same trustee meeting in November 2014, IMB trustees also voted to approve Zane Pratt, age fifty-seven, as vice president for global training. Platt, in an effort to strengthen the cross-cultural experience of his new executive team, asked Pratt to come off of the mission field to serve in this capacity. Pratt, a proven veteran mis-sionary of two decades in central Asia, also had theological training experience serving as dean and professor of Christian missions at The Southern Baptist Theological Seminary from 2011 to 2013. Pratt combines a missionary heart with keen theological acumen.

---

21 Tess Rivers, "Trustees: IMB's Platt Unfolds Five-Point Strategy," BP, November 10, 2014, http://www.bpnews.net/43691/trustees-imbs-platt-unfolds-fivepoint-strategy.

Alongside Pratt, Traeger, and Meador, Platt also decided to retain the leadership of veteran missionary and former field leader John Brady. Brady, age fifty-nine, like Pratt added wisdom, organizational insight, and cross-cultural ministry experience to the newly formed executive team. Brady, the son of IMB missionary Otis W. Brady of British Guiana, grew up as a missionary kid with the IMB in South America.[22] He was a lifelong Southern Baptist and lifelong "IMBer," and he had been serving as vice president for global strategy in Richmond since November 2012.[23]

By the start of 2015, a leader was needed to lead the newly developed Support Services Team (operations), and a new leader was still needed to lead the newly named Mobilization Team. God provided a new and highly competent leader for the Support Services Team in one of the most unexpected places. Rodney Freeman, who was serving as an IMB trustee from New Jersey, also happened to serve as vice president of global facilities management at Merck & Co. Freeman, age forty-six, like Platt and Traeger did not have any previous cross-cultural missionary experience but brought a wealth of business and organizational intelligence to the IMB.[24] Freeman, in his previous role at Merck & Co., was responsible for leading a global staff of more than 950 professionals and managing a budget of more than $1 billion to service more than 400 sites.[25]

The last key hire for Platt's executive team would take some time. In the spring of 2016, the veteran executive and IMB leader Clyde Meador decided to retire. Meador, seventy-two at the time of his retirement, had served with the IMB for forty-one years.[26] Meador provided a

---

22   David J. Brady, *Not Forgotten: Inspiring Missionary Pioneers* (Maitland, FL: Xulon, 2018), 49–63.

23   Laura Fielding, "Trustees: Global 'Harvest' at Hand, Elliff Says," BP, November 19, 2012, http://www.bpnews.net/39190/trustees-global-harvest-at-hand-elliff-says.

24   Rodney Freeman, interviewed by Julie Schaeffer, "Extensive Lab Work," *American Builders Quarterly*, September 18, 2013, https://americanbuildersquarterly.com/2013/09/18/merck.

25   Anne Harman, "Trustees: IMB Opens New Pathways for Service," BP, May 13, 2015, http://www.bpnews.net/44753/trustees-imb-opens-new-pathways-for-service.

26   I personally remember walking with Clyde Meador out of the IMB building on his last day of work before his retirement. Clyde and I served together in the president's

steady and calming presence in the early days of Platt's leadership, and people across the IMB were grateful for his leadership and legacy.[27]

In August of 2016, IMB trustees affirmed Edgar Aponte as the new vice president for mobilization.[28] Aponte, a native and government diplomat of the Dominican Republic, originally came to the United States (Washington, DC) to serve in the ministry of foreign affairs. During his time in politics, Aponte became a follower of Christ and sensed a call to ministry. He earned a master's degree from The Southern Baptist Theological Seminary and completed a PhD in systematic theology from Southeastern Baptist Theological Seminary. Aponte brought youth, vibrancy, a diverse perspective, and a passionate desire to see the IMB grow in mobilization and cooperation among Southern Baptists.

Two years after his election as president, Platt finally had in place his executive team, a diverse mixture of leaders from across the SBC. Brady and Pratt represented the strong heritage and legacy of IMB missionary work and the wisdom of decades of leadership, while Traeger, Freeman, and Aponte brought new and innovative perspectives to the organization. There was a generational transition that was taking place in IMB leadership, and it was welcomed by IMB missionaries around the world. This was a new day at the IMB with a whole host of new leaders ready to lead Southern Baptist mission efforts into the future.

A CALCULATED RESET, FINANCIAL REALITIES, AND A DIFFICULT DECISION (FALL 2015 TO SPRING 2016)

In a very short amount of time, Platt and his newly formed team began to set the stage for change. In February 2015, less than six

---

office, and I have always had immense respect for him and his wife Elaine. His more than four decades of service to the IMB was monumental and in many ways unparalleled in recent history.

27 Michael Logan, "IMB's Clyde Meador to Retire after 41 Years," BP, May 10, 2016, http://www.bpnews.net/46828/imbs-clyde-meador-to-retire-after-41-years.

28 Julie McGowan, "Trustees: IMB Announces New Mobilization VP," BP, August 25, 2016, http://www.bpnews.net/47443/trustees-imb-announces-new-mobilization-vp.

months after his election, Platt unveiled a calculated reset of IMB structure. Under the new structure, the IMB would consolidate offices and have four main teams across the organization that would work under the direction and supervision of Platt and Traeger.

In the new structure, Global Training would be led by Zane Pratt; Global Engagement, representing all of the work IMB missionaries do around the world, would be led by John Brady. Support Services would be led by Rodney Freeman upon his hire in May 2015. Mobilization would be led by an interim leader initially, and then by Edgar Aponte upon his hire in August 2016.

The IMB had gone through many minor and major resets throughout its history. Meador, in commenting on the reset, argued that "recalibration . . . has been used by God."[29] As expected there was some excitement and some hesitation. But Platt tried to keep the focus on the mission and vision of the organization. He argued, "Strategy and structure are not the ultimate answer to seeing Christians and churches engaging unreached people with the Gospel. . . . What that means is that more than we need a streamlined structure or a simplified structure, we need the power of God to do what only He can do. This is why I am calling everyone across our IMB family—from trustees to personnel to otherwise—to fast and pray, because only God can do this work."[30] The structural and organizational reset that was announced in February 2015 inevitably led to some further changes at the next trustee meeting in May 2015.

Trustees at the May 2015 meeting in Louisville, Kentucky, announced new streamlined guidelines for appointing new missionary personnel. During the previous decade, IMB trustees had considerable debates and disagreements regarding policies that were affecting aspiring missionary candidates.[31] In an effort to

---

29 Anne Harman, "Platt Unveils 'Reset' of IMB Strategy Structure," BP, February 26, 2015, http://www.bpnews.net/44286/platt-unveils-reset-of-imb-strategy-structure#.

30 Harman, "Platt Unveils 'Reset' of IMB Strategy Structure."

31 See Harman, "Trustees: IMB Opens New Pathways for Service." The article notes, "Prior to the May board of trustees meeting, miscellaneous policies existed for career, apprentice, Journeyman, ISC and Masters program missionary appointees. Specific policy regulations covered issues of faith and practice such as levels of education,

move beyond these debates, Platt and the trustees determined it was time to streamline the new missionary guidelines and align all missionary requirements with the Baptist Faith and Message. These changes were contested but in the end were approved by the board.[32] Platt in support of these policy changes stated, "To be as clear as possible, this is no lowering of the bar for potential missionaries. This is a raising of the bar in all the areas that matter most. . . . We will continue to train our missionaries and work as missionaries in ways that faithfully represent Southern Baptist churches and Southern Baptist conviction."[33] The impetus for these changes was a desire to provide more Southern Baptists with opportunities to engage in global mission around the world.[34] The purpose of these changes was to provide clearer doctrinal alignment and increased avenues for more Southern Baptists to serve with the IMB.

Soon after, Platt had the opportunity to communicate clearly his vision and plan to Southern Baptists at the annual meeting in Columbus, Ohio, in June 2015. Platt shared his desire to mobilize and unleash a "limitless" missionary force through the IMB. He stated, "I want to lead the IMB to blow open that funnel to create as many pathways as possible for Southern Baptists to get the gospel to unreached people." Laura Fielding noted, "At the end of the IMB's report, the audience loudly applauded and cheered Platt, some even giving a standing ovation. No messengers asked questions from the floor."[35] Coming out of that annual meeting, momentum for the IMB continued to increase, excitement abounded across the SBC,

---

history of divorce, teenage children in the home, the practice of a private prayer language, and greater specificity around baptism than the Baptist Faith & Message."

32 To read more about the specifics of the policy changes in May 2015, see David Roach, "IMB to Align Missionary Requirements with BFM," BP, May 15, 2015, http://www.bpnews.net/44772/imb-to-align-missionary-requirements-with-bfm.

33 Harman, "Trustees: IMB Opens New Pathways for Service."

34 Platt, in a clarifying article to Southern Baptists, explains the goal and purpose behind these changes here: David Platt, "IMB & Churches: 'Limitless Missionary Teams,'" BP, May 14, 2015, http://bpnews.net/44755/imb-and-churches-limitless-missionary-teams.

35 Laura Fielding, "Platt Envisions 'Limitless' Missionary Pathways," BP, June 18, 2015, http://www.bpnews.net/44986/platt-envisions-limitless-missionary-pathways.

and Platt was casting a compelling vision to Southern Baptists in regard to the future of its global mission efforts.

Financial Realities

With all the excitement and momentum, there remained a critical problem for Platt and the IMB. In his address to the SBC messengers in Columbus, Platt made mention of the financial challenges facing the IMB. Platt stated, "In 2009, IMB had a record-high 5,600 missionaries overseas. Today the number has dropped to 4,700 and is fast on its way to 4,200, primarily because IMB is not financially able to support their missionary force on the field. Last year, IMB operated with expenses nearly $21 million more than income."[36] The news of the financial shortfall seemed to resonate in the room in June but also seemed to be quickly forgotten by Southern Baptists after the annual meeting.

The reality is that the budget shortfalls at the IMB had been taking place every year for several years. Each year, IMB leaders would hope and pray for increased giving to the Cooperative Program and the Lottie Moon Christmas Offering, but neither would see any substantial growth or increase. Over time, this led IMB leadership to begin selling global property and reaching into reserves to make up the budget shortfalls. Something drastic needed to be done. Platt was the right man at the right time to help lead the IMB to a place of short-term financial responsibility and long-term organizational stability.

A Difficult Decision

Due to the budget shortfalls that had continually plagued the IMB since 2008, IMB leaders decided in August 2015 that the time to act was now. The relatively new executive leadership team gathered together late into the night at the headquarters in Richmond and unanimously decided that something significant must be done to get to a balanced budget. Between 2009 and 2015, the IMB had spent

---

36   Fielding, "Platt Envisions 'Limitless' Missionary Pathways."

$210 million more than it had received. In other words, the gap between what was budgeted and what was spent at the IMB between 2009 and 2015 exceeded an average of $35 million annually. That pattern of operation could not continue, and this new assembly of IMB leaders was left with no viable alternative other than to work immediately to reduce the number of personnel at the IMB.

As the leadership team gathered that day in August to address this growing problem, a number of options were explored and considered.[37] Platt would later write an open letter to Southern Baptists recounting the process of decision-making:

> When staff leadership realized the severity of our financial situation, we knew that we needed to take significant action. We spent hours on our knees praying and at tables discussing potential options for balancing our budget, ranging from sending fewer missionaries to cutting various costs. We poured over financial models and looked at the long-term impact of each of our options. However, with 80% of our budget being devoted to personnel salary, benefits, and support expenses, we inevitably realized that any effort to balance our budget would require major adjustments in the number of our personnel. When we gathered with our trustees at our most recent meeting, the same conclusion was clear. Though board policy did not require an official trustee vote, and though these brothers and sisters agonized over the thought of many missionaries stepping off of the field, there was resolute and resounding recognition across the room that our financial situation required such action.[38]

37　I was involved in this meeting, and we met from early in the afternoon until late into the night. All of the facts were carefully evaluated; and all viable options were considered, debated, and discussed. Much time was devoted to prayer and earnestly seeking the Lord. There was a strong desire to determine suitable alternatives, but in the end, there was a consensus around the room that it was the right decision at that time.

38　"IMB's Platt Sends Open Letter to SBC Family," BP, September 4, 2015, http://www. bpnews.net/45432/imbs-platt-sends-open-letter-to-sbc-family.

People wanted to know why the IMB did not just ask the churches to give more money. The problem was that the headlines coming out of IMB meetings for years had been sounding the alarm to these financial issues but often fell on deaf ears.[39] Platt was clear that no blame should be assigned to any previous group of IMB leaders. He expressed his thankfulness for the resources that God did provide during those years and for the missionaries who were able to stay on the field and proclaim the gospel.

Robin Hadaway, veteran IMB missionary leader and Southern Baptist missions professor at Midwestern Baptist Theological Seminary, applauded Platt for his courageous and bold leadership in light of these financial realities. Hadaway wrote,

> As a missions veteran, I must admit to having some reservations about David Platt's election as IMB president. After fifteen months, I no longer have these doubts. I believe only an outsider could have taken a fresh look at the procedures, positions, and roles that have evolved over the organization's 170-year history. I applaud Platt for examining missions through different eyes and adjusting strategy, structure, and personnel to fit the twenty-first

---

39 A sampling of headlines shared in Platt's open letter: 2008—"IMB reports cautionary finance news that could have a significant impact on the Board's work around the world next year." Later that year, our trustee chair said to churches, "I am sounding the alarm. The IMB budget is under strain to support growth in our missionary force." 2009—"Economic challenges . . . IMB anticipating another tough financial year . . . IMB in budget shortfall crisis [that] could affect 600 positions." 2010—"IMB lamenting financial declines, trying to balance budget . . . IMB sending 30 percent fewer long-term personnel than would be sent if there were no financial constraints." 2011—"IMB having difficulty balancing budget . . . IMB lowering the missionary force." 2012—"IMB preparing for another sobering financial report . . . IMB working through a painfully difficult process of trying to balance the budget." 2013—"IMB urging for greater support from churches . . . IMB laments Christian callousness . . . IMB trustees vote for substantive proposal changes across the SBC." 2014—Just two months before Platt stepped into his role, one article read, "IMB must soon come to grips with the demands placed on us by years of declining Cooperative Program receipts and Lottie Moon giving. We will be hard-pressed to continue supporting a mission force of our current number, much less see a greatly needed increase in the number of fully supported career missionaries on the field."

century. . . . He wisely has chosen to voluntarily reduce personnel by offering a generous retirement incentive so those who remain can be fully supported. I applaud Platt's administration for looking at the worldwide situation with fresh eyes and determining the jobs that need to be done in this new age of missions.[40]

Yet, in the end, desperate times called for desperate measures, and the IMB announced a plan in September 2015 to address directly the budget shortfall and move the organization to a financially stable position.

Phase one of the plan included a voluntary retirement incentive (VRI). The goal of this first phase was to offer as generous a voluntary retirement incentive as possible to all eligible staff and missionaries age fifty and older with five or more years of service. Phase two would be a Hand-Raising Opportunity (HRO) in which any person working at the IMB who was not eligible for retirement would also have the opportunity to transition voluntarily out of the IMB. The initial news of the VRI caused some to wonder why the IMB was asking older, seasoned, and experienced missionaries to transition. This is a logical question and one that the leadership team deliberated about in the process of making their decision. Platt outlined four reasons for coming to this conclusion.

First, he stated the value of every person in the IMB and his desire to call every person at the IMB to ask, "Is the Lord leading me to a new phase of involvement in mission?" This was not an issue of age or generation, but something that was made available to people of all ages across the IMB. Second, the plan was always to make this as voluntary as possible. Platt wrote, "I want to be crystal clear: we are not asking people to leave the field. If someone is thriving on the field and senses the Lord leading them to stay

---

40   Robin Dale Hadaway, "Understanding the IMB Financial Crisis," *SBC Life*, December 1, 2015, https://www.baptistpress.com/resource-library/sbc-life-articles/understanding-the-imb-financial-crisis.

on the field, then I trust they will stay on the field."[41] IMB leadership wanted to put that decision into the hands of each individual person. Third, freezing any new missionary sending would send a negative message to SBC churches and cripple the organization's future growth. Fourth, cutting or freezing new missionary sending would not address IMB's need to fix the long-term cost structure.

In the end, Platt greatly lamented being in this position and having to make this decision, but he, along with all of his leadership team, believed this was the right decision. He stated, "My preference is not to stop sending new missionaries to the field, and my preference is not to see existing missionaries leave the field. As I've mentioned at different points, the path we are walking is not ideal in any way, but after much prayer and discussion, other leaders and I believe the path we are walking is the best option we can take in a sea of non-ideal options available to us."[42]

After months of low morale at the IMB and with a pressing need to move to a financially stable position, a bombshell was dropped on the Southern Baptist world on February 24, 2016. Exactly 1,132 IMB missionaries and stateside staff decided to transition out of the organization during the two-phase plan to balance the IMB budget.[43] In the planning stages of the two-phase plan, the IMB had announced the need to reduce the total number of personnel by 600 to 800 people. But 1,132 people was a staggering number. Almost overnight the number of IMB missionaries went from around 4,800 to less than 3,800. The last time the number of IMB missionaries was below 4,000 was in 1993. This news was noteworthy in the SBC and in the broader evangelical world.[44] As expected, the news of

41   Anne Harman, "IMB Announces Voluntary Retirement Incentive Details," BP, September 10, 2015, http://www.bpnews.net/45462/imb-announces-voluntary-retirement-incentive-details.

42   Harman, "IMB Announces Voluntary Retirement Incentive Details."

43   "IMB: 1,132 Missionaries, Staff Accept VRI, HRO," BP, February 24, 2016, http://www.bpnews.net/46374/imb-1132-missionaries-staff-accept-vri-hro.

44   Sarah Eekhoff Zylstra, "Southern Baptists Lose Almost 1,000 Missionaries as IMB Cuts Costs," Christianity Today, February 24, 2016, https://www.christianitytoday.com/news/2016/february/southern-baptists-lose-1132-missionaries-staff-imb-cuts.html;

retiring and transitioning missionaries was somber and sorrowful. September 2015 to February 2016 was a volatile and challenging time at the IMB. But Platt and his team led well through that season amid much change and transition.

IMPLEMENTATION OF THE VISION (SUMMER 2016 TO SUMMER 2018)

By the summer of 2016, Platt had been in his role for almost two years. The first two years proved to be trying and challenging on a number of levels. Much change and transition had occurred. Nonetheless, in less than twenty-four months, Platt had cast a compelling vision, assembled his team, implemented an organizational reset, and moved the organization to a financially stable position. As a result, the stage was now set for implementation of the vision.

A Balanced Budget and a Record Lottie Moon Offering

In the aftermath of the VRI/HRO and just before the 2016 SBC annual meeting in St. Louis, Platt and Southern Baptists received a much-needed jolt on June 7, 2016. By God's grace and in many ways in response to the VRI/HRO, Southern Baptists rallied behind Platt and the IMB by generously giving $165.8 million to the Lottie Moon Christmas Offering. The generous offering was the highest total in the 127-year history of the offering and surpassed the previous all-time record of $154 million by $11.8 million. This was monumental.[45] Within a few months, the IMB would celebrate a balanced budget for the first time in several years.[46] From a

---

Lonnie Wilkey, "Nearly 1,000 Missionaries Return Home," *Baptist and Reflector*, March 8, 2016, https://baptistandreflector.org/nearly-1000-missionaries-return-home; Adelle M. Banks, "Southern Baptist Foreign Missionaries Drop by Nearly 1,000," *Religion News Service*, February 24, 2016, https://religionnews.com/2016/02/24/southern-baptist-missionaries-drop-by-1000-with-volunteer-departures.

45   Julie McGowan, "Lottie Moon Offering Reaches Nearly $165.8 Million," BP, June 7, 2016, http://www.bpnews.net/46994/lottie-moon-offering-reaches-1658-million.

46   Julie McGowan, "Trustees: IMB Celebrates Balanced Budget," BP, November 11, 2016, http://www.bpnews.net/47882/trustees-imb-celebrates-balanced-budget.

financial standpoint, the IMB was now back on solid ground and in a position to grow. Platt expressed his thanks to Southern Baptists and reminded them of the urgency of the mission:

> As an IMB family, on behalf of unreached people around the world, we are deeply grateful for the generosity of Southern Baptists who have given for God's glory among the nations. In addition, we as an IMB and SBC family look forward to exploring in the days ahead how our cooperative giving can fuel an ever-increasing mission force taking the Gospel to those who have never heard it. Our times are too urgent, our opportunities are too great, and our Gospel is too glorious to settle for anything less than wholehearted abandon as a convention of churches to seeing Christ proclaimed in every place and among every people group in the world.[47]

New and Optimized Pathways to the Mission Field

As the IMB looked to the future, Platt and his leadership team realized that for the IMB mission force to grow substantially in the future that the organization needed to explore new pathways for service alongside the established pathways. In his address to the SBC messengers, Platt commented on the rate of population growth around the world and the staggering reality of global lostness. In response to those numbers and statistics, he declared, "Our goal as a group of 40,000 churches is not just to send a couple of hundred more missionaries. We want to send thousands more missionaries, and the potential for doing that is real if we'll create the pathways for that to happen."[48] Platt envisioned new pathways designed to mobilize and send professionals, students, and retirees to join alongside fully funded IMB career missionaries. This idea

---

47   McGowan, "Trustees: IMB Celebrates Balanced Budget."

48   Julie McGowan, "IMB 'Standing Strong,' Platt Reports," BP, June 16, 2016, http://www.bpnews.net/47071/imb-standing-strong-platt-reports-at-sbc.

resonated with many and generated some excitement, but there were some who were skeptical of this approach, both inside and outside the IMB.

Though he wanted to expand the mobilization efforts of the IMB, create new pathways, and broaden the missionary force, Platt always remained committed to the established pathways and the essential role of fully funded career missionaries. In the same address in which he called for the mobilization of professionals, students, and retirees, he also championed the priority and indispensable nature of fully funded career missionaries. He knew that for the IMB to be strong and to have a substantial and sustaining presence among the unreached for decades to come that fully funded career missionaries were vital. He said to the SBC messengers, "Let me be crystal clear: the IMB is still going to send full-time, fully-funded career missionaries just like we've always sent. They are the priceless, precious, critical core of our mission force."[49] The vision was to continue sending fully funded missionaries through established pathways and to surround them with an increasing force, which would include professionals, students, and retirees. It was always a both-and approach to see more Southern Baptists go to the nations.

The call for new pathways resulted in a new initiative in five key cities around the world.[50] The Global Cities Initiative (GCI) was a pilot initiative intended to mobilize and meaningfully integrate professionals, students, and retirees onto existing IMB teams in these five cities. Michael O'Neal, a missions pastor of an SBC church in Georgia, highlighted the purpose behind the GCI pilot:

---

49   McGowan, "IMB 'Standing Strong,' Platt Reports."

50   The five pilot cities chosen were London, Dubai, Shanghai, Kuala Lumpur, and a major city in South Asia (unnamed for security concerns). Each city had a designated city leader who was tasked with developing a strategy to reach the city and working to integrate people coming through new pathways onto their teams. This pilot project was the starting point for an emerging urban emphasis at the IMB. Over time, the role of city leader grew in prominence across the IMB and developed as a training ground for emerging and innovative leaders in the IMB. The urban cohorts that emerged from this pilot provide a unique forum and format for helpful dialogue, discussion, and collaboration that spans affinities and teams.

As a missions pastor, one of the greatest lessons that I've learned is that churches need to offer multiple pathways for members to be on mission. If churches are going to impact London—or any other global city, for that matter—then we must go beyond one or two short-term mission trips every year that involve only a few people. And, though we are thankful for their amazing work, it's going to take more than a relative few IMB missionaries. We need to mobilize the whole body of Christ, encouraging people to leverage their God-given gifts, passions, and vocations to engage cities short-term, mid-term, and long-term.[51]

The GCI pilot was instrumental in the development of the Team Associate (TA) role with the IMB.[52] Team Associate was a new pathway for SBC members who want to serve as missionaries but who receive their funding through non-IMB sources. In time, the TA role started to gain some traction with some partner churches and has made a real contribution to IMB work around the world.[53] One TA in a large urban city in Asia noted that when they arrived in their city in 2017 there were fourteen total people on the city team, and all of them were IMB funded. By the spring of 2019, there were over sixty team members (the majority of them coming through the TA pathway), and some of them were working in businesses and schools that would not have had a gospel witness had the IMB not

---

51 Michael O'Neal, "Global Cities and Marketplace Initiatives: Pathways to Limitless Sending," imb.org, February 16, 2017, https://www.imb.org/2017/02/16/global-cities-and-marketplace-pathways.

52 For a description of a Team Associate see, https://www.imb.org/go/options/team-associate.

53 In 2019, there were more than 130 TAs serving with IMB teams around the world. That is more than 130 Southern Baptists who were serving as missionaries on IMB teams, but not on IMB payroll and not receiving Cooperative Program or Lottie Moon Christmas Offering resources through this newly created pathway. If you combined TAs and Seconded workers, the IMB in the spring of 2019 had more than two hundred people actively serving alongside IMB teams who were not receiving Cooperative Program or Lottie Moon Christmas Offering resources. That makes up around 6 percent of the current IMB mission force.

created new pathways and expanded their mission force to include these non-IMB-funded missionaries. The process of providing new and optimized pathways certainly did not occur overnight, and the team responsible for implementing these new initiatives repeatedly encountered hurdles and obstacles to their work.[54] Nevertheless, Platt's dream for mobilizing professionals, students, and retirees and for developing new pathways to facilitate their sending and joining of IMB teams became a reality and continues to add value to IMB work today.

Theological and Missiological Clarity

Coming into this role from the pastorate, Platt had a particular passion to help the IMB clearly articulate its core theological and missiological convictions. In a changing world, theological and missiological convictions need to be regularly and clearly defined and articulated. Therefore, soon after he was elected as president he began collaboratively meeting with the senior leaders in Richmond and affinity leaders from around the world to work on defining some of the key terms that were central to IMB missions strategy.

This process ensued for more than a year until finally there was an agreed-on list of key terms and definitions. Platt and other leaders spent considerable time meeting, praying, and discussing how the IMB defines *gospel, evangelism, conversion, disciple, disciple-making, calling, IMB missionary, missionary teams, unreached people* and *places*, and *church*.[55] Defining these key terms took work and concentrated effort, but defining the terms helped provide a layer of clarity in the IMB that did not exist previously.

After clarifying these terms, Platt and the leadership team believed it would be valuable to add even more clarity and attempt to define further not only the theological meaning of these terms

---

54 Many were influential in the development and optimization of these pathways, but Sebastian Traeger, John Brady, Edgar Aponte, Scott Logsdon, Rodney Freeman, Matt Burtch, Sam Lam, Hal Cunningham, and Lukas Naugle were all instrumental in the development and implementation of these new pathways.

55 For definitions of these key terms see, https://www.imb.org/beliefs-key-terms.

but also the missiological application of missionary work around the world. This led to a meeting with selected field leaders in the Middle East in 2016 to define the missionary task. In other words, the IMB has thousands of missionaries scattered around the world, but what exactly are those missionaries doing? What is their over-arching goal and purpose? What is the task that they are trying to accomplish? After several days of meeting and deliberating about the nature of the missionary task, this ad hoc group emerged with a clear definition and description of the missionary task. The missionary task includes six primary components: entry, evangelism, disciple-making, healthy church formation, leadership develop-ment, and a strategically planned exit.[56]

Clarifying the missionary task was significant for the IMB during this period of time. After more deliberation and discussion with a variety of groups and audiences, Platt and the leadership team determined it would be good to compile the key terms, the newly clarified missionary task, core missiological convictions, charac-teristics of a healthy church, and guiding statements about what the IMB is and what the IMB does into one unified and clarifying document. This document, under the leadership and influence of the vice president for training, Zane Pratt, became later known as the Foundations document.[57]

The Foundations document took more than a year to be compiled and completed. The document went through a series of revisions and edits. Feedback from across the IMB was solicited, debated, and discussed at length in several different settings. Pratt gave critical leadership and oversight to the project, but in many ways this was a collaborative document shaped by IMB leaders from around the world. Finally, in May of 2018, the document was complete. In an effort to bring clarity and unity, the IMB leadership

---

56   This understanding of the primary components of the missionary task was de-veloped and adopted by the IMB leadership team in the summer of 2016. "Six Components of the Missionary Task," https://www.imb.org/topic-term/six-components-missionary-task.

57   It is available at their web store: https://store.imb.org/imb-foundations-magazine.

team invited several hundred leaders from around the world to attend a "Foundations" meeting in Southeast Asia in 2018. The purpose of the meeting was to highlight these theological and missiological foundations and to ensure clarity, alignment, and unity toward this approach to mission work around the world. The Foundations document was released to all the SBC messengers at the 2018 annual meeting in Dallas, Texas. Since that time, it has been adopted and utilized for training by scores of churches across the SBC, and it is now required reading in many of the seminaries across the SBC. The work and energy that leaders across the IMB put into this effort will be valued for years to come.

Reshaped Vision for Missionary Assessment and Expanded Partnerships

Out of a conviction that the local church is God's primary instrument for the accomplishment of the Great Commission, the IMB began to evaluate and revise the missionary assessment process. To be clear, the IMB has a strong record of evaluating and assessing missionaries for service. However, in an effort to heighten and increase both the role of the local church and the receiving missionary team on the field, some adjustments and modifications were recommended and implemented.[58]

Beginning in the winter of 2018, the IMB determined that the local church was best positioned to provide the initial level of assessment for new missionary candidates. There was a learning curve for both the local church and the IMB in this reshaped process, but the result was a greater level of collaboration from the church and a more well-rounded and comprehensive assessment process. In addition to the church, missionary team leaders also were given an expanded role and responsibility in the latter part of the process as it related to team matching for new missionary candidates. In

---

58   Working alongside Scott Logsdon and Zane Pratt, I had the opportunity to lead the assessment and deployment team during this time of change and transition and help implement a reshaped vision for missionary assessment.

the revised assessment process, missionary team leaders would interview individual missionary candidates as the final step in the matching process. This step ensured that the sending church, the IMB assessment team, and the receiving missionary team were all on the same page and in agreement concerning the selection and matching process for new missionaries.[59] The reshaped assessment process helped increase the IMB missionary candidate pipeline significantly in 2019–2020.[60]

The IMB leadership team also expanded the IMB's partnership during this era. Platt desired to see IMB grow in partnering and networking with like-minded organizations, and under his leadership partnerships expanded at the IMB. Perhaps the most notable partnership was the deepening relationship between the IMB and NAMB. The IMB and NAMB have coexisted for more than a century and been involved in varying levels of cooperation during that time. However, the friendship of Platt and NAMB president Kevin Ezell was unique and helped establish a much stronger level of partnership and cooperation between the two entities. In the summer of 2015, the IMB and NAMB partnered together to host the SEND conference in Nashville, Tennessee. The conference drew more than thirteen thousand people and provided a visible avenue for the IMB and NAMB to work together for the spread of the gospel across North America and around the world. In commenting on the conference, Billy Godwin of the *Christian Index* commented, "The respective leaders of these two Southern Baptist missions sending agencies—Kevin Ezell and David Platt—appeared on the platform together numerous times. They clearly exhibited a great deal of mutual affection and respect

---

59 Changes made to the assessment process are visualized and explained at the IMB website here: https://www.imb.org/go.

60 Ann Lovell, "Chitwood Announces Five-Year Plan, Trustees Elect Vice Presidents," imb.org, January 30, 2020, https://www.imb.org/Chitwood-announces-plan. Paul Chitwood notes, "Our missionary pipeline is growing again. In just over a year, we've been able to increase the number of candidates in the career pipeline by more than 400% and the number of combined long-term, mid-term, and team associate candidates by nearly 300%."

for one another. . . . The camaraderie between Ezell and Platt was one of the most encouraging aspects of the conference. The positive and cooperative spirit between the two leaders underscored the synergy that must exist between being on mission at home and to the nations."[61] NAMB was not the only organization the IMB grew in partnership with during this time. Organizations like Together for the Gospel (T4G) and the Cross Conference also grew in their relationship with the IMB. The result of these expanded partnerships and relationships was a new connection with pastors (T4G) and college students (Cross Conference). In particular, these expanded partnerships helped the IMB establish relationships with a younger generation and an emerging demographic in the SBC.

Lingering Challenges

While there is much to celebrate about the developments that occurred from 2016 and 2018, some lingering challenges remained. The IMB was increasingly competing with other missions organizations for new missionary candidates. When the IMB was established in 1845, there were not many comparable competitors. Over time, new organizations develop, SBC pastors and churches consider other options for sending missionaries, the "market" for sending missionaries becomes more saturated, and competition naturally increases. For better or worse, in the twenty-first century, there is increased competition when it comes to missions sending.

Along with the increased competition was the reality that the Cooperative Program continued to be flat with only minimal increases over the last decade. Those two factors—increased competition and flatlined Cooperative Program giving—are significant challenges for the IMB. The Cooperative Program, along with the Lottie Moon Christmas Offering, helps fund and sustain the IMB

---

61   Billy Godwin, "SEND North America Conference Will Leave a Lasting Impact," *The Christian Index*, August 25, 2015, https://christianindex.org/20150825-send.

mission force on an annual basis. If the Cooperative Program is not growing, then the ability to grow the mission force is limited.

In addition to those lingering challenges was Platt's desire to preach and pastor again. Platt, without a doubt, believed God providentially led him to the IMB. He loved the IMB, he loved the mission and vision, and perhaps most importantly, he loved the missionaries of the IMB. However, he continued to have a burning desire and passion to preach and pastor in a local church.

Early in 2017, an opportunity was presented to Platt to serve as an interim preaching pastor at a megachurch in northern Virginia, McLean Bible Church. He began preaching as an interim pastor, but in the fall of 2017, the church wanted Platt to be their teaching pastor on a full-time basis. They were amenable with Platt remaining as the IMB president but wanted him to preach at McLean each week as well. At that time, Platt was living in Richmond, Virginia, and commuting one hundred miles north every Saturday and Sunday to preach at McLean. This arrangement was not sustainable long-term for Platt or his family.

Between the fall of 2017 and the spring of 2018, Platt fasted, prayed, and sought the Lord's guidance and direction in his life. Over time, he sensed the Lord leading him to commit full-time to preaching and pastoring at McLean and to resign from his role as president at the IMB.[62] This was a grueling and heart-wrenching decision for Platt. He loved the IMB and desired to keep serving the missionaries and churches of the SBC, but out of a desire to obey the leading and guidance of the Holy Spirit, he believed God was calling him to pastor McLean Bible Church.

The news of Platt's transition was sobering for many inside and outside the IMB. Furthermore, Platt's pending transition raised questions for people across the SBC. *SBC This Week* wrote,

---

62 David Roach, "David Platt to Transition out of IMB Presidency," BP, February 12, 2018, http://www.bpnews.net/50350/david-platt-to-transition-out-of-imb-presidency; Kate Shellnutt, "David Platt Is Ready to Leave the IMB," *Christianity Today*, February 12, 2018, https://www.christianitytoday.com/news/2018/february/david-platt-leaving-imb-president-mclean-bible-pastor-sbc.html.

To Platt's credit, the financial issues he inherited have
largely been resolved, and the IMB is operating with a
balanced budget once again. However, Platt's impending
transition now raises questions about the future direction
of the 172-year-old missions sending agency. Platt was
seen by many in the SBC as the obvious choice to lead the
IMB when he was hired in August 2014. His appointment
was even met with great excitement by Southern Baptists
and non-Southern Baptists alike. He and his team had
implemented a new strategy of "limitless missionaries"
during his less-than-four-year tenure—a strategy that
now hangs in the balance for missionaries who've been
sent during that time and are scheduled to be commissioned in the coming months.[63]

Platt agreed to continue serving as president until the IMB Trustees
found a successor. In September 2018, after serving as president
for just over four years, Platt officially resigned as president of the
IMB. The IMB trustees named Clyde Meador as interim president
effective immediately.

Platt's official resignation from the IMB was met with mixed
emotions. Some were sad, some were frustrated with him, while
others were excited for Platt to be back in the pulpit preaching on a
weekly basis. Nevertheless, in the span of four years, Platt's leadership was vital in helping position the IMB for future impact in the
twenty-first century. Under his leadership the IMB achieved a balanced budget, celebrated a record Lottie Moon offering, optimized
and created new pathways, provided theological and missiological
clarity, reshaped the missionary-assessment process resulting in an
increase in missionary applicants, and expanded partnerships for
future mobilization. While the duration of Platt's presidency may
have been shorter than desired and his tenure was not perfect, the

---

63   "IMB President David Platt to Leave Missions Organization," SBC This Week, Feb-
      ruary 12, 2018, https://sbcthisweek.com/imb-president-david-platt-resigns.

impact was immediate. In a short period of time, he led the IMB to reset organizationally, reach a fiscally healthy position, and in the process led several key initiatives that positioned the organization for the future. There was significant change at the IMB between 2015 and 2018, but in retrospect, Southern Baptists will look on Platt's tenure with gratitude for making hard decisions, moving the organization to a healthy financial position, and preparing the IMB for maximal impact in the twenty-first century.

THE IMB IN THE TWENTY-FIRST CENTURY: CHALLENGES AND OPPORTUNITIES

On November 15, 2018, trustees of the IMB unanimously elected Paul Chitwood to serve as the thirteenth president of the IMB.[64] Chitwood, a graduate of Cumberland College (now the University of the Cumberlands) and a two-time graduate of The Southern Baptist Theological Seminary, came to the IMB after serving as a pastor of several churches in Kentucky and most recently serving as the executive director of the Kentucky Baptist Convention. The search for a new president took place throughout much of 2018 (February to November), but in the end, the trustees unanimously elected Chitwood. Like Platt before him, Chitwood had never served overseas with the IMB as a field missionary. However, his experience as an IMB trustee and serving in pastoral and denominational life helped equip and prepare him for this role.

Challenges
Chitwood, forty-eight at the time of his election, took office immediately. Upon his election, Chitwood was met with some timely challenges. Prior to his departure as president, Platt had launched a study and internal investigation regarding the way in which the IMB

---

64   David Roach, "Paul Chitwood Elected Unanimously as IMB President," BP, November 15, 2018, http://www.bpnews.net/51968/paul-chitwood-elected-unanimously-as-imb-president.

had handled past allegations of abuse and sexual harassment. Platt had launched the study, but the responsibility now fell to Chitwood to continue the work.[65] This endeavor would take considerable time and attention in his early days as IMB president.[66]

In addition, Chitwood immediately began working to form his leadership team. With Platt's departure, Traeger and Aponte both transitioned out of the IMB, which created an EVP opening and an opening in the area of mobilization. Meador, who had come back to work at the IMB after his retirement, served briefly as interim EVP and then as interim VP for mobilization and later interim VP for support services. Nonetheless, in February 2019, trustees unanimously elected Todd Lafferty to serve as the EVP for the IMB.[67] Lafferty, fifty-nine at the time of his election, was a veteran IMB field leader for twenty-nine years. Lafferty's election as EVP was applauded and appreciated by many within the IMB.

However, after Lafferty's election, the next phases of team formation for Chitwood proved to be more challenging. The same day that trustees elected Lafferty as EVP, they also affirmed Chitwood's selection of Roger Alford to fill a newly created role of vice president for communications. However, after less than two months, Alford determined it was not a good fit for him and left the newly created position.[68] On August 12, 2019, IMB trustees announced the election of Mark MacDonald to serve as VP for marketing and communication. Regretfully, the excitement regarding this announcement was short-lived as the IMB released a statement on August 29, 2019,

65   "Chitwood to Continue IMB Abuse & Harassment Study," BP, December 12, 2018, http://www.bpnews.net/52110/chitwood-to-continue-imb-abuse-and-harassment-study.

66   "Trustees: IMB Appoints Missionaries, Hears Abuse Prevention Update," BP, September 27, 2019, http://www.bpnews.net/53670/trustees-imb-appoints-missionaries-hears-abuse-prevention-update.

67   Julie McGowan, "Trustees: IMB Elects EVP, Appoints 19 Missionaries," BP, February 7, 2019, http://www.bpnews.net/52384/trustees-imb-elects-evp-appoints-19-missionaries.

68   "IMB Communications Director Alford Decides 'He's Not the Right Fit' for the Role," The Alabama Baptist, April 12, 2019, https://www.thealabamabaptist.org/imb-communications-director-alford-decides-hes-not-the-right-fit-for-role.

stating that they had determined MacDonald would not be a good fit and that they had decided to go in a different direction.[69] In October 2019, Chitwood would announce to IMB staff that VP for Support Services Rodney Freeman would transitioning out of his role and that Derek Gaubatz would be transitioning out of his role as general counsel. In time, God provided leaders to fill these critical roles, but the initial team formation phase proved to be challenging.[70]

In addition to team formation, other notable challenges remain for the IMB in the days ahead. With the emergence of the COVID-19 virus and the reality of a global pandemic, the IMB once again finds itself facing an arduous challenge and formidable threat. With the threat of this virus looming around the world, will the IMB be able to see substantial annual increases in Lottie Moon Christmas Offering giving over the next few years? Will giving to the Cooperative Program substantially increase in the years ahead? Will more churches see the value of the IMB and actively engage in praying, giving, and going? Will the IMB be able to engage and mobilize adequately the next generation of Southern Baptists? Will the IMB be able to adapt constantly to a rapidly changing world? These concerns and many others are sobering realities that Chitwood and his leadership team are faced with as the IMB moves into the future.

Opportunities

While Chitwood was faced with some initial challenges upon his arrival at the IMB, he also stepped into a role with great opportunities. After more than a year of listening and learning and eventually getting his leadership team in place, Chitwood was ready to seize the opportunities and communicate his plan to Southern Baptists. During the January 2020 trustee meetings in California, Chitwood

---

69 Julie McGowan, "Updated: IMB to Continue Focus on Communication, Marketing," BP, August 12, 2019, http://www.bpnews.net/53430/updated-imb-to-continue-focus-on-communication-marketing.

70 Lovell, "Chitwood Announces Five-Year Plan, Trustees Elect Vice Presidents." In January 2020, Charles Clark was announced as vice president of mobilization and Price Jett as vice president of finance, logistics, and technology.

laid out a five-year plan for the IMB.[71] Chitwood's fivefold plan was built on IMB's vision and mission to engage unreached people and places with the gospel of Jesus Christ. Each goal presented by Chitwood was quantified with numerical targets.

The first goal was to mobilize 75 percent of Southern Baptist churches to support the IMB through prayer and financial giving. Currently, less than half of Southern Baptist churches report on the Annual Church Profile that they give to the Lottie Moon Christmas Offering. The IMB has an opportunity to help mobilize churches across the SBC to pray and give more faithfully for global mission. Second, in terms of sending, the IMB has a goal to send an additional five hundred fully funded missionaries by 2025. This goal was based on a number given to Chitwood by IMB field leaders. Third, Chitwood wants IMB to mobilize five hundred global partner missionaries on IMB teams. The IMB will not fund these missionaries, but they will be embedded on IMB teams. This is an attempt to increase the number of Southern Baptists serving overseas, but not limiting the number based on the IMB budget. Fourth, there is a goal to engage seventy-five global cities with a comprehensive strategy. Demographers forecast that by the year 2100, more than 80 percent of the world population will be living in cities.[72] If these urbanization forecasts come anywhere close to these projections, this will have tremendous implications for the IMB and Great Commission work around the world. The IMB must be intentional and effective in proclaiming the gospel, making disciples, and planting churches in global cities in the decades to come. Fifth, to fund and maintain a strong mission force, the final goal is to increase Lottie Moon Christmas Offering receipts 6 percent annually to sustain the five hundred additional missionaries.

In an effort to reach these goals, Chitwood and his newly established team of leaders are working hard to strengthen relationships

---

71 Ann Lovell, "Chitwood Announces 5-year Plan for IMB; Appoints 21 New Missionaries," *Kentucky Today*, January 30, 2020, http://kentuckytoday.com/stories/chitwood-announces-five-year-plan-for-imb,24015.
72 "Urban Population, 1950–2100," FutureTimeline.net, https://www.futuretimeline.net/data-trends/12.htm.

with churches, associations, and state conventions across the SBC. In many ways, Chitwood's primary focus since stepping into this role has been to help the IMB reconnect with some of its most established and traditional partners. This emphasis has been well received, and a continued emphasis on the centrality of the local church in global mission remains central to the IMB's approach in the twenty-first century. It will be exciting to see how Chitwood and his leadership team continue to lead Southern Baptist to pray, give, and go in the decades to come.

CONCLUSION

Titles change. Organizational structures are reorganized. New missionaries are appointed, and aging missionaries retire. One thing that remains the same through it all is that the gospel of Jesus Christ continues to be proclaimed every day around the world. By God's grace, gospel proclamation, in every corner of the world, has been a reality through the IMB for the last 175 years. That is a staggering and breathtaking reality. Through many ups and downs, economic crises, global pandemics, terrorist activity, and other obstacles, the IMB continues year after year to send people out who boldly share the gospel, make disciples, and plant churches for the glory of God.

Organizational leaders come and go, but the real heroes of the IMB always have been and always will be the anonymous and unknown missionaries who are faithfully serving Christ in some of the most difficult and hard-to-reach places on the planet. It is the resilience, humility, and Christ-centered commitment of these Spirit-empowered brothers and sisters that makes the IMB unique, distinct, and indescribably special. Challenges will remain and will be constant, but one day all of those challenges will be swept away when the Lion of the tribe of Judah receives the praise due his name from every tribe, language, people, and nation. Until then, may God bless the work and efforts of the IMB far into the twenty-first century and beyond.

AFTERWORD

I T HAS OFTEN BEEN SAID THAT "the more things change, the more they stay the same." In a certain sense, this maxim well describes the 175-year trajectory of the International Mission Board of the Southern Baptist Convention. Taking the gospel to the nations was the primary purpose of the founding of the Southern Baptist Convention in 1845—our "one sacred effort" as it was called. Although the origins of the SBC are tainted by a sinful commitment to the perpetuation of slavery, current IMB president Paul Chitwood helpfully notes how God has nevertheless used Southern Baptist churches and their commitment to missions to help advance the gospel: "Only God's redeeming love and the reconciling power of the Gospel could result not only in repentance, but in a convention of churches today that is among the most diverse in the world and whose membership includes thousands of African American churches and many other ethnicities. That diversity, from such a regretful beginning, causes this celebration of what God is doing through Southern Baptists to be even more joyous."

According to the IMB, since 1845 Southern Baptists have sent almost 25,000 missionaries who have served in 189 different countries around the world with a combined 228,000 years of service. Chitwood further notes concerning the financial generosity of the people called Great Commission Baptists, "Since 1888, Southern Baptists have given approximately $4.7 billion to the Lottie Moon Christmas Offering. . . . Since the introduction of the Cooperative Program in 1925, Southern Baptists have contributed almost $3.6

billion to international missions through that initiative." So much has been done, yes, that this volume has chronicled in great detail. But so much work remains.

Now, 175 years after our founding, the unfinished task of fulfilling the Great Commission must propel Southern Baptists to continue to push back lostness throughout the world, knowing this gospel endeavor is our primary mandate until Jesus returns. Indeed, the 175th anniversary of the formal launching of Southern Baptists' international missions effort is an appropriate time to recenter and recommit ourselves to the Great Commission.

From our simple yet complicated beginnings, Southern Baptists have grown into the largest non-Catholic denomination in the world, with a complex and diverse array of missions and ministries that touches on every calling rightly ordered from God's Word. Nevertheless, having begun with this "one sacred effort," Southern Baptists should not allow any other matter, no matter how worthy, to distract us from our God-given calling to take the gospel to every nation. It should be our mission that in as much as it depends on us—and we know that it ultimately depends on the Lord—we should not rest until every man and woman, boy and girl, in every nation has been told the good news that God is reconciling sinners in his Son, our Savior, Jesus Christ. This book concludes, but our work continues. Until Christ comes, Great Commission Baptists must go!

—Adam W. Greenway
President, Southwestern Baptist Theological Seminary